The Global Economy
A Concise History

Edited by
Franco Amatori - Andrea Colli

The Global Economy
A Concise History

First published 2020
by Routledge
2 Park Square, Milton Park, Abingdon, Oxon OX14 4RN

and by Routledge
711 Third Avenue, New York, NY 10017

Routledge is an imprint of the Taylor & Francis Group, an informa business

and by G. Giappichelli Editore
Via Po 21, Torino – Italia

© 2017 Franco Amatori - Andrea Colli (Edited by), *Il mondo globale. Una storia economica -* Giappichelli Editore
© 2019 Franco Amatori - Andrea Colli

British Library Cataloguing-in-Publication Data
A catalogue record for this book is available from the British Library

Library of Congress Cataloging-in-Publication Data
A catalogue record for this book has been requested

ISBN: 978-0-367-26508-3 (hbk-Routledge)
ISBN: 978-88-921-1734-1 (hbk-Giappichelli)
ISBN: 978-0-429-29355-9 (ebk-Routledge)
ISBN: 978-0-367-26507-6 (pbk-Routledge)

Typeset in Simoncini Garamond
by G. Giappichelli Editore, Turin, Italy

The manuscript has been subjected to the double blind peer review process prior to publication.

CONTENTS

pag.

LIST OF ILLUSTRATIONS

Figures

Tables

Chapter 1
THE STRUCTURAL CHARACTERISTICS OF PREINDUSTRIAL ECONOMIES

SUMMARY: 1.1. From the Neolithic Revolution to the Bronze Age urban revolution. – 1.2. The structural features of agrarian economies. – 1.3. Late-mediaeval economies and the impact of the Black Death. – Bibliography.

In order to understand pre-industrial economies, we must imagine a radically different world from the one we know today. To paraphrase economic historian Carlo M. Cipolla, an Englishman in the mid-18th century had more in common with a Roman contemporary of Julius Caesar than with one of his own great-grandchildren (who had, however, no idea about personal computers or mobile telephones).[1] Cipolla intended to illustrate the rates of growth and the pace of change in economic and social structures: not completely static, but certainly very slow before the Industrial Revolution, and increasingly rapid, at times even frenetic, thereafter. To a great extent, the change of pace derives from the transformation of prevalently agrarian economies into industrial economies. And yet, the Industrial Revolution did not arise from a void: some areas (it is a matter of debate as to how many), mainly in Europe, had already begun to accelerate centuries before this, differentiating themselves from the rest of the world and launching what is now commonly known as the "Great Divergence". This chapter aims to briefly describe the structural characteristics of pre-industrial agrarian economies and their semi-immobility, which only a wide-ranging trauma could shake (the Black Death of the 14th century is the best example). The two following chapters will tackle the timing and development of this divergence: firstly between continents, and then between northern and southern Europe.

1.1. From the Neolithic Revolution to the Bronze Age urban revolution

Until 10-12,000 years ago, agrarian societies simply did not exist. People

---

[1] C.M. Cipolla, *Before the Industrial Revolution: European Society and Economy, 1000-1700*, London, 1993.

lived in groups of hunter-gatherers, finding food provided spontaneously by nature. The groups were limited in size and not very numerous, given that the global population is estimated at no more than six million. Then the situation changed: in different parts of the world (Near East, China, Central South America) and independently of each other, some of these groups settled down, built villages and began to cultivate the land. In other areas (Northeast America, perhaps the Sahel, equatorial Africa and New Guinea) this transition took place "autonomously", but later. In even more areas of the world, agriculture was imported along with the seeds of plant species that had been domesticated elsewhere. This is the case of Central and Western Europe, where wheat from the Near East was introduced between 6000 and 3500 BCE. In general, the autonomous transition to agriculture occurred in areas where there was a relative abundance of wild species of both plants and animals suitable for domestication.

This was the first "agricultural revolution" in history, and also marks the first acceleration in population growth. At the start of the Common Era, the world population had increased by over 40 times and stood at 250 million. The growth rate was very slow by contemporary standards (less than 0.04% per year), although much higher than was typical in pre-agrarian societies. But what about the per capita availability of resources, or living conditions? There is more doubt about this kind of improvement, since the classical idea – that human beings "discovered" agriculture and became farmers following a crucial invention – has largely been replaced by the idea that people started to cultivate the land and to create permanent settlements when forced to do so by demographic pressure. The assumption is that they already possessed some key skills derived from simply observing nature; for example, how to propagate plants by placing seeds in the ground. Therefore, agriculture was not such a momentous discovery, and living conditions actually worsened in many ways. The human diet became increasingly dependent on cereals and hence impoverished, as appears from the reduced stature of skeletal remains. Diseases became more numerous and more frequent due to increased population density and close proximity with domesticated animals and their parasites. Lastly, peasants were obliged to work longer and harder than their hunter-gatherer ancestors to produce what they needed for survival.

However, the appearance of agrarian societies also brought some definite benefits. For example, they were more complex, and could coordinate labour and the use of resources in ways unimaginable in a society of hunters and gatherers. On the other hand, this involved a greater degree of social-economic inequality. Diversification of tasks and the development of a more complex social structure allowed the accumulation of skills and knowledge, whose transmission from one generation to the next was facilitated by the invention of writing (circa 3200 BCE in Mesopotamia). These advantages developed fully only after another major historic development: the urban revolution of the Bronze Age. The first cities began to appear in different parts of Europe and Asia from approximately 3000 BCE. This is associated with a sharp increase in economic and social complexity, also because the cities were able to organise activities across a vast surrounding area. At the same time, the first states began to form, with characteristics – according to authoritative social anthropologist Jack Goody – not generally observable in other parts of the world.[2] In particular, the Eurasian states soon developed the ability to impose systematic forms of taxation on their own citizens, enabling them to channel resources towards new and increasingly complex uses. There was also a remarkable growth of social stratification, which meant the emergence of new aspirations, providing an impetus to consumption, technological innovation and the general advancement of knowledge.

In comparison with the Neolithic Revolution, the urban revolution was much more local, and initially limited to Europe and Asia. This was essentially the start of a sort of proto-divergence between Eurasia (not surprisingly the area with the most advanced pre-industrial economies) and the rest of the world. Much of traditional historiography has underlined the differences between West (Europe) and East (especially East Asia) in order to explain the emergence of European supremacy, forgetting that essentially all contenders for the leading position in pre-industrial economic development are in Eurasia. Therefore, before tackling the issue of the Great Divergence, it must be explained why other parts of the world had no chance of achieving supremacy. Jared Diamond has recently provided an environmental answer.[3] According to this theory, the Asian species of domesticated plants and animals (subsequently exported to Europe) were superior to those found in the Americas and Oceania. For example, wheat and barley are more nutritious than maize, while cows and horses have a greater capacity for work and are more versatile than llamas (the llama is the only large domesticated mammal native to the Americas, while Eurasia has 13), and so on. In addition, the Eurasian landmass has an east-west axis, unlike the north-south axis of the American landmass, which is also extremely narrow at the Isthmus of Panama. Humans and their domesticated animals could expand much more easily along latitude than longitude, for the simple reason that this did not involve changing climate zone. People on the move also take ideas with them, and there is evidence that innova-

---

[2] J. Goody, *The Theft of History*, Cambridge, UK, 2006.
[3] J. Diamond, *Guns, Germs and Steel*, New York, 1997.

tions spread much more rapidly in ancient Eurasia than in the Americas, where even the more advanced cultures were separated from each other by daunting natural and environmental barriers.

These factors were already present well before the first Europeans "discovered" the Americas and could exploit Europe's other technological and bacteriological advantages. These derived mainly from the original environmental advantages, enabling more efficient and productive agriculture together with a higher population density and states with a more complex form of organisation. Lastly, American societies suffered (in comparison with Eurasia) the effects of a delayed start: as they moved outwards from Africa and migrated to other continents, humans reached the American continent approximately 14,000 years ago, and took a further 2,000 years to complete the journey from their entry point in the north (Alaska) down as far as Patagonia in the south.

At the arrival of Columbus (1492), there were only two American empires (Inca and Aztec) capable of mobilising resources on a large scale, whereas Eurasia had many states in more or less advanced conditions, including the world's most developed states. As observed by Goody, we must highlight the organisational, institutional and cultural analogies within the vast expanse of Eurasia before indicating the differences. Organisational and structural analogies are naturally connected with the emergence of complex state structures; for example, the Roman Empire at its height encircled the Mediterranean, including much of Europe, the Middle East and North Africa, and the Chinese Empire was even larger. However, the analogies are also related to essential economic and family institutions, ranging from private property, to inheritance systems, educational structures, and the family. For example, in Eurasia (but not elsewhere) all children received a share of the paternal inheritance, including daughters (through their dowry). This required the pursuit of complex and often endogamous matrimonial strategies to avoid excessive dispersion of inherited assets. These strategies were inherent in intensive exploitation of the land. The following chapters will take up some of these themes, highlighting that although differences between the institutions in different parts of Eurasia have been at various times evoked as possible factors of divergence, on this wider chronological and geographical scale it is actually the fundamental elements of analogy which are striking and which differentiate the two continents from all others.

Sub-Saharan Africa, where the first hominids appeared and thence migrated worldwide, is separated from Eurasia by the desert and by the Red Sea, but is nevertheless still much easier to reach than the American continent. Africa's urban revolution took place much later, and its cities were never as large, numerous and capable of organising ample territories as their Eurasian counterparts (here again, environmental factors seem to have been an important obstacle). The prevailing methods of cultivation, typical of an itinerant and less productive agriculture, were accompanied by a less diversified society, in which the inheritance of land rights had nothing like the central importance it had in the agrarian societies of Europe and Asia. Consequently, even the family structures were very different from those of Eurasia, and placed much less emphasis on the pursuit of complex matrimonial strategies.

1.2. The structural features of agrarian economies

Eurasian agrarian societies were much more complex than their predecessors based on hunting and gathering, but were also much less complex and stratified than contemporary industrial or post-industrial societies. This was also because the vast majority of the population lived in small villages. Even in a highly urbanised region like Italy, no more than 20-25% of the total population lived in cities at the start of the 14th century (before the Black Death). On average, the urban population of Western Europe was about 6-8% of the total. Therefore, one reason for paying particular attention to the rural population is that it was much more numerous.

Another reason why agrarian societies were less complex is due to the limited division of labour, based (at least in the countryside) less on differences in ability than on the age and gender of the members of each family group. The fundamentally important skills and knowledge were common among all or almost all of the population, engaged in different activities according to the seasons. The lower level of complexity was associated with a more limited range of needs, and most of what was needed for consumption and production was made or reproduced on a local basis: seed, livestock, implements and simple clothing. Only a few types of goods were imported from outside by acquiring supplies marketed in the nearest city: most metal tools and goods, salt and higher quality textiles.

Productivity was generally low, and the traditional agrarian societies were capable of producing only a limited surplus above what was needed for immediate subsistence and to constitute reserves of seed to sow the next crops (this also placed a great constraint on the growth potential of the urban population). In addition to limiting economic development, this meant that the population was very much at the mercy of harvest fluctuations due to climatic and meteorological factors. In particular, long and intense spring rains could cause considerable damage to cereal harvests, causing them to fall well below the minimum subsistence level. In general, agrarian societies were able to tolerate a year of "normal" hardship by using their available reserves (according to one estimate, an average of one in four years saw poor harvests in the pre-industrial era). However, two or more consecutive years of poor harvests were usually enough to cause a famine, always associated with a net reduction in births and, especially in the worst cases, a notable increase in death rates. The fragility of agrarian economies could be aggravated by a population increase, given the limited possibilities of achieving a rapid increase in output. This "Malthusian" [4] interpretative model should not be rigidly applied, since it is known that Eurasian agrarian societies did not always survive merely at subsistence level, but were able to enjoy lasting and progressive improvements in living conditions, at least in certain periods and areas. Nevertheless, it remains an extremely useful means of understanding the dynamics of the pre-industrial era.

The vulnerability of agrarian societies to crop failure poses the question of their resilience, meaning their capacity to deal with these crises. One fundamental aspect to underline is the capillary solidarity system in villages, based on a dense fabric of various degrees of family ties. Matrimonial strategies were central to this system. European and Asian inheritance mechanisms assigned daughters an important share of the patrimony, thus necessitating "rational" management of marriages. The choice of marriage partner was usually the result of careful consideration by the respective families, and did not necessarily reflect the preferences of the young couple directly involved. Complex matrimonial alliances, and the kinship ties which these created between lineages and across the generations, constituted the essential framework of a strong solidarity system, which could be activated when needed and allowed agrarian societies to deal relatively successfully with these crises. The exception was, of course, the most terrible disasters, which were devastating not only in terms of the huge numbers of victims, but even more so in terms of the consequent collapse of social organisation within the community.

The importance of self-consumption in agrarian societies has already been mentioned. Around 90% of produce was consumed where it was

---

[4] According to the "classical" interpretation of the theories propounded by English economist Robert T. Malthus (1766-1834), in conditions of constant technology the population tends "naturally" to grow more rapidly than resources. Consequently, the balance between population and resources can be maintained in the mid- to long term only by periodic mortality crises (epidemics, famines and wars, all directly or indirectly triggered by a shortage of food and other resources). Only a significant innovation in agricultural technology can allow substantial population growth, but not a lasting improvement in living conditions (for instance, in terms of calories available per capita), since the (fragile) balance between population and resources will return in the long term to subsistence level under the effects of population growth itself.

produced, either directly by the producer or else bartered in the village (the use of money was highly unusual in rural communities). Only about 9% of total production was sold for money in the market of the nearest city. Just over 1% of produce travelled beyond the reference territory of a single city to become a part of the long-distance trade conducted by the merchant-capitalists residing in the largest cities.

In pre-industrial agrarian societies, the city was the site of trade and of the market. This latter was always subject to strict and thorough controls; it was what French historian Fernand Braudel famously called a "regulated market". The cities also tended to concentrate the production of the more complex manufactured goods and dispensed certain essential services to urban residents and those of the surrounding country area, since they hosted the principal magistratures, civil institutions (city government, law court) and ecclesiastical institutions (bishoprics). However, many city residents were still engaged in rural activities, at least to a partial extent. There were very few exceptions to this rule. At the start of the 14th century, Florentine banker and chronicler Giovanni Villani was astonished at the peculiar behaviour of Venetians, writing that they "did not plough, nor sow, nor harvest grapes" (*illa gens non arat, non seminat, non vindemiat*); although Venice was the greatest commercial power in the Mediterranean, it did not yet possess a large agricultural hinterland.

Exceptions like Venice were fundamentally important in the pre-industrial era, especially during the Middle Ages and at the dawn of the early modern era, due to their capacity for technological, institutional and behavioural innovation, and the following chapters will return to this subject. They were the fundamental centres of the commercial and proto-financial capitalism that was so important in maintaining and strengthening both cultural and economic contacts between the different regions of the enormous Eurasian landmass.

One last explanation is required. This brief description of agrarian societies has placed them inside a static framework. However, as already said, although the pace of change was extremely slow and not at all comparable with that of industrial societies, agrarian societies were by no means immobile. On the contrary, they were capable of notable progress, such as technological improvements. The heavy plough was introduced into Europe in the 7th century, with important improvements made between the 9th and 12th centuries, and was mostly used in central and northern regions where soils were more difficult to work. The three-year crop rotation system took hold from the 8th century[5] and iron agricultur-

---

[5] This system divided the land into three parts. One was used to grow cereals, which

al implements spread from the 12th century. These innovations enabled important increases in agricultural productivity. Another crucial innovation was the water mill, already known during the Roman Empire but widespread only from the 6th-7th centuries. Initially used for milling flour, over time the water mill proved as versatile as it was powerful, and was adapted for different applications, from fulling cloth to iron-working. Most of these "European" innovations are also found in the more advanced regions of Asia, which is actually where many of them originated, confirming the ease with which men and ideas travelled across the Eurasian landmass. For example, the first form of heavy plough appears to have been invented in China between the 1st and 2nd centuries CE, after which its use spread towards the West.

Figure 1.1. Technological innovation in the Middle Ages

Water wheel   Heavy plough

1.3. Late-mediaeval economies and the impact of the Black Death

Agrarian societies were therefore capable of making progress, but the times required for progress and for social and economic changes were generally slow and almost imperceptible, unless there was an exceptional occurrence. Here, the principal event was the Black Death, which triggered an accelerated phase of transformation of social and economic structures.

The plague was well known in the ancient world, but had disappeared from the Mediterranean and Europe in the 8th century, retreating to certain specific areas of Asia, such as the Himalayan area, where it remained endemic. According to the prevalent theory, the plague's return to Europe is directly connected with the formation of the Mongol Empire, one of the

gave high yields but quickly depleted the soil of nutrients; one was left to rest (fallow); and one was used for pulses, helping to re-establish the fertility of the soil. Crop rotation was practised each year, so that cereals were grown on the same land every three years.

major events in Eurasia during the last centuries of the Middle Ages. From around 1206, the year Temüjin succeeded in uniting all the tribes under his leadership and had himself proclaimed as Genghis Khan ("universal chief"), the advance of the Mongols impacted first on Central Asia, then continued under his successors towards China and Eastern Europe. After many military campaigns, the Mongols finally succeeded in subjugating the whole of China in 1279 under the dominion of Kublai Khan, founder of the Yuan dynasty. In Asia, they overran Tibet, Korea and vast areas of the Indian sub-continent, while in Europe they advanced towards Poland and Hungary after the conquest of Russia, devastating vast territories and posing a constant threat to the entire continent for decades.

The Mongol Empire was the greatest territorial empire the world had ever seen, and its formation was a fundamentally important event in Eurasian history. Not only did it overturn pre-existing states and political equilibria, but its chief importance is that it improved communications and favoured the exchange of goods and ideas across an enormous area. The Mongols were able to create an efficient communications network within their vast Empire by strengthening and integrating the existent road system and fully reviving the ancient Silk Road, which had already linked China and India with the Mediterranean area during the Roman Empire. This was Eurasia's principal trade route before the ocean shipping routes were established. In 1271, a young Venetian merchant called Marco Polo set out on a journey along the Silk Road that would take him as far as the city of Xanadu and the court of Kublai Khan.

Marco Polo's adventures represent the movement of men and goods which flourished for over a century, due to the relative stability and security provided by the Mongol Empire (the period is also known as *Pax Mongolica*). Unfortunately, just as men and goods travelled the trade routes, so did pathogens. It was precisely the improved efficiency of the road networks under the Mongols which allowed the plague to spread from the Himalayan region, first (in the early 1330s) infecting Central Asia, and probably part of China, before reaching the Middle East and Black Sea in 1346. In the Crimea, the plague came into contact with the Republic of Genoa, one of Europe's greatest economic powers, which like Venice had built up an articulated commercial empire in the Mediterranean area. The Genoese colony in Kaffa was infected by the Mongol army besieging the city. Genoese galleys fleeing from the epidemic in 1347 took the plague firstly to Constantinople, then Europe's largest city, to different regions of Italy, and also perhaps as far as Marseille in France. In 1348 the Black Death spread from these areas to the rest of Italy, to central and southern France, northern Spain, southern England, the Balkans, the Middle East and much of North Africa (from Egypt to Algeria). The plague continued its spread until 1352 or 1353, affecting the whole of Europe and the Mediterranean area, except perhaps for some very restricted areas, especially those in the extreme north.

Figure 1.2. Marco Polo's travels along the Silk Road

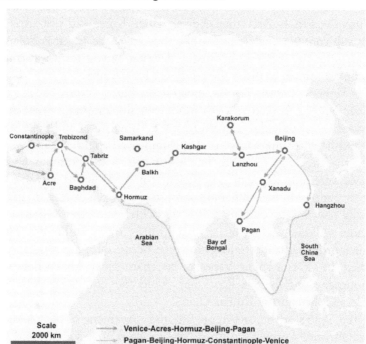

In Europe and the Mediterranean area alone, the Black Death is estimated to have killed at least 50 million people. This was undoubtedly one of history's worst pandemics, eliminating in just a few years 33 to 60% of the entire European population. According to contemporary chroniclers, the death rates in Italy were 60% in Florence and Siena, 50% in Orvieto and 45% in Prato and Bologna. Estimates for the entire peninsula range from a minimum of 30% to a maximum of 50-60%, and are essentially the same as the European average.

The Black Death caught Europe largely unprepared. Despite their considerable wealth and cultural development, not even the continent's most advanced areas, with Italy in the lead, could do a great deal to control the disease and limit mortality. The plague's arrival in Europe and the fact that it subsequently became endemic led to a process of institutional adaptation and consolidation of public health services in which the Italian merchant republics led the way. For example, the first permanent lazaret (or plague hospital) was built in 1423 on an island in the Venetian Lagoon. Here it must be emphasised that the plague caused a shock to the existing social and economic structures, accelerating the rate of change, and some interpretations see it as constituting Europe's first specific advantage (and therefore divergence) factor in comparison with Asia.

In effect, the damage to the European economy during the epidemic and in the period immediately afterwards, caused by the breakdown of production and trade, huge losses of life and human capital, and the collapse of the overall product, were amply compensated by a large number of "beneficial" effects. In general, the survivors enjoyed a sharp "re-adjustment" of the relationship between the population and natural resources, which had become obviously precarious by the start of the 14th century, as shown by some of the worst famines in European history: in particular, the "Great Hunger" of 1315-1317.[6] Suddenly, more land became available than could be cultivated. It was thus possible to reorganise agricultural production more efficiently, abandoning marginal lands and redesigning the countryside and even the settlement patterns, although we now know that the reorganisation of settlements and consequent abandonment of many villages had already begun during the decades prior to the Black Death. Very recent research has demonstrated how the plague brought about a vast redistribution of wealth, resulting in greater equality; this is the only instance of a substantial and generalised reduction in economic inequality recorded during the entire Middle Ages or early modern era.[7]

On the whole, the new balance between the population and resources (and the more equal distribution of these resources) allowed large strata of the population to achieve higher living standards. This was also helped by the fact that city workers could obtain higher wages, allowing them to stay above subsistence level in the long term.

The higher living standards in Europe following the Black Death were consolidated by the plague's permanence in the continent, and may have constituted a divergence factor compared with China, "unlucky" enough to have suffered less from the plague also thanks to its cleaner and less crowded cities. The paradox is that one type of advantage (the quality of the urban environment and public health levels) may actually constitute a relative disad-

---

[6] Italy was the only area of Europe spared by the famine, but was severely affected by two others in 1328-1330 and 1346-1347.

[7] G. Alfani, T. Murphy, *Plague and Lethal Epidemics in the Pre-Industrial World*, in *Journal of Economic History*, 77(1), 2017, pp. 314-343.

vantage (less capacity to accumulate surplus and to raise living standards), although this sort of paradox is not infrequent during the course of history. For instance, following the establishment of the Atlantic routes, the states (like Venice and Genoa) which had benefitted during the Middle Ages from their central position in the Mediterranean area then found themselves imprisoned within the very same area, while other areas formerly excluded from the major commercial routes could now take full advantage of the new opportunities.

Figure 1.3. Impact of the Black Death on real wages

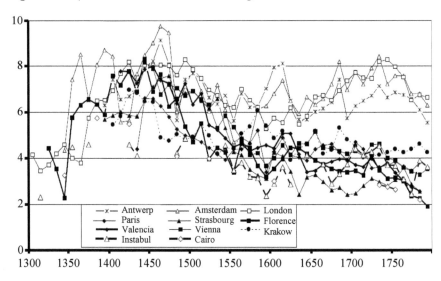

Source: S. Pamuk, "The Black Death and the Origins of the 'Great Divergence' across Europe, 1300-1600", in *European Review of Economic History*, 2007, 11(3), p. 297. The graph shows real wages of unskilled workers converted to indexes.

Bibliography

Braudel F., *Civilisation matérielle, économie et capitalisme, XVᵉ-XVIIIᵉ siècle*, Paris, 1979.

Cattini M., *La genesi della società contemporanea europea*, Modena, 1994.

Chaunu P., *Histoire, science sociale; la durée, l'espace et l'homme à l'époque moderne*, Paris, 1974.

Cipolla C.M., *Before the Industrial Revolution: European Society and Economy, 1000-1700*, London, 1993.

Diamond J., *Guns, Germs and Steel*, New York, 1997.

Goody J., *The Theft of History*, Cambridge, UK, 2006.

Livi Bacci M., *A Concise History of World Population*, Oxford, 2017.

Malanima P., *Pre-Modern European Economy*, Leiden, 2009.

Chapter 2
THE "GREAT DIVERGENCE"

SUMMARY: 2.1. Opening closed worlds. – 2.2. The Great Divergence: causes and timing. – 2.3. Beyond Eurasia: America, Africa and Oceania. – Bibliography.

Pre-industrial societies were not static. Although changes took place slowly, they could lead to evident – but sometimes fragile – progress. However, it is beyond discussion that the rate of change increased sharply in the transition from the Middle Ages to the early modern age. From this point of view, the traditional date of the "discovery" of America[1] in 1492 is still useful to mark the start of a new phase of transformation and renewal that would upset human societies and consolidated equilibria on a global scale, continuing until the 18th century and the start of the Industrial Revolution. As during all phases of change, not all players were able to take advantage of the new opportunities offered, meaning that there were both winners and losers. The relative advantage of the great Eurasian societies (constructed and consolidated following the Bronze Age urban revolution) now increased, giving rise to the direct supremacy some of these civilisations exercised over those of other continents. New balances of economic and military power then emerged within Eurasia, together with the gradual development of European supremacy. This process, known as the "Great Divergence", has been the object of intense debate and will be the focus of particular attention.

2.1. Opening closed worlds

The ancient Silk Road was a fundamental communications artery linking Europe and eastern Asia; it connected the major civilisations of the two continents and allowed the transit of people, ideas and merchandise (silk,

---

[1] There is now solid archaeological evidence that Viking merchants and explorers arrived in North America (Newfoundland) almost five centuries before Columbus. However, their presence in America was always sporadic and temporary, except for the colonies founded in Greenland around 980, which were abandoned during the 14th and 15th centuries.

spices, tea, precious stones). Together with the wider area around the Mediterranean, Europe was never a strictly "closed world". In addition to the Silk Road, equally ancient caravan routes crossed the Sahara into Central Africa, which however remained essentially an unknown and mysterious region to Europeans. Very few people were able, like Marco Polo, to travel beyond the confines of this vast European and Mediterranean area, and very few types of merchandise were sufficiently precious to make their long-distance trade profitable. Consequently, the process leading to the opening of new trade routes and to the integration of increasingly vast areas into a sort of constantly expanding world economy is fundamentally important. As French historian Pierre Chaunu observed very effectively several decades ago, the process of opening up these closed worlds between the mid-15th and mid-16th centuries marks a fundamental breakthrough in the history of humanity, and lies at the origin of an extremely important process of change.[2]

This process began in 1434, when Portuguese explorer Gil Eanes sailed for the first time beyond Cape Bojador in Western Morocco. This was not only a starting point, but also the end of a journey begun a couple of centuries before, when the great Italian mercantile republics (Genoa and Venice) first sent their maritime trade expeditions beyond the Mediterranean.[3] Their ships mostly sailed northwards, where the Italians used their business skills to open and consolidate commercial routes linking the Mediterranean directly with the large markets of Flanders and England. They found plentiful raw materials, semi-finished products (wool, metals), and a demand for spices; their bases in the Levant gave the Italians the monopoly of this trade. However, they were unable to venture any further south than the port of Safi in Morocco, a centre for gold, spices and ivory transported by caravan from Central Africa. The same technical difficulties that prevented them from sailing further south became even more evident when the Italians attempted to venture westwards. For instance, Genoese merchants and explorers Ugolino and Vadino Vivaldi in 1291 rediscovered the Canary Islands (already known to the Romans as the Fortunate Isles) and then sailed into the open Atlantic with the aim of reaching the Indies, but their two galleys never returned.

The first and most serious technical problem the Italians encountered on these early expeditions was technological: although their galleys were

---

[2] P. Chaunu, *Du pluriel à un singulier*, in P. Léon (ed.), *Histoire économique et sociale du monde*, Vol. I, Paris, 1970.

[3] In 1277, for the first time the Republic of Genoa sent its annual fleet west, towards the North Sea, followed by the Republic of Venice at the start of the 14th century.

well-suited to trade and warfare in the Mediterranean, they were not capable of ocean voyages. Easy to manoeuvre and powered essentially by rowers, with sails used only occasionally, once the galleys were outside the Mediterranean they were unable to sail far from the coastline without running serious risks, and their low sides offered inadequate protection against ocean waves. In the North Sea and the Baltic, however, traders mostly used round high-sided cogs, which were capable of carrying very heavy loads. These ships enabled the success of the Hanseatic League, an alliance of trading cities led by Lübeck, which monopolised trade in the Baltic and Northern Europe for much of the Middle Ages. The cogs, however, were unsuitable for long-distance Atlantic voyages; having only one sail, they were too slow and also difficult to manoeuvre.

Portugal's success where the powerful and enterprising Italian republics had failed and its new role in pioneering the great exploration of the Atlantic were due first of all to great advances in naval technology. They resulted from a combination of northern and Mediterranean shipbuilding principles. Hence the innovations were born of contacts and ideas exchanged between different peoples, enabled by the maritime trade routes between the Mediterranean and Baltic. At the same time came the fundamentally important invention of the sternpost rudder, which made sailing ships much more manoeuvrable. The Portuguese had been deep-sea fishermen for centuries and had become increasingly involved in the trade along their coasts, assimilating also the most advanced commercial methods of the time. They were thus in an ideal position to take advantage of innovations in naval technology. The caravel, symbol of the first phase of exploration and establishment of the new Atlantic routes, was developed in Portuguese shipyards around the mid-15th century under the direction of Prince Henry the Navigator, with the specific aim of expansion into the Atlantic.

Figure 2.1. The evolution of naval technology: from galley and cog to caravel

Galley – used in the Mediterranean

Cog – used in the North Sea and Baltic

Caravel – vessel symbolising the opening of the Atlantic routes

The rounding of Cape Bojador in 1434, at a distance of 2,000 km from the Portuguese coast, marked a technical and psychological breakthrough. Europeans possessed no knowledge of the winds beyond that point, and any reasonable hope of a safe return home depended on having suitable ships and good navigation skills. The Portuguese pushed on southwards with the aim of reaching the Indies by circumnavigating Africa, although they were completely unaware of the continent's enormous size. It took them almost forty years to reach the Gulf of Guinea for the very first time, mid-way along the route from north to south. One indication of their increasing ability is that it took much less time for them to complete the second half of the journey; in 1488, explorer Bartolomé Diaz returned to Lisbon after successfully rounding the Cape of Good Hope at the southern tip of Africa for the first time.

In the meantime, the Portuguese had begun to establish permanent trading bases along the African coast, establishing important trades in valuable goods, such as gold, ivory and spices of the Gulf of Guinea, which soon became an important supply centre also of slaves. They were still far from their target destination in the Indies, but believed that it was almost in reach. This is why when Genoese explorer, Christopher Columbus proposed an alternative route to the Indies, the Portuguese declined the offer, preferring to complete the project they had begun decades before. In fact, once they had rounded the Cape of Good Hope, the winds and currents that had hampered their southward journey now drove the Portuguese rapidly northwards. In 1498, Vasco da Gama reached Calicut in India, thus realising a dream the Portuguese had pursued for almost a century.

Columbus found a better reception for his bizarre idea in Spain. In the same year (1492) as they completed the Christian *reconquista* of the Iberian Peninsula with the conquest of the kingdom of Granada,[4] Spanish sovereigns Isabella of Castile and Ferdinand of Aragon financed Columbus' expedition to reach the East Indies and particularly China by sailing westwards, with the evident intention of taking control of trade routes not under Portuguese domination. As is known, Columbus did not reach India, but made landfall in the Americas, launching an entirely new phase of exploration and colonisation, which gradually brought this area of the world into the nascent world economy. It was the Portuguese who eventually managed to sail to the East Indies; they reached the Malacca Peninsula in

---

[4] The *reconquista* was the period of almost 750 years during which the Christian kingdoms in the north of the Iberian Peninsula gradually "reconquered" the regions that the Arabs had taken from the Visigoth kingdom in 711, known collectively as *Al-Andalus*.

Malaysia in 1510, China in 1513, and Japan in 1543. These brilliant results were achieved just as the Mediterranean was engaged in a bitter struggle with the expanding Ottoman Empire, which threatened the possessions of the Republics of Genoa and Venice in the Levant. Even more serious was that the Ottomans threatened to interrupt the traditional channels (still controlled by Italian merchants) via which Europe received its supplies of spices.

For several decades, the Portuguese maintained a sort of monopoly of the maritime trades between Europe and the Far East. Their technological and military superiority allowed them to come very close to completely replacing Arabs in the rich Indian Ocean trade. The Portuguese presence in Asia not only involved the profitable but complex trade with Europe, but also included control of many local activities; they exercised a kind of economic dominion, which would in time be succeeded by the more direct control of other European powers.

Figure 2.2. West meets East: the Portuguese in Japan

The geographical discoveries and establishment of new communication routes had an inestimable economic, social and cultural importance in opening up Europe's "closed world". In the late Middle Ages, only around 1% of total production was traded over long distances inside the various "closed worlds": Europe and the Mediterranean, the Far East, and Central America. Now however, the ancient trading areas were connected in a sort of world economic system, expanding continually in progressive waves from an epicentre in Europe, a system integrating existent communication routes as it developed, from the Silk Road and other ancient caravan routes to the Arab trade routes on the Indian Ocean. The goods in transit across this new economic space were only a small part of the total trade, around 1:10,000 in 1550.[5] However, this tiny fraction would succeed in breaking the boundaries of the "closed worlds", in questioning long-established balances, and in profoundly changing the way people viewed the world and their own role in it. This was a major turning point in history; once this space had been established, the path forward was inexorably mapped out, and so it can be said that the period 1434-1550 marked the start of a kind of "proto-globalisation".

2.2. The Great Divergence: causes and timing

The great process of opening up the world between the end of the Middle Ages and the start of the early modern age was led by some of the great Eurasian civilisations. These were undoubtedly the most likely to launch this process, given their wealth of institutional and technological advantages (accumulated since the urban revolution of the Bronze Age) as well as their environmental and demographic advantages (Eurasia contained by far the greatest share of the world population, and almost all the world's most densely populated areas). For this reason, it is quite easy to answer the question: "Why Eurasia?" However, the change originated in the West, so the next question must be: "Why Europe and not Asia?" This second question is about the causes of the so-called "Great Divergence", and is not easy to answer.

The meaning of the term Great Divergence must be clarified. The expression is very popular nowadays and refers to two aspects. Firstly, it indicates the process by which Western Europe gradually emerged as the richest and most powerful area of the world. On the other hand, it also indicates the capacity of this world area to overcome the limitations typical of pre-industrial agrarian economies, consenting a relative improvement in living conditions and the start of the Industrial Revolution. Obviously, better living conditions helped to consolidate European supremacy in the long term, but only a few historians indicate that they may have been the principal cause of the Great Divergence.

There is no doubt that Europe had achieved a position of global supremacy by the 19th century, with most of the planet either under direct domination or else in a condition allowing Europe to impose its own rules and interests. Although there are differing ideas as to when the Great Divergence actually began, many indicators suggest that development was al-

---

[5] P. Chaunu, *Du pluriel à un singulier*, cit.

ready differentiated in the period *before* the Industrial Revolution. For example, urbanization rates generally reflect the level of relative economic development, and it can be seen that Asia (China and India) had similar and even slightly higher urbanisation rates than Western Europe in the late Middle Ages, while Eastern Europe lay far behind. However, Western Europe began to overtake Asia during the 16th century, and the difference became more pronounced over time, due to the combined effect of accelerated growth in Europe and the slow decline seen in Asia from the 17th century.

Figure 2.3. Urbanization levels in Europe and Asia (1300-1850, %)

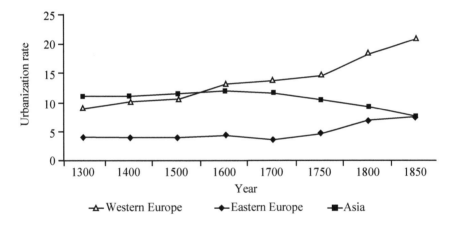

Source: D. Acemoglu, S. Johnson, J.A Robinson, "The Rise of Europe", in *American Economic Review*, 2005. In the graph, Asia refers only to India and China.

In 1500, the most advanced Asian civilizations (India, China and Japan) were at least level with Europe in science and technology. Asia, and particularly China, was still ahead of Europe in some fields, and many key breakthroughs occurred there well before they reached Europe. For example, while printing existed in China (in the sense of mechanized writing) from as early as 868 CE, it developed in Europe only during the 15th century. However, if the East was more advanced than the West throughout the Middle Ages, why did the balance begin to tip the other way in the 16th century? This is known as the "Needham Question", after the author of a monumental history of Chinese science and civilization. Answering this question means asking questions about what was undoubtedly one of the crucial factors in European dominance: its technological and scientific supremacy.

There is no agreement among historians on the origins and causes of the Great Divergence. In general, explanations can be classified as belonging to three broad categories: 1) demographic; 2) institutional; 3) geographical and geopolitical.

Demographic explanations

Eurasia's high population density, linked to the spread of advanced agricultural technologies and the relative "original" abundance of plant species suitable for domestication and human consumption, is one factor explaining why such a major historical process as the great opening of the world began here and not elsewhere. A few decades ago, a similar theory was put forward to explain Europe's supremacy compared with Asia. According to this theory, the population in the Mediterranean area was more concentrated than that of the enormous Chinese Empire or Indian sub-continent, and communications were therefore easier. These conditions not only enabled the rapid diffusion of ideas and innovations, but also provided the critical mass and (due to the constant pressure on the limited resources available in a relatively restricted area) the incentives to produce innovations.

More recently, economic historian Gregory Clark has suggested a different demographic explanation for the origins of the Great Divergence. According to Clark, the decisive impulse came from the Black Death (so that the origins of the Great Divergence lie in the 14th century). When the plague returned to Europe in 1347, it remained endemic for centuries, profoundly changing the biological environment and causing a regime of high mortality, which provided a "solution" to the Malthusian trap. By destroying the population, the successive plagues afflicting Europe over several centuries[6] prevented the population from "destroying" all possibilities of any improvement in *per capita* income obtained via technological progress.[7] In other words, by reducing people's life *expectancy*, the plague paradoxi-

---

[6] The plague was endemic in Europe until the end of the 17th century. Thereafter, serious epidemics did occur, but were always caused by the arrival of infection from outside Europe (North Africa or the Middle East).

[7] G. Clark, *A Farewell to Alms. A Brief Economic History of the World*, Princeton, 2007. Before Clark, historians providing demographic explanations for the Great Divergence had insisted more on fertility than on mortality. According to a school of interpretation led by demographer John Hajnal, some typical Western European social institutions, in particular the relatively high marriage age, contributed to a reduction in the average number of children per couple, thus slowing the rate of population growth. J. Hajnal, *European Marriage Patterns in Perspective*, in *Population in History. Essays in Historical Demography*, 1965, pp. 101-143.

cally brought about an improvement in their *conditions* of life. The proof is, for example, the permanent rise in real wages which began in various parts of Europe immediately after the Black Death.

Institutional explanations

Economic, social and political institutions are also often used to explain the origins of the Great Divergence. The underlying idea is that Western Europe's typical institutions were 1) different from the typical institutions of East Asia, and 2) more apt to enable the emergence of societies capable of introducing economic and technical-scientific innovations. For example Joseph Needham, who built on ideas already proposed by renowned German sociologist Max Weber, underlined the importance of the spread of universities in Western Europe. According to Needham, the universities fostered the development of knowledge, triggering the "scientific revolution" of the Renaissance, symbolised by Galileo Galilei (1564-1642), the first scientist to formalise the principles of the scientific method. For Needham, the age of Galileo was when Europe began to overtake China in some fundamental scientific fields (mathematics, astronomy and physics). In the economic sphere, he sees the mercantile cities as playing a similar role to universities, as crucibles of advanced economic institutions, and the chosen residence place of the bourgeoisie, whose mentality and culture made them interested in enterprise and innovation. On the other hand, since the strongly centralised state systems of the great Asian empires were based on (very advanced) agrarian societies, they not only restricted the development of trade and the emergence of "capitalistic" economic elites, but also impeded scientific progress.

The economic doctrine of neo-institutionalism (according to which every society needs institutions in order to organise interaction between producers, consumers and the state, and the efficiency of an economic system depends ultimately on that of its institutions) has inspired many writers to propose different combinations of institutions as the possible cause of the Great Divergence. These range from market conditions (theorised as being more widespread, efficient and "free" in Europe than in Asia), to the progressive improvements in private property rights in the West, to the different degree of interest taken by the political institutions in the requests of the economic elites.

Some aspects of the institutional explanations are difficult to refute. For example, it is fairly evident that, for different reasons in each case, the state and governmental structures of the great Asian empires (Chinese Empire, Indian Mughal Empire, Japanese Shogunate, and Ottoman Empire) became increasingly inefficient, rigid and incapable of protecting their peoples from a European interference which was often extremely aggressive, especially in economic terms. Nevertheless, it is also difficult to deny the existence of some astonishing similarities across Eurasia, of which the institutions are perhaps the most important, as underlined by Pomeranz, Goody and many others.[8] Those who refuse an institutional explanation usually identify demographic, geographical or geopolitical factors as the cause of the Great Divergence, and often bring its beginnings much further forward in time.

Geographical and geopolitical explanations

Why did European ships reach China, if Chinese ships did not reach Europe? This is not a purely rhetorical question, because even in this field the Chinese started out with an advantage. Between 1413 and 1433, Admiral Zheng He led various diplomatic and exploratory missions towards the West, sailing with dozens of ships and thousands of men as far as Mogadishu and Mombasa in East Africa. However, he ventured no further, despite having made an impressively long voyage (proof of the remarkable development of Chinese naval technology and navigation science), before the Portuguese were able to complete even the first stage of their travels by rounding Cape Bojador. According to some, Zheng He did not attempt to circumnavigate Africa (like the Chinese merchants who had preceded him to the Gulf of Aden and East Africa) because he encountered the same problems the Portuguese faced on their southbound voyage along the Africa's western coast. There was, however, one fundamental difference: the Portuguese tackled these problems on the first stage of their voyage, whereas the Chinese were already very far from home; at this point, they simply decided it was not worth going any further, and began the long journey back.

This line of reasoning can be set within the wider category of possible "geographical" explanations of the Great Divergence, identifying environmental obstacles as the source of a possible long-term advantage. Jared Diamond in particular has suggested that the origin of European supremacy compared with Asia (apart from the many advantages possessed by the entire Eurasian landmass) lay in the natural barriers (mountain ranges, rivers) breaking Europe up into fragmented areas, making it relatively unsuited to the emergence of single great empires. On the contrary, European geography favoured the appearance of relatively small states in continual competi-

---

[8] K. Pomeranz, *The Great Divergence: China, Europe, and the Making of the Modern World Economy*, Princeton, 2002; J. Goody, *The East in the West*, Cambridge, UK, 1996.

tion, which were more likely to innovate because they were always attempting to gain advantages over their rivals. Diamond suggests that the great Asian empires (particularly China and Japan) were often ready to forbid potentially useful technological innovations, preferring to preserve social stability because they had no direct competitors, thus there was no significant short-term cost if they rejected progress.[9] For example, the Japanese progressively abandoned firearms during the 17th century, as the Shogunate attempted to prevent the outbreak of civil wars like those which had devastated the country in previous decades. Similarly, China abandoned ocean navigation following Zheng He's expeditions, partly because of the enormous expense these ventures entailed, and partly because the faction promoting such expeditions was no longer in favour at the Imperial court.

Other writers highlight the advantages enjoyed by some parts of the world as a result of their geographical position and specific environmental features. In particular, Kenneth Pomeranz has stressed the importance for Western Europe of enjoying relatively easy access to the Americas, where supplies of essential resources could be obtained. The fact was that both Western Europe and Asia were faced with a crucial ecological problem during the early modern age. In both areas, the law of diminishing returns meant that intensive and advanced agricultural systems ran the constant risk of becoming trapped in an increasingly labour intensive economy.[10] According to Pomeranz, this was effectively the fate of the great Asian empires. Europe was able to avoid this trap only because the discovery and subsequent exploitation of the Americas, with their natural resources and fertile soils, enabled Europe to pursue a capital intensive model of development. In addition, in certain specific areas of the continent (in particular England), there was a relative abundance of some key resources near densely populated areas, especially of coal. The replacement of wood with coal allowed more intensive land use and the development of energy intensive production sectors, which was to be a decisive factor in launching the Industrial Revolution. Pomeranz, however, tends to minimise Europe's relative ad-

---

[9] J. Diamond, *Guns, Germs and Steel*, New York, 1997.

[10] The law of diminishing returns postulates that while the other factors remain constant, the addition of one production factor to a production process determines (at least beyond a certain threshold) a diminishing output for each unit of the added factor. Thus, if land suitable for agriculture is available in a finite quantity, and if agricultural systems are already quite intensive, the need to increase output (in particular, to feed a growing population) will make it necessary to intensify cultivation by using a larger workforce, but with diminishing returns. According to Pomeranz, this was the case in China, Japan, and possibly also in northern India. K. Pomeranz, *The Great Divergence*, cit.

vantage during the early modern age, maintaining that a true divergence in living conditions and development levels between West and East appeared only in the 19th century, and that Europe and Asia would have developed in essentially similar ways without Europe's privileged access to New World resources.

Many historians, like Pomeranz or even more so, emphasise the exploitation of non-European peoples as an essential factor in the West's achievement of supremacy. In particular, several decades ago, American sociologist Immanuel Wallerstein built on some of Braudel's ideas, interpreting the creation of the first global "world-economy" in terms of the progressive institution of a system articulated in a core, a semi-periphery and a periphery.[11]

According to this interpretation, the dominion (especially economic, but also political and military) of the centre imposes an unequal trade system which consolidates the supremacy of the centre, but at the same time it tends to make the relative underdevelopment of the peripheries into a permanent condition. The origin of the process is held to be the small advantage that some areas of Western Europe had in terms of accumulation of capital: this small advantage increased and became permanent with the gradual formation of the world-economy and its expansion to cover the entire globe.

As should be evident from this summary of some different interpretations (there are also many others) of such a complex and important issue as the Great Divergence, there are no simple explanations, and opinions can differ widely. One aspect, however, must be underlined: the concept of the Great Divergence refers to a condition of Western supremacy, which has been greatly eroded in recent years by the emergence of other economies, in particular China. There are many who foresee China's return to the position of supremacy it appears to have enjoyed until around 1500. However, there are also many who theorise that the conditions for this to occur do not exist, at least in terms of economic development (measurable, albeit imperfectly, via GDP *per capita*) if not in terms of the total size of the Chinese economy. From the point of view of world economic history, the question is important, because the first case would mean that the Great Divergence was merely an interlude (albeit a relatively long one, up to a maxi-

---

[11] For Braudel and Wallerstein, a "world-economy" is not necessarily a "world" economy, since various world-economies co-existed at different times. According to Braudel, it is rather "a fragment of the world, an economically autonomous section", with definite borders and a system of internal trade (similarly to the "closed worlds" we discussed earlier) as well as an internal hierarchy between a core and a periphery. F. Braudel, *The Perspectives of the World*, Berkeley, 1984, p. 70.

mum of five or six centuries) in human history, and not the major and irreversible turning point that almost all historians took for granted until just a few decades ago.

2.3. Beyond Eurasia: America, Africa and Oceania

The inevitability of European supremacy compared with Asia is a matter of lively debate. However, no academics appear to believe that Western Europe's role in launching the great process of expansion and construction of a world economic system could have been played by the great Central American civilisations, the kingdoms of sub-Saharan Africa or Australian aborigines, because these cultures were at a disadvantage from the outset.

On the contrary, when Europe had its first contacts with these civilisations, European technological and military superiority was so evident that Europeans were able to impose their interests almost without any hindrance. The most famous case involves Central and South America, where there were actually two empires capable of mobilising vast resources: the Inca and Aztec Empires. The story of Spanish *conquistador* Hernán Cortés is emblematic. After landing in Mexico in 1518, he overthrew the powerful Aztec Empire in just three years with only 600 men and 15 cannons, although he did receive help from local rivals of the Aztecs and also resorted to treachery in order to capture Emperor Moctezuma. A similar fate befell the Inca Empire, conquered by Francisco Pizarro in 1532-1533. These easy victories were not only due to the superior quality of European weaponry and the use of gunpowder and horses, unknown in the Americas before then; an even more important factor was the involuntary "bacteriological weapon" of pathogens brought by the European explorers and *conquistadores*, against which the *indios* had absolutely no immunities. Plague, smallpox and even the common cold were devastating for the native populations. On the other hand, Europeans found the American biological environment relatively healthy, and the only important disease to travel in the opposite direction, from the Americas to Europe, was syphilis.

In the Americas, the Spanish looked in vain for the spices which had been the first objective of the Columbus expedition, finding instead large quantities of precious metals, obtained in the first instance by stripping the *indios* of their possessions, and then by exploiting the great gold and silver deposits that were gradually discovered. The natives were forced into a system of compulsory labour (*encomienda*). Miners were subjected to harsh working conditions and separated from their families for up to 10 months a year; both factors not only increased mortality rates but also reduced the birth rate. The result was an unprecedented demographic collapse: the population of Central Mexico, estimated as 6.3 million in 1548, had fallen to 1.9 million in 1580 and amounted to barely 1 million in 1605. Population decline in the area under the Inca Empire (Peru) was equally dramatic, and in North America it is estimated that between 1500 and 1800 the indigenous population fell from approximately 5 million to scarcely 60,000.

Although the Spanish and Portuguese actions in Central and South America played a major role in eroding the structure of native societies, thus contributing to their demographic collapse, the Europeans did not aim to destroy the local populations. On the contrary, they encountered an important problem when the native workforce dwindled, since it would have been impossible to replace the losses with immigration from the thinly populated Iberian Peninsula. The solution was found in the slave trade, of which the Portuguese were initially the unrivalled leaders. Subsequently they would face competition, in decreasing order of importance, from England, France, Spain and the Dutch Republic. Between 1500 and the trade's final abolition in 1870, 9.5 million people were forcibly shipped from Africa to the Americas. Most of this trade took place after 1700 (before this, only 1.5 million slaves were imported to the Americas), and was mainly directed towards the flourishing sugar plantations of Brazil and the Caribbean.

The Spanish and Portuguese built up vast and articulated colonial empires in the Americas. Since the Spanish colonies incorporated the pre-existing states, they immediately included a vast hinterland, although the degree of control effectively exercised over this territory varied from area to area. In Africa and in Asia, however, the Iberians adopted a very different strategy. In Africa, the Portuguese went no further than establishing a solid network of outposts, trading posts and forts, concentrating only on gaining control of the coasts and shipping lanes, trading with local peoples to obtain African goods (including slaves from the Gulf of Guinea, mostly provided directly by the African kingdoms who had taken them captive in war or raids). The Portuguese also pursued a similar strategy in Asia from their Indian bases in Goa and Calicut, the Malacca Peninsula and Macao in China. In Asia, the Spanish limited their control almost exclusively to the Philippines (colonized from 1565), also because the Treaties of Tordesillas (1494) and Zaragoza (1529) divided the world into precise spheres of influence along lines of longitude, helping to prevent the latent conflict between the two great European colonial empires from leading to open warfare.

Figure 2.4. The Spanish and Portuguese colonial empires circa 1600

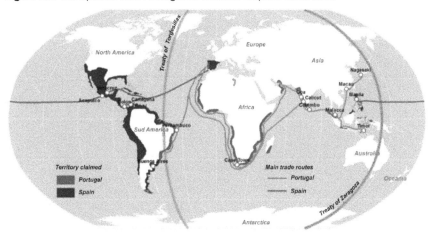

Other areas of the world (much of North America and Oceania) were colonised and incorporated into the world economy with more or less of a delay, and by other actors: mainly the French, English and Dutch. The case of North America is discussed in the next chapter.

From the early 17th century, the Dutch were the first to explore Oceania, a continent with a complex and fragmented morphology. They were then followed by the French, while the English arrived last on the scene. British naval officer and explorer Captain James Cook was the first European to arrive in New Zealand (1769) and on Australia's east coast (1770). This was far more hospitable than the island's west coast where Dutch and French explorers had alternated for over 150 years, without ever considering it economically advantageous to set up colonies or trade with the local peoples. Only about twenty years after Cook's voyage did the English found their first Australian colony at Botany Bay (1788), partly as a reaction to the loss of most of their North American colonies, which had now grown to a point where they were able to rebel and gain their independence.

Bibliography

Braudel F., *Civilisation matérielle, économie et capitalisme, XVᵉ-XVIIIᵉ siècle.* Paris, 1979 (English ed. *Civilization and Capitalism, 15ᵗʰ-18th Centuries,* Berkeley, 1979-1984).

Chaunu P., *Du pluriel à un singulier,* in P. Léon (ed.), *Histoire économique et sociale du monde,* Vol. I, Paris, 1970.

Clark G., *A Farewell to Alms. A Brief Economic History of the World*, Princeton, 2007.

Diamond J., *Guns, Germs and Steel*, New York, 1997.

Goody J., *The East in the West*, Cambridge, UK, 1996.

Livi Bacci M., *A Concise History of World Population,* Oxford, 2017.

Pomeranz K., *The Great Divergence. China, Europe, and the Making of the Modern World Economy*, Princeton, 2002.

Chapter 3
NEW PLAYERS, NEW INSTITUTIONS

SUMMARY: 3.1. From south to north. – 3.2. Origins of the Little Divergence. – 3.3. On both sides of the Atlantic. – Bibliography. – *Demographic transition*.

During the first stage of the great opening of the "closed worlds", which began towards the end of the 15th century with the circumnavigation of Africa and Columbus' first voyage to the Americas, the principal players were definitely the Portuguese and Spanish. They took full advantage of the opportunities created during the Middle Ages by the great Italian trading powers. So southern Europe drove the changes in this early phase of expansion. Nevertheless, the great Spanish and Portuguese empires were already beginning to struggle in the 17th century, as new and determined rivals began to emerge, mostly in northern Europe. The process allowing these new players gradually to gain superiority over southern Europe, not only in military terms, but more importantly in economic, social and institutional terms, is known as the "Little Divergence". The Great and Little Divergences together form the complex and fascinating framework for the shifts affecting the global economy during the early modern era.

3.1. From south to north

Since ancient times, Europe's economic centre had always been in the south, close to the Mediterranean. This situation was consolidated during the Roman Empire; even after it ceased to exist, many of the principal Roman cities continued to play a leading role in medium- and long-range trade, and from the 11th century were fully involved in the rise of the communes. The leading role of southern Europe, particularly Italy, lasted throughout the Middle Ages, and was threatened at certain stages only by the Hanseatic cities of the Baltic coast and by Flanders. Inside Italy itself, four great mercantile cities were engaged in a long and often hard competition for supremacy: Florence, Genoa, Milan and Venice. In the century and a half following the Black Death, the economic centre of Europe and the Mediterranean was Venice.

The development of the great Atlantic trade routes, following Columbus' landfall in the Americas and Vasco da Gama's arrival in India, dealt a hard blow to Venetian supremacy. Her territorial expansion on the mainland of northern Italy[1] ended after the crushing defeat at the Battle of Agnadello (1509), when Venice faced a coalition of France, the Holy Roman Empire and various other Italian states,[2] and repeated clashes with the Ottoman Empire only aggravated the situation. At this point, it seemed likely that Europe's economic centre would shift westwards, towards Seville and Lisbon, the principal ports of Spain and Portugal. However, despite the immediate advantages these two countries gained from their vigorous colonial and commercial expansion, especially from the 16th century, the medium- and long-term situation was much more complex. Portugal was a small state, limited by its scarce demographic and economic resources, which led it to rely on foreign operators, especially those based in the Flemish city of Antwerp, to redistribute and sell spices in the rich markets of northern Europe. Moreover, Portugal's almost incredible success in creating a vast commercial empire on the African and Asian coasts immediately attracted determined rivals (the Dutch and English *in primis*), who proved to be extremely difficult opponents for the Portuguese.

In some respects, Spain also overreached itself. Besides possessing an enormous colonial empire, it had acquired direct control of two of Italy's principal states (the State of Milan and the Kingdom of Naples) following the "Italian Wars" (1494-1559), and actually dominated most of the peninsula. Spain also had extensive possessions in central and northern Europe, corresponding to the territories controlled by the ancient Duchy of Burgundy, including the extremely wealthy Low Countries.[3] Spanish supremacy on the continent meant inevitable conflict with Western Europe's major powers, particularly France and England. The situation was further complicated by the long period of religious wars, linked to the Protestant

---

[1] From the end of the 13th century, Venice had begun a dynamic process of territorial expansion beyond her limited possessions in the Lagoon area by incorporating various important *signorie* (Padua, Treviso, Verona, Vicenza), thus creating tension with the principal Italian states.

[2] The coalition, known as the League of Cambrai, aimed to end the Venetian expansion, and possibly also to share out Venetian territories on the mainland. Following Agnadello, Venice managed to break up the League and recover some of its lost territories. However, the risks involved, and the changes in the Italian political situation at the end of the "Italian Wars" (1494-1559), led Venice to give up any ambition of further territorial expansion in mainland Italy.

[3] Charles V Habsburg (1500-1558), King of Spain and Holy Roman Emperor, inherited the crowns of Castile and Aragon (Spain) from his mother Joanna of Trastámara, and the territories of the Duchy of Burgundy from his Habsburg father, Philip the Handsome.

Reformation, conventionally considered as beginning on 31st October 1517, when German theologian Martin Luther nailed his Ninety-Five Theses to the door of All Saints' Church in Wittemberg. Lastly, the way in which the American colonial empire was exploited, as well as the kind of colonial products imported, created problems and not only advantages. In fact, colonial exploitation was often ruthless and "extractive", causing great suffering among the native populations and the slave work-force imported from Africa; many see this as compromising the future development prospects of the colonized territories. Regarding the products imported, these were mainly precious metals. Since the Spanish economy was relatively backward in the early 16th century, the influx of large quantities of precious metals not only caused notable market imbalances, but also slowed down the development of local production. In fact, the inflation generated by American silver and gold meant that Spanish goods became more expensive than those imported from abroad. Additionally, only a small share of this American gold and silver actually remained in Spain, given the crown's reliance on the great foreign bankers (originally the Germans, thereafter the Genoese), so that the influx of American precious metals is thought to have actually hindered economic development in the medium to long term, rather than aiding it.

The structural weaknesses of the Spanish and Portuguese empires are only one of the reasons why the Iberian Peninsula could not become Europe's economic centre. The other reason is the considerable strength and enterprise of the more advanced areas of Northern Europe. Instead of shifting westwards, the continent's economic centre actually moved northwards to Antwerp in Flanders. The area boasted long-standing mercantile and manufacturing traditions, especially in the textile industry, and had always taken advantage of its favourable geographical position, allowing it to act as a centre of international trade linking the Mediterranean and the Baltic.

Of the great Flemish cities, Antwerp was most able to exploit the new opportunities offered by the expansion of the Atlantic trade routes, and it also enjoyed the considerable advantage, at least in this stage, of being a Spanish possession. Growing quantities of spices arrived in Antwerp from the earliest years of the 16th century, imported by the Portuguese from Africa and Asia (pepper and nutmeg), together with sugar from the Antilles, and non-colonial goods, including English cloth (finished and dyed in Flanders) and French and Spanish wines. American silver and gold also arrived in the city, transferred by the Spanish in the Low Countries to finance their activities in continental Europe and to buy massive quantities of goods for their developing American colonies. Antwerp thus became also a fundamental financial centre, due to the bases established there by the great bankers of Augsburg, particularly the Fuggers, who were Emperor Charles V's great financiers.

Antwerp was Europe's economic capital for almost all the first half of the 16th century. The city's fortunes began to wane with the first bankruptcy of the king of Spain, Philip II (Charles V's son) in 1557, which had a very serious impact on the city's activity as a financial centre. This was followed by a long series of rebellions and wars by the Low Countries against Spanish rule, starting in 1566 and soon taking on a religious character, since the rebel provinces were also largely Protestant. Antwerp also rebelled, but was re-taken by the Spanish in 1585. The city's port was then blockaded for almost twenty years by the rebels, to the benefit of the cities of the Northern Low Countries, especially Amsterdam.

For several decades, the problems of the Low Countries tipped the balance again towards southern Europe, especially Genoa, which had become the centre of European finance. This was also due to the city's privileged relationship with the Spanish crown, which it gained by supplying financial services after the 1557 bankrupcy had seriously damaged the German bankers of Augsburg.

Spain's decline during the 17th century, however, also meant the decline of Genoa, and Europe's economic centre shifted back to Northern Europe, to the city of Amsterdam. From 1585, the Northern Low Countries had effectively obtained their independence, although the situation was ratified only after many decades of war against Spain. This was eventually achieved with the Treaty of Münster, included in the Peace of Westphalia (1648), which put an end to the devastating Thirty Years' War and the wars of religion in a continent now divided into Catholic and Protestant areas.

Figure 3.1. Amsterdam citizens celebrating the independence of the Dutch Republic (Treaty of Münster, 1648)

The revolt of the Northern Low Countries created the Dutch Republic, a new power that was to play a crucial role in the European economy and the nascent global economy throughout much of the early modern age. The new country's biggest port, Amsterdam, obtained the trade routes formerly belonging to Antwerp. Additionally, when Portugal entered into a personal union[4] with Spain, the Dutch Republic immediately seized the chance to take control of Portugal's trade routes and colonial possessions. The final result was that the Portuguese were able to keep their possessions in South America and Africa, but in Asia were mostly replaced by the Dutch, and managed to retain only their important bases at Goa (India) and Macao (China).

In order to wage war against Portugal, and then to manage the expansion and administration of a colonial Empire that soon became global (Figure 3.2), the Dutch made effective use of an innovation: the privileged trading companies. These were mostly founded in England, the Dutch Republic and France from the 16th century, in order to exploit the commercial opportunities offered by the new trade routes, and to make up for lost time in comparison with the Portuguese and Spanish "first comers". These companies of merchants had a long-term charter (for 15-20 years and renewable) and possessed special privileges, such as the exclusive right to use certain routes or trading monopolies for certain goods. The major companies were also given the right to stipulate commercial and diplomatic treaties in the areas of the world where they operated, to recruit and maintain a fleet and army, and to govern the bases and territories they obtained outside Europe.

The Dutch East India Company (VOC – *Vereenigde Oostindische Compagnie*), founded in 1602, had all these characteristics, as did its major rival the English East India Company (EIC). The considerable commercial success of these companies also helped diversify trade with Asia, accompanying spices (dominant throughout the 16th century) with Indian cotton, Chinese silk and porcelain, indigo, cane sugar and other products. The Dutch West Indies Company (WIC – *West-Indische Compagnie*) was founded in 1621 to manage trade and colonies in the Americas, and one of its prerogatives was that it was authorized to carry out privateering, plundering the Spanish galleons which transported gold and silver to Europe.

---

[4] The two separate crowns of Spain and Portugal were united in the "person" of the same monarch from 1580 until the union was dissolved in 1640, following a Portuguese uprising.

Figure 3.2. The Dutch colonial empire

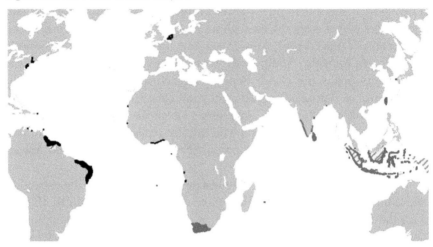

Note: Areas under WIC control in black, and under VOC control in dark grey. Territories acquired during the 19th century in light grey.

In their wars against the Portuguese, the Dutch Republic had often obtained the help of another emerging northern European power: England. In Asia, the English took from the Portuguese the important fortress of Hormuz, which controlled the Strait of Hormuz and consequently, all the trade between India, the Levant and Europe which passed through the Persian Gulf. During the 17th century, the English consolidated their presence in India, while the Dutch still dominated the rich Indian Ocean and East Asia trades.

During the first two centuries of the early modern era, however, the English had concentrated more on colonial and commercial expansion to the west, particularly in North America, than towards the already crowded east. England and Holland soon became rivals for the Asian routes in the 17th century, but the competition between the two was much more intense in the North Sea and Baltic. The Navigation Acts, introduced in 1651 and strengthened during the following decades, established that all goods arriving in England's ports and those of her colonies had to be transported by English ships. This measure reflected mercantilist principles perfectly,[5] and was clearly aimed at wresting at least some of the international colonial

---

[5] Mercantilism was the prevalent economic doctrine in Europe from the 16th century to the first half of the 18th century. Mercantilists held that the State had the duty to protect its own commerce, encourage exports and discourage imports as far as possible. A positive trade balance would, it was maintained, enable the accumulation of gold and silver reserves, thus increasing the nation's wealth.

trade from the Dutch, who also controlled a large share of the trade carried out along the English coast. The Navigation Acts were followed by three wars with the Dutch Republic between 1652 and 1674, at the end of which England emerged in a generally stronger position, having been helped at some stages by France, another great European state aiming to carve itself a share of international trade at the expense of the Dutch. It was only from the beginning of the 18th century, however, that the English fleet became so enormous that England could dominate the seas of the entire world. The economic centre of Europe then began to shift towards London, a city already on the way to becoming Europe's leading metropolis (Table 3.1), whose supremacy would be further consolidated by the Industrial Revolution.

In the gradual movement of Europe's economic centre from Venice to Antwerp, to Genoa, then Amsterdam and finally to London, the general trend was a definite shift from south to north, accompanied by the gradual differentiation in economic development between the two ends of the continent: the "Little Divergence". There remains one last aspect to underline before providing a detailed analysis of the causes behind this process.

Historians now agree that the decline of the more advanced areas of southern Europe, especially of Italy, was relative (i.e. due to higher growth rates in the north than in the south) and not absolute. Venice, for example, remained a principal European and world economic centre throughout the 17th century, while Spain enjoyed a period of exceptionally rich art and culture in the 16th and 17th centuries, known as the "Golden Century" (*El Siglo de Oro*). In fact, the relative underdevelopment of southern Europe did not actually become evident and deeply enrooted until the 18th century.

3.2. Origins of the Little Divergence

The Little Divergence between northern and southern Europe has been the object of much debate among academics, like the Great Divergence between Western Europe and Asia. There have been many different and sometimes contrasting interpretations of its causes, timing and development. As with the Great Divergence, some offer geographical/geopolitical or demographic interpretations, while others insist on the importance of institutional factors.

Geographical, geopolitical and demographic explanations

Italy's great mercantile republics had enjoyed the relative advantage of a central position in the Mediterranean, but this actually became a disadvantage in the passage from the Middle Ages to the early modern era. Venice was now imprisoned in the Mediterranean, unable to take a leading role in the nascent Atlantic trade, while its traditional trade with Asia through its Levantine bases was impeded by the inexorable expansion of the Ottoman Empire. Historians who view the expansion of the new trade routes as the primary cause of the Little Divergence tend to consider it as starting in the 16th century.

The first line of demographic interpretation to mention relates to the theories of demographer John Hajnal. He argued that some social institutions typical of Western Europe, particularly the relatively late age at marriage, allowed more effective regulation of fertility, thus leading to a gradual improvement in living standards and a more rapid accumulation of human capital.[6] What had a decisive effect on raising the age at marriage was that neo-local behaviour was more common in Western Europe (i.e. young married couples did not live with their parents) than in Eastern Europe, where the culture was patri-local (i.e. young married couples lived with the husband's parents). Another difference was that it was much more common in Northwestern Europe for young people of both sexes to spend the first stage of their working life in the service of other families (life-cycle service), which also helped them to accumulate the resources they needed to start their own family. According to Hajnal, in time this practice created a workforce that was more economically and psychologically mobile and independent. This was not only a pre-condition, but constituted a real cause of the divergence between north and south that culminated with the Industrial Revolution.

Hajnal's theories and those he inspired have plenty of followers, but are also crticised, and some recent demographic interpretations of the Little Divergence have underlined other aspects. Gregory Clark has supplemented his interpretation of the Great Divergence by suggesting that the emergence of England in Europe (seen as the outcome of a long-term process starting as far back as the 13th century) can be explained by the exceptional fertility of the country's elites, and by the downward social mobility of many young members of these elites. This was mostly caused by the division of inheritances among many descendants, and was increased by the high fertility rate. The consequence was that the good practices (*memes*) typical of the more dynamic and economically capable members of society also spread among the lower social classes. However, Guido Alfani has

---

[6] Hajnal traced an imaginary line connecting Trieste in Italy with St. Petersburg in Russia during the pre-industrial period; to the west, the age at marriage was relatively high and fertility was relatively low, while to the east, the opposite was the case.

emphasized the role of the terrible plagues in the 17th century, which had more devastating impacts on southern European populations. For example, it is estimated that 30-35% of the population of northern Italy died in the terrible plague of 1629-1630, with a death toll of approximately 2 million. In England, however, the total number of deaths due to the various plagues of the 17th century amounted to no more than 8-10% of the total population in 1600. Plague devastated the more economically advanced area of Italy just as the commercial and industrial competition with Northern Europe became more intense, and the shock it caused to Italy's economic and social structures was so vast that it set the major Italian states on a lower growth path.[7]

Institutional explanations

An exogenous shock caused by the plague is also the crucial component of one recent institutional interpretation of the Little Divergence. According to economic historians Tine de Moor and Jan Luiten van Zanden, the Black Death not only helped consolidate the European marriage pattern (EMP) already described by Hajnal, but also helped to consolidate and extend the labour market, especially in Northwestern Europe, strengthening female participation in this market and reducing inequality between the sexes.[8] These authors have also suggested that the so-called "Industrious Revolution" was essentially the continuation and intensification of this process. The Industrious Revolution led to increased working hours and participation in the labour market from the mid-17th century. It also originated in a revolution in consumption, as families started to demand luxury goods they were unable to produce directly (such as coffee, tea, sugar and tobacco from the colonies), and which had to be purchased on the market in return for money earned with labour.

According to Dutch economic historian Jan de Vries, this process preceeded and facilitated the Industrial Revolution. In fact the Industrious Revolution, which also involved women and adolescents, mostly concerned Flanders and England, where the putting-out system was very widespread, especially in the textile sector (wool and linen). This extremely flexible production system involved a city-based merchant-entrepreneur who organized a rural workforce. Only the final stages of the production process

---

[7] G. Alfani, *Plague in Seventeenth Century Europe and the Decline of Italy. An Epidemiological Hypothesis*, in *European Review of Economic History*, 17, 2013, pp. 408-430.

[8] T. de Moor, J.L. van Zanden, *Girlpower. The European Marriage Pattern (EMP) and Labour Markets in the North Sea Region in the Late Medieval and Early Modern Period*, in *Economic History Review*, LXIII, 2010, pp. 1-33.

were entrusted to skilled urban workers. The merchant-entrepreneur supplied the rural workers with raw materials, stored the semi-finished products in his warehouses, and then marketed the final product.

The labour market is just one of the institutions that may have contributed to the Little Divergence, and different authors have proposed different "institutional combinations" as causes or co-causes.

– *Economic institutions (guilds, stock exchanges, privileged companies)*. During the Middle Ages, most urban manufacturing in both southern and northern Europe was regulated by the guilds, which were associations of master craftsmen with their apprentices and assistants. The guilds established the rhythms and methods of work, imposed their own quality standards, and controlled the levels of pay and profits. This production model began to have problems in the 17th century due to the competition with cheaper goods (especially in the textile sector), mostly produced in the Low Countries and in England. According to a traditional theory, the decline of the guild system in the north was paralleled by its "defensive" rigidification in the south, leading to a gradual differentiation in the efficiency of the manufacturing sector. In the north, as these economic institutions declined, new ones emerged, for example the privileged companies and stock exchanges. This made it easier than ever before to sell shares, including those in the privileged companies; the Amsterdam Stock Exchange was actually founded in 1602 by the Dutch East India Company. Although stock markets had existed in other areas of Europe since the 14th century, especially in Italy, the Amsterdam Stock Exchange is generally considered the first real stock exchange. In many ways, the stock exchanges represented the height of global commercial capitalism that developed during the early modern age.

– *Legal rights (private property, citizenship) and political institutions*. Following the principles of neo-institutionalist economic theory, many academics have underlined the importance of legal rights and the political institutions as potential divergence factors. Economist Douglass C. North has focused on the emergence of "full" and "secure" private property rights, reducing the uncertainty of economic activity, and thus reducing transaction costs,[9] promoting cooperation between economic actors and reducing

---

[9] "Transaction costs" are all the expenses involved in gathering information required in order to establish the value of traded goods, to ascertain ownership rights over the goods and the reliability of the trading partner, and to define, protect and render effective the agreement (e.g. a contract) on which the trade is based. D.C. North, R.P. Thomas, *The Rise of the Western World. A New Economic History*, Cambridge, Mass., 1973.

conflicts. This was the outcome of a complex process of institutional development, which distinguished Europe from Asia, and England from most of Europe. More recently, economic historians Maarten Prak and Jan Luiten Van Zanden have underlined the importance of the consolidation and extension of citizenship rights, intended as a set of mutual rights and obligations regulating the relations between governmental institutions and specific categories of people.[10] This theory holds that the consolidation of civil rights in some areas of Europe, particularly in England and the Dutch Republic, reduced the cost of transactions between individuals and the state, increased the fiscal capacity of the State, and expanded the range and quantity of public goods it provided, including those promoting the accumulation of human capital and economic growth, like education and health. This process is also linked to the emergence of new political institutions and the start of a gradual process of "democratisation". North, together with Barry Weingast, had already underlined the strong impetus the English economy received with the Glorious Revolution of 1688,[11] followed by the establishment of a constitutional monarchy firmly under Parliamentary control. The Bill of Rights (1689) established some fundamental rights, including the right to free elections and to freedom of speech in Parliament. It also obliged the Crown to request Parliament's consent for new taxes and for the abrogation of existing legislation. The Constitution and Parliament made citizens (and creditors) more inclined to trust the State, more willing to provide it with increased resources, and meant that they were better protected from an arbitrary exercise of power; in other words, their property rights were more secure.

Economists Acemoglu, Johnson and Robinson have recently proposed an interesting summary of some of the geographical and institutional theories about the Little Divergence.[12] Starting with the fact that most growth occurring after 1500 in Western Europe involved states which had easy access to the ocean and chose to engage in Atlantic trade, these authors ob-

---

[10] J.L. van Zanden, M. Prak, *Towards an Economic Interpretation of Citizenship. The Dutch Republic between Medieval Communes and Modern Nation States*, in *European Review of Economic History*, 10, 2, 2006, pp. 121-147.

[11] D.C. North, B.R. Weingast, *Constitutions and Commitment: The Evolution of Institutions Governing Public Choice in Seventeenth-Century England*, in *Journal of Economic History*, 49, 4, 1989, pp. 803-832. The "Glorious Revolution", promoted and supported by some members of the English Parliament with help from the Dutch Republic, resulted in the exile of James I Stuart and the enthronement of William I of Orange, previously *Stadtholder* (military governor) of the Dutch Republic.

[12] D. Acemoglu, S. Johnson, J.A. Robinson, *The Rise of Europe. Atlantic Trade, Institutional Change and Growth*, in *American Economic Review*, 2005, 95, pp. 546-579.

serve that the most successful states were those with the least "absolutist" political institutions, in other words England and the Dutch Republic. The relative political openness in these countries created the best conditions for the economic elites to promote the institutional innovations needed to take full advantage of the opportunities offered by the Atlantic trade, which then led to a gradual divergence from the more politically rigid states: France, Spain and Portugal. Divergence also occurred with respect to those non-absolutist states (the Republics of Genoa and Venice) that did not enjoy the advantage of easy access to the Atlantic.

The institutional theories used to explain the Little Divergence also present some controversial aspects. These range from criticism of the "myth" of full property by economist Elinor Ostrom (who underlines how – in certain conditions – shared rights and collective property may actually prove to be economically efficient), to defence of the positive role played by the urban guilds in terms of knowledge transfer, technological innovation, and the financial and coordination services they provided to their members. Most importantly, the guilds served to redress the informational imbalance between buyer and seller, since the corporations provided guarantees regarding quality and the "fair price". Another controversial aspect of the institutional theories involves the debate concerning the effective nature of citizens' rights in pre-industrial societies.

Lastly, to conclude this brief overview of the theories proposed as explanations for the Little Divergence, there are those inspired by Max Weber, viewing the Protestant Reformation as the reason for the emergence in Central and Northern Europe of new attitudes favouring economic activity and the development of capitalism. According to Weber, these attitudes generally distinguished Protestantism from Catholicism, but were particularly strong among Calvinists, whose belief in predestination led them to seek worldly success as a kind of reassurance of their own salvation. Although Weber's theories are still widespread among social scientists, they remain unsupported by solid empirical proof.

3.3. On both sides of the Atlantic

While the Spanish and Portuguese concentrated their attention on Central and South America, which were more densely populated and gave their colonisers more immediate benefits, North America was the focus for the countries whose involvement in colonialism began relatively late. The French were among the first to set foot in this area, beginning their exploration of the Newfoundland and Nova Scotia (known as *Acadia*) coasts and the Gulf of St Lawrence in the 1520s. As early as 1534, explorer Jacques

Cartier claimed vast territories for the French crown in what would become known as New France. However, the French were relatively slow to
colonise the area; after an unsuccessful attempt in 1534, the first French
colony, Port-Royal, was not founded until 1603. One reason for this was
lack of interest by the French Crown. However, from the 16th century the
French had managed to create a flourishing and profitable trade network
(especially in valuable furs) with the Native Americans, with whom they
managed almost always to entertain good relations.

The English were the last to arrive on the continent, after the French,
the Dutch (the WIC was founded in 1621) and the Spanish, who controlled
Florida in the south. Jamestown, the first English colony, was founded in
1607 on Chesapeake Bay in what would later become Virginia, and the Pil-
grim Fathers founded Plymouth in Massachusetts in 1620. This was the
start of a very singular type of colonial migration, involving the Puritans;
this Protestant sect was in open conflict with the Church of England, and
sought greater religious freedom in America, aiming to create a society in
keeping with its own principles. In general, England did not prevent Puri-
tan emigration, but actually encouraged it (according to some historians,
the aim was to get rid of a particularly unruly element of the population).
By 1620, at least 20,000 Puritans had crossed the Atlantic, contributing
greatly to the rapid growth of the English colonies, and helping to incul-
cate some features still widespread in American society, ranging from enterprise and hard work to religious fervour.

There was a stark contrast between the development of the French and
English colonies during the 17th century. Despite considerable expansion
of the area under French control and the establishment of a dense network
of trading trails protected by a system of forts and military outposts, the
French colonies had difficulties attracting emigrants from Europe, partly
because the mercantilist ideology of the French crown tended to have a
negative attitude to any loss of population from the mother country. The
English colonies, on the other hand, had the fastest population growth of all
the European colonies at this stage, and this allowed the development of a
more diversified economy. New England soon succeeded in establishing
flourishing trade and shipbuilding activities alongside its farming, fishing
and logging sectors. In 1664, when the English conquered the Dutch city of
New Amsterdam (renamed New York), they gained possession of all the
North American colonial territories of the Dutch Republic.

Expansion of the English colonies inevitably led to conflict with the
French. Starting in the last decades of the 17th century, a series of wars saw
the the two countries' colonies on opposing sides. With some difficulty, the
English gradually expanded the area under their control, helped by the fact

that their colonies had larger populations. Nonetheless, France still controlled vast areas of North America in 1750, and these separated England's "thirteen colonies" on the Atlantic coast from the Canadian territories claimed by the Hudson Bay Company, founded in 1670. When a new conflict began in 1754, it was the first war to start in the colonies and then spread to Europe: the "Seven Years' War" (1754-1763). The peace treaty marked the end of New France, since virtually all the French colonies in North America were transferred to England.

Figure 3.3. The colonies and European claims in North America (1750)

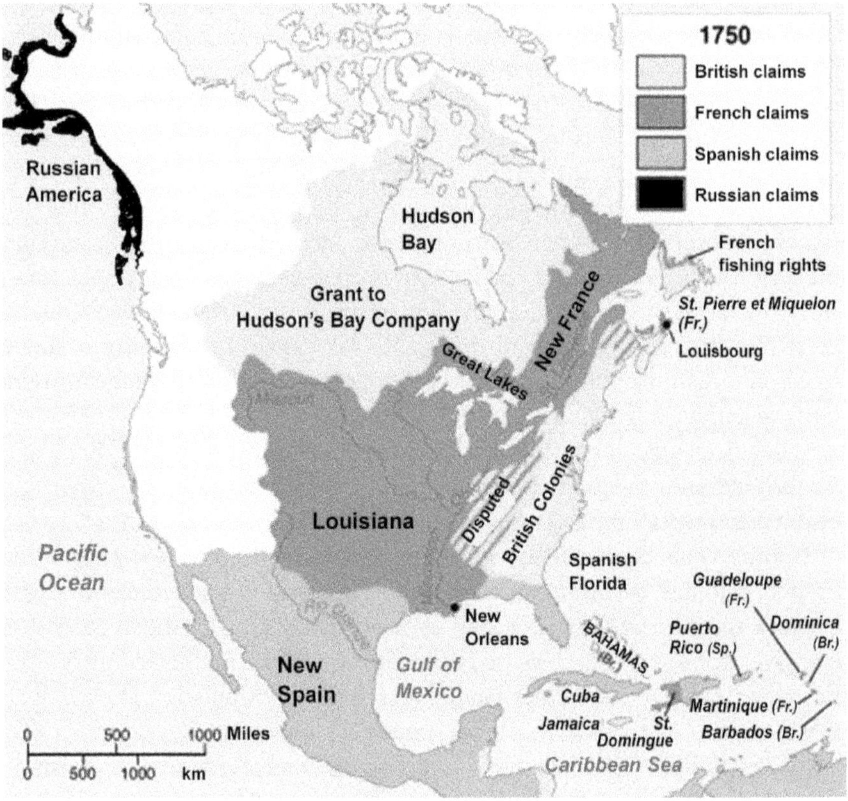

Their fundamental role in the war against France gave the thirteen English colonies the hope of gaining representation in the London Parliament. Consequently, when the English government increased taxation, from 1765, the colonists' protests were less about the level of fiscal pressure than about the illegitimacy of imposing taxes on a people without any political representation (the rebels' slogan was "no taxation without representation"). After years of more or less open tax revolt, armed rebellion finally broke out in 1775. The American War of Independence soon expanded into a global conflict when France and Spain allied with the American colonists, and lasted for years. When the Treaty of Paris (1783) finally forced England to recognize the independence of the United States of America, a new power appeared which was destined to play a leading role in the world economy.

Table 3.1. The five largest cities of Europe and the Mediterranean (1300-1800, population in thousands)

	1300	1400	1500	1600	1700	1800
1	Paris 250	Cairo 250	Istanbul 280	Istanbul 700	Istanbul 700	London 948
2	Cairo 220	Paris 200	Paris 200	Paris 300	London 575	Paris 550
3	Granada 150	Granada 100	Cairo 180	Naples 275	Paris 500	Istanbul 500
4	Venice 110	Tunis 100	Adrianople 127	Cairo 250	Cairo 330	Naples 430
5	Damietta 108	Venice 100	Naples 25	London 200	Naples 300	Cairo 263

Source: M. Bosker, E. Buringh, J.L. van Zanden, *From Baghdad to London. Unravelling Urban Development in Europe, the Middle East, and North Africa, 800-1800*, in *Review of Economics and Statistics*, 95, 4.

Bibliography

Acemoglu D., Johnson S., Robinson J.A., *The Rise of Europe. Atlantic Trade, Institutional Change and Growth*, in *American Economic Review*, 95, 2005, pp. 546-579.

Alfani G., *Calamities and the Economy in Renaissance Italy. The Grand Tour of the Horsemen of the Apocalypse*, London, 2013.

Cattini M., *L'Europa verso il mercato globale*, Milan, 2006.

North D.C., Weingast, B.C., *Constitutions and Commitment. The Evolution of Institutions Governing Public Choice in Seventeenth-Century England*, in *Journal of Economic History*, 49, 1989, pp. 803-832.

Van Zanden J.L., *The Long Road to the Industrial Revolution. The European Economy in a Global Perspective, 1000-1800*, Leiden-Boston, 2009.

DEMOGRAPHIC TRANSITION

Demographic transition denotes the passage from the high fertility and mortality typical of pre-industrial Europe to the low fertility and mortality of contemporary developed societies. The death rate falls quickly at the beginning of the transition, but the birth rate takes longer to drop. The combination of the two processes causes rapid population growth, which then slows down as birth rates gradually fall.

Demographic transition in Europe and the West in general occurred during the 19th century and lasted about 150 years. The process occurred later in developing countries and is still ongoing in some cases.

Although this long period was not homogeneous, population growth rates were relatively low (from 0.1% to 0.5% per year) under the **old demographic regime**, and could vary greatly according to the biological, environmental and social context. Birth rates were high (an average of 4-5 children per woman), as were death rates (3-4%), especially for children (between a third and half of children did not live to reach reproductive age), and life expectancy at birth was low (25-35 years).

The slow growth rate was further limited, or abruptly arrested, by what English economist Thomas Malthus defined as "preventive" and "positive" checks (*An Essay on the Principle of Population*, 1798). Preventive checks are methods families use deliberately to limit births, in particular by raising the age at first marriage. This happened especially in times of falling incomes when families had difficulty in providing their sons and daughters with the means to form a new family. For societies in which extra-marital conception was rare, this practice reduced the fertile period available to married couples, lowering the birth rate and slowing the natural population growth. Positive checks, on the other hand, caused sudden rises in death rates, due to events such as epidemics, and to a lesser extent to famines and wars. For these reasons, the old demographic regime was characterized by a fluctuating population, although there was a slight long-term trend towards growth.

Various factors favoured **demographic transition** in the 19th century and thereafter. While opinions regarding this issue continue to differ, it can generally be stated that the falling death rate (approximately 1% in the second half of the 20th century) was a decisive factor in rapid population growth. Mortality fell due to gradual improvements in per capita income, personal hygiene and living conditions, better nutrition as a consequence of increased agricultural productivity, and the regression of various epidemic diseases. These were not linear processes, so that increased urbanisation actually forced a larger share of the population into unhealthier living conditions, although at the same time they had easier access to public health care.

These factors combined to increase life expectancy in a context in which the fertility choices of families did not initially change, leading to a sharp rise in the natural population growth (0.5%-1.5% per year). Despite the substantial waves of emigration in the last few decades of this period, Europe's population rose from around 125 million to over 450 million between 1750 and 1914.

This phase of demographic expansion settled to lower levels in the passage from transition to the **modern demographic regime** of low birth and death rates and a high life expectancy at birth, which had risen to over 80 years by the end of the 20th century.

The narrowing of the gap between birth and death rates is due to the physiological slowing of the decline in mortality and to the fall in birth rates, connected with the social changes set off by the Industrial Revolution. In modern industrial and urban society the cost of raising children has gradually increased, as they begin contributing to family income at a later age and require greater investments in education; this has led families to limit fertility in an attempt to maintain family living standards unchanged. This has also been enabled by new methods of voluntary birth control, more efficient than the traditional practice of marrying later in life.

In this final stage, which characterizes contemporary Europe and the other advanced societies, the natural rate of population growth has dropped back to levels like those of the old demographic regime (approx. 0.1-0.5% per year), but within the context of a total population which is now much larger.

The diagram in Figure 3.4 is a good general illustration, although there is considerable variation between different countries in the duration of the transition, the speed of realignment of birth and death rates, and the gap between them.

Figure 3.4. The main phases of demographic transition

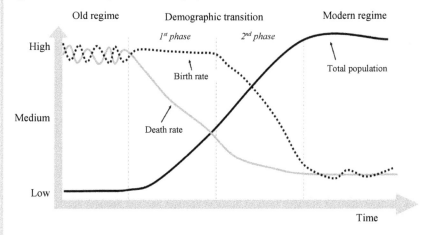

Chapter 4

THE INDUSTRIAL REVOLUTION: TECHNOLOGY AND SOCIETY

4.1. A long-term process

In the 19th century, for the first time in history, rapid population growth in Europe and North America was accompanied by rapidly rising incomes and levels of productivity. The structure of the economy changed radically during the century, as a growing share of the population moved from agriculture into industry and services. In some sectors of the economy, family firms were replaced by joint-stock companies; trade became increasingly global and some radical changes affected social life and ideologies, such as urbanization and secularisation. On a world scale, growth spread in certain specific areas of the West, leading to a notable divergence in living standards between the developed and underdeveloped nations. In two centuries, Europe's GNP multiplied by 50 and per capita income by almost 20. This new world, marked by geographical, environmental and social imbalances, would provide the context for modern economic development, and began to form with the first Industrial Revolution, which started in England and then spread through Western Europe and the United States during the central decades of the 19th century.

Historians have underlined, however, that there was actually no dramatic acceleration in England's GDP during the "classical" period (1760-1830). Despite extraordinary innovations, per capita economic growth during those decades was actually very small: 0.2-0.5%. Only industrial output grew more rapidly, perhaps between 2.6 and 3% according to the most optimistic estimates. This led to a debate, especially during the 1980s and 1990s, about the actual idea of "Industrial Revolution", which was considered an inappropriate concept to describe such a gradual change.[1]

---

[1] N.F.R. Crafts, *British Economic Growth during the Industrial Revolution*, Oxford, 1985.

However, the economic changes between the start of the 18th century and the mid-19th century effectively constituted a revolution, since they proved to be irreversible, and the world as it is today would be a very different place if they had never occurred.

The low growth rates estimated for *per capita* GDP in the period 1760-1830 can mostly be explained by the rapid rise in England's population, which grew from 6 to 13 million between 1750 and 1850. It is also unrealistic to imagine a sharp rise in productivity and innovation in every single economic sector. The first "modern" sectors grew very quickly (for example, cotton grew by 7% a year, and iron by 3% between 1770 and 1815), but these were initially just a very small share of the economy. The dualism of "modern" and "traditional" sectors obviously implies that the macro-economic statistics are very slow to reflect the impact of innovations. In addition, GNP does not always explain what is happening in terms of technological innovation, because it does not measure product or quality innovation, and also because the acceleration of production indicators registers a time lapse, which may be considerable, between the first adoption of important innovations and their generalized effects. The Industrial Revolution was not a macro-economic event bringing an immediate acceleration in the growth rate, but an "incubation" period during which the foundations of economic development were laid.[2]

In reality, the transformation of Great Britain's economy and society was a long-term process, beginning before the 18th century and continuing during the 19th century. It was not simply a case of industrial change, but involved a radical transformation of trade, agriculture and transport, accompanied by a demographic revolution and intense urbanisation. In the 160 years leading up to 1870, there was a growth of 240% in real *per capita* output, a truly revolutionary result given that the British population grew from 6.7 to 26.4 million during the same period. This may appear slow in comparison with modern day standards, but the lasting increase in per capita output associated with rapid population growth was absolutely unprecedented.[3] At the same time, it should be noted that the growth rate accelerated most notably after 1830. The Industrial Revolution started after a long period of changes, and so this account will begin with the earlier changes which laid the foundations for the acceleration occurring in the second half of the 18th century.

---

[2] J. Mokyr, *Accounting for the Industrial Revolution*, in R. Floud and P. Johnson, *The Cambridge Economic History of Modern Britain*, 2004, p. 14.

[3] B. A'Hearn, *The British Industrial Revolution in a European mirror*, in R. Floud, J. Humphries, P. Johnson, *The Cambridge Economic History of Modern Britain*, 2014, pp. 1-52.

4.2. Foreign trade, empire, mercantilism

An initial impetus came from foreign trade and the Empire. In the two hundred years following 1670, overseas trade grew faster than the population and the production of goods and services; in 1870, it accounted for over 60% of GDP. In the mid-17th century, England was a small nation of 5 million inhabitants, but this population had grown 20% during the previous fifty years. The population figure is important, because during the same period, plague and the Thirty Years' War killed over 9 million people in the Mediterranean areas and Germany, while the total population of the British Isles, Scandinavia and the Netherlands rose from 11 to 14 million (Table 4.1). While Italy and Germany spent decades rebuilding their economies, the merchant communities in the Northern and Atlantic ports became stronger during the second half of the 17th, directing their investments westwards, on routes offering a way out of the crisis afflicting the European trade circuits.

English success was inextricably linked with naval supremacy, since mercantilism admitted no form of pacifism. The English merchants, traditionally supported by the Crown, entered into competition with the Dutch in every area of trade, and three trade wars were fought against the United Provinces before the two rivals were forced into an alliance when threatened by France. Between 1689 and 1815, England and France were continually at war: eight great wars necessitated considerable expansion of the state budget, of which 80% was used to meet military expenditure and pay interest on the public debt. The debt grew very rapidly but it was supported by the country's rapid economic and population growth, aided by the efficiency of the tax system, Parliamentary control and a financial system which enjoyed the confidence of investors.[4]

All of fiscal and state financial policy was directed towards promotion of exports and protection of the trade systems by pursuing three interconnected strategies. The first of these was achievement of a trade surplus to ensure that the nation had the money it needed to pay for imports of raw materials and goods not available in England. The second was to open up new markets to create employment in trade and industry. The third strategy was to expand maritime routes and develop the merchant fleet, national defence and shipping services. The Navigation Acts, especially the measures introduced during the 1660s, caused the shift to a single and all-encompassing

---

[4] N. Zahedieh, *Overseas trade and empire*, in R. Floud, J. Humphries, P. Johnson, *The Cambridge Economic History*, cit., pp. 392-420; R. Findlay, K. O'Rourke, *Power and Plenty,* Princeton and Oxford, 2007.

national monopoly in the general interest, without any special privileges (except for the Levant Company and the East Indian Company). However, despite this rigid system based on nationalism and protectionism, competition was allowed within the country itself.[5]

During their "apprenticeship", the British accumulated naval and trading experience, overtaking their Dutch rivals in terms of tonnage in the first few decades of the 18th century, then widening the gap until 1780, when their fleet was actually twice that of the Dutch. Foreign trade became increasingly intercontinental, also due to the protectionist policies of the other European states. Around 1770, 40% of the British fleet was operating in the Atlantic. Great Britain imported raw materials for shipbuilding, together with dyestuffs, linen, Indian cotton and silk fabrics, porcelain and other goods not available in Britain itself (wines, rice, sugar, tea, coffee, citrus fruits, spices, raw cotton). Trade with Asia had a remarkable impact upon Britain's industrialization, due to the attempt of domestic manufactures to replace Asian goods such as Chinese porcelain and Indian cotton cloth. As the manufacturing sector gradually expanded, so did imports of raw materials (60% in 1854-56). Regarding exports, the main driving force was provided by exports to the colonies, which were the destination throughout the 18th century for a growing variety of manufactured goods, including linen cloth and a vast array of other articles. At the same time, re-exports accounted for a third of all exports, and played a crucial role in overall growth (Table 4.2), especially products like sugar and tobacco, which had now become widespread consumer goods. The African slave trade in the Americas boomed in the 18th century, when English merchants dominated the trade (transporting over 2 million slaves), making enormous profits, although not always continuously. The role these profits played in industrialisation is a matter of controversy, but they had an essential impact on the Atlantic trade system, which could not have existed without the plantations based on slave labour.

Implementing protectionist policies, the state had a fundamental role in the development of domestic manufactures such as linen, cotton, iron and steel, potteries, malt, beer, spirits, leather, soap, candles, paper and glass. British mercantilism also included a policy of attracting skilled workers, a practice which dated a long way back. In the 17th and 18th centuries, England's policy of welcoming specialized immigrants from Europe brought the most innovative techniques in mining, metallurgy, glass-making, pottery and gold-working, as well as in the manufacture of arms, clocks and scien-

---

[5] D. Ormrod, *The Rise of Commercial Empires*, Cambridge, UK, 2003.

tific instruments, in the wool, silk and linen sectors, in hydraulic engineering and in agriculture. During the course of the Industrial Revolution, the British continued to import every type of innovation that could be improved and commercially exploited.[6]

4.3. Early structural transformation

Another fundamental component preceding and accompanying the Industrial Revolution was the agricultural revolution. This was another outcome of a process taking centuries to complete, which began in the 15th century and ended towards the middle of the 19th century. One of its most important features was the expansion of arable land, from 21 million acres in 1700 to 36 million by 1850, helped by extensive land reclamation work. Given that the population grew from 4.2 to 8.7 million between 1600 and 1800, while the workforce in the primary sector remained more or less stable, it is likely that *per capita* output more than doubled during these two centuries.[7]

In the past, many historians believed that increased productivity was mainly achieved with new crop rotation systems and *enclosures* of the *open fields* traditionally regulated by the village community. In fact, during the 18th century, millions of acres of land were privatised by Acts of Parliament, and around 20% of English land was enclosed between 1700 and 1850. However, even if enclosures and the increasing size of farms stimulated investments, it must be noted that open fields and smaller farms also proved capable of increasing their output in order to participate in agricultural trade. The rise in productivity cannot be attributed to one single institution or innovation, but was due to a series of changes: land reclamation and drainage, and canal building; the production of high-yield seeds; the spread of soil fertilisation; the use of leguminous plants and new crop rotation systems; the greater availability of meat and dairy products due to animal breeding and the introduction of foreign breeds; the increased production of peas, beans and potatoes, and the development of market gardening around the cities.[8]

On the whole, the greatest incentive was probably the rapid increase

---

[6] C.H. Wilson, *England's Apprenticeship, 1603-1763*, London, 1965; W.J. Ashworth, *The Industrial Revolution. The State, Knowledge and Global Trade*, London, 2017.

[7] E.A. Wrigley, *Poverty, Progress, and Population*, Cambridge, UK, 2004, pp. 42-43.

[8] R.C. Allen, *Agriculture during the industrial revolution*, in R. Floud, P. Johnson (eds.), *The Cambridge Economic History*, cit., pp. 96-116.

in urban growth. There was a sharper rise in all the typically commercial products, such as milk, meat or wool, showing that agriculture was now a commercial activity, directed at supplying a growing urban population. Grain exports were encouraged by Corn Laws, introduced between 1663 and 1670 and maintained in place until 1846. For the first time in Europe, the traditional aim of favouring consumers (to prevent possible revolts) was abandoned, as a new strategy was adopted in favour of the producers, who were well represented in the country's Parliament. High import duties were imposed when domestic grain prices were low, and lower duties when domestic prices rose. When domestic cereal production was abundant and prices fell, cereals could be exported, and export premiums awarded. These measures ensured self-sufficiency and good profits for farmers.

The precocity of the economic transformation taking place in England is also shown by recent data on the occupational structure of the population.[9] These new data demonstrate that 37.9% of English adults (men and women) were already employed in the manufacturing sector in 1710, while 48.7% were employed in agriculture or mining, and 13.4% in the tertiary sector. The agricultural population fell to 34% of the total in 1817, while the tertiary sector grew more rapidly, to 24% in 1817 and 35% in 1871 (Table 4.3). Agricultural work underwent the greatest decline; half of the workforce was employed in agriculture in 1700, but by 1871 it employed just one in five workers. Therefore, at the start of the 18th century the English economy was much more "industrial" than was previously thought, while the shift towards the secondary sector was relatively modest in the 70-80 years after 1760. These data have two important implications. Firstly, production rose dramatically, although the percentage of those working in the secondary sector grew slowly, meaning a sharp increase in *per capita* output in the manufacturing sector. Secondly, if the fastest rate of growth between 1710 and 1817 was in tertiary sector employment, services should then have a central place in any discussions of the Industrial Revolution. The explanation may lie in an intensification of transport or commercial services, such as warehouses, and a slower growth of productivity in the tertiary sector than in the secondary sector.

The Agricutural Revolution made it possible to sustain an exceptionally high rate of population growth between 1750 and 1850, greater than that of the other European states. Between 1681 and 1841, England's population actually trebled from 5.1 to 14.9 million, with an average annual growth

---

[9] L. Shaw-Taylor, E.A. Wrigley, *Occupational structure and population change*, in R. Floud, J. Humphries, P. Johnson, *The Cambridge Economic History*, cit., p. 69 (e Table 4.3).

rate of 6.7% (Table 4.4); for the first time in European history, prolonged demographic growth was not accompanied by rising food prices. Two-thirds of this growth in the 18th century have been attributed to the increase in birth rates, due in turn to the lower marriage age. The factors underlying the lower death rate included the decline of epidemic diseases, improved hygiene, and smallpox vaccinations. Population growth was linked to rapid urbanisation, which caused enormous social problems due to inadequate provisions regarding housing standards or hygiene and sanitation. Growth in England was much higher than on the Continent, and the number of residents in cities of at least 10,000 trebled between 1700 and 1870. While urban growth in the 17th century had involved almost exclusively London, it was mostly the industrial cities and ports (Birmingham, Manchester, Leeds, Liverpool and Sheffield) which grew in the 18th century, so that by 1801 they had over ten times the number of residents than just a century before. At the start of the 18th century, most manufacturing workers lived in the country, but by 1870 most were in the cities.

This sustained population growth and urbanization would not have been possible – in a country where just 7% of the surface area was forested – without the growing availability of coal at stable prices. Output was already 3 million tonnes per year in 1700, rising to 15 million by 1830, and 68 million by 1850 (Table 4.5). Until 1775, it was mostly produced for family consumption. Coal became the daily fuel in homes and British factories because it was a cheap and readily available energy source, with abundant and easily exploited coalfields situated near watercourses and seaports. Nonetheless, engineers and architects had to experiment with ventilation systems, chimneys, and new "coal-fired houses" in order to make the fumes bearable. This "great reconstruction" was a vital element of growth during the period 1570-1800, a collective innovation unique in Europe. At the same time, alongside the traditional manufacturing processes using coal (salt production, brewing and dyeing), new industries developed as the initial drawbacks were overcome, including soap and sugar factories, paper mills and glassworks, brickworks and potteries, together with the processing of lead, tin and copper.[10]

4.4. The technological revolution: stages, sectors and innovations

The growth of domestic trade, like the coal boom, was sustained by the range of improvements in the transport sector, which underwent an in-

---

[10] E.A. Wrigley, *Energy and the English Industrial Revolution*, 2010; R.C. Allen, *The British Industrial Revolution in Global Perspective*, Cambridge, UK, 2009.

crease in productivity comparable to that of the most revolutionary industries.[11] The greatest impulse towards expansion came from the increase in national income, but the transport sector probably grew at double the rate. By 1870, Great Britain had already experienced a transport revolution with the railways, although they were not the only factor, given that trains began to play an important role only after 1830. The foundations date back to the mid-18th century with the construction of turnpike roads, which was most intense between 1751 and 1772, and navigation canals. Private ventures supported by *ad hoc* Acts of Parliament overcame an obstacle that had become evident in the British economy early in the 18th century, in spite of the many navigable rivers and the form of the island itself, which made the inland regions easy to reach. The main advantage of navigable rivers was that transport costs were 20-25% less than for road transport, although river transport was not available in all areas.

Entrepreneurial ventures were backed by the instutions, but the market was subject to competition between concession holders and between the different means of transport. Speeds improved slowly before 1750, with the major changes taking place in the subsequent 80 years: according to estimates, the average speed of a stage coach was 1.96 miles per hour in 1700, 2.61 in 1750, and almost 8 mph in 1820. Obviously, the railways brought the most revolutionary change in transport, since the average speed in 1865 was over 23 miles per hour. The cost of internal transport also fell steeply, probably by 40% just in the second half of the 18th century. In around 1825, before the railways, all the country's major cities and towns were linked by good roads, usable at all times of year; trade could count on an integrated system of roads, canals, rivers and coastal shipping routes, transporting merchandise to and from the industrial hinterland.

It was also thanks to the changes outlined here that at a certain point technology became the essential driving force of a growth that was persistent and irreversible. The technological revolution can be sub-divided into three stages, starting from the discontinuous progress made between 1760 and 1820, which laid the groundwork for the subsequent transformation of the economy. Between 1760 and 1780 there was a striking increase in the number of legally patented inventions, in particular Watt's steam engine, the spinning machines and Cort's iron "puddling". This first wave involved limited but important sectors of industry, with innovations making low-pressure steam engines available, mechanical spinning machines,

---

[11] D. Bogart, *The transport revolution in industrialising Britain*, in R. Floud, J. Humphries, P. Johnson, *The Cambridge Economic History*, cit., pp. 368-391.

and machinery powered by water or steam, so that the output of cotton yarn rose dramatically. This type of innovation did not stop once the initial objective had been reached, as had previous innovation clusters in the early modern age, but it was then followed by a second stage after 1820. This was no less important than the first, and involved a large number of micro-innovations and improvements that brought a sharp reduction in production costs. Companies adapted the new technologies, extending their use to a much greater number of industries, and improving production processes. The innovations introduced in this second stage include mechanical weaving (improved only after 1820), Roberts' *self-acting mule* for spinning yarn, the adaptation of new textile machinery for other fibres (linen and wool), new blast furnaces in the iron industry, improvements to the steam engine (the high-pressure version suitable for transport and the railway), progress in chemistry, gas lighting, high-precision engineering and the telegraph.

During the first stage, *per capita* income remained stable, but this second wave of innovation was the critical period, and this is reflected in the statistics, given that the new technologies were in widespread use after 1830. The second wave was a bridge between the first and second Industrial Revolutions, in which the changes taking place were no less revolutionary, since they had a wider and more solid scientific base.[12]

The three most innovative sectors of the Industrial Revolution were cotton and textiles, energy and the iron industry. In the cotton-spinning industry, the rising demand for yarn drove the design of machinery produced during the 1760s and 1770s: the *jenny*, the *water frame*, and the *mule-jenny*. Productivity grew at an impressive rate: in 1812 a spinner could produce as much yarn as 200 workers before invention of the *jenny*. Continual improvements were made to machinery throughout the period of the Industrial Revolution, including the use of iron instead of wood, and the increased number of spindles. It had taken Crompton's 1769 *mule* 2,000 hours to produce 100 lbs of yarn, but Roberts' self-acting mule reduced this 135 hours in 1825. The added value of cotton production rose from under £500,000 in 1760 to around £25 million by the mid-1820s. This sensational progress and the incredible expansion of the cotton industry explain why many have seen this as the leading sector.[13]

[12] J. Mokyr, *The Enlightened Economy. An Economic History of Britain 1700-1850*, New Haven and London, 2009.

[13] D.S. Landes, *The Unbound Prometheus. Technological Change and Industrial Development in Western Europe from 1750 to the Present*, Cambridge, Mass., 1969.

The Industrial Revolution's most famous invention was the steam engine. Although it was improved by James Watt between 1769 and 1787, it began to have a decisive role only after 1830 (Table 4.6), allowing the revolution to continue, ensuring that productivity grew rapidly as its use became widespread. This became possible only after further improvements and technological development, when new applications and combinations with existent techniques were found, a century after the first machine was produced. Its permanent success arrived in the early 1830s with the development of the high-pressure steam engine.

It is natural to associate the steam engine with the Industrial Revolution, because it was one of the most revolutionary inventions, able for the first time to convert thermal energy into mechanical energy, a new technology that opened up an unprecedented series of opportunities and found a vast range of applications. Nevertheless, it is important to reiterate that its impact on industry was quite limited until the early decades of the 19th century. The steam engine was developed and improved during a century and a half of experimentation, with mechanics and engineers continually engaged in making micro-innovations.

The 18th century expansion of the coal industry enabled not only urbanization and the growth of traditional industries, but also allowed the expansion of the new iron and steel industry following Henry Cort's invention of puddling in 1783-1784. The coalfields provided the location and aided the development of many of Great Britains' first industrial regions, enabling many improvements in the iron industry, such as larger blast furnaces and more complex smelting techniques. David Landes invited historians not to exaggerate the importance of iron for the 18th century; despite the progress made, the sector cannot be compared with the cotton industry. However, the growing availability of inexpensive metal had positive impacts on the other industries, since high quality forged iron was being produced at a low cost by the last decade of the 18th century. In these three sectors, therefore, the famous words of T.S. Ashton's schoolboy – that "about 1760 a wave of gadgets swept over England" – is not entirely unfounded. However, to present a truthful picture of the economic change in act, it must be stressed that every innovation was actually the result of a long-term process of preparation and development.

Furthermore, the most famous inventions represent just the tip of the iceberg; many other pervasive innovations were less spectacular, but had a profound impact on economic activities. Most registered patents involved a wide range of small products and processes, suggesting the idea of widespread inventiveness on a smaller scale. Although these developments were specific to certain activities, they had a decisive combined effect on the economy in terms of employment and production figures.[14] For example, food preservation was improved by Appert's invention of canning, and other innovative processing improvements involved bakeries, brewing (which became a large-scale specialized industry), sugar, chocolate, tobacco, and coffee. Chemistry provided innovations like the chloralkali process using sodium chloride, which was widely applied in various industries, while chlorine was used to bleach cloth. New and more accurate machine tools were developed; these were essential in the construction of machinery and enabled standardisation. The paper industry was revolutionised when Robert in France invented a way to produce a continuous sheet and accelerate production. English developments in other fields also followed those on the Continent in glass-making, gas lighting, and many other manufacturing sectors, including optics, glass bottles, pottery, and various kinds of machine tools.

Lastly, it must be recalled that the process of innovation does not merely mean reducing production costs, since the most important long-term economic developments include the increase in consumer goods, product innovation and improved product quality. Besides the famous Wedgwood porcelains, Great Britain also witnessed the expansion of a wide range of small articles, and both show that the growing middle class enjoyed an improved standard of living. In brief, innovation was a wider and more pervasive process, involving a great number of "small" inventions throughout all sectors of a society generally inclined towards innovation.

Technological innovation was not in itself a novelty, but there had never previously been such a rapid sequence of reciprocal demands involving innovations and the manufacturing sectors. Acceleration of one stage of the production process in weaving, for example, caused a bottleneck in the spinning industry, which was unable to meet the increased demand for yarn and thus required innovations to redress the balance. The same happened between the different manufacturing sectors, so that now industrial activity could develop only if it were based on broad internal diversification and interconnection, extending the reciprocal demands to traditional agricultural and service activities.

Some historians have identified the central event of the Industrial Revolution in the establishment of the factory system, of the industrial companies using complex machinery powered by inanimate sources of energy, and which required substantial capital investments to achieve economies of scale. The theory is that concentration of production made it more effi-

---

[14] K. Bruland, *Industrialisation and technological change*, in R. Floud, P. Johnson, *The Cambridge Economic History*, cit., pp. 117-146.

cient, and launched an age of social mobility in which entrpreneurs and innovators, together with the mass of consumers, enjoyed the fruits of their entrepreneurial spirit. Others, however, have highlighted how the factory system created an exploited industrial proletariat without rights (this was especially true for women and children), subjected to harsh factory discipline and unprecedented working hours, forced into unhealthy overcrowded housing in cities with filthy streets. In this situation, workers could no longer decide for themselves how much and how long to work, since the implacable pace was now set by machinery, and this meant that social conflicts would be concentrated in the factories.

Irrespective of the point of view adopted, the big factory is mostly associated with the second Industrial Revolution more than with the first.[15] It is true that a growing share of many manufacturing sectors (especially the textile industry) gradually became concentrated in the factories during the first half of the 19th century, and that numbers of workers grew in sectors like shipbuilding and civil engineering, together with some steelworks. However, historians have shown that small family businesses were predominant during the first Industrial Revolution. Factories actually spread slowly and discontinuously, and their expansion was accompanied and supported by the proliferation of small businesses and factories that also used dispersed forms of labour and domestic manufacturing. In the textile sector, only 10 percent of factories employed more than 100 workers in 1841, and very few had a workforce of over 150; even in 1871, the average number of workers in iron foundries was just over 20. The reasons why these structures existed are quite clear. The economies of scale and of diversification associated with big business were not yet present in most sectors, not even in the cotton industry, where the technology in use at the time did not require necessarily large factories. Different sectors continued to use the *putting-out* system, often connected with a factory, such as weaving, the Birmingham ironworks, and many other sectors relying on manual skills. Nevertheless, the factory system gradually expanded as technology gradually improved, and as the use and cost of machinery increased.

The demand for new consumer goods, such as sugar, tea, printed cottons and *chinoiserie*, and the average increase in annual working hours contributed to launching British industrialisation, but falling prices may have been much more influential. Average real income is estimated to have increased by 68% between 1688 and 1851, so that many middle-class families were able to increase their consumption of non-essential goods, alt-

---

[15] P. Hudson, *Industrial organisation and structure*, in R. Floud, P. Johnson, *The Cambridge Economic History*, cit., pp. 28-56.

hough general data seem to indicate a stagnation in living standards in the decades 1780-1840.[16]

In the mid-19th century, Great Britain was the leading industrial nation, the first to overcome the problems and difficulties which had previously impeded modern economic growth. A divide opened up between Britain and the other European countries regarding the use of raw materials like cotton and coal; the steam engine provided Britain with 1.29 million hp, compared with 370,000 hp in France and 260,000 hp in Germany. The gap was wider in the industrial sectors and narrower in terms of average income, which grew rapidly, however, between 1820 and 1870 (Table 4.7). British supremacy was the result of over a century of technological and economic leadership, but Britain would soon be equalled by the other European countries and by the United States.

Table 4.1. European population in millions (1500-1700)

	1500	1550	1600	1650	1700
Scandinavia	1.50	1.70	2.00	2.60	2.90
England	2.30	3.00	4.10	5.20	5.10
Scotland	0.80	0.90	1.00	1.00	1.20
Ireland	0.80	0.90	1.00	1.50	2.00
Netherlands	0.95	1.25	1.50	1.90	1.90
Belgium	1.25	1.65	1.30	1.75	1.90
Germany	9.00	12.60	16.20	9.50	14.10
France	16.40	19.00	20.00	20.50	22.00
Switzerland	0.60	0.75	0.90	1.00	1.20
Italy	9.00	11.60	13.30	11.50	13.40
Spain	6.80	7.40	8.10	7.10	7.50
Portugal	1.00	1.20	1.10	1.20	2.00
Austria-Bohemia	3.50	3.60	4.30	4.10	4.60
Poland	2.50	3.00	3.40	3.00	2.80
Total	**56.40**	**67.35**	**78.30**	**71.85**	**82.60**

Source: S.A. Conca Messina, *A History of States and Economic Policies in Early Modern Europe*, London-New York, 2019.

---

[16] S. Horrell, *Consumption, 1700-1870*, in R. Floud, J. Humphries, P. Johnson, *The Cambridge Economic History*, cit., pp. 237-263.

Table 4.2. English foreign trade 1663-1774 (£ million per year)

	1663-1669	1699-1701	1752-1754	1772-1774
Total exports (incl. re-exports)	4.1	6.4	11.9	15.6
Re-exports only	0.9	1.9	3.4	5.8
Total imports	4.4	5.8	8.2	12.7
Imports of raw materials and foodstuffs		4.0	6.3	10.5

Source: R. Davis, *English Foreign Trade, 1660-1700*, in *Economic History Review*, VII, 1954, p. 160; Id., *English Foreign Trade, 1700-1774*, *ibid.*, XV, 1962, pp. 300-303.

Table 4.3. Occupational structure in England and Wales 1710-1871 (% adult workers)

Sector	1710	1817	1851	1871
Primary	48.7	34.6	27.7	21.3
Secondary	37.9	41.3	42.6	43.5
Tertiary	13.4	24.2	29.7	35.2

Source: L. Shaw-Taylor, E.A. Wrigley, *Occupational structure and population change*, in Floud R., Humphries J., Johnson P. (eds.), *The Cambridge Economic History*, cit., p. 69.

Table 4.4. Population of England 1600-1871 (millions)

Year	1600	1701	1751	1801	1841	1851	1871
Population	4.1	5.2	5.9	8.6	14.9	17	21.2

Source: L. Shaw-Taylor, E.A. Wrigley, *Occupational structure*, cit., p. 73.

Table 4.5. Coal production in the United Kingdom 1700-1850 (million tonnes)

1700	1750	1775	1800	1815	1830	1850
2,9	5.2	8.8	15	22.2	30.3	68.4

Source: Mokyr J., *The Enlightened Economy*, cit., p. 101.

Table 4.6. Stationary power sources in Great Britain 1760-1907 (hp x 1000)

	1760	1800	1830	1870	1907
Steam	5	35	160	2,060	9,659
Water	70	120	160	230	178
Wind	10	15	20	10	5
Total	85	170	340	2,300	9,842

Source: R.C. Allen, *The British Industrial Revolution*, cit., p. 173.

Table 4.7. Per capita GDP in Europe 1500-1870, United Kingdom in 1820 = 100

	1500	1700	1750	1820	1870
United Kingdom	57	73	87	100	187
Netherlands	67	109	109	107	162
Belgium	58	69	76	77	158
France	n.a.	n.a.	n.a.	72	110
Italy	83	71	76	65	88
Spain	63	61	58	62	71
Sweden	64	66	67	70	97
Poland	50-54	38-42	34-37	41	55
Russia	n.a.	n.a.	n.a.	40	55
Turkey	n.a.	35	38	40	52

Source: S. Broadberry, K. O'Rourke (eds.), *The Cambridge Economic History of Modern Europe*, Vol. 1 (1700-1870), Cambridge, UK, 2010, p. 2.

Bibliography

Allen R.C., *The British Industrial Revolution in Global Perspective*, Cambridge, UK, 2009.

Ashworth J.W., *The Industrial Revolution. The State, Knowledge and Global Trade*, London, 2017.

Crafts N.F.R., *British Economic Growth during the Industrial Revolution*, Oxford, 1985. Floud R., Johnson P. (eds.), *The Cambridge Economic History of Modern Britain*, Vol. I, Cambridge, UK, 2004.

Floud R., Humphries J., Johnson P. (eds.), *The Cambridge Economic History of Modern Britain*, Vol. I, 1700-1870, Cambridge, UK, 2014.

Findlay R., O'Rourke K.H., *Power and Plenty. Trade, War and the World Economy in the Second Millennium*, Princeton and Oxford, 2007.

Landes D.S., *The Unbound Prometheus. Technological Change and Industrial Development in Western Europe from 1750 to the Present*, Cambridge, Mass., 1969.

Mokyr J., *The Enlightened Economy. An Economic History of Britain 1700-1850*, New Haven and London, 2009.

O'Brien P.K., *Inseparable Connections. Trade, Economy, Fiscal State, and the Expansion of Empire, 1688-1815*, in P.J. Marshall (ed.), *The Oxford History of the British Empire*, Vol. II, Oxford, 1998.

Wrigley E.A., *Energy and the English Industrial Revolution*, Cambridge, UK, 2010.

Chapter 5
WHY EUROPE? WHY BRITAIN?

SUMMARY: 5.1. Why Europe? Culture, institutions, economic incentives. – 5.2. Why Britain? A peculiar combination of factors. – Bibliography. – *The industrial revolution*.

Why did the Industrial Revolution take place in Europe? Why was Britain the first industrial nation?

Before the Industrial Revolution, Europe was not the only area of the world with well-developed markets and a Smithian division of labour. According to some historians, especially Americans, "surprising similarities" between Europe and Asia still existed in the 1700s. This theory has become increasingly unconvincing in recent years, since it underestimates many aspects that were specific to Europe and very evident in the century when the Industrial Revolution began. Certain processes have already been highlighted which were strongly divergent in the long term: Europe's geopolitical and commercial expansion, the creation of vast overseas empires, acceleration of the economy and urbanization, and a philosophical and religious culture setting man at the centre of the universe, thus leading to developments like the Renaissance, the scientific revolution and the Enlightenment. This chapter will provide a more detailed study, especially of certain aspects: the competitive (and conflictual) relations between states and their mercantilist intervention in the economy; market mechanisms and the state's role in promoting economic growth; the ability to defend trade, and the military revolution; the existence of developed financial systems controlled by private operators and low interest rates; the tradition of representation for social classes, and experimentation in some countries with "inclusive" institutions that gradually enabled wider distribution of economic benefits. In brief, the Industrial Revolution was not a sudden event, but represented the outcome of pre-existing processes of cultural, social, istitutional, technological and economic development which were a feature of Europe as a whole, and came to fruition particularly in the 18th century, when the Industrial Revolution began.[1]

---

[1] P. Vries, *Escaping poverty. The origins of modern economic growth*, Vienna, 2013.

5.1. Why Europe? Culture, institutions, economic incentives

In order to answer the question "Why was Europe the starting point of industrialization?" it is necessary to focus firstly on the interplay of culture, institutions and economic incentives that made Europe different from the other areas of the world.

Long-distance trade was a vital necessity for commercial cities and the small states like Portugal, the United Dutch Provinces and England. European enterprise, the discovery of new territories and the new routes between the different continents originated in the need to seek out markets, raw materials, slaves, and trade goods, also because state income in the more commercialized states depended on customs and excise duties. Europeans faced dangers and travelled great distances to obtain goods that were unavailable in their homelands; for example, they took American silver to China, where it was in short supply, reaping enormous profits. China, on the other hand, believed that it was self-sufficient, since the enormous empire could collect taxes from millions of peasants; this gave fewer incentives to commercial ventures, which effectively stopped at the beginning of the early modern age. Overseas expansion, precious metals (vital at the time for the development of trade), coal, and the American plantations were the result of deliberate decisions taken by the European states and entrepreneurial groups, as were the many innovations enabling European expansion.

The fiscal-military state played a central role in European economic expansion, because no medium- or long-distance trading venture was possible without military protection. Unlike the Eastern empires, Europe was a patchwork of states, and this political pluralism created competition and rivalry in the attempt to acquire markets and control resources. It was inevitable that the cost of war rose dramatically, and the competitive ability of the European political formations came to depend on their economic and financial resources. This political and military antagonism made it increasingly evident that the wealth of the state depended on the fiscal capacity of its subjects. States were forced to invest in military and naval power to defend their own trading activities; they introduced innovations that contributed to the destructive effects of warfare, but were also adapted for civilian uses and improved mining, metallurgy and shipping. European technology was "mobile" because the competing states readily welcomed foreigners, Jews, religious dissenters, merchants and craftsmen, importing their capital and specialized skills. This naturally provided a strong stimulus to the arms market and to the demand for experts and technicians, encouraging investments aimed at improving the efficiency and productivity of the military apparatus. The competition between Europe's political formations often implied imitation of the best practices of other states, and was the main reason for the subsequent institutional "convergence" as state structures became increasingly similar during the 18th and 19th centuries.[2]

At the same time, since competition often led to war, which was increasingly expensive, the public debt rose, providing a strong incentive to financial innovations and mobilization of capital. The existence of a sizeable debt guaranteed by the state government was not a feature of the Asian empires, but played an important role in European growth, since the financial elites worked to deploy the available financial resources. Unsurprisingly, European interest rates were by far the lowest in the world. Because repayment of interest on the public debt required more efficient fiscal systems and more sources of income, countries unable to obtain resources from a vast peasant population were more active in implementing mercantilist shipping and trade policies. It is no surprise that the intellectuals, merchants and politicians across Europe were increasingly interested in debating the issue of economic growth: this is another specifically European feature.

In addition, only the European states implemented a real economic policy. The importance of the state's role in the economy is shown by comparing Europe and China, the largest of the Eastern empires. Between 1700 and 1850, the Chinese state was weak, and government policies were essentially directed towards maintaining social stability, ensuring the survival of the population and internal order; there were no measures aimed at change or at supporting for the merchants engaged in foreign trade. On the other hand, European states and merchants, especially those engaged in international trade, were highly motivated towards competition and expansion. Concepts like benchmarking, "state export-oriented", "import substitution" and "external market capture" originated in the activities and ideas of European writers and governments, and state policies were responsible for the development of many industrial sectors.[3]

Although based on military strength, there are at least two reasons why European expansion was not just a "primitive accumulation" consisting of the mere subtraction of resources. For instance, Europeans had a systematic desire to gather geographic data, to discover new fishing grounds and improve their ships, to acquire knowledge, territories and markets, and to accumulate a set of scientific and technical advances which all contributed decisively to European supremacy. Moreover, everything they discovered

---

[2] P. Vries, *State, economy and the Great Divergence. Great Britain and China, 1680s-1850s*, London, 2015.

[3] P. Vries, *Escaping poverty*, cit.

was economically exploited, transformed and enhanced, thus providing further incentives to investment, trade and innovations. For example, although the slave trade (at its height in the 1700s) was absolutely terrible and destructive for Africa, it was dictated by economic objectives, i.e. to increase the workforce and investments, and to exploit vast territories and their raw materials. Contact with Europe transformed the Americas, as the productive potential of the New World was enhanced by ecological and technological exchanges.

The development of commerce had important effects on the design of precision instruments like telescopes, barometers, thermometers and clocks. These improvements were connected with the scientific revolution and were fundamentally important in the long term. The new knowledge of astronomy and geography drove Europeans to question even the traditional religious texts and authorities, and they developed an original scientific approach, based on independent research by scientists and on mathematics. The Renaissance and the experimental scientific method were the prerequesites for the Enlightenment, a cultural movement with no equivalent elsewhere in the world, in the period when the Industrial Revolution began. David Landes has written that these developments have a single cultural root which is specific to the West, namely the central role assigned by Judaeo-Christian tradition to man's rational manipulation of nature.[4]

The "cultural" interpretation of the Industrial Revolution as a European feature has been re-proposed in an original and convincing way by Joel Mokyr. He maintains that the Industrial Revolution began at the end of the 18th century because the Enlightenment demonstrated an extraordinary interest in technology, generating the intellectual and practical developments he has called "industrial enlightenment". Although the first Industrial Revolution began when science and technology were still apparently "separate" and it was based to a large extent on practice, technicians were already identifying and codifying regularities and experimental procedures in the early modern age. This historical process intensified during the Enlightenment, when there was a growing convergence of technical and scientific knowledge.

Knowledge, "useful knowledge" advanced during the 18th century based on experiment and experience, trial and error, with models and patterns established by the compilation of data and codification of material applications. The convergence of technology and science was a gradual

---

[4] J.A. Goldstone, *Why Europe? The rise of the West in World History 1500-1850*, Boston, 2008; D.S. Landes, *The Wealth and Poverty of Nations. Why Some are So Rich and Some So Poor*, New York, 1998.

process, but it was possible because specialists in every field had already been trained in the systematic documentation of experimental procedures. The academies and other scientific institutions also contributed to this convergence of science and technology; this enabled the development and spread of the second stage of the Industrial Revolution, when the connection between science and technology becomes evident, and subsequently closer. Since the scientific approach and advances in "useful knowledge" were European developments and were key elements of the Industrial Revolution (given that technology is essentially knowledge), it was therefore a European development and not only British; this is shown by the fact that British technologies were rapidly assimilated and adapted, and the United Kingdom was equalled and overtaken relatively rapidly by other countries. According to Mokyr, Europe would have still had its Industrial Revolution even without British technological leadership, although it would have taken a partly different course.[5]

Interest in technology is evident from handbooks about the various production sectors that were published well before the *Encyclopaedia*. Once again, production and dissemination of books in Europe was unequalled elsewhere in the world. China published an average of 474 new editions per year between 1644 and 1911, whereas the European average was already 5,000 titles in 1600, and the number of new books continued growing. China's political authorities controlled printing, but in the West it stimulated cultural debate, encouraging intellectual freedom and unorthodox tendencies. There was also an enormous disparity between East and West, which is evident from the correlated data on literacy rates: far more Europeans were able to read and write than their counterparts in other parts of the world, and literacy rates increased substantially during the two centuries before the Industrial Revolution. It may be debated how far this also reflects a Great Divergence in the availability of human capital, but it is highly likely that the increasing number of books reflected improvements in living standards.[6]

Some historians maintain that the rise of Europe was also helped by Western Europe's family structures (based on the nuclear family) and by the transformation of labour and consumption known as the "industrious revolution", which can be defined succinctly as a labour-intensive process of economic growth. According to the model proposed by Jan de Vries, the increase in consumption (and in working hours) occurred between 1650 and 1850, in northwestern Europe (Britain, the Netherlands, and

---

[5] J. Mokyr, *The Enlightened Economy*, cit.

[6] J.L. van Zanden, *The Long Road to the Industrial Revolution*, cit.

some regions of France and Germany), in the major continental cities, and in the North American colonies, while Eastern and Southern Europe did not participate fully. A middle class of small landowners, farmers and professionals was formed, who enjoyed a higher standard of living and increased the demand for consumer goods, so that the range of goods became much more ample in the second half of the 17th century. In short, these changes in family behaviour constituted an "industrious revolution" with positive impacts on trade, stimulated by new types of consumption: this preceded and prepared the ground for the Industrial Revolution, which was then led by technology and by organizational changes in production.[7]

5.2. Why Britain? A peculiar combination of factors

In a context as favourable to economic growth as Europe, why did Great Britain become the first industrial nation? Firstly, Britain had the advantage of possessing different elements favouring economic growth and technological progress, or of developing these before the other countries. Of course, both material and immaterial factors are involved.

One evident advantage concerns geography. As an island, Britain was less vulnerable to direct threats posed by a neighbouring power, and the British domestic market was far more unified than those of France or Germany, for example, because there were many navigable rivers providing merchants with easy access to cities, and this meant that transport costs were low, especially for bulky goods. In addition, over twenty English ports were capable of accommodating coastal shipping. Another factor was that the country's lack of high mountain ranges enabled the early development of canals and of a capillary network of internal water-borne transport. Not least, the country's position allowed the English to participate in the expansion of the economy circulating around the North Sea, and subsequently of the Atlantic trade.

It is no surprise, therefore, that economic policy gave special consideration to the interests of the merchant classes engaged in foreign trade. This was a fundamental component of the first Industrial Revolution, because foreign trade provided a growing abundance of land and raw materials (starting with raw cotton), without encountering increased prices. With regard to exports, production of yarn and textiles could continue to grow

---

[7] J. de Vries, *Industrious Revolution in Europe. Consumer Behaviour and the Household Economy, 1650 to the Present*, Cambridge, UK, 2008.

without prices collapsing, because Britain enjoyed a much larger export market. This trade allowed the marketing of excess production which the domestic market could not have absorbed.[8]

However, it must be stressed that Great Britain's rise to dominance in foreign trade in a competitive mercantilist context was not only due to the growth of commerce, but also owed much to the firepower of the Royal Navy as it protected foreign trade and the markets acquired with military strength. In any case, no major European state showed any intention to adopt free market rules, and none was powerful enough to oblige the others to do so. During the course of the "long 18th century" (1689-1815), Great Britain and France were at war with each other for at least 64 years out of 126, and Britain emerged victorious from every conflict (except for the American War of Independence). This had important implications for the future balance of the international economy. In Britain, the state spent vast sums of money to achieve its aims and accumulated a substantial public debt; it interfered constantly in production and trade, and was particularly protective towards foreign trade; it had a navy which proved decisive, was engaged in numerous wars and had a key role in building the Empire and in international trade; it created and regulated the country's monetary and financial system efficiently. The fiscal-military state and mercantilist policies were not alone sufficient to bring about economic development, although in the historical context they were the conditions required for Britain to emerge as the first industrial nation.[9]

Another typical characteristic of Britain was its unusual factors of production. The innovation was often driven by the need to replace relatively scarce factors and resources, such as wood, water power, and manpower, with other relatively cheaper alternatives, such as coal, the steam engine, capital, process innovation and labour-saving machinery. It mainly involved diminishing returns in the energy supply. France and Germany had vast forests, but coal was scarce, and although the demand for timber was growing and prices therefore rising, the relative timber shortage remained a local concern. In Britain, without the economic and technological valorization of coal, the Industrial Revolution would probably have been impossible or would have stopped. Coal made it possible to create a new economy (defined the "mineral economy" by historian Tony Wrigley) capable of aggirare diminishing returns of the traditional energy system (the "organic economy"), based on the products of the land or on limited sources. Coal was a

---

[8] R. Findlay, K. O'Rourke, *Power and Plenty*, cit.

[9] P. Vries, *State, Economy and the Great Divergence*, cit.; J.W. Ashworth, *The Industrial Revolution. The State, Knowledge and Global Trade*, London, 2017.

source of energy equivalent to millions of acres of woodland. The Americas also provided additional agricultural land with an area corresponding to two-thirds of English farmland, thus making it possible to obtain sugar, cotton and other goods cheaply from agriculture. Mercantilism and British military power transformed the New World into an almost inexhaustible reserve of land-intensive products and an outlet market for goods, labour and capital.[10]

The differences between Britain and the other European countries were just as evident in the manufacturing sectors employing the largest numbers of workers, the textile industries, where the cost of labour had a great impact, and was relatively higher in Britain. Although the putting-out system had spread because there was an inexpensive rural workforce, expansion inevitably encountered diseconomies of scale when it surpassed certain limits, entailing increased distribution and control costs. The enormous growth of demand for cotton yarns and cloth spurred interest in labour-saving machinery, in part because English salaries were, according to the data collected by Robert Allen, the highest in the world. In short, expansion of the modern economy between 1500 and 1750 contributed to the establishment of a very unusual structure: British salaries were high compared with other countries, while the cost of energy was cheaper, thanks to coal. Consequently, the most revolutionary technologies were exceptionally profitable in Great Britain: the steam engine, the mechanized cotton spinning factory and the use of coal instead of wood in the manufacture of iron, steel and other metals. The situation was different in the other European countries, where rural areas were less industrialized, the putting-out system had greater margins for expansion, and – most importantly – there was a large reserve of relatively cheap labour. In other words, the search for improved production systems was directed by the relative costs of the production factors.[11] This assessment challenges the traditional view that industrial progress was more likely to happen in areas where labour was relatively abundant and cheap (Pollard). However, we need to consider that the labour of women and children accounted for a large share of the workforce in the textile industry.

The economic incentives were not sufficient; suitable human capital was also required. Britain probably had a higher number of specialists, together with better institutions and commercial structures. The Industrial Revolution would not have occurred without the widespread availability of engineers (employed in the private sector more often than on the conti-

---

[10] E.A. Wrigley, *Energy and the English Industrial Revolution*, cit.

[11] R.C. Allen, *The British Industrial Revolution*, cit.

nent), technicians and scientists able to adapt and improve the macro- and micro-innovations. They worked alongside thousands of specialized workers, trained in an efficient apprenticeship system, who developed and passed on their practical skills. It has been estimated that in 1700 over a quarter of all British males aged 21 had completed a practical apprenticeship. The men responsible for British leadership up to 1850 were specialized workers (mechanics, metallurgists, clockmakers, precision instrument makers and carpenters), used to a daily work of adapting inventions and "useful knowledge" to meet local needs.[12]

Another British peculiarity concerns the political institutions. The Industrial Revolution found a favourable context due to an original political system, which was anti-absolutist and pluralistic. Since the economic institutions are one of the fundamental causes of growth, but depend on the political institutions, the parliamentary system has been assigned a determining role in English originality. It was not a democratic system, but the benefits of economic activities were widely distributed, since Parliament represented groups with a broader ability to enforce the respect of property rights, limiting and counter-balancing the Crown's political power and the possible vested interests of restricted groups; the British system was more "inclusive". At the same time, Parliamentary control made it possible to increase taxes and the public debt when necessary in order to make public investments considered advantageous for the productive classes (such as strengthening the navy in defence of the overseas trades liberalized within the mercantile system). In addition, the Glorious Revolution of 1688-1689, which was led by a broad coalition of interests in order to prevent a restricted group from monopolising power, is also considered to have made the political system more open towards the needs of the economic operators by strengthening property rights, improving the financial systems, dismantling the foreign trade monopolies and removing barriers to industrial expansion.[13]

Great Britain's judicial system was also different from that of the other European states. While most had a system based on a corpus of written laws, which took an extremely long time to change, the United Kingdom had its *Common Law* based on the precedents established by previous judicial decisions. This system could adapt more rapidly to social and economic changes than the *Civil Law* system of Roman-Germanic tradition.

Lastly, English society of the early modern era was different from other

---

[12] J. Mokyr, *The Enlightened Economy*, cit.

[13] D. Acemoglu, J.A. Robinson, *Why Nations Fail. The Origins of Power, Prosperity and Poverty*, London, 2013.

European societies: there was a smaller divide between the social classes and social mobility was greater. Income was more equally distributed, and contemporary accounts describe an 18th century "middle class" enjoying a high standard of living: the main source of rising demand. This may have contributed to a greater standardization of consumption, which differentiated Britain sharply from France and was essential in the development of mechanized production to overcome the limits (volume and price) of traditional manufacturing.

Many factors favoured the first Industrial Revolution: the growth of trade and shipping; the creation of a strong and dynamic state; a growth-oriented economic policy; agricultural innovations and the possession of particular production factors; the economic institutions supporting enterprise and innovation; the scientific institutions, "a culture of growth", a pragmatic approach and so on. These conditions, however, were not absent elsewhere in Europe, where they existed to a larger or smaller degree, and were sometimes just as developed when considered singly. Why was Britain the first industrial nation? The most convincing answer is still that of Peter Mathias: no other European country possessed these and other elements at the same time (and so early on). It was the combination of these factors in one single country that made it unique.[14]

Bibliography

Ashworth J.W., *The Industrial Revolution. The State, Knowledge and Global Trade*, London, 2017.

Broadberry S., O'Rourke K. (eds.), *The Cambridge Economic History of Modern Europe*, Vol. 1, 1700-1870, Cambridge, UK, 2010.

de Vries J., *Industrious Revolution in Europe. Consumer Behaviour and the Household Economy, 1650 to the Present*, Cambridge, 2008.

Findlay R., O'Rourke K., *Power and Plenty. Trade, War, and the World Economy in the Second Millennium*, Princeton and Oxford, 2007.

Goldstone J.A., *Why Europe? The rise of the West in World History 1500-1850*, Boston, 2008.

Pomeranz K., *The Great Divergence. China, Europe and the Making of the Modern World Economy*, Princeton, 2000.

Vries P., *Escaping poverty. The origins of modern economic growth*, Vienna, 2013.

---

[14] P. Mathias, *British Industrialization: Unique or not?*, in *The Transformation of England*, London, 1979.

THE INDUSTRIAL REVOLUTION

The term **Industrial Revolution** appeared for the first time in Arnold Toynbee's book *Lectures on the Industrial Revolution in England* (1884). The word "revolution" served to underline the momentous fracture that the author saw occurring between 1760 and 1830 in England's economy and society. The Industrial Revolution had been a period marked by rapid urbanization, an accumulation of capital, the growth of agricultural productivity and rising incomes.

This interpretation of the revolution as a fracture was very popular with historians, and prevailed until the mid-1970s. For Eric Hobsbawn (Industry and the Empire, 1968) the Industrial Revolution was "the most fundamental transformation of human life in the history of the world"; Ronald M. Hartwell (The Industrial Revolution, 1970) defined it as "the greatest discontinuity in history, greatest in terms of changes in institutions and organization, or in terms of output" and again, according to David Landes (The Unbound Prometheus, 1969), "the Industrial Revolution has been like in effect to Eve's tasting of the fruit of the tree of knowledge: the world has never been the same".

This interpretation of the **Industrial Revolution** as a great fracture was questioned during the 1970s, when the the long and intense period of growth following the Second World War came to an abrupt halt. The consolidation of industrial society appeared problematic in the light of the ecological and energy problems which exploded during the decade. The Industrial Revolution was viewed as "less revolutionary", and thus lost much of its eversiveness and significance as a moment of radical discontinuity, scaled down almost to a kind of side-show.

New cliometric studies have also scaled down the growth of the fundamental variables – income, savings, investments, fixed capital, installed power – during the decades immediately before and after 1800, and have underlined the persistence of marked regional and sectorial imbalances, even within Great Britain. Some academics maintained that English growth was gradual up to 1830, and some even proposed using the word "evolution" instead of revolution.

Revisionist interpretations, therefore, supported the idea of a slow development, starting in the early modern period, but did not deny the uniqueness of the Industrial Revolution. The new studies intended to analyse the multiple factors which had contributed to the Industrial Revolution. In addition, there was now mention of the revolution's social consequences and of the social fractures caused by the self-regulated market. Academics finally tried to understand why the **Industrial Revolution** had taken place in England, and whether England had been one of the models for modernization, or an exception. This revision ended up questioning one of the pillars of traditional interpretation, which considered English development as the normative model, or at least as the yardstick for all the industrial development processes.

The new current of study viewed the **Industrial Revolution** as a gradual process, no longer seeing it as a break with the past. It underlined continuity with the proto-industrial developments of previous eras; in particular, Franklin Mendels (*Proto-industrialization*, 1972) maintained that the so-called Industrial Revolution marked the birth of modern industry, but not of industry *tout court*, which already existed. Concepts like **proto-industrialization** and **industrious revolution** were introduced, implying a reformulation of the periodization of the Industrial Revolution. Attention was shifted onto the centuries of the early modern period, and thus onto the slow sedimentation from the Late Middle Ages of the technological, financial, social, demographic and institutional prerequisites which had produced the growth occurring in the 18th century.

This revision of traditional historical interpretation also brought greater interest in the development process of the Asian countries, especially in questioning the idea of a "European miracle" and the periodization of the so-called Great Divergence, in other words, the East overtaken by the West. For many years, comparisons between *the West and the Rest* had concluded that the other countries were backward compared with the Western model of development. The academics of the California School intended to review this **eurocentric** position, analyzing the economic, demographic and socio-political dynamics of the different East and South Asian situations in the pre-industrial period in order to make a comparative evaluation of the presumed European exception. They also focused on understanding the system of relations and interdependence between the various areas of the world in order to enhance the definitions of the concepts of **centre** and **periphery**. Given this outlook, according to recent studies, industrialization is not the necessary outcome of a sedimentation of prerequisites, just as these prerequisites are not necessarily connected with a European or Western specificity. Industrial modernity can even be unpredictable, caused by chance events and unusual circumstances.

The academics who have studied the complex subject of the **Industrial Revolution** have essentially tried to answer two great questions: 1) Which factors and variables favoured/determined industrialization and long-term growth? 2) Why England?

The most significant **variables** used by historians to explain the process of industrialization include 1. the institutions; 2. the "production factors": labour, energy/technology and capital; 3. demographics.

1. The **institutions** are defined by economist Douglass C. North (The Rise of the Western World, 1973) as "the rules of the game in a society or, more formally, the humanly devised constraints that shape human interaction". The institutions are endogenous, that is to say that they originate within a precise context and in certain conditions, and therefore differ from country to country. Institutions can be formal, such as the government, property laws, economic policies, the market regulations, or informal, such as socially acceptable behaviour, habitual business practices, and the degree of mutual trust between parties during commercial transactions. From an institutionalist point of view (D.C. North, *Institutions, Institutional Change and Economic Performance*, 1990), the economic *performance* of a country depends on the "incentive structure", i.e. on the greater or lesser stimuli to enterprise created by a given institutional framework.

The two macro-categories of **institutions** with an impact on development and growth are **political** and **economic**. The political institutions correspond not only to the form of government (absolutist state, oligarchic republic, constitutional state or autocracy) but also to the groups which actually exercise political power. The political institutions choose the economic institutions, and therefore define the constraints and opportunities for the economic subjects. In turn, the economic institutions determine the growth and distribution of resources, and provide an explanation for the divergences in economic development of between different countries.

In the case of England, for example, the limits placed on the monarch's power (following the Civil War of 1642 and the Glorious Revolution of 1688) prepared the ground for the development of property rights, for a new distribution of economic resources and for financial and commercial expansion. The growth of an economic system requires an efficient administration of justice, especially the protection of property rights, and also requires "political" protection to avoid requisition by the government and an overwhelming tax burden. If property rights are uncertain, businesses are smaller, investments in fixed capital are low, poor technology is used, and long-term contracts are avoided.

Furthermore, the inadequacy (or absence) of legislation regarding patents limits the incentives to innovate, in England, the 1624 patent legislation increased earnings from innovations and thus encouraged technological progress. In France and the rest of Europe there was no law regarding patents until 1791.

The fiscal systems, judicial systems, commercial law and financial tools are just some examples of the **institutions** which have developed over the centuries to guarantee the security of property and the rights pertaining to it, in order to limit abuses of political power towards private individuals and regulate the relations between private individuals by means of contractual tools. The progressive regulation of economic relations between individuals has played an important role in building a system of incentives designed to stimulate the maximization of wealth and income. The institutional balance – political and economic – can therefore be considered a fundamental factor underlying the differences in wealth and prosperity between nations.

2. With reference to the variable regarding the availability di **labour, energy/technology and capital**, as underlined also recently by economic historians like Kenneth Pomeranz and Robert Allen, Great Britain had an unusual combination of high salaries and cheap energy during the 18th century. This situation provided English businesses with an incentive to invent *labour-saving* technologies replacing human labour with capital (machines) and energy (inanimate).

According to Allen, high real salaries were the result of English growth at the international level. The expansion of English trade and its colonial empire had favoured the growth of the cities, the centres of commercial and financial activity: in turn, urbanization encouraged a better division of labour and therefore led to higher salaries. The high real salaries also gave the population spending power, which stimulated product innovation, and literacy rates increased because more people could afford the cost of education.

Another similar advantage Great Britain enjoyed was the availability of cheap raw materials, since its coalfields provided cheap energy. This *carbon coke* proved to be a decisively important element for the energy revolution and the invention of the steam engine. At this point, a virtuous circle was established, linking increased coal consumption, mechanization of production processes, expansion of the steel industry and the transport revolution.

On the other hand, England was favoured by the accumulation of capital in the agricultural and trade sectors, which could be used to launch entrepreneurial ventures. Moreover, at the outset, only a modest amount of capital was required for investments in industrial plants, and the barriers to entry were low: the most expensive investment was the steam engine. The credit provided by the great merchants and provincial banks was used to support companies' circulating capital (raw materials, a warehouse for finished products, liquidity reserves, workers' salaries). Towards the mid-18th century the cost of capital was lower than the cost of labour in Great Britain, and this was a further incentive to mechanization, since businessmen found it profitable to use labour-saving technologies, intensifying the use of two cheaper factors, i.e. energy e capital.

Here it is important to remember that some authoritative interpretations see the technological innovations of the first Industrial Revolution as facilitated by a favourable cultural context (Joel Mokyr writes of the Industrial Enlightenment, describing it as a European feature and not exclusively English), featuring a scientific approach, interpretation of natural phenomena, experimentation, and analysis and solving of technical problems.

3. With regard to the link between economic growth and **demographic changes**, as industrialization took hold, population cycles took a new course. The traditional societies of the past underwent alternating periods of expansion and stagnation, with high average birth and death rates (the latter due to famines, epidemics and wars). From the mid-18th century, the population in Western Europe's developed countries began to grow at an annual rate of 1% and population growth became irreversible.

Average birth rates increased as the great demographic disasters (plagues) disappeared, the subsistence crisis was alleviated by increased agricultural productivity, and the international trade in cereals grew. The improved relationship between population and resources (a constraint which had always impeded the economic growth of the traditional societies), provided the cities with food supplies and favoured migration to the cities; this meant that there was an increasing workforce in the areas where industrial activities were taking hold. Population growth favoured the modernization of agriculture: the land became more profitable and more could be produced by a smaller number of workers. To sum up, population growth stimulated the growth of production, which led to further population growth.

Given this long-term perspective, the **Industrial Revolution** marked the new course of modern economic development, because the typical constraints of economic growth intraditional societies were overcome, the constraints connected with the relationship between population and resources. It occurred in a particular political and cultural context which favoured innovation, while structural factors (the relative cost of production factors) marked Britain's particular course of growth. The spread of technological innovation made it possible to overcome diminishing returns in agriculture and to support the urbanization processes launching the period of sustained economic growth.

Chapter 6
AN UNSTOPPABLE PROCESS

The Industrial Revolution set off a dynamic self-propelling process that has never stopped in the last two centuries, although it has not been homogeneous in terms of intensity, rapidity and geographical area. Technological and scientific progress produced innovations applied to the production process, triggering complex mechanisms of adaptation and response to new problems with attempts to improve, accelerate and organise industrial production. The very essence of this dynamism is constant technological progress, which is increasingly sophisticated and expensive, although the economic development of a region or country can be a bumpy road. Since the Industrial Revolution began in Britain in the last two decades of the 18th century, no country has been able to choose the station where it joins the industrialization train. The "first comer" had a group of heterogeneous "followers" in pursuit, and Britain's consolidated leap forward meant that each country subsequently beginning its industrialization process would encounter very different technological and economic conditions. Each latecomer to industrialization pursued its own particular path towards modernity, which was original, impossible to reduce to a simple model or theory, but certainly not accidental. Historical and economic research should consider the objectives, the responses to technological challenges, the means and tools, the timing and the social, political, cultural and economic outcomes of these processes in the different areas, regions, and nations of the world. This chapter presents and some factual prompts. It examines the comparative context in order to explain the dynamics of the economic scenario irreversibly transformed by British industrialization.

6.1. The dynamics of "peaceful conquest" in European industrialization

At the start of the 19th century, the technological core of Britain's Industrial Revolution, continental Europe also experienced mechanization of production processes, and authoritative claims have been advanced that Great Britain never possessed a monopoly of technological creativity, even during the first stage of industrialization. Many new industries were actually introduced to Britain from continental Europe in the second half of the 18th century or early 19th century. These include some processes used in the paper industry, food processing, and manufacture of textiles like linen and silk, and also chemicals (chlorine for bleaching cloth, or sodium carbonate used in the production of glass and soap), gas-lighting and machinery, such as the Jacquard loom. However, even if the "Industrial Enlightenment"[1] was a European development, it is undeniable that in the 19th century the European countries became debtors, imitators and followers of the British model and its efficient use of innovations in industry.

Not only was "useful knowledge" widespread in Europe, but some areas of the continent also proved quite early on that they could establish manufacturing industries and participate in the international trade circuits by exporting their industrial products. The regions most ready to implement mechanization and industrial development were in north-western Europe; from the English Channel coasts, industrialization spread to northern France, Belgium, the Rhineland, Alsace and the Protestant cantons of Switzerland; further eastwards, it affected parts of Saxony, Bohemia and Silesia, and Lombardy to the south.

In a study now considered a classic of economic history, Sidney Pollard defined the spread of industrialization from Britain to continental Europe as a "peaceful conquest": a kind of "epidemic" that crossed national borders and "contagiously" in neighbouring regions, according to specific local factors, and outcomes were not homogeneous. This is an appealing approach, which analyses the region and not the nation-state. It shows European industrialization in the 19th century as a unique process, in which an extremely important role was played by "spontaneous" forces, which were present and reactive and not due to the particular political context of the state. Moving beyond the image of national industrialization processes as single seeds sprouting in different pots, Pollard traces a single of European industrialization,[2] a

---

[1] J. Mokyr, *The Enlightened Economy*, cit.

[2] S. Pollard, *Peaceful Conquest. The Industrialization of Europe, 1760-1970*, Oxford, 1981.

shared plot where plants with common roots grew in the same climate. The model also applies well to Britain itself, where the development chronologies were uneven, accompanied by regional specificities and temporary industrial centres.

This perspective recognised the importance of a region's political-institutional and judicial context, and therefore of the context provided by the particular state of reference, but also underlined that the factors of contagion were mostly the advantages of the area's geographical location, natural resources, and very much connected with its historical development, in terms of the relevant social and entrepreneurial capacities.

However, the two approaches – regional and national – are not mutually exclusive. No one nowadays attempts to deny the importance of the regional dimension and its virtuous processes. At the same time, however, it is impossible not to recognise that economic activity has been determined by national interests and policies, in a competition to emulate the most developed country, together with conflicts and power struggles. While the ferment during the first industrialization may still be considered "spontaneous" – although caused by a combination of different factors – and the "peaceful" spread of knowledge may be seen as a stimulus to industrialization, the following stage requires examination of the choices made by the various countries in their efforts to reach the cutting-edge of development in the global competition.

6.2. The universal banks

In the second half of the 19th century, the technological pattern of the second Industrial Revolution was already traced, and the race to catch up involved increasingly complex and expensive production processes.

In the space of just a few decades, Germany became Europe's leading industrial country as its process of industrialization was concentrated on heavy industry: iron and steel, chemicals, electricity and mechanics. Entrepreneurs' were no longer able to sustain economic activity in these sectors using their own financial resources. The large industrial factories and the most advanced technologies now required the intervention of a new actor, the universal bank, which drew on the French *Crédit Mobilier* experience of important investments in infrastructures, but was also active across the territory, with a network of branches able to collect savings. The universal banks (or mixed banks) assumed the risk of directing resources towards long-term investments, and in the mid-19th century they were essential in promoting the industrialization of a country following the course pioneered by Britain just a few decades earlier.[3]

After political unification in 1871, historians consider the efficiency of its articulated banking system as a strategic element in the rapid development of the German economy, together with institutional modernization, and the customs union already consolidated in the previous decades. It took just half a century for German heavy industries to lead Europe by the eve of the First World War. The German banks also acquired a major role with their financial backing for industry, and for the development of the railways. A strong central bank, the *Reichsbank* (founded Berlin 1876), was the hub of the activities of the universal banks, like the Deutsche Bank and Dresdner Bank, which focused on long-term finance. The local components of the banking system, like the savings banks, cooperative banks and private banks, were left to engage with small and medium businesses, and to provide short-term finance to agriculture or the building industry.

Thus, the spectacular growth and solidity of the universal banks was the distinctive element of the German development model, which saw the emergence of *capital intensive* companies in the leading sectors of the second Industrial Revolution. Economic historians attribute the consolidation of companies like Thyssen, Siemens, and AEG to the active role played by the German credit institutions: between 1870 and 1913, the share of German industrial capital controlled by the universal banks rose from 6% to 20%, and half of these *assets* were held by the five major Berlin banks. In 1913, the three largest companies quoted on the German stock exchange were banking companies. One estimate for the same period is that the credit provided by the universal banks constituted half of the total net investments in German industry.[4]

6.3. The state's role in the backward countries

After the mid-19th century, the conditions for access to industrial development gradually became more difficult with the increased cost of production plants, technologies and machinery in the new driving sectors, and also because of the increasingly marked relative backwardness of the countries which decided to focus on industrial development. In tsarist Russia, for example, state intervention became necessary towards the end of the century,

---

[3] R. Cameron, *Banking in the Early Stages of Industrialization. A Study in Comparative Economic History*, Oxford, 1967.

[4] J.R. Fear, *German Capitalism*, in T.K. McCraw (ed.), *Creating Modern Capitalism: How Entrepreneurs, Companies, and Countries Triumphed in Three Industrial Revolutions*, Cambridge, Mass., 1997, pp. 135-182.

and some remarkable results were achieved using powerful tools like subsidies, commissions and customs duties to favour companies and entire sectors of industry.

If it is clear that the economies which were starting up or in a phase of accelerated development are not those of more advanced systems, another important aspect also emerged in this process of growing industrialization: countries which started to industrialise later could use technologies that were already mature, and build more modern and efficient factories than the countries preceding them, which had carried out laborious experimentation. This was especially true in comparison with the pioneering work done in Britain. Economic historian Alexander Gerschenkron's research in the 1970s examined precisely the problem of the relative advantage of backward countries in a historical perspective. His work looked at the necessary strategic action of "substitutive factors" for individual entrepreneurship and private capital (i.e. the universal banks, the state and public finances), and at the potential imbalances created by the massive effort required to locate resources and direct them towards the development, support or protection of the national industrial system.[5]

Public intervention in national industrialization deserves closer study. In addition to tsarist Russia, the cases of Meiji Japan, and of Italy between the end of the 19th and start of the 20th centuries, also provide some important elements for consideration.

Japan was the only Asian country in the 19th century whose government reacted to European industrialization with an initiative viewing industry and economic development as crucial for the country's continued political independence. In 1868, a "revolution from above" ended the Shogunate system and returned the emperor to power (Meiji Restoration). In just a few decades, Japan was completely transformed by energetic state intervention in the political, military, banking, educational institutions and the economic system. Since the "unequal treaties" made it impossible to apply protectionist tariffs, the Japanese state decided to invest directly in industry: it built new factories in different sectors, brought technicians in from abroad, and guaranteed subsidies and commissions to industrial companies. The traditional interpretation of Japanese industrialization underlined the role of state initiative and the dominant role of the samurai, whose entrepreneurial activity as industrialists, bureaucrats, and bankers made them systematic modernisers of Japan's economy and society. However, the most recent historical research has highlighted that success of the central initia-

---

[5] A. Gerschenkron, *Economic Backwardness in Historical Perspective*, Cambridge, Mass., 1962.

tive, imposed from above, required a widespread social and economic response from a population culturally ready to embrace the process of forced industrialization as a positive national value. It was not only a case of transforming a peasant class into industrial manpower, but also of mobilising widespread entrepreneurship, which was energetic and provided capital that was mostly derived from trade. The *chonin*, who were merchants and craftsmen active in the urban centres, represented the most socially and economically dynamic class, which had already emerged during the Tokugawa period; it possessed the entrepreneurial vocation and financial resources of the market economy, and was capable of meeting the challenge of industrialization when it was launched by the state's nationalist initiatives.[6]

Although it was generally backward, there was important entrepreneurial and economic activity in some areas of Italy, and the process of industrialization was started by concentrating decisively on the initiative of Gerschenkron's "substitutive factors".

The universal bank model was imported at the end of the 19th century from Germany (*Banca Commerciale Italiana* and *Credito Italiano*, both based in Milan), and played an important role in the consolidation of a widespread industrial base in the Giolittian era, with the formation of the Milan-Turin-Genoa triangle. Most importantly, it provided decisive support at the national level for the highly capital-intensive steel and electricity sectors.

However, the state had dealt early on with the challenge of choosing industrialization, which many people saw as an unnatural hazard, "a heresy" for a country that was mostly agricultural until the 1880s, and whose place in the global economy depended mainly on primary sector exports.

The transport revolution involving steamships and railways sent this economic situation into an irreversible crisis. The first awareness of the processes taking place at the world level and its ambition to play a role in international politics, therefore spurred drove the Italian state to consolidate the country's strategic steel sector. It created a modern steelworks at Terni, entrusting its construction and management to a private entrepreneur, Vincenzo Stefano Breda. Steel production at the time was mostly directed towards the armaments industry, and the state intervened immediately to support Terni with commissions, subsidies and customs protection. When poor management decisions and inexperience brought the company to the brink of bankruptcy just three years after its foundation, the state

---

[6] J. Kocka, A.D. Chandler, K. Yamamura, P.L. Payne (eds.), *Evoluzione della grande impresa e management. Stati Uniti, Gran Bretagna, Germania, Giappone*, Turin, 1986.

once more carried out a first "rescue" operation and printed paper money through the country's largest bank (which was to become the Bank of Italy a few years later). This type of rescue was repeated three more times during the course of the following half century. In 1887, the state rescued a company (Terni), in 1911 it rescued the entire steel sector, and in 1922 it was the turn of the industrial activities of two great banks, the *Banca Italiana di Sconto* (including *Ansaldo*, Italy's largest industrial company with a workforce of 110,000) and the *Banco di Roma*. Finally, in 1933 the state rescued all the industrial shareholdings of the three great universal banks: the *Banca Commerciale Italiana*, the *Credito Italiano* and the *Banco di Roma*. This led to the creation of the IRI, the "institute for industrial reconstruction", which meant that the Italian state became an "entrepreneur state".[7]

In both cases, Japan and Italy, state-owned enterprises and state intervention directed industrial growth and economic modernization, pushing forward at a stage when the countries able to exploit the technologies and specific organizational demands of the second Industrial Revolution (the United States and Germany) were world leaders. However, historiography has highlighted that the successful combination of the first and second Industrial Revolutions, especially in Italy, took advantage of a socio-economic and entrepreneurial fabric that was already dynamic, despite the existence of significant imbalances in certain sectors and territories.

Moreover, it had been evident from the first half of the 19th century that a simple intervention from above to trigger industrialization was not alone sufficient to ensure extensive development that could be self-sustaining over time. This was seen when some peripheral countries attempted industrialization through state intervention in order to maintain and develop their military and political power.

Egypt during the 1820s and 1830s is an exemplary case, the first backward non-Western society to attempt economic modernization through state intervention to achieve industrialization. This ambitious experiment in forced industrialization was led by Muhammad Ali, an Albanian-born general of the Ottoman sultan, who gained political and military control of Egypt, proclaiming himself its ruler in the confused aftermath of the Napoleonic Wars. Looking to the British and French examples, he grasped the connection between economic power and political-military power, and developed a grandiose industrialization project based on cotton. The project involved massive state investments to encourage cultivation of the raw material and create spinning and weaving industries. It also included the recruitment of European experts, and state monopolies to control marketing.

---

[7] F. Amatori, A. Colli, *Impresa e industria in Italia dall'Unità a oggi*, Venezia, 1999.

The problem, however, was Egypt's socio-economic situation, since there were no workers who could spontaneously accept industry's discipline. The use of a servile workforce had disastrous results on the efficiency of the industrial system, and the attempt to train a native class of technicians and entrepreneurs was unsuccessful. In short, the impulse from above was not countered by Egyptian society, and the government initiative to enforce industrialization failed within a few decades.[8] At the time, and in later studies, British high-handedness was seen as largely to blame, preventing the enterprising Egyptian leader from introducing high customs barriers to defend Egyptian production. This makes no sense, however, because "unequal treaties" also prevented Japan from implementing protectionist tariffs.

6.4. Industrialization and the reactivity of the socio-economic fabric

A recent study focused on France leads once again to the theme of a diffused model of European industrialization. Michael S. Smith traces France's economic development after the Second World War back to its 19th century roots. This is not a process based on national specificities, but simply a variation of the diffusion of industrial, technological and organizational progress in the West's most advanced regions, especially in Europe.[9] The *business history* perspective converges here in the explanation of a development process rooted in the 19th century European dynamics of the spread of technological skills, entrepreneurial and organizational competence, and in a reactive social fabric consisting of different-sized industrial and commercial companies, capable of reacting to the impulses created by state economic policy decisions and foreign investments, by effective application of new technologies, and by European continental integration.

Although Germany is typically the country where the energetic activity of the universal bank represented an extremely important substitutive factor, there were also some very dynamic entrepreneurs among its merchants and craftsmen. Jürgen Kocka estimated that one million craftsmen were active in Germany at the start of the 19th century, and David Landes recalls that a massive number of vehicles crossed the frontiers when the customs union (*Zollverein*) between the German states took effect on 1st January 1834.

---

[8] D.S. Landes, *The Wealth and Poverty of Nations. Why Some are so Rich and Some so Poor*, New York 1998, cit., pp. 392 ff.

[9] M.S. Smith, *The Emergence of Modern Business Enterprise in France, 1800-1930*, Cambridge, Mass., 2006.

The mixed bank of German origin that began operating in Italy at the end of the 19th century is seen by some academics as the *deus ex machina* of the first period of Italian industrialization. However, the question is how and why this economic actor took a foothold in the country. The Italian reality was that industrial capitalism dependent on state action existed alongside a strong *Manchesterian* component, the "enterprising society" without which development is impossible. Some of Italy's major 19th century entrepreneurs must be mentioned. For example, the woollen mills belonging to Alessandro Rossi of Schio made him Italy's leading entrepreneur at unification; having studied British industry, he then replaced all machinery and re-organized the family company, achieving success at a European level. As a young graduate from Milan Polytechnic, Giovanni Battista Pirelli, discovered the rubber industry when a grant enabled him to travel abroad in search of a "new" industry. At first, Pirelli's success was based on state commissions, and the company's most important activity involved military telegraph cables, but it soon moved into the civilian market. Pirelli's use of the most advanced technologies allowed it to compete on the global market and build manufacturing plants in Spain, South America and even Britain, the heart of world capitalism. Similarly, while some steel producers were involved almost exclusively in supplying the state's military needs, the Falck family, newcomers from Alsace, focused on the flourishing market of the industrial triangle, using technologies that were valid but not excessively expensive enough to require state protection.

Together with the great figures like Rossi, Pirelli and Falck, a widespread business class had accumulated capital, invested in mechanization of production, and consolidated the trade networks, especially in Northern Italy and in the textile sectors (silk, cotton, linen and wool).

In conclusion, industrial development has historically been the combined result of exogenous impulses and endogenous responses: the meeting of an impulse from above and an impulse from below. Without the activity of the universal bank and the state in Germany, Russia, Italy and Japan, these countries would have been unable to experience what is defined as industrial *take-off*, but the development promoted "from above" would not have been self-sustaining without the active collaboration of social and economic forces already operating in the national structure, which were ready to accept the challenges of modernization.

Bibliography

Bonelli F., *Il capitalismo italiano. Linee generali d'interpretazione*, in *Storia d'Italia, Annali I, Dal feudalesimo al capitalismo*, Turin, 1978.

Cameron R., *Banking in the Early Stages of Industrialization. A Study in Comparative Economic History*, Oxford, 1967.

Chandler A.D., Kocka J., Payne P.L., Yamamura K. (eds.), *Evoluzione della grande impresa e management. Stati Uniti, Gran Bretagna, Germania, Giappone*, Turin, 1986.

Gerschenkron A., *Economic Backwardness in Historical Perspective*, Cambridge, Mass., 1962.

McCraw T.K. (ed.), *Creating Modern Capitalism. How Entrepreneurs, Companies, and Countries Triumphed in Three Industrial Revolutions*, Cambridge, Mass., 1997.

Mokyr J., *The Enlightened Economy. An Economic History of Britain 1700-1850*, New Haven and London, 2009.

Pollard S., *Peaceful Conquest. The Industrialization of Europe, 1760-1970*, Oxford, 1981

Smith M.S., *The Emergence of Modern Business Enterprise in France, 1800-1930*, Cambridge, Mass., 2006.

Chapter 7
A NEW WORLD BALANCE

7.1. The Second Industrial Revolution

The Second Industrial Revolution was marked by major technological innovations and the systematic application of scientific knowledge to industrial production processes. It also involved new forms of company organization to deal with the increased size and complexity of emerging sectors, which became the leading industries in the most developed economies (iron and steel, chemicals and mechanical engineering). Industries used electricity, a source of energy with a vast range of applications and a profound impact both on production systems and on daily life. These constitute the pillars of the Second Industrial Revolution, which led to a shift in the world's economic balance of power in the last decades of the 19th century. At the end of the century, the more dynamic economies of the United States and Germany actually overtook Great Britain. After a long period of British economic supremacy, this new American leadership was based on its extremely large capital – and management-intensive companies, on standardised mass production, and on the central role of new scientific knowledge applied to industry.

7.2. A new leading figure: big business

With the Second Industrial Revolution, an assertive new actor appeared on the economic scene – big business. This was not a spontaneous development, since it required a suitable judicial and institutional, economic and cultural framework, together with prerequisites involving transport (railways) and communications (telegraph). Businesses exploited the new networks to reach wider markets, relying on a constant relationship of trust with suppliers and customers, and re-organising their own internal systems of production and distribution, based on established and regular routines.

The completely new management and financial requirements of railway and telegraph systems meant that a new kind of company emerged in this two sectors, requiring such a large financial commitment that the difficulty of maintaining both possession and control together soon became evident. For the first time, the development of vast railways systems required an increasingly formalized management organization and precisely defined relations of authority, responsibility and communication within company functions.

New management tools like the organizational chart, *line* and *staff* were the managerial response to the complexity of the new company units. However, the decisive factor underlying the birth of big companies was the wide range of mechanical, electrical and chemical production processes invented, tried and improved in the United States and Western Europe after 1870. These became available for industry just as the new communications and transport networks were completed. The new processes ranged from petroleum distillation to mass processing of foodstuffs like sugar, vegetable oils, tobacco, alcoholic beverages and wheat. They included canning machinery and packaging innovations, which were fundamental for the food industry and for chemical consumer goods. They ranged from manufacture to assembly of inter-changeable mechanical parts for armaments and agricultural machinery, sewing machines, typewriters and cars. Another decisive innovation was the Gilchrist-Thomas converter (patented in 1879) used in the steel industry, the fundamental sector of modern industrialization. It was also possible to use electricity, a flexible energy source whose interaction with chemistry and metallurgy enabled the large-scale production of widely used products like chlorine, calcium carbide and aluminium.

This pivotal set of innovations meant that the Second Industrial Revolution differed from the previous period in that production processes now used more energy, enabling the high-speed production of massive quantities of goods.

This meant a significant division between two types of industry. Some sectors, such as clothing, textiles, wood and leather, were not actually affected by this transformation and continued to use traditional labour-intensive processes and simple technology. Even here, the growth of demand led to increased size, but the expansion of manufacturing plants only meant additional machinery and workers, without any significant reduction in unit costs; small and large factories remained equally competitive. Conversely, increased factory size in the sectors typical of the Second Industrial Revolution meant that radical reorganization was required. Machinery was positioned so that the different stages and processes in the manufacture of the finished product took place in a continuous sequence inside the same factory, which was regularly supplied with large amounts of fossil fuel. This made it possible to achieve a significant reduction in unit costs as the volume of output increased (economies of scale), giving larger factories an incomparable advantage over smaller ones.

The economic advantages of the bigger factories could be maintained only if there was a constant flow of materials through the production plant. This could not be achieved just by improving factory organization, but also required constant coordination between suppliers, distributors and consumers, and it therefore became essential to create a vast organization.

During the first stage of industrialization, an entrepreneur could achieve success by using the skills of a technological expert and a good salesman, but the critical entrepreneurial tactic of the Second Industrial Revolution was the creation of an extensive managerial hierarchy, and for economies of scale to be effective, companies were unable to avoid vertical integration. This was necessary to protect against possible risks created by suppliers, to overcome the difficulties created by independent distributors when products required specialised services, or when the quantities of a single product manufactured by the plant exceeded the distributors' possibilities of offering competitive costs. When a company grew by vertical integration, then production, supply and distribution required supervision by managerial staff, so it was essential to establish a central office to coordinate the entire complex of operations.

One novel aspect of the large companies was its direct relationship with the market due to its investment in a distribution network. This provided a constant stimulus to improve and research new products, creating stable and virtuous communication between the functions of production, marketing and "research and development", in order to exploit the economies of scope through product diversification.

In the space of a few decades, this process of continual company growth during the Second Industrial Revolution began to have an effect not only on the competition between companies within the nation, but also on the international economic equilibrium.

The technology and organizational conditions in which a limited number of large production plants met domestic demand, and sometimes even world demand, for a certain product, inevitably required the creation of an industrial structure where the focus of competition shifted from prices to function and strategy, which involved constant improvements in company functions, and research into new products and markets. In the same way, the need to achieve the lowest possible costs via technology took company expansion beyond national borders. This usually began with the creation of a marketing network, followed by investments in production: these complex decisions were dependent on technological specificity, the size of present markets and future forecasts, on the costs of transport, supply and distribution, and on the customs system.

7.3. Technological change: constraints and opportunities

The technological changes of the Second Industrial Revolution created a set of constraints and opportunities. The potential of the innovations could be exploited only by investing in a vast company organization, which was never a simple or automatic transition. It involved many uncertainties, including the risk of upsetting traditional power balances and depriving the owners of complete control over the company. The world's three most advanced nations – Great Britain, the United States and Germany – did not grasp the opportunities offered by the Second Industrial Revolution in the same way.

In the United States, the *big corporations* were already established in all sectors affected by technological development before the First World War, from heavy industry to the manufacture of consumer goods. During the 20th century, this became the successful model for other countries to imitate. Controlled by a central office and functional departments, the corporations integrated production and distribution, tending towards multinational expansion.

During the years immediately before the First World War, some British companies were also capable of integrating production with an adequate marketing network, and could therefore compete at the world level: these included Dunlop (tyres), Courtaulds (synthetic fibres), and Pilkington (glass). However, most British companies were still manufacturing consumer goods that required relatively unsophisticated technology and smaller investments in production and distribution. The greatest difference with the American model was, however, that the family owning the company played an active management role alongside a limited managerial staff.

Development was different in Germany, where the big corporations became established in the iron and steel industry, chemicals, and heavy machinery. These highly technological sectors required an extensive and competent managerial staff alongside the owners; above all, they required substantial investments to launch and maintain their position. Differently from the other two countries, Germany saw the emergence of the dynamic universal banks, which took a vigorous role in the ownership and management of large corporations, especially in their initial phases.

Other variables defining the development of the most advanced economic systems during the Second Industrial Revolution include market characteristics, economic competition regulated by public authorities, the social fabric, and cultural attitudes towards big businesses.

7.4. Towards a new global scenario

At first glance, British industry appeared to possess the advantage of vast domestic and international markets. In 1870, Great Britain had the highest *per capita* income of the three most industrialised nations, and between 1870 and 1914 British exports provided almost 30% of national income. Nevertheless, more careful study reveals little dynamism in the domestic and foreign markets of British companies, and little potential to stimulate responses to the challenges created by the technological innovations of the Second Industrial Revolution. A comparative perspective makes it possible to understand why Britain, the industrial pioneer, was gradually overtaken by the United States, and in Europe, by Germany. The well-being, modernization, urban and industrial growth achieved by Britain in the mid-19th century came to represent an element of rigidity, providing little incentive for entrepreneurs to seek out more efficient forms of organization in order to exploit the most advanced technology. Low urbanization levels and population density drove the American corporations towards forward integration, but the high population density in British cities did not drive improvement of what was already a widespread and consolidated distribution system. In the same way, Britain's modern cities, housing structures and transport systems did not require the same widespread interventions in the second half of the century as the growing German cities, where the need for metal frames and electrical wiring systems drove the most modern industries.

The British economy eventually also encountered a kind of "pioneer's disadvantage" in the strategic railway sector, which was the first big business, but did not have the overwhelming impact on the general economic equilibrium in Britain as it did in the United States and Germany during the same decades.

In America, besides effectively creating an enormous unified internal market, the railways also required the formation of a specialised staff able to manage enormous companies, and led to the concentration of the capital market in Wall Street. In addition, they provided a testing ground for regulation and for modern industrial relations.

Railways had a similarly important impact in Germany, with the additional factor that new financial institutions, the universal banks were created precisely to support this new sector; after completion of the railway network in the 1880s, the banks were active in providing long-term financial support for other industrial sectors.

The size of domestic and foreign markets is another significant variable for understanding the changes to the world scenario in the second half of the 19th century. Given the dimensions of the American domestic market, US exports accounted for only a small share of national income, no more than 5% per year between 1870 and 1913. The United States sold cotton abroad, together with wheat, tobacco and meat, but also traded new goods like refined petroleum, canned foods and light engineering goods.

Britain's foreign trade was much more important during the same decades, accounting for 27-30% of national income, although the products were mostly those typical of the first Industrial Revolution: textiles, iron and coal. Foreign markets were also extremely important for Germany, but the structure of its exports was very different from Britain's, as it mostly involved the chemicals and machinery of the second Industrial Revolution. The markets able to absorb these products were in Eastern and Southern Europe, where industrialising countries needed supplies for their textile factories and metalworking industries, and for the construction of railways, telegraph networks and electricity grids. In 1913, Germany was the world's leading exporter of chemical products, electromechanical goods and industrial machinery (28.5%, 35% and 29% of the world total, respectively). These industries required continual investment in innovations and large-scale business management.

The question of regulating competition among companies offers some interesting starting points for a detailed comparison. Academics have spoken of the "American paradox"[1] regarding the result of the antitrust legislation introduced around the turn of the century. The opposition of the state and judiciary to the gigantic industrial corporations was embodied in a series of laws and judicial interventions aimed at preserving free competition in the contest to acquire wealth, although the result was actually the opposite of what was intended. Despite the resilience of small industrialists and tradesmen, antitrust legislation was unable to prevent big companies from working together to control markets or to limit the economic power of big business. During these decades, the large corporations continued their research into internal efficiency, proving insuperable in the new high-technology and capital-intensive sectors.

When it came to regulating economic activity, more differences emerged between Britain and Germany. In the birthplace of Adam Smith and liberalism, agreements to control competition were allowed and unimpeded by the laws of the land. In Britain, large companies existed alongside

---

[1] T.K. McCraw (ed.), *Creating Modern Capitalism. How Entrepreneurs, Companies, and Countries Triumphed in Three Industrial Revolutions*, Harvard, 1998.

small companies and traditional commercial activity, and there was no need for any eventual antitrust policy. Unlike their counterparts in the United States, German corporations were free of any pressure from political and judiciary power. Cartels regulating market behaviour spread throughout the country in the last two decades of the century and were eventually protected by law in 1897, when the German Supreme Court declared that they were beneficial to the public interest.

The social and cultural climate in the different countries at the end of the 19th century is also important in defining the global economic equilibrium. Research has shown that American society offered a particularly favourable terrain for the large bureaucratic and hierarchical organizations represented by the big companies, and also for other institutions capable of providing a "new order" based on efficiency, regularity, continuity and systematic controls, such as political parties, trade unions, pressure groups and professional associations.[2]

The rapid industrial development driven by the technology of the Second Industrial Revolution actually posed a difficult challenge in all countries involved. It tested society's cultural attitudes, and the capacity of the national school and university systems to meet the demands of industry. German society, with its consolidated tradition of bureaucratic efficiency serving the state, appeared to welcome and support big business, creating collaboration between entrepreneurs and managers. Conversely, in 19th century British society there was considerable resistance to the more modern industrial economy. Intellectual elites and vast sectors of public opinion shared a widespread feeling of rebellion, while "third generation" entrepreneurs resembled gentlemen rather than industrialists engaged in promoting the managerial hierarchies imposed by the new technological and organizational conditions. Economic historian David Landes describes this negative attitude in 1969, in a passage from his *Unbound Prometheus*, "(...) now it was the turn of the third generation, the children of affluence, tired of the tedium of trade and flushed with the bucolic aspirations of the country gentleman. (...) Many of them retired and forced the conversion of their firms into joint-stock companies. Others stayed on and went through the motions of entrepreneurship between the long weekends; they worked at play and played at work. Some of them were wise enough to leave the management of their enterprises to professionals (However), Nor were corporate enterprises significantly better. For one thing, family considerations often determined their selection of managing personnel (...).[3]

---

[2] R.H. Wiebe, *The Search for Order. 1877-1920*, New York, 1967.

[3] D.S. Landes, *The Unbound Prometheus*, cit., pp. 336-7.

Another sharp contrast opposing the United States and Germany to Britain can be seen in the response of school and university systems to the needs of industry during these decades. Late 19th century Germany boasted the world's best science faculties, which trained the scientists and engineers required by the companies operating in the various sectors: the chemical, mechanical, and electrical sectors and the steel industry. Its various *Technische Hochschulen* trained technicians specifically for industry, and its *Handelshochschulen* provided training in the economic, financial and legal aspects of business management.

University education in the United States also adapted rapidly to the demands of industry. Before 1880, American colleges concentrated on training the technicians essential to the constructions of railways, but in the last two decades of the century, schools like the Massachusetts Institute of Technology, Purdue and Cornell began holding courses for mechanical, electrical and chemical engineers. MIT soon took on a central role through its close contacts with big business corporations like DuPont, Standard Oil, General Electric and General Motors. During the same years, alongside the centres offering advanced technical training, students in *business schools* began for the first time to study the strategy and management practices of the big industrial corporations.

The British system was unable to offer anything similar, which provides another confirmation of a negative attitude towards technology, science and industrialism. The last decade of the 19th century was a particularly significant turning point in the economic history of all three countries, allowing an evaluation of their reactivity to the challenges of the second Industrial Revolution. In this period, the imbalance between offer and demand caused by application of new technologies to the production processes led to a general drop in prices, both in Europe and in the United States. The first reaction everywhere was an attempt to control the market with agreements between companies.

However, the use of this kind of agreement soon proved so ineffective in the American economic situation (devoid of legal protection, then illegal) that company *mergers* became common. The classic example is John D. Rockefeller's gigantic Standard Oil Trust, which began to develop in 1882. In this case, the consequence of merger was a radical process of technical and organizational renovation, involving selection of the most efficient production plants, coordination of the product flow from oil wells to consumers, and a strictly centralised administration. In the space of a few years, the company had achieved its target of reducing production costs and achieved a correspondingly a substantial rise in profits.

Not all mergers were straightforward, but despite the difficulties encountered, the *merger movement* was a general tendency, and the most effective reaction to the demands of highly technological industrialization. It led to the creation of a new kind of company, which differed from the sum of its parts, capable of managing the changes in production and organization and able to dominate the markets, even at the international level, by cutting the unit costs of production.

Mergers also took place in Britain, although the dimensions and numbers involved were smaller than in the United States. Most importantly, the results differed in terms of organizational quality. British mergers took the form of business federations; each company maintained its managerial independence, but all would cooperate on single stages of the production process (for example, purchasing, research or price-fixing). The most widespread model of British *merger* was therefore an agreement at the highest level, which did not substantially change the national model of corporate ownership.

Although German capitalism was "organised", it was no match for the dynamic strength of its American counterpart with the technical and organizational efficiency of its vast corporations.

The processes triggered by the second Industrial Revolution caused a definitive shift in the global equilibrium, and the story of British industry after 1880 seems to be largely a story of missed opportunities and delays. The country's loss of position involved the leading industrial sectors: chemicals, metallurgy, electro-mechanics, heavy engineering, and mass production of light engineering goods. Britain's American and German competitors certainly benefitted. The problem was structural; the real leaders of the Second Industrial Revolution were the big companies, and their lack of success in the British economy meant that the world's first industrial nation was doomed to suffer long-term economic decline after a century of absolute world supremacy.

Table 7.1. Infrastructures, transport costs and price convergence (1870-1915)

The reduction in transport costs

American Export Routes transport cost (deflated)	1869/71-1908/10	from 100 to 55%
American East Coast Routes transport cost (deflated)	1869/71-1911/13	from 100 to 55%
British Tramp transport cost (deflated)	1869/71-1911/13	from 100 to 78%

Price convergence of some products

Liverpool/Chicago difference in wheat prices	1870-1912	from 58 to 16%
London/Cincinnati difference in bacon prices	1870-1913	from 93 a 18%
Philadelphia/London difference in pig iron prices	1870-1914	from 85 to 19%
London/Boston difference in wool prices	1870-1915	from 59 to 28%
London/Buenos Aires difference in hide prices	1870-1916	from 28 to 9%

Source: Table uses data from K.H. O'Rourke, J.G. Williamson, *Globalization and History. The Evolution of a Nineteenth-Century Atlantic Economy*, Cambridge, Mass., 1999.

Table 7.2. Railways in operation (1870 and 1913, km)

	1870	1913
Belgium	2,897	4,676
France	15,544	40,770
Germany	18,876	63,378
Italy	6,429	18,873
United Kingdom	21,500	32,623
Spain	5,295	15,088
Austria-Hungary	6,112	44,800
Russia	10,731	70,156
United States	85,170	400,197
Japan	0	10,570

Source: Table uses data from B.R. Mitchell, *European Historical Statistics*, London, 1992; Id., *International Historical Statistics: Africa and Asia*, London, 1982; Id., *Historical Statistics: The Americas and Australasia*, London, 1993.

Table 7.3. Per capita income levels (1820, 1870, 1913, United Kingdom = 100)

	1820	1870	1913
Austria*	74	57	69
Belgium	74	81	82
France	69	57	69
Germany**	63	59	76
Italy	62	45	50
United Kingdom	100	100	100
Spain	61	42	45
Russia***	43	31	30
United States	73	75	105
Japan	40	23	27

* Current area
** German Federal Republic
*** USSR

Source: Table uses data from A. Maddison, *Monitoring the World Economy*, Paris, 1995.

Table 7.4. The distribution of industrial production. % shares of United States, United Kingdom and Germany (1870 and 1913)

	1870	1913
United States	23	36
United Kingdom	32	14
Germany	13	16

Source: Table uses data from A.D. Chandler, *Scale and Scope.*, cit., p. 19.

Bibliography

Amatori F., Colli A., *Business History, Complexities and Comparisons*, *Routledge*, London 2011.

Chandler A.D., *Scale and Scope. The Dynamics of Industrial Capitalism*, Harvard, 1990.

Landes D.S., *The Unbound Prometheus. Technological Change and Industrial Development in Western Europe from 1750 to the Present*, Cambridge, New York, 1969.

McCraw T.K. (ed.), *Creating Modern Capitalism. How Entrepreneurs, Companies, and Countries Triumphed in Three Industrial Revolutions*, Harvard, 1998.

Wiener M.J., *English Culture and the Decline of the Industrial Spirit 1950-1980*, London, 1985.

WORKPLACE ORGANIZATION

Between the 1870s and the First World War, the economies of the industrialised countries experienced a season of rapid production growth based on new energy sources and technology. The novelty of this period was the completely new alliance of science, technology and industry. Scientific research was increasingly directed towards its potential applications in industry and was increasingly often carried out in the laboratories of the big companies, which systematically applied the result to their production processes. There were also important innovations in the organization of industrial production, introduced in order to improve the flow of production (conveyor belts, lifts, and hoists) and to increase productivity (machinery ensuring the production of uniform pieces, which then had to be assembled). However, the most important process in the reorganization of production was the more rational and scientific use of the workforce in the large factories, always with the aim of cutting the cost of labour and increasing its productivity.

This **organizational revolution** was led by American engineer Frederick Winslow Taylor (1856-1915). Taylor was well-acquainted with the shop-floor, and had observed, examined and analysed its every aspect from being a young apprentice to becoming manager of some of America's greatest steel companies. In his best-known work, *Principles of Scientific Management*, published in 1911, Taylor describes a chaotic factory without one single production method on which everybody agrees, with dozens of different ways to perform a single operation, and where the workmen exploit this lack of a unified production process to do as little work as possible. With his studies of *scientific management*, Taylor intended to provide a response to the problems caused by the growth of American industrial companies. These may be summarised as the profound contrast between a level of technological progress allowing mass production and the organizational backwardness of factory production processes, still marked by imprecise and obsolete criteria, a mixture of approximation, practical experience and arbitrariness.

For Taylor, the solution lay in increased productivity created by his system, powerful enough to permanently eliminate all contrasts between company interests and those of the workers. Taylor's proposed scientific organization can be summarised in his famous **four fundamental principles**: identification of the best working methods; selection and training of the workforce; development of respect and collaboration between management and workers; a strict division of tasks between the workers and the different levels in the management hierarchy. The aims were to achieve the best management of the company's human and material resources. By applying the scientific method, management could understand not only the possibilities of increasing productivity, but also be aware of the limits to what it could be require of the workforce, whose efforts were to be recompensed with adequate pay rises.

The best proof of Taylor's modernity is probably provided by the comparison with Charles Eugene Bedaux (1886-1944). A French-born engineer who emigrated in 1906 to work in the United States, Bedaux had personal experience of the obstacles impeding the application of "orthodox" Taylorism in American companies. The organizational revolution propounded by Taylor actually affected all company activity, from the planning offices to the departments, and was both laborious and costly. Some solutions were greeted by businessmen and managers with widespread scepticism, for instance the division of workshop management on a functional basis. There was also strong resistance from technical managers to **Taylorist organisers'** attempts to deprive them of their traditional margins of independence.

The **Bedaux system** was elaborated a few years after the publication of Taylor's *Principles*, as the low-cost (and low management effort) to genuine Taylorist organization. It was a piece-work system, presented as a scientific measurement of work, and consisted essentially of "sampling" work by measuring the time it took a worker to carry out each single operation. The quantity of work which could be done during that time was then standardised and this determined the basic rate of pay. The reduction of the effort incorporated in the different labour tasks to a single unit of measurement provided elements for an immediate comparison between the efficiency levels of the departments and the shop floors, enabling quantification of the results achieved. However, the Bedaux system only involved the production area, and avoided any suggestions about organizational methods.

The most complete application of Taylor's ideas to industrial activity was made by Henry Ford, the car industry giant, who is considered the creator of the integrated form of labour organization and factory system regulation known as Fordism. From Taylor, Ford adopted the attention paid to ensure maximization of time and effort, but the most important step towards **mass production** was his adoption of the *standardized and synchronized system*, in other words, the sequential connection of assembly operations using automated systems to move the parts to the workers. This is the principle of the assembly line which Ford introduced in 1913 at his Highland Park factory in Michigan, and would become the symbol of 20th-century industrial organization. Ford did not stop, as Taylor had, at the division and sub-division of the operations, but aimed to keep the work moving so that every processed part was moved and conveyed to the workers, enabling them to work in the best possible way. The results achieved with the assembly line were immediately outstanding. Before the Highland Park factory became operational, it took 728 minutes of work to produce a Model T, Ford's "car for everybody", according to the slogan with which it was launched in 1908. The assembly line reduced the time to no more than 90 minutes, and drastically cut unit costs of production: the price of a Model T fell from $950 in 1908, when it appeared on the market, to $360 in 1917 and $290 in 1927, when it went out of production.

The historical limit of mass production arrived with the first petrol crisis in 1973, although signs of crisis appeared even before this. For example, after the mid-1960s, the average profit levels of the big corporations had halved in the United States, and fallen by a third to half in the European countries. The crisis of the **Taylor-Fordian production model** had a series of causes. Between the end of the 1960s and the start of the 1970s the market in the most developed economies had become not only less able to absorb growing shares of durable and mass goods, but also increasingly fragmented into different consumer groups. This made the market unstable and unpredictable, given that demand and customer needs changed continually. Instability and market saturation were caused by the increased interdependence of economies, which implied increased competition on a world scale, due for example to the emergence of newly industrialised countries, like those in Southeast Asia, which could produce the same mass goods at much lower costs.

From the end of the 1960s, **market diversification** and the market's reduced ability to absorb stock upset the organizational values of the past and replaced them with new principles, in the search to find new technological and organizational systems that could promote forms of production for small batches, at the same costs.

The need for a response to diversification and market saturation with better quality diversified products at competitive costs was behind a new model of industrial organizational which merged once again from within the car industry. The **Lean Production model** was developed and systematised during the early 1970s by Taiichi Ohno, an engineer working for the Japanese car company Toyota. According to Ohno, the new situation of slow growth created by the petrol crisis required a redefinition of the flow of production, so that it no longer began at the top, but from the bottom, with the requirements of the market dictating production. This reduced stock to a minimum, because materials were purchased only when needed and in the required quantity. **Toyotism**, as the Toyota Production System soon became known, had three basic principles. *Just-in-time* meant that each component arrived on the line exactly when needed and in the quantity required; "self-activation" allowed workers to safeguard high quality standards by intervening to eliminate problems on the line; and workers were organised into groups to enhance responsibility, quality control and self-managed teamwork. The effectiveness of this new organizational system is borne out by Toyota's outstanding results. In 1950, the company was almost insignificant, but just over 30 years later – in 1983 – it manufactured 3.4 million vehicles with just over 130,000 workers, whereas America's General Motors produced 5 million cars with 460,000 workers, Ford made 2.5 million cars with over 160,000 workers, and Chrysler totalled just over a million cars with 140,000 workers. In the same year, each Toyota worker produced 56 cars, compared to 16 for Chrysler, 12 for Ford, and 10 for General Motors.

From the end of the 1980s, the lessons learnt from the **Japanese model** spread to American industry and then to Europe. In most industries, the old impersonal assembly line system was replaced by teamwork; each unit of the team or group has to demonstrate management ability and participate actively in the organization scheme. Pressure towards a leaner industrial organization and the massive introduction of automation have drastically reduced the size of the workforce.

In this framework, the spread of teamwork has made it possible to recover a degree of independence, operational autonomy, and even control and self-regulation, completely lacking in the traditional Taylor-Fordian model. However, increased autonomy and improved working conditions have been offset by the loss of the stability guaranteed by the Fordian model. Work has become **flexible**, less standardised and perhaps more satisfying, but also more temporary and unstable, and much less protected. Companies increasing use of flexible forms of work, pay, working hours and job duration has introduced novelties regarding the form and the content of work and has modified the jobs market at the levels of employment and composition. One example is the shift from the traditionally homogeneous working conditions of most paid workers towards increasing differentiation, resulting in a vast array of professional figures and working conditions.

Chapter 8
THE WESTERN MODEL AND ITS LIMITS

SUMMARY: 8.1. Tsarist Russia. – 8.2. Reform from above: Imperial Japan. – 8.3. The Meiji Restoration. – 8.4. China in the late Qing period. – 8.5. Latin America. – Bibliography. – *Mass emigration from Europe.*

The previous chapters have traced the different economic development paths of the European countries and United States from the 19th century, as they embarked on what Simon Kuznets termed "modern economic growth".[1] Development was facilitated by a cultural context favouring innovation, and by the technology and skills already developed in the pre-industrial age, fitting broadly into the framework outlined by Alexander Gerschenkron. The substitutes for a widespread entrepreneurial fabric (the state, the universal banks, or foreign capital) combined with the capacity to sustain and create a favourable environment for innovation and drove the convergence of technology and *per capita* GDPs in Europe.

However, in the 1860s, the states considered in this chapter still belonged to the *ancien régime* in all respects. Their modernization was a consequence of exogenous shocks, of the industrial modernity that had transformed the West, revolutionizing international relations and changing geopolitics worldwide. Equilibria that had existed for centuries were shattered by the new demands of trade and industry, the gradual integration of the world market, and the increasing density of business relations. These countries were forced to change, although with differing degrees of success.

8.1. Tsarist Russia

In 19th century Europe, Russia symbolized reactionary absolutism. The country's level of urbanization was limited; over 90% of the population lived and worked on the land in 1860, the burgher class was extremely small, and power was concentrated in the autocratic figure of the tsar.[2] The

---

[1] S. Kuznets, *Modern Economic Growth. Rate, Structure and Spread*, New Haven, 1966.

[2] A.S. Milward, S.B. Saul, *The Development of the Economies of Continental Europe. 1850- 1914*, London, 1977.

nobility held over 90% of the land not belonging to the Crown, and industry was seriously backward, apart from some cotton and sugar factories. Russia was the country where serfdom survived the longest, with peasants subjected to the harshest treatment, and where the factories operated by the nobility also used serfs as manpower.

Production in the primary sector was based on the agricultural estates: cultivation was extensive and the rotation system was backward, while the climatic conditions were unfavourable. The nobility gradually increased pressure on the peasants, provoking over 470 uprisings between 1855 and 1861.[3] These social tensions were a cause of concern for the monarchy, which was hesitant to launch industrialization because this implied a process of institutional review, although it was well aware that industrialization would increase Russian military power.

Modernization proceeded unevenly, driven by the conflicts (or military defeats) involved in territiorial expansion, such as the Crimean War (1853-1856), which played a crucial role; it was triggered by tsarist ambitions to expand towards the Mediterranean, and saw Russia opposed by the Western powers. The fall of Sebastopol following an eleven-month siege showed the world that Russia was no longer the power that had defeated Napoleon, and the humiliating Treaty of Paris (1856) imposed an urgent need for change on Tsar Alexander II. However, the effects of his reforms were limited by the inherent need to preserve his autocratic power and protect the interests of its legitimating base, the nobility.

Between 1855 and 1861, Alexander II abolished serfdom, corporal punishment and courts for different classes of society. The peasants ceased to be "goods" and became a class of taxpayers. Although peasant families worked the land and claimed rights over it, the question of ownership had to be resolved without alienating the nobility. The solution was a compromise which appeared as a revolutionary change, but was actually a conservative process of revising the traditional structure of agriculture. A share of the land belonging to the Crown and nobility was granted to rural families via a complicated scheme of repayment, with the village community standing as guarantor. This system was designed to limit the expulsion of manpower, but the peasants' uncertainty about their ownership of the land actually discouraged them from any attempts at improvement. This created a situation that was diametrally opposed to the agricultural individualism that was replacing the community spirit in the European countryside.

---

[3] J.M.K. Vyvyan, *Russia in Europe and Asia*, in J.P. Bury (ed.), *The New Cambridge Modern History*, X, Cambridge, 2008 [1967].

The most significant outcome of the reform was that it expanded the potential tax base on which the State could increase its income. In the long term, however, the discontent of the peasantry increased, since their conditions actually worsened with the division of the land into small plots and with the increase in population from 74 to 132 million between 1860 and 1900. Although Alexander II escaped six assassination attempts, he was killed by an anarchist's bomb in 1881. While the reign of Alexander III marked a return to authoritarianism, it was followed from the mid-1880s by a greater commitment to modernization under Nicholas II. From 1893, Finance Minister Sergei Witte used a combination of subsidies, customs tariffs and high prices to attract foreign capital, which greatly accelerated development. Here was another case in which change was forced on Russia: any form of industrial development based on domestic factors was hampered by the absence of an entrepreneurial class and local bourgeoisie, and by the limited domestic market. The Russian model of modernization combined the agents of industrialization typical of the most backward nations (i.e. the state) and foreign capital, in a way that would subsequently be repeated in many developing countries. Before the October Revolution, 36% of all Russian shares were in foreign hands; the greatest proportion were held by French investors, but there were also British and Belgian investors. In 1914, foreign entrepreneurs controlled 90% of the capital of mining companies, 50% of the chemical industry, 40% of the mines and 28% of the textile industry.[4] In the second half of the 19th century, construction of the railways drove the growth of the mining and steel industries. Donbass in the Ukraine was the world's seventh biggest coalfield, and French businessmen exploited the nearby mineral deposits of Krivoj Rog.[5] Between 1830 and 1860, total iron production increased from 180,000 to 450,000 tonnes; during the 1890s, blast-furnace cast iron output increased by 190%, compared with an increase of just 18% in Great Britain and 72% in Germany.[6] The railways were largely financed by the State, expanding from 1,626 km in 1860 to 10,731 in 1870, and to 62,000 km before the First

---

[4] R. Portal, *The Industrialization of Russia, 1861-1917*, in H.J. Habakkuk, M. Postan (eds.) *The Cambridge Economic History of Europe*, VI, *The Industrial Revolution and After*, Cambridge, UK, 1966.

[5] The name Donbass was coined when exploitation of the area's resources began at the end of the 19th century. This transnational coalfield includes the Donets and Dnieper river valleys, and its important resources make it the focus of the current conflict between Russia and Ukraine.

[6] Many reasons for the commitment to the iron and steel industry were connected with military needs. When evaluating the entity of the increase, it must be noted that the starting point was extremely low.

World War. The monetary system was also reformed in order to attract foreign capital. Since the silver standard was not sufficiently stable, it was abandoned in favour of the gold standard.

Despite the enormous efforts made to modernize Russia, the economic results were actually mediocre. Production remained concentrated in just a few areas. The development of heavy industry was substantial in terms of quantity, but quality levels were poor. Moreover, light industry and the manufacture of consumer goods were deliberately neglected. Russia's oil output was second only to that of the United States, but its extraction and refining methods were extremely backward. Nonetheless, the oil and gas industries made an indelible mark on Russia's history, economy and foreign policy. In 1900, the Russian manufacturing sector employed three million workers (not all were industrial), an insignificant share of the total population. The divide between the areas of industrial modernity and the huge and stagnating agricultural sector remained immense. In 1895, life expectancy at birth was 32 years (compared with 47 in Belgium), and in 1913, 70% of the population was illiterate.[7] Russia remained a backward country.

8.2. Reform from above: Imperial Japan

The Tokugawa period was the last stage of the Japanese feudalism which began in 1183 with the reintroduction of the *shōgunate*. The Tokugawa clan's domination of Japan (1600-1867) ended a period of feudal anarchy, intensified after 1543 by the arrival of the Portuguese, who introduced firearms to Kiusu. Following the victorious battle of Shekigahara (1600), Tokugawa Ieyasu, head of the victorious coalition, increased his family estates by acquiring lands from his adversaries and consolidating alliances with the related clans. The *shōgunate* conferred on him by the Emperor became hereditary. However, the dominant coalition controlled a smaller area of territory than those of their rival feudatories,[8] and this prevented the creation of a centralized state similar to the typical model of the European monarchies.

Politically, Japan was a confederation of around 250 semi-independent units, in a system known as "centralized feudalism". The *han* (feudal holdings) recognized the supremacy of the *shogun*. However, the centrifugal tendencies of the feudal lords (*daimyōs*) persisted, and so the reigning dynasty created an institutional structure centred on particular mechanisms of

---

[7] D.V. Glass, E. Grebenik, *World Population. 1850-1950*, in H.J. Habakkuk, M. Postan (eds.), *The Cambridge Economic History of Europe*, cit.

[8] E.H. Norman, *Japan's Emergence as a Modern State. Political and Economic Problems of the Meiji Period*, New York, 1940.

social and political control designed to contrast these tendencies. The first step was to ensure control of Japan's important cities, Edo (later named Tokyo), Kyoto (the principle manufacturing centre) and Osaka (the country's largest rice market), where the peasants had achieved relative independence from the nobility. The feudal territories were strategically redistributed, and the *daimyō* enemies of the ruling dynasty were consigned to the outlying edges of the state, separated by buffer *han* under the control of allied clans. The law known as *buke shohatto* defined the duties of the military class, while imperial authority was relegated to religious-sacral functions. A policy of isolationism (*sakoku*) was imposed on the whole country. Apart from one Dutch settlement on the artificial island of Deshima in Nagasaki Bay, Westerners were expelled from Japan in order to preserve local society from the disruptive influence of individualistic European values.

The system of alternating residence (*sankin-kōthai*) was introduced between 1635 and 1642. This obliged the *daimyō*s and their entourage to reside for six months of the year in Edo, where they had to use their wealth to maintain a lifestyle appropriate to their rank. When depating from the city, they were obliged to leave their sons behind, essentially as hostages. The Tokugawa power model gave *sankin-kōthai* a central role: it prevented the *daimyō*s from accumulating resources they could use to overthrow the reigning dynasty, and it allowed them to be kept under control. In the long term, however, it had the opposite effect. The migration of the social elite to the capital led to the creation of a communications network also used by other travellers, which allowed a rudimental integration of the domestic market and the formation of regional markets. The fashions of the capital spread among the nobility resident on the regional *han*, thus triggering an "industrious revolution" that over 150 years later became an "industrial revolution". The economy became increasingly monetized; extra-agricultural production consisted of a wide range of useful and elegant luxury goods, made essentially without using machinery, and growing demand attracted increasing numbers of craftsmen to the cities, especially to Edo.

The *sankin-kōthai* indirectly encouraged the deruralization of local society. Differences in salaries between advanced and backward regions began to shrink from the mid-1700s. At the same time, the nobility's need to convert their agricultural incomes into money favoured the growth of Osaka, thus giving greater prominence to the mercantile families, who increasingly became the bankers of the *bushi*, using the money they accumulated to obtain political influence. The *daimyō*s depended financially on the merchants (*chōnin*) in order to maintain their own consumption habits. Crushed by their debts, feudatories were often obliged to dismiss the former military minor nobility (*samurai*), which created another source of discontent. The country was shaken by riots in cities and rural areas, and the idea of overthrowing the regime devloped in the rich Osaka area, one of the Tokugawa system's centres of power. There was a widespread desire for restoration of Imperial power, the same authority that had previously provided legitimation for the dominant clan.[9] The decline of the Tokugawa system was evident as early as the 18th century.

When US Navy Commodore Perry forced Japanese ports to accept US ships in 1853, other countries rapidly followed his example. However, the outcomes were not the same as in China, since Japan was not completely unprepared for contact with the West. The Dutch base on Deshima had provided the Japanese government with a window to the outside world, the great Western feudal domains of Satsuma and Chushu had always maintained their contacts with foreigners through smuggling, and the study of foreign books had been allowed in Japan since 1720. The local government was aware of the consequences of Western intervention in China, from the Opium War to the "unequal treaties", seen as warning about how to deal with foreign interference. The emergency obliged Japan to change course: Prime Minister Abe Mashairo attempted to reunite the country, asking for support from the nobility outside the government (*bakufu*), the educated classes and merchants. Although the intention was to foster unity and a shared sense of purpose, internal divisions were actually highlighted, and discontent increased after the unavoidable signing of "unequal treaties".

The economy worked against the government as imports of cheap British cotton led to the collapse of spinning, a task performed by peasants and the daughters and wives of the masterless samurai, the *rōnin*. At the same time, foreign demand for silk forced domestic prices higher, which created problems for Japanese weavers. The mobilization of these groups provided the bases for the *Sonno Jōi* revolutionary movement,[10] which was supported by Chūshū and Satsuma *hans* and demanded restoration of the emperor. Chūshū created a popular militia, challenging the principle that only the *bushi* were entitled to use arms. When repression of the *bafuku* proved unable to restore order, the politically isolated government suspended hostilities and dissolved the army.

8.3. The Meiji Restoration

The Meiji Restoration was the founding event of the modern Japanese state. The fact that it is known as a "restoration" and not as a revolution shows that the political upheaval was viewed as occurring within the tradi-

---

[9] E. Collotti Pischel, *Storia dell'Asia orientale. 1850-1949*, Urbino, 1994.

[10] A slogan: "Revere the emperor, expel the barbarians".

tional framework, since the new regime continued to derive its legitimacy from the Imperial family.

After 1868, the first problem facing the rapidly reunified ruling class was the defence of Japanese independence. This need dominated the entire political project of the Meiji Restoration, and its success was firstly due to the fact that Japanese society was "more similar" than Chinese society to Western society, and so provided more favourable conditions for the development of modern capitalism.[11] Moreover, experiences like the 1857 Indian Mutiny and the Taiping Rebellion in 1851-1864 had made Westerners more cautious towards local governments, and they were aware now that destabilization might lead to popular uprisings. Subsequently, once Japan had consolidated its role on the Asian chessboard and obtained revision of the "unequal treaties", its adoption of an imperialist culture represented a step towards achieving international legitimation. Since Japan lacked raw materials and relied on imported food, it was driven to conquer new territories in order to obtain resources without much further exploitation of its own ecosystem.

The action of the State proved crucial in the capitalistic transformation of the Japanese economy, although some studies valorize the role of the samurai oligarchy, whose unconditional adhesion to the *bushido* (a code of honour) is believed to have created an extremely cohesive group. Focus on explanations that were based on the national elite had the advantage of interpreting Japanese development in such a way as to give the credit to the traditional *bushi* ruling class (the military nobility and officer caste).[12] These interpretations recognize that modernization was planned at the highest levels of local political society, but view what had once been the minor warrior nobility as the optimizing agent of economic effort. The samurai stood midway between Schumpeter's demiurge innovator and the bureaucrat in pursuit of national prestige.

The real situation was much more complex. One study of a very small sample of entrepreneurs from the first Meiji period highlights that around 75% of them were not actually *bushi* but were often *chonin*.[13] On the oth-

---

[11] E.O. Reischauer, J.K. Fairbank, A.M. Craig, *East Asia. Tradition and Transformation*, London, 1973.

[12] According to E.H. Norman, many *samurai* voluntarily became *rōnin* (masterless) to achieve freedom from all forms of loyalty towards the *bakufu*, learnt foreign languages and became "the intellectual harbingers of the opening of Japan to the World". *Japan's Emergence as a Modern State*, New York 1940, p. 17.

[13] K. Yamamura, *Entrepreneurship, Ownership and Management in Japan*, in P. Mathias, M. Postan (eds.), *Cambridge Economic History of Europe*, VII, Cambridge, UK, 1978.

er hand, many politically protected merchants in the service of the *bakufu* had received "the privilege of the name and of the sword", making them socially equivalent to the *samurai*, and in the late Tokugawa period some warriors had been obliged to work in order to supplement their incomes. The same line of reasoning can be applied to the foundation of the banks: many *samurai* deposited the money they received as compensation for the loss of their privileges, but other social classes also provided inputs of entrepreneurial talent and money.

However, the problem of raising sufficient capital to develop economic activity beyond the artisanal level of the local industries was not immediately resolved. Bankers were not ready to finance a "novelty" like industry, and often preferred to use their capital in agriculture or trade. The government played an important role in expanding infrastructure investments, promoting pilot factories in new sectors (from cement to sugar) and introducing Western technology, and also in introducing two key institutions of the modern state: universal education and conscription.[14] The advanced training institutes would provide the personnel for companies, replacing the businessmen from the merchant class.

The effort of modernization involved a large public debt. In order to restore balance to the public finances, the government conceded control of the pilot factories to the families traditionally associated with political power. The great industrial conglomerates (*zaibatsu*), which formed from the mid-1880s, developed from the mercantile companies and were initially more expert in obtaining political favour than in evaluating the potential of new industrial ventures. Japanese society fully understood the lesson taught by the West in both manufacturing and finance. A strong currency was needed for the increasing imports required to support accelerated industrialization. Since there was no need to increase exports of food or industrial products, and the ruling class did not identify itself as exporters of agricultural products, it was relatively easy to adopt the *gold standard*, which represented another step towards becoming one of the so-called "civilized countries".

8.4. China in the late Qing period

China fell under the dominion of the Qing dynasty during the 17th century. The Manchu conquered Beijing in 1645, but it took 40 years for them to pacify the entire country with the final subjugation of Taiwan. The reigning dynasty was at its height in the 18th century, when the Empire extended

---

[14] E.K. Tipton, *Modern Japan. A Social and Political History*, London, 2011.

over an area of 10 million km², equalling the size of the Ming Empire. The population grew from approximately circa 275 million in 1700 to approximately 350 million in 1800 and some urbanization also occurred.[15] The economy was still based on agriculture, benefitting from the introduction of some New World crops and early maturing rice varieties, and also making massive use of fertilisers (also imported) derived from cotton, colza and soya residues. The population increase led the Qing to encourage agriculture in Southern Manchuria, and the new lands were improved with grandiose hydraulic engineering projects. The standard of living is believed to have remained high until this stage, constituting a sort of pre-modern "agricultural miracle", although development was still "natural" and there were no Promethean leaps forward.

Existing potential was exploited, without any changes to the social, cultural and economic framework. To paraphrase Elvin, whose viewpoint is strictly Western, quantitative growth did not accompany qualitative change (unimaginable in a system already organized as high-yield intensive agricultural system) and the country remained caught in a "high level equilibrium trap".[16] However, it is doubtful that there were tensions or even any awareness of this issue.

Industrialization was not a priority in a multi-ethnic empire which viewed itself as the Middle Kingdom, and whose ideological construct was based on Confucianism and values like frugality, disapproval of profit, and the subordination of each person to their natural superior. This was the antithesis of Western culture's natural law (or Locke's philosophy). Terms like industry, society, science, economy and nation did not exist, and were imported from Japan in the aftermath of impacts from abroad. Qing sovereigns based their power on political and cultural objectives, not on economic aims. Emperor Kangxi financed the publication of traditional local works to legitimate Manchu domination of China, and the Manchu used the term "China" to indicate the Empire, as had the Ming. However, although the name was the same, the Empire was not, because it now consisted of a vast area including Central Asia and Manchuria. Mongols, Tibetans and Manchu all became "Chinese".

The appearance of broadly economic concerns was a reaction to the first phase of globalization and to imperialism, in which Britain played a key role. Having won the Seven Years' War (1756-1763) and consolidated

---

[15] K. Vogelsang, *Geschichte Chinas*, Stuttgart, 2012.

[16] M. Elvin, *The High-Level Equilibrium Trap. The Causes of the Decline of Inventions in the Traditional Chinese Textile Industry*, in W.E. Wilmott (ed.), *Economic Organization in the Chinese Society*, Stanford, 1972, pp. 137-172.

its control over a part of the Indian sub-continent, Britain intensified its trade with Asia. Tea was an essential British import; annual imports of 400,000 lbs at the beginning of the 18th century rose to 2.8 million lbs over the century, bringing a consequent deterioration in the terms of trade.[17] British products had few admirers in China's rural and self-referential society, and Indian cotton did not suffice to pay for imports: every year, millions of silver Mexican dollars were shipped to China. The solution was to replace this precious metal with opium from Bengal. Opium exports allowed India to balance its trade deficit with Britain. China's balance of trade became negative. The opium trade and its consumption not only threatened the health of China's population, but also increased local corruption and caused administrative disorder. Tension mounted until it broke out in the "Opium Wars" of 1840 and 1860, which many historians have identified as marking the divide between traditional and modern China. These conflicts highlighted the weakness of central authority and fuelled discontent. Internal tensions caused peasant uprisings, and the dynasty only held on to power because it had the support of Western countries interested in defending what they had acquired. The "unequal treaties" were extended to people and goods, but also to property rights. New ports were opened to international trade. The imposition of reparations related to war damages in silver coinage meant that the copper coinage lost its purchasing power and the peasants became impoverished. The Chinese authorities were concerned about the consequences of Western military superiority, and realized that it was time for change, favouring Chinese culture as the basis but Western studies for practice.[18] This "philosophy" laid the basis of the Self-Strengthening Movement in the 1860s. Some Imperial counsellors suggested enhancing heavy industry. This choice occurred amid setbacks and contradictions that emerged in all their seriousness with the disastrous conflict against Japan (1894-1895). The Treaty of Shimonosheki not only imposed new reparations on China but also opened up new ports to foreign shipping, allowing the establishment of industries. The defeat highlighted that it was quite unrealistic to attempt to conciliate ethnocentrism, the Confucian superstructure and its bureaucratic-mandarin culture with technology and skills that were essentially the mature fruits of an alien culture, which was overwhelmingly energy-intensive, Promethean and Faustian in nature.

China's self-consolidation and selective integration of Western technol-

---

[17] G. Borsa, *La nascita del mondo moderno in Asia orientale. La penetrazione europea e la crisi delle società tradizionali in India, Cina e Giappone*, Milan, 1977, p. 178.

[18] J.A.G. Roberts, *A History of China*, London, 1999.

ogy gave an industrial veneer to the areas where there was a foreign presence, but also strengthened the regional governors at the expense of Imperial power. Openness to international trade and the intensification of Chinese emigration to the Americas and other areas of Asia led to the formation of a commercial middle class and an entrepreneurial class, but the liberalization of trade and the installation of industries faced obstacles that limited their potential, such as customs tariffs and the subdivision of the region into spheres of influence. In the meantime, the nature of Western economic penetration also changed, and exports of manufactured goods were followed by capital in the form of loans and direct investments. The school and army reforms implemented after the anti-Western Boxer rebellion destroyed the reigning dynasty's ability to dominate the bureaucratic-intellectual class. Chinese students sent abroad for further studies, especially to Japan, became critical towards traditional society and turned increasingly towards an ethnic nationalism (Chinese-han) that was lethal for the Manchu dynasty. China avoided dismemberment only due to rivalry between Western powers and the American "open door" principle, but the Empire was now in a state of full-blown crisis that created the conditions for Sun Yat-Sen's republican revolution.

8.5. Latin America

Latin America was deeply influenced by Spanish and Portughese colonization, in contrast with Anglo-Saxon North America. The border between Mexico and the United States, the "tortilla curtain", has always been a "hot spot" and is still militarized at present, marking both a cultural and socio-economic divide.[19] Centuries of Iberian domination have given the Latin American countries a common cultural substrate, based on consumption models and a socio-cultural behaviour imbued with Western values, which is easily penetrated due to the lack of a linguistic barrier, and has been consolidated by centuries of mass emigration from Europe. At first, the colonizers imported African slaves to compensate for the lack of a native workforce, and then they attracted immigrants from Europe. For this reason, the impact of human activity on Latin America was not the result of a gradual process. Settlements essentially sprang up in mining areas, plantations and port cities.

The persistence of slavery until the end of the 19th century left indelible

---

[19] A. Rouquié, *Amérique Latine. Introduction à l'Extrême Occident*, Paris, 1996; T. Torrans, *Forging the Tortillia Curtain. Cultural Drift and Change along the United States-Mexico Border, from the Spanish Era to the Present*, Fort Worth, 2000.

traces and delayed technological progress. A black slave was considered both "an animal and a machine" and humans were used more than draught animals in Brazil as late as the 1940s. Following the abolition of slavery, the growth of international demand drove the cultivation of cash crops,[20] requiring a fresh supply of labour. The response was to attract European immigrants, often from Italy and Iberia, who mostly settled in the temperate zones of southern Brazil and Argentina. Between 1857 and 1930, over three million Europeans settled in Argentina, where the influx of emigrants meant doubled the population every twenty years up to 1914, while over four million immigrants settled in Brazil. Uneven population distribution is a structural feature of the entire subcontinent. Aside from the pre-Columbian settlements, many towns were founded on the coast, whose large populations were due to their function as hubs of Brazil's important international trade.[21]

The consequences of independence, spurred by the Napoleonic invasion of Spain in 1808, did not bring an institutional shift towards democracy. Much of the traditional order remained intact; although the creoles had led the emancipation movement, their sole aim was to replace the Spanish.[22] Conflict ceased around 1830, bringing new republics nominally based on European models, but unable to adapt to what was a profoundly different social and political situation, or come to terms with the disappearance of Bolivar's dream of creating the United States of Latin America. The power vacuum left by the collapse of Spanish domination was filled by the *caudillos*, "strong men" whose personal militias took control in many regions. Economic development began in the late 19th century, stimulated by external factors. The Latin American countries specialised in exporting raw materials and staples, but imported manufactured goods. Growth was essentially limited to the mining industries or processing commodities, and a particularly important sector involved processing of the food products that also supplied the urban centres.

The railways built in the second half of the 19th century were financed by foreign capital, mostly British and French. They were not constructed to allow integration of the national markets but to link mines and plantations

---

[20] The American plantation economy originated in Brazil, the world's leading exporter of sugar from 1580 to 1680. The sugar trade during this period made Brazil extremely important for its motherland, Portugal. W. Reinhard, *Kleine Geschichte des Kolonialismus*, Stuttgart, 1996.

[21] M. Carmagnani, *L'altro Occidente. L'America Latina dall'invasione europea al nuovo millennio*, Turin, 2003, pp. 270-271.

[22] D. Bushnell, N. Macaulay, *The Emergence of Latin America in the Nineteenth Century*, Oxford, 1994.

to the ports. The entire economy of the continent was shaped by the needs of international trade, while the social and political fabric was permeated by the agrarian elites, who constituted the ruling class in almost every region. The great estates were a deeply rooted feature of the region and a legacy of the colonial era. Their creation was connected with the transformation of the *encomienda,* an institution that granted the use of farmland and groups of natives to an *encomendero.* In return, the *encomendero* ensured the evangelization envisaged in the 1494 division of the subcontinent between the Spanish and Portuguese crowns along the meridian 370 leagues west of the Capo Verde Islands. The *encomienda* did not initially imply that land was inherited, but the institution moved rapidly in this direction. From the start of the 19th century, the tendency to expand the size of land holdings was consolidated. The laws regulating secularization of *mortmain* allowed Church property to come under the ownership of local oligarchies, which created the great Mexican *haciendas.* The authoritarian regime of Porfirio Diaz (President 1876-1880, 1884-1911) gave the country its first veneer of industrialization and a protectionist trade policy. The State also used foreign capital and dispossessed the peasants to create an industrial workforce.[23] In 1910, millions of hectares of land changed hands, leading to the Morelos State uprising led by Emiliano Zapata (1910-1917).

In Argentina, the 1870s saw the start of the *conquista del desierto*, a military campaign to wrest Patagonia from the native population. The State distributed vast areas of land along the border, which had increased in value due to the railways built with British capital. The history of Brazil was similar. In the 1890s, the State offered vast areas of territory to big international companies that often used "front men" to drive away or even kill the peasant families who farmed the land. These land ownership conflicts have not been officially recognised, but may represent the "real history" of Brazil's foundation, and have been depicted with crude realism by Jorge Amado in *Tocaia grande.*[24]

The fragility of the political institutions was counterbalanced by the power of the great landowners. The mobility of production factors was limited, while labour relations were asymmetrical and developed in a context of unequal mutual relations around the *cacique* (local chief), who was an intermediary between his subordinates and the rest of Brazilian society, who used mechanisms of favouritism and patronage. On the other hand, foreign investors, who were mostly Anglo-Saxon, used these semi-colonial

---

[23] R.C. Allen, *Global Economic History. A Very Short Introduction*, Oxford, 2011.

[24] J. Amado, *Tocaia grande. A Face Obscura*, Rio de Janeiro, 1984.

mechanisms to their own advantage with the creation of "enclave econo-mies".

Table 8.1. 'Traditional' and 'new' products taken from the Americas at the start of the 20th century

Countries	Traditional products	New products
Argentina	leather, hides	frozen beef, wool, wheat, maize, linen
Brazil	gold, diamonds	cotton, cacao, coffee, natural rubber
Chile	wheat, mineral copper	saltpeter, copper ingots, wool, refrigerated mutton
Mexico	silver coins	silver ingots, copper ingots, coffee, sisal, natural rubber, cotton
Peru	alpaca, medicinal herbs	cotton, natural rubber, sugar, copper ingots

Source: M. Carmagnani, *L'altro Occidente*, cit., p. 234.

Bibliography

Bairoch P., *Victoires et déboires. Histoire économique et sociale du monde du XVIe siècle à nos jours*, Paris, 1996.

Collotti Pischel E., *Storia dell'Asia orientale. 1850-1949*, Urbino, 1994.

Fairbank J.K., Kwang-Ching L. (eds.), *The Cambridge History of China*, Vol. II, *Late Ch'ing 1800-1911*, Cambridge, UK, 2008.

Milward A.S., Saul S.B., *The Development of the Economies of Continental Europe. 1850-1914*, London, 1977.

Rouquié A., *Amérique Latine: Introduction à l'Extrême Occident*, Paris, 1996.

von Glahn R., *The Economic History of China. From Antiquity to the Nineteenth Century*, Los Angeles, 2016.

MASS EMIGRATION FROM EUROPE

The **first phase of globalization** involved a massive opening of the markets, accompanied by new mobility of production factors, especially labour. Between 1815 and 1914, no fewer than 40 million Europeans left their homelands and crossed the world's oceans to the United States, Latin America, Canada, Australia, New Zealand and South Africa. Emigration took place on an unprecedented scale.

The first wave of departures (up to the end of the 1890s) mostly involved Northwestern Europe, while most emigration in the second wave (up to the eve of the "Great War") came from Southern and Eastern Europe. In general, there was a greater tendency to emigrate from island or coastal countries, where access to the sea gave benefits in terms of travel time and transport costs.

The United Kingdom was the country with the greatest number of emigrants, due to the combined effects of three factors. Firstly, it had the advantage of linguistic affinity with the main destination of overseas emigration (United States). Secondly, the British had overseas territories, colonies and dominions where land and mineral deposits were plentiful (Australia, South Africa, Canada). Lastly, the Irish potato famine of 1845-1846 caused a fifth of Ireland's population (1.75 million) to emigrate in the following eight years, and this exodus continued uninterrupted until the First World War, although less intensely. While Italy had the second largest number of emigrants for the entire period between the Congress of Vienna and the Great War, it actually led the other countries in the period 1890-1913; as over 3.6 million emigrated during the first decade of the 20th century (Figure 1 and Table 1). This enormous wave of emigration involved the entire country, but the northwestern, northeastern/central and southern regions contributed very different proportions of the entire figure (Table 8.3).

This huge wave of emigration was due firstly to **demographic causes**. Between the start of the 19th century and the First World War, Europe's population increased by 243 percent, rising from 188 to 458 million, and growing more than in the previous three centuries in both absolute and relative terms. This growth was caused by the net fall in ordinary mortality, the infrequency of famines and epidemics, and maintenance of the high birth rate (demographic transition). In addition to putting increased pressure on available resources, this population growth also meant that the labour market was congested. The consequences were particularly intense in rural areas, where there was less birth control and so the population increased more than in towns and cities. At the same time, the introduction of technical innovations (e.g. seed selection, improved tools, modern machinery like the steam-powered threshing machine) increased productivity and favoured the spread of large agricultural estates, reducing the numbers of small peasant farmers and making large numbers of workers surplus to requirements. This process was accentuated by the agrarian crisis caused by imports of American and Russian wheat into Western Europe from the 1870s to 1890s. The final result was that millions of workers left the European countryside and crossed the oceans in search of farmland or a salaried job.

The great migrations of the 19th-20th centuries also involved the craftsmen and workmen of countries where industrialization did not occur so easily and which could not absorb enough of the growing internal offer of labour. Some of these workers moved to other European states. They were welcomed by more dynamic countries, such as Germany, France, Belgium and Switzerland, which became destinations for migrant Poles, Slavs, Italians, Spanish and Portuguese, employed in seasonal jobs or in mining, building and "low-level" services. The other workers moved to North America, responding to the local demand for miners, labourers and workmen, who were needed to expand the railway network and create urban infrastructures.

However, the demand for men and women to employ in both primary and secondary sectors was limited by the desire to prevent migrants whose language, culture and lifestyle differed greatly from their potential new homelands. Thus, the United States and South American states on the Atlantic initially discriminated against Asians, and then also against Europeans. This racist approach meant that they selected workers by favouring those who would integrate most easily into their new community. Nonetheless, other considerations were less important than the measures to attract workers, as used by the same countries in the 17th century. For instance, the Homestead Act (1862) in the US granted 160 acres of land to every individual of any origin who was over the age of 21.

In some cases (Uruguay, Argentina) the borders were also opened to those who left Europe for political and not economic reasons. This second type of emigration involved much smaller numbers, and originated with the popular revolts that shook Europe from the 1820s, reaching a height with 1848-1849 Revolutions and the Paris Commune of 1871. During the first phase, a mass of political refugees found asylum within Europe itself, taking advantage of the tolerance, if not the manifest benevolence, of the French, Swiss, Belgian and British governments. This possibility disappeared, however, at the turn of the century, when sharpening social conflict led to borders being closed to "subversives" (especially socialists and anarchists), who were then expelled from the European countries which had previously hosted them - both their homelands and the host countries. They had no other choice but to emigrate across the ocean.

Another component of this great wave of European emigration is often overlooked when data are analysed and concerns ethnicity and religion. An eloquent example is provided by the Jews forced to leave Russia to escape the persecutions ordered by the tsarist government in the 1880s.

The enormous waves of migration marking the first period of globalization were facilitated by certain **technological, social and legislative factors**. The first was the revolution in sea-going transport, which meant that the most advanced Western countries had iron passenger ships with steam-powered propellors. These steamships were not only larger and more robust than traditional wooden sailing ships, but were also much faster, which drastically reduced the time it took to cross the oceans: while the voyage from Liverpool to New York took six weeks at the start of the 19th century, at the end of the 1830s it took only fifteen days, and had been cut to just seven days by the end of the century. Shorter travelling time was reflected in transport costs, and fares fell. Another factor making travel less expensive for emigrants at the same time was the expansion of the European railway networks, which made it cheaper for emigrants to reach their departure ports.

One social factor which contributed to emigration was the "migration network". These formed during the 19th century, as immigrants gradually formed consolidated communities in their new countries, ready to share information and hospitality with relatives, friends and former colleagues who wanted to follow in their steps. Although their aim was to make money and their methods were rarely orthodox, emigration agents also operated in a similar way. They acted as intermediaries for the shipping companies, governments, landowners or industrialists who required manpower on the other side of the Atlantic. The agents' task was to illustrate the opportunities for potential emigrants, organize their journey, offer free passages (especially for Argentina or Brazil), and sometimes also to create contacts between the migrant and a future employer.

The laws introduced in the principal European states of the time played a fundamental role in favouring emigration. These measures reflected the ideals propagated by the French Revolution, and also by the free trade movement in Europe from the mid-19th century, leading to removal of the barriers which had impeded the free circulation of people during the early modern age. Britain and the Scandinavian countries recognised the right to expatriate in the 1830s, Germany in 1867, and the Hapsburg and Russian Empires did so at the end of the century. Italy allowed its citizens complete freedom to leave the country only in 1901, although many had already left before this date, illegally boarding ships in foreign ports.

The most important **consequences** of mass emigration from Europe in the 19th and 20th centuries involved demographics, the labour market and public accounts.

The movement of millions of people had a profound effect on redistribution of the world population; it relieved the demographic pressure on Europe and increased the low population of the New World. This extraordinary mass of immigrants allowed the host countries to complete colonization of their territories, and the United States obtained the manpower it needed to build roads, bridges and railways, and to employ in the mines and traditional factories, and in the capital intensive and modern labour-intensive factories. In this way, **globalization** eventually also affected the labour market, broadening it to an unprecedented extent. The result was an increase in average salaries across Europe, although the effect on convergence was not so uniform: there was still a wide gap between wages in Northwestern Europe and in Southern and Eastern Europe. In the same way, there were substantial and permanent differences in pay between immigrants of different nationalities in their new countries (Tables 3 and 4). However, this did not reduce their "remittances", the money they sent home. Those who left Europe were mostly men, who hoped to be reunited as soon as possible with their families by either returning home or bringing their relatives to join them overseas. In the meantime, they usually sent home some their overseas earnings. This flow of money gradually increased, and came to represent a substantial revenue item in the balance of payments of the main emigrant countries (as in the case of Italy), which was often in deficit.

Figure 8.1. Migration from Europe by decade (1851-1911, in thousands)

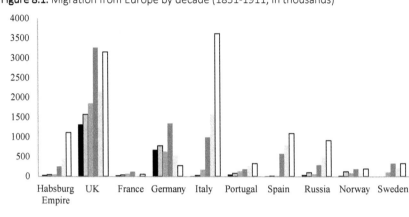

■ 1851-60 ▫ 1861-70 ▪ 1871-80 ■ 1881-90 1891-90 ▫ 1900-11

Table 8.2. Rates of emigration from Europe and immigration to America by decade (1850-1910, x 10,000 residents)

	1851-60	1861-70	1871-80	1881-90	1891-00	1901-10
Emigration from Europe						
Hapsburg Empire			2.9	10.6	16.1	47,6
Belgium				8.6	3.5	6,1
Great Britain	58.0	51.8	50.4	70.2	43.8	65,3
Denmark			20.6	39.4	22.3	28,2
Finland				13.2	23.2	54,5
France			1,5	3.1	1.3	1.4
Germany		14,7		28.7	10.1	4.5
Ireland			66.1	141.7	88.5	69.8
Italy			10.5	33.6	50.2	107.7
Netherlands			4.6	12.3	5.0	5.1
Norway			47.3	95.2	44.9	83.3
Portugal			28.9	38.0	50.8	56.9
Spain				36.2	43.8	56.6
Sweden			23.5	70.1	41.2	42.0
Switzerland			13.0	32.0	14.1	13.9
Immigration to America						
Argentina	38.5	99.1	117.0	221.7	163.9	291.8
Brazil			20.4	41.1	72.3	33.8
Canada	99.2	83.2	54.8	78.4	48.8	167.6
Cuba						118.4
United States	92.8	64.9	54.6	85.8	53.0	102.0

Source: T.J. Hatton, G. Williamson, *The Age of Mass Migration. Causes and Economic Impact*, New York, 1998.

Table 8.3. Average annual emigration per 1,000 residents and distribution of total ex-patriates in Italy by macro-area (%, 1876-1913)

	1876-80		1881-90		1891-00		1901-10		1911-13	
	% pop.	% exp.	% pop.	% exp.	% pop.	% exp.	% pop.	% exp.	% pop.	% exp.
North-West	6.64	46.0	7.46	31.4	6.02	17.9	12.60	18.9	15.91	21.2
North-East/Centre	4.71	41.2	7.87	41.8	12.94	48.8	17.98	34.4	20.73	35.2
South	1.27	12.8	4.35	26.8	7.64	33.3	21.65	46.7	23.18	43.6

Source: E. Sori, *L'emigrazione italiana dall'Unità alla seconda guerra mondiale*, Bologna, 1979.

Table 8.4. Immigrants to USA working in industry and mining (1911)

	Wage earners	Average weekly wage ($)
Armenians	594	9.73
Bohemians/Moravians	1.353	13.07
Bulgarians	403	10.31
Canadians (French)	8.164	10.62
Canadians (others)	1.323	14.15
Croats	4.890	11.37
Danes	377	14.32
Dutch	1.026	12.04
English	9.408	14.13
Finns	3.334	13.27
Flemish	125	11.07
French	896	12.92
Germans	11.380	13.63
Greeks	4.154	8.41
Russian Jews	3.177	12.71
Other Jews	1.158	14.37
Irish	7.596	13.01
N. Italians	5.343	11.28
S. Italians	7.821	9.61
Lithuanians	4.661	11.03
Macedonians	479	8.95
Magyars	5.331	11.65
Norwegians	420	15.28
Poles	24.223	11.06
Portuguese	3.125	8.10
Romanians	1.026	10.90
Russians	3.311	11.01
Ruthenes	385	9.92
Scots	1.711	15.24
Serbs	1.016	10.75
Slovacchi	10.775	11.95
Slovenes	2.334	12.15
Swedes	3.984	15.36
Syrians	812	8.12
Turks	240	7.65

Source: F. Fauri, *Storia economica delle migrazioni italiane*, Bologna, 2015.

Table 8.5. Real salaries in Europe (1850-1913, indices, Great Britain 1905 = 100)

	1850-59	1860-69	1870-79	1880-89	1890-99	1900-13
Belgium	45.5	52.8	64.2	73.9	85.6	86.9
Denmark			41.0	52.6	70.6	94.2
France		46.2	52.0	60.4	65.1	71.2
Germany	52.5	55.4	62.3	68.5	78.1	85.9
Great Britain	59.4	59.0	70.3	83.5	99.4	98.2
Ireland	44.4	43.6	51.7	64.5	87.3	90.9
Italy			26.2	34.2	37.4	46.4
Netherlands	45.7	48.9	62.8	79.9	88.1	77.8
Norway	27.2	30.7	40.1	45.8	67.5	83.8
Portugal	18.8	19.6	20.1	27.4	23.3	24.6
Spain	30.4	28.0	27.6	25.5	26.8	30.4
Sweden	24.2	34.6	39.0	51.1	70.7	92.2

Source: T.J. Hutton and J.G. Williamson, *Global Migration and the World Economy. Two Centuries of Policy and Performance*, Cambridge, Mass.-London, 2008.

Chapter 9
THE FIRST PHASE OF GLOBALIZATION

SUMMARY: 9.1. The (first) Great Depression and neomercantilism. – 9.2. The gold standard and the City at its height. – 9.3. Imperialism. – Bibliography. – *International monetary systems.*

From the end of the Napoleonic Wars to the Crimean War (1853-1856), the European geopolitical system rested on the balance of power and the Concert of Europe, a common set of interests and ideas shared by the major monarchies, who aimed to prevent or oppose potential eversive threats. However, in mid-century, the spread of the Industrial Revolution increased the differences between the continent's regions, remodelling the balance of power and transforming relative comparative advantages. The single economies were synchronized by the opening of the Suez Canal (1869), the Panama Canal (1881-1914), the spread of railways in Europe and the United States, the introduction of agricultural machinery, the reduction in the time and cost of transport, the massive movements of long-term capital, and the temporary relaxation of protectionist trade barriers enabled by the generalised adoption of the *Most favored nation* clause (1860).[1]

Between 1800 and 1913, the volume of world trade multiplied by twenty-five times, mostly concentrated in the area between North America, Western Europe, Australia and New Zealand.[2] This growth strengthened international relations and spurred a "reactive nationalism"[3] which drove industrialization. The aim of obtaining power led the nation-state to promote itself as the model of political and economic organisation and socicultural identity. At the same time, exceptionally liberal migration policies combined with integration of national economies and led to the formation of a world labour market. This caused enormous migration from some European countries, and to a lesser extent from India and China,[4] towards the

---

[1] J.A. Frieden, *Global Capitalism. Its Fall and Rise in the Twentieth Century*, New York, 2006, p. 5.

[2] J. Ostherhammel, N.P. Petersson, *Globalization. A Short History*, Princeton, 2005.

[3] W. Rostow, *How It All Began. Origins of the Modern Economy*, London, 1975.

[4] K. O'Rourke, J. Williamson, *Globalisation and History. The Evolution of a Nineteenth-Century Atlantic Economy*, Cambridge, Mass.-London, 1999.

"New Europes": first of all the United States, followed by South Africa, Australia and Latin America. Between 1850 and 1914, 60 to 70 million people left their homelands, including 40 million Europeans (Table 1).

Prices oscillated widely during the 19th century, and their fluctuations spread across the world with an exceptional speed and intensity. Between the 1850s and 1890s, a crisis occurred in every decade. The economic cycles were not ignored by classical economics, but were not included in its theoretical framework. Economists based their interpretation on Say's law: the production of goods generated an aggregate demand sufficient to buy what had been produced, the economic system tended towards equilibrium, and the market was always able to correct itself. However, the empirical evidence suggested otherwise, and this required theoretical reflection. Interest in price and production fluctuations increased during the Napoleonic Wars, when prices rose sharply for real reasons (the shortages caused by war) and for monetary reasons (inflation). When the conflict ceased and stocks of goods were released onto the market, production also increased at the same time, and this led to a general fall in prices. The discovery of gold in California and Australia in the mid-1800s furthered this reversal. Between 1870 and 1890, the combined effects of global over-production, agrarian and financial crises pushed the world economy into the longest period of deflation in its history.

About ten years earlier, Clément Juglar had identified a cyclical trend by systematically using data about historical price series from three different countries. Crises were not isolated occurrences, but were part of a three-stage process; they preceded liquidation, which was followed by recovery. The length of these cycles, on which William Stanley Jevons roughly agreed, ranged from six to eight years. Juglar's interpretation was that an excess of credit caused the cycles, while Jevons attributed them to sunspot activity. Statisticians and economists concentrated on the instability of the system: study of fluctuations in production and prices revealed that production tended to increase in the long term, but was subject to variable oscillations. The state of the art remained more or less unchanged for another sixty years. Only in 1921, did Joseph Kitchin identify a short cycle of approximately three and a half years by studying the variations in wholesale prices and interest rates in the United States. The Kitchin and Juglar cycles were in turn placed located within a longer wave, identified by Nikolai Kondratiev in 1926. He defined periods of 50 years, initially linked to the discovery of new goldmines and then to the substitution and expansion of capital goods, which included phases of economic growth and degrowth. In the 1930s, Joseph Schumpeter identified fluctuations as the essence of capitalism: growth originated from the "creative destruction" constantly moving the economy. As Juglar had supposed, and as Hyman Minsky clarified, development and crisis were the two sides of the same coin: prosperity harboured the seeds of depression. Schumpeter demolished Smith's "circular flow" model and inserted credit and technological progress into economic analysis, justifying economic fluctuations with the action of the economic system's great demiurge – the entrepreneur. Using credit, the entrepreneur transformed the system, combining production factors in new ways, identifying new markets, adopting new technologies: his actions explained the four phases of these economic cycles (recovery, prosperity, recession, crisis). Economic development actually tends to destroy the context in which it operates, replacing this with a new social structure. Innovations, which were also discontinuous, occurred in clusters, which then generated the Kondratiev cycle.

Figure 9.1. Kondratiev waves: graph showing world economic cycles (1800-2000)

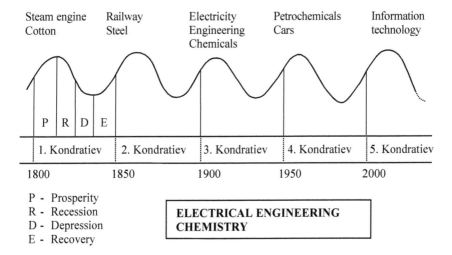

P - Prosperity
R - Recession
D - Depression
E - Recovery

**ELECTRICAL ENGINEERING
CHEMISTRY**

9.1. The (first) Great Depression and neomercantilism

The Great Depression was a new experience. Between 1873 and 1896, prices dropped by 22% in the United Kingdom and 32% in the US, falling unequally but inexorably also in the other countries and starting a deflation process probably never experienced before.[5] The economy had become a victim of its own success. New *competitors* had entered the global market,

---

[5] D.S. Landes, *The Unbound Prometheus*, cit.; J.A. Frieden, *Global Capitalism*, cit.

and the crisis was caused – surprisingly – by excess, and not by scarcity. It not only involved the prices of manufactured goods that a poor market struggled to absorb, but also affected raw materials and agricultural products: silk, wheat, rice and tea.

The advent of big industry had transformed competition. As Friedrich List and Karl Marx agreed, the huge and growing profits linked with economies of scale had become the stigma of modern development. Reality refuted Smith's theories, but the existence of situations between the norm, competition, and the exceptional case of the monopoly was adopted by economic theory from the early 1930s, when Joan Robinson and Edward Chamberlain coined the eloquent oxymoron of "monopolistic competition". Nor was this the only subversive novelty at the end of the century. Economic transformation was accompanied by a political upheaval. As the 20th century advanced, salaried managers increasingly replaced entrepreneurs in the large US *corporations* and also to a lesser extent in the most progressive European countries. This posed an unsettling question: was it still the aim of business to maximize profits? Faceless bureaucrats were threatening the supremacy of Sombart's captain of industry and the individual flair of Schumpeter's entrepreneur.[6]

This was the period of Friedrich List's posthumous success. Having launched a battle that eventually drove him to suicide, he worked to identify and publicize the true causes of the wealth of nations.

Ideologically opposed to Smith and Ricardo, List wanted to use nationalism to convey the ideology of industrialization.[7] It was imperative to develop manufacturing as the condition for achieving military power. Once the technology for industrial development had been imported from Britain, protectionism was the strategy implemented to equal (and then overtake) the *first comer* by using the same methods Britain had used to challenge the United Dutch Provinces with its Navigation Acts.[8] This was the heresy. By requiring protective measures to safeguard the nation's industry, the state implicitly placed itself above the individual. This approach constituted an unprecedented attack on the ideas of Ricardo, who had imagined a planet where the interdependence of single economies derived from production specialization and free trade. List's vision, initially unorthodox, perfectly suited the spirit of the age. The *laissez-faire* policies and globalization that

---

[6] The quote from F. Taylor is in G. Berta, *L'imprenditore. Un enigma tra economia e storia*, Venice, 2004, p. 78.

[7] A. Gerschenkron, *Economic backwardness in historical perspective, a book of essays*, Cambridge, Massachusetts, 1962.

[8] F. List, *Das nationale System der politischen Ökonomie*, 1841.

had created prosperity were now blamed for the human and material costs of deflation. Farmers and industrialists, victims of *free trade*, pressurized politicians for a change of direction. Apart from Britain and some other small countries that depended on exports (like the Netherlands and Denmark), the late 19th century response to the Great Depression was protectionism.

International trade grew more slowly, but did not stop. Before the Great War, the world economy was more integrated than it would be at the end of the Second World War, when multilateralism was embraced due to the lessons drawn from past experience and in homage to US interests.

9.2. The gold standard and the City at its height

The twenty-year Great Depression coincided with the transition of the leading players of the Industrial Revolution and a vast group of their followers to the gold standard. Countries with radically different economies attempted to advance along a path England had traced when it adopted the *gold standard* in 1819.

The movement gained strength between 1873 and the early 20th century. When it disintegrated for good in 1929, the mechanism involved at least 46 countries. In the first half of the century, however, apart fom Portugal (which was bound to the United Kingdom by the Methuen Treaty of 1707), the monetary systems of the major European countries were based on bimetallism or on the *silver standard.* The bases for change were created during the *laissez-faire* period, as the enormous growth in the volume and value of trade favoured the use of gold for international payments. The spread of industrialization had the same effect, expanding British exports of producer goods and placing England at the centre of the world trade system. The superiority of British banking and shipping made the sterling the centre of the international monetary system, and the London Stock Exchange became "the economic temple of the West".[9]

The gold standard was not immediately adopted by all countries, and there was plenty of tenacious resistance. In 1865, France's suprematist ambitions led to the creation of the Latin Monetary Union (LMU), which included Belgium, France, Italy and Switzerland: the silver content of the coins was unified at 0.835. Napoleon III and the French *haute banque* supported the LMU because his ambition was to create a franc-based monetary area against Germany. Another Frenchman, Felix Parieu, a historical

---

[9] G. Berta, *L'ascesa della finanza internazionale*, Milan, 2013, p. 16.

supporter of international monetary cooperation, theorized that a common currency would lead to the creation of a European union, parliament and commission. However, events took a different course. Italy was engaged in a difficult process of *nation building* and its Third War of Independence when it adopted a purely fiat money system in 1866. The consequent sale of Italian government bonds (*Rendita italiana*) by French investors caused silver to flow out towards France, immediately demonstrating the weakness of the Latin Monetary Union and the others that have followed it until today: the difficulty of unifying different monetary systems without coordinating economic policies. France's defeat at Sédan (1870) eliminated the political base of French continental supremacy, and the LMU converted *de facto* to the *gold standard*. In 1873, the newly unified Germany took advantage of French reparation payments to adopt the gold standard system, followed by its neighbours and traditional trading partners: Denmark, the Netherlands, Norway and Sweden. When continental Europe's first industrial country adopted the gold standard as important silver deposits were being discovered, there was a chain reaction. The sale of German silver depressed the price on the world markets, and the other countries were faced with a difficult choice: inflation or the abandonment of bimetallism?

In the same year, the government suspended the minting of silver coins in the USA, where silver had still the value of legal tender. However, faced with pressure from both farmers and the owners of silver mines, the US government reintroduced convertibility a decade later (1879), followed by the the Sherman Silver Purchase Act (1890). The aim was to ensure that individuals and businesses damaged by industrial changes would accept the Mc Kinley Tariff, a duty introduced to protect the domestic market. The price of silver rose, triggering some short-lived speculation. In 1894, following abolition of the Sherman Act, President Grover Cleveland put a stop to the free minting of silver coinage, while the discovery of new gold deposits made it cheaper and drove up the prices of agricultural products, facilitating acceptance of the *gold standard*. The cultural legacy of this dispute was a fantasy story for children, *The Wonderful Wizard of Oz*, by L. Frank Baum (1900). The story describes the adventures of the orphan Dorothy and her companions,[10] who travel along a yellow brick road to reach the Emerald City (Washington D.C.), where the residents wear green-tinted

---

[10] Dorothy's travelling companions are the Tin Woodman (representing unemployed factory workers), the Scarecrow (farmers ruined by deflation), and the Cowardly Lion, indicated as the 1896 US presidential candidate William Jennings Bryan, known for his powerful oratory castigating the "Cross of Gold". H. Rockoff, *The "Wizard of Oz" as a Monetary Allegory*, in *The Journal of Political Economy*, 98, 1990, 4, pp. 739-760; M. Friedman, *Capitalism and Freedom*, Chicago, 1962.

glasses (the colour of dollars) and see everything in terms of money. The road represents the gold standard, and Dorothy's silver shoes, which allow her to return home when she claps the heels together, represent the interests connected with silver. The meaning of the allegory is clear. As Milton Friedman later stressed, the United States would have recovered from deflation if it had created inflation (reflation) by coining silver. Clapping the silver shoes together implied that success was possible only with the collaboration of all parties involved.[11]

Although the gold standard also prevailed because of powerful financial interests favouring *free trade,* it must be specified that the nations adhering to it had different monetary systems. The pure *gold standard* was quite rare, while the *gold exchange standard* was more usual.[12] On the other hand, the countries involved in the intensification of mutual trade would gain substantial benefits from stable exchange rates. If fluctuation of the exchange rates were kept within the *golden points*, fewer occasions required arbitrage, guarantees were provided for international trade, economic actors had a clearer view of the situation, and prices were likely to be more stable. In Great Britain, for example, average inflation between 1870 and 1913 settled at -0.7% and in the United States at $+0.1$.[13]

The *gold standard* ensured that a country's internal stability depended on its international stability. The money supply was directly linked to the inflow or outflow of gold, and therefore to the positive or negative balance of trade payments. Deficits and surpluses were automatically levelled by the market mechanisms and by the realignment of relative prices: if exports outweighed imports, gold would enter the country (and vice versa). Prices would therefore increase, so that the economic actors and consumers would prefer foreign products, thus allowing a realignment of the exchange rates. The widespread adoption of the gold standard made gold an international currency shared by all countries in the system, where it circulated in currencies with different denominations. Because the national currencies were exchanged at a fixed rate, the international monetary system was unified and homogeneous.[14]

---

[11] M. De Cecco, *Moneta e impero*, Turin, 1979, p. 79.

[12] B. Eichengreen, *Globalizing Capital. A History of the international Monetary System*, Princeton, 1996.

[13] N. Ferguson, *The Cash Nexus. Money and Power in the Modern World, 1700-2000*, London 2001.

[14] The mechanism was actually mediated by the central banks, which obtained the same effects by regulating the bank rate, making indebtedness more or less expensive. The principles of the *gold standard* were first described by David Hume in 1750.

There were other reasons for the appeal of the *gold standard*. Since it removed the risk of exchange and compelled the countries involved to pursue "healthy" (orthodox) fiscal and monetary policies, it reduced the cost of servicing the public debt, compressing what is today defined as *spread*, and rewarding virtuous countries. The fixed exchange rate implicitly involved the commitment to keep "a tidy house", meaning an uncompromising adherence to solid economic basics. Two further conditions were essential (but subsequently vanished): the cooperation and independence of the central banks, which had to conduct a credible defence of the exchange rate. This naturally came at a price. As highlighted by Obstfeld-Taylor's *political trilemma*, only two of three desirable macro-objectives (fixed foreign exchange rates, free circulation of capital, independent monetary policy) can be achieved at the same time. The system collapsed in the 1930s, as the crisis imposed the massive use of an expansionary monetary policy to shore up the economy, and cooperation between the central banks ceased, also because of the issues of inter-allied debts and war reparations.

9.3. Imperialism

The gradual integration of the international markets was counterbalanced by the rise of nationalism, which aimed to expand international trade in order to increase national power, thus contributing to an antagonistic vision of international relations. The colonial period expresses this rivalry and is a central element of globalization, because it integrated peripheral areas into a single world system. The long period of peace, the spread of industry, and the technological and scientific developments put a Eurocentric stamp on the world, creating peripheral areas with which Europe could trade a growing quantity of manufactured goods. Although the European colonizers were relatively few and their home countries relatively small, their empires were vast (Table 9.2). The Congo, for example, was eighty times the size of Belgium. In parallel with this political expansion on a vast scale came shorter travelling times. Improvements in transport had made the planet smaller, as in the first novel about globalization, *Around the World in Eighty Days,* where Jules Verne described: "one of the greatest novelties of its time, a process expanding the borders of the economy that is no less incredible than the results of science applied to technology".[15]

Improved weaponry increased Europeans' military power, and medical

---

[15] G. Berta, *L'ascesa della finanza internazionale*, cit., p. 11.

progress gave them better resistance to disease, making it easier for them to penetrate new territories. This was a historic turning point. In previous centuries, Europeans had been almost unassailable on the seas, but largely unable to penetrate the hinterlands of Asian or African countries. Now industrialization and a handful of inventions had given them the power to dominate the world.[16] The race to build empires took on a new strategic dimension; political leaders presented the newly annexed territories to the masses as necessary and inevitable. Governments played on national pride and stoked organismic metaphors, which were further fuelled by the evolutionary theories of Herbert Spencer and William Graham Sumner.[17] The concepts of competition and survival through natural selection were known to the educated public, and were easily transferred to market mechanisms by suggesting that aggressive behaviour was an expression of progress.[18] A dynamic economy required outlet markets and sources of raw materials, making it necessary to incorporate all regions that their incapable inhabitants would have failed to develop. In the words of Kipling, this was *The White Man's Burden*, Europe's civilizing mission.[19]

However, the importance of imperialism was not limited to the economy, and the imperialist countries considered it as a fundamental element of their national identity. According to Lord Salisbury (Robert Cecil, Marquess of Salisbury), London would have sunk into poverty and decay without imperialism. One of the major figures of British imperialism, Cecil Rhodes, saw space as the emblem of hope. These visions produced a metaphysical principle identifying space as a primary factor. A kind of mysticism evoked a spirit of adventure, propagating the idea that character-building experiences came through contact with the unknown, as represented by the wilderness.

The Great Depression offered an economic and theoretical justification for colonialism. The leading countries and the main areas of influence were no longer those of the early modern age: Spain, Portugal and the Netherlands were now peripheral powers in decline. New leaders emerged on the scene: Belgium, Japan, Italy and Germany. For the recently unified nations, colonialism might represent the ideal culmination of the unification

---

[16] D.R. Headrick, *The Tentacle of Progress. Technology Transfer in the Age of Imperialism*, Oxford, 1988.

[17] D. Rodrick, *The Globalization Paradox. Democracy and the Future of the World Economy*, Oxford, 2011.

[18] J.K. Galbraith, *A History of Economics. The Past and the Present*, London, 1987.

[19] F. Romero, *Storia internazionale del Novecento*, Roma, 2009, p. 15.

process. At the same time, the withdrawal of Great Britain into its vast imperial markets was a centrally important factor in the development of international economic relations in the twenty years before the First World War.[20] It was thanks to its Empire, especially India, that the world's first industrial country achieved global supremacy in international trade during the second half of the 19th century. Dependent on the rest of the world for foodstuffs and raw materials, Britain's preservation of its trade monopoly with its colonies allowed it to obtain the surplus needed to pay for its imports. The incapacity of the British economy to meet the challenge of the Second Industrial Revolution turned this country towards the areas it dominated politically, supporting the costs of their domination.[21] The circle was squared because trade in the colonies was a prerogative of the imperial administration, which naturally favoured British products.

The first theoretical reflections about imperialism were formulated during the Boer War (1899-1900) by John Hobson, a left-wing liberal. He interpreted the conquest of new territories as the result of a change in economic competition, which was developing in the direction of trade monopolies that would eventually lead to conflict between states. Imperialism was seen essentially as the result of the return to mercantilism. Hobson believed that this could be avoided by implementing institutional and fiscal reforms, and with the introduction of generous wage policies to sustain the domestic demand, an idea that was already present in Adam Smith's mind. Hobson's ideas influenced Lenin, who in 1916 focused on the theme of the transformation of the struggle for the domination of international markets into a struggle among nationalist states.

However, 19th century imperialism was different from that of the mercantilist period, when governments had entrusted overseas expansion to the privileged companies, granting them trade monopolies with the newly annexed territories. The companies had organized the economy, created militias and issued their own coins. The East India Company functioned like a state within the state; it had absolute dominion over India and plundered its resources. Its administrators, like Robert Clive, accumulated fortunes that scandalized London society, and parliamentary enquiries led to greater state vigilance over Indian affairs. However, the British government took over direct control of the colony only after the *sepoy* mutiny in 1857, although it left some areas under the formal rule of their *rajah*.

---

[20] D.K. Fieldhouse, *Economics and Empire. 1830-1914*, Ithaca, 1973.

[21] N. Ferguson, *Empire: How Britain Made the Modern World*, London; J. Gallagher, R. Robinson, *The Imperialism of Free Trade*, in *The Economic History Review*, VI, 1953, I, pp. 1-15.

The Conference of Berlin in 1885 legitimated the colonial possessions of European powers only if these were actually annexed and organized as territories, thus launching the "Scramble for Africa". Great Britain preferred a system of *indirect rule* for its dominions, especially in the peripheral areas, which ensured the survival of native institutions. Local chiefs administered justice, kept law and order, set the taxes and allocated jobs in the plantations and public works to their subjects. On the other hand, the French generally chose a system of *direct rule*, in line with the republican ideals of their constitution. They aimed to achieve the gradual cultural assimilation of the native populations, leading them to become *citoyens*. The policy had some unusual effects; although the natives could not actually achieve the same rights as the whites, indigenous children attending French primary schools used textooks telling them that the "Gauls" were "our common ancestors".

The Congo was a very different case. The region was explored and annexed by American journalist Henry Stanley with support from Belgian King Leopold II, who aspired to establish a personal domain in the heart of Africa. Bismarck encouraged the project, considering it a folly, but also a useful way to guarantee free trade and contrast the ambitions of Great Britain, France and Portugal. The Congo Free State came into being, with Leopold II as its absolute monarch. Within the space of a few years, the region's resources (starting with ivory) were systematically plundered, with the aim of making the maximum profit from the minimum investment. The unprecedented violence used against the natives and the natural environment inspired Joseph Conrad's *Heart of Darkness*.[22] The European elites were scandalized by what they perceived to be the opposite of Western colonialism's "civilising mission", and an international protest movement eventually forced Leopold to surrender his personal dominion to the Belgian state in 1908.

Table 9.1. Total gross emigration from Europe (including Russia, millions)

Periods	Emigrants	Periods	Emigrants
Before 1850 (total)	1.0	1881-1890	7.8
1851-1860	2.2	1891-1900	6.8
1861-1870	2.8	1901-1910	11.3
1871-1880	3.2	1911-1915	6.7

Source: P. Bairoch, *Storia economica e sociale del mondo*, Turin, 1999, p. 464.

---

[22] J. Conrad, *Heart of Darkness*, London, 1899.

Table 9.2. Size of colonies (million sq.km)

Home country	1826	1876 (a)	1913 (b)
United Kingdom	9,000	22,470	32,860
France	100	970	10,590
Netherlands	1,200	2,020	2,020
Spain	400	430	350
Germany	–	–	2,940
Italy	–	–	1,530
United States	–	–	310
Japan	–	–	290
World	11,200	26,490	55,330

Note (b)-(a) = 28,840,000 sq.km annexed by the colonial powers over 37 years. The present surface area of the United States is 9,373,000 sq.km.

Source: P. Bairoch, *European Trade Policy, 1815-1914*, in P. Mathias, S. Pollard (eds.), *The Cambridge Economic History of Europe*, Vol. VIII, Cambridge, 1989, pp. 1-160.

Bibliography

Bairoch P., *Victoires et déboires. Histoire économique et sociale du monde du XVIe siècle à nos jours*, Paris, 1996 (it. translation: *Storia economica e sociale del mondo. Vittorie e insuccessi dal XVI secolo ad oggi*, Turin, 1999).

Bordo M.D., Taylor A.M., Williamson J.G. (eds.), *Globalization in historical perspective*, Chicago, 2003.

Fieldhouse D.K., *Economics and Empire. 1830-1914*, Ithaca, 1973.

Frieden J.A., *Global Capitalism. It's Fall and Rise in the Twentieth Century*, New York, 2006.

Headrick D.R., *The Tentacle of Progress. Technology Transfer in the Age of Imperialism*, Oxford, 1988.

O'Rourke K., Williamson J., *Globalisation and History. The Evolution of a Nineteenth-Century Atlantic Economy*, Cambridge, Mass.-London, 1999.

Rodrick D., *The Globalization Paradox. Democracy and the Future of the World Economy*, Oxford, 2011.

INTERNATIONAL MONETARY SYSTEMS

An **international monetary system** is a set of regulations and laws defined by international treaties and integrated with conventions and practices accepted by the member states, regarding the criteria for regulating international payments, the system of exchange rates between the currencies of the member states, and financial aid between central banks or states in the event of a crisis involving the balance of payments. The need for an international monetary system increases with the growth of trade between countries and therefore with **international specialization**, aside from the fact that no **international capital market** can exist without a **foreign exchange market**.

In the case of the **international *gold standard***, in force from approximately 1870 to 1914, practices and conventions were so deeply rooted in the routine procedures of governments and central banks that the absence of treaties regulating its operation created no problems. However, after the Second World War, with the **Bretton Woods system** (1944-71) and the **European Monetary System** (EMS), in force from March 1979, it became the norm to draw up formal agreements establsihing the regulations.

As Maurice Obstfeld and Alan Taylor have highlighted, the inevitable interdependence of open economies makes it impossible for the *policy makers* of a country to achieve more than two of the following objectives at the same time: a stable exchange rate; a monetary policy directed towards "internal" objectives like full employment and stable prices; the free movement of international capital. The **"impossible trinity" of the open economies** means recognition that 1. fixed exchange rates are compatible with an independent monetary policy only on conditions that capital mobility is limited; 2. fixed exchange rates and free mobility of capital imply foregoing an independent monetary policy; 3. an independent monetary policy and free movement of capital can co-exist only if fixed exchange rates are abandoned.

The choice of **economic policy** objectives has an immediate effect on the balance of the international monetary system. Therefore it should not be surprising that the ideas underlying the establishment of the *gold standard* differ from those behind the monetary agreements in the second half of the 20th century. Between 1870 and the First World War, economic policy was actually subordinated to objectives connected with "external" balance (stable prices, an even balance of payments, lower public debt costs), while the internal objectives of economic policy (for example, to contrast unemployment) were not on the government agenda.

Above all, the ***gold standard*** meant respecting three fundamental norms: convertibility of the national currency into gold at a legally-defined fixed rate; full convertibility of paper money; free trade in gold. There was also an unspoken rule: any variation in the stock of money in circulation would be directly proportional to the variation in gold reserves. In theory, the *price-specie-flow* mechanism should have automatically ensured that countries on the *gold standard* maintained an even balance of payments. In practice, however, the adjustment process was controlled by the **central banks**; they bought domestic State bonds when a balance of payments deficit meant that gold left the country, reducing the supply of money in circulation and raising interest rates, or sold domestic bonds when an export surplus brought gold into the country, increasing the money supply and reducing interest rates.

The *gold standard* ensured long-term price stability and similar price movements among the participant countries, since price levels in all countries were determined by the relationship between the demand and offer of gold, and no single country had a decisive influence on price levels. Expectations based on the fixed exchange rates also meant that financial speculation helped restore balance in the system. The other side of the coin was the deflationary pressure caused by the ratio to gold, since it was impossible to increase monetary aggregates in proportion to the growth of the real economy; falling prices of raw materials (wheat, raw cotton, coal) during the Great Depression (1873-1896) led many states to erect tariff barriers as protection for their domestic manufacturers and to wage trade wars against each other. It should be remembered that the countries in deficit with the balance of payment paid for this with higher unemployment levels.

Governments abandoned the *gold standard* during the First World War and financed much of their massive military spending by stamping banknotes. As a result, prices were higher everywhere at the end of the war in 1918. During the 1922 Conference of Genoa, a group of countries, including the United States, Great Britain, Italy, France and Japan, agreed on a generalized return to the *gold standard*. Aware that the supply of gold might be insufficient to meet the central banks' requirements for their reserves, the Conference of Genoa established a **gold exchange standard**, a monetary system based on the convertibility of national currencies into a foreign currency directly convertible to gold, like the US **dollar** or **British sterling**. If the *gold exchange standard* theoretically made it possible to save gold and strengthen the reserves of the central banks with convertible foreign currencies, it was not actually possible to restore the gold standard's automatic effects on the balance of payments and the money supply required by the economic system. Attempts to restore a more flexible *gold standard* were finally abandoned after the **1929 Crisis**: Great Britain abandoned convertibility to gold in 1931, followed by the United States in 1933, while the other countries did so during the 1930s.

A new international monetary system did not arrive until the **Bretton Woods Conference** (New Hampshire, USA) in July 1944. The objective was to reduce the serious imbalances in the balance of payments of the 44 participant countries, thereby avoiding a new age of the kind of protectionism that destroyed the international economy after the Great Crisis. Two proposals were advanced at the Conference. The **White Plan** proposed by the US Treasury Secretary was based on the return to fixed exchange rates and the creation of a "International Monetary Stabilization Fund" to provide countries with loans to shore up their currency. The **Keynes Plan** proposed by the British government's economic advisor advocated the creation of a Clearing Union (a central world bank) to control international payments and lend a new currency, the *bancor*, based on gold.

The American plan won the day, and the international monetary system adopted a new **gold exchange standard** centred on the **American dollar** (the only currency convertible into gold at $35 per ounce/28.5 g). The United States therefore became the only country not obliged to guarantee the parity of its currency with others. The main duty of the USA was now to maintain sufficient gold reserves to guarantee dollar convertibility, while the other countries had to guarantee the parity of their currencies in US dollars (maximum deviation ± 1%).

Bretton Woods was therefore an attempt at a "great compromise" between the need for stable exchange rates to favour trade and investments, and the need to allow the possibility of independent national economic policies, for example, to contrast unemployment. Firstly, the fixed exchange rate system was made more flexible, providing the possibility of agreement on allowing countries to devaluate their currency in order to cope with with structural disequilibria in their balance of payments. Although no other country except the USA could freely use the monetary policy, the introduction of strict limits on the movement of capital allowed the various countries to pursue their internal economic policy objectives via their fiscal policies.

The weakness of the system was the double role of the US dollar as the international means of payment and the reserve currency of the national central banks. In other words, it was not possible to increase international liquidity unless the US Federal Reserve increased its gold reserves to maintain parity. Conversely, devaluation of the dollar in relation to gold would lead to generalised inflation. The repercussions on US monetary stability were important. Firstly, the dollar reserves accumulated by the central banks grew until they exceeded those of the Federal Reserve, and the United States could no longer guarantee the convertibility of the dollar. Secondly, the rapid growth in prices and money supply meant that the dollar was overvalued in relation to gold; from the 1960s, international liquidity could be guaranteed only by a persistent US balance of payments deficit.

The Bretton Woods system gradually lost credibility, making dollar devaluation increasingly likely, and this finally occurred on 15th August 1971, when US President Nixon declared that the dollar was no longer convertible to gold. In February 1973, all links between the dollar and foreign currency were permanently severed, and the gold standard was replaced with a **flexible exchange system**.

Although flexible exchange rates are required in order to reconcile the pursuit of internal economic objectives (low inflation, full employment) with external objectives (an even balance of payments) in a system allowing the free international circulation of capital – as shown by the Obstfeld-Taylor **"impossible trinity"** (see above) – various attempts were made to restore **fixed exchange systems**, at least on a regional basis.

The best known of these is the **European Monetary System (EMS)**, a regional agreement in force from March 1979, which established a central parity with the **German mark** for the bilateral exchanges of the member countries. The purpose of the EMS was to create a European "stable currency zone" and stable exchange rates.

Following the high **inflation** and **unstable exchange rates** of the 1970s, European governments felt the need for a return to more stable exchange rates and greater **economic and monetary cooperation**. The EMS eventually included Germany, France, the United Kingdom, Italy, Spain, Netherlands, Belgium, Denmark, Portugal, Ireland and Luxemburg, but collapsed in 1992-1993 following a serious exchange crisis, triggered by market expectations of a re-evaluation for the most unstable currencies, which could no longer support the extreme restrictions of German monetary policy. The first countries to abandon the EMS in September 1992 were the United Kingdom and Italy; as a result of the excessively rigid nominal exchange rate against the mark and their own insufficiently restrictive fiscal policies, both countries had become much less competitive than a few years previously.

Chapter 10
THE GREAT WAR: THE END OF A WORLD

SUMMARY: 10.1. Interpretation of the war: discontinuity and social revolution. – 10.2. Total war: industrial planning and mobilization. – 10.3. The geopolitical and economic consequences. – Bibliography.

10.1. Interpretation of the war: discontinuity and social revolution

The First World War ended a period of peace and progress that had lasted almost uninterrupted since 1870. The conflict weakened Europe, which lost its political and economic supremacy for good, and it also shaped world geopolitics until 1989. International trade was seriously damaged, and the international monetary system ceased regulating the relations between currencies.

The First World War was defined as "great" not just because of the numbers of countries or troops involved, the scale of destruction and death it caused or the duration of the conflict itself, but also because it was revolutionary and levelling, cutting across all social classes. It was a kind of incubator for the transformations that were to occur in the 20th century. The war modified politics, society, culture and the economy, marking the end of positivism and liberal individualism. It led to the development of a new collectivist concept of the state, which guaranteed new rights for its citizens, redefining and reshaping the relations between political power and capitalism. The state broadened its prerogatives of intervention, vigilance and control, not only in economic affairs but also in social issues. In the period between the two wars, the state also implemented population and public health policies, entering into the most private spheres of individual and family life to compensate for the generation gap caused by the loss of so many young people in war.

The 1919 constitution of the Weimar Republic was written immediately after Germany's defeat, and was an ideal representation of the classless society born in the trenches. It was the archetype of an original conception of the national community, providing an ideal model for the new 20th century democracies. It enshrined a new concept of the citizen-state relationship, making the state responsible for satisfying citizens' essential needs (work, education and health). It redesigned the connections between collective and individual rights and exalted the dignity of intellectual and manual work. It revolutionised the relations between capital and labour, income and profit, income and labour, to the benefit of the community.

The economy would ensure that all had "a truly human life" and private initiative would also be regulated in this sense. Property rights were protected, but property was to be used for "the common good. Every citizen had the "moral duty" to use his or her "energy" in a way that was useful for society. Every German was guaranteed work that paid a living wage, but if this were not possible the government would provide. The state was given the right to confiscate land for redistribution to ex-soldiers. It also had the power to nationalise companies if these were judged to be strategically important for the benefit of society, and could impose industrial concentration in certain sectors of public interest. The state had the right to plan the production, distribution and use of goods, and also to control prices, imports and exports. It obliged entrepreneurs to collaborate with technicians and workmen to improve working conditions and to allow the company to achieve "overall economic development".

There was an even more radical representation of the "new economy" in the constitution of Fiume in 1920, during a revolutionary episode combining politics, poetry and aesthetics that even Bolshevik leaders viewed with interest. The *Charter of Carnaro* was inspired by Gabriele D'Annunzio and written by trade unionist Alceste De Ambris; it proclaimed the Free State of Fiume to be "a direct democracy" based on "productive work", aiming to elevate the "prosperity" of all its citizens. It guaranteed the right to primary education and to "paid work" with a minimum wage appropriate for the cost of living, it provided for unemployment benefit, health care, and an old age pension. The Republic considered property to be merely "a social function" and not an "absolute right or individual privilege": the prerogative of property "over any means of production or trade" was legitimated only by the work that made it benefit the country's economy. The state recognised the right to citizenship only of those who contributed to the "material prosperity" and "civil development" of the nation, defined as "productive citizens". The Republic also created corporations, which grouped all the workers of a certain sector; these bodies were completely independent in terms of production and function, and also enjoyed the right to "collective" ownership of all kinds of asset.

The First World War was the first episode in what can be ideally defined as the "Second Thirty Years' War". The Battle of Verdun (February-

December 1916) was one of the bloodiest clashes of the Great War, since the objective of German strategists was not to break through the enemy front but to test the enemy's resistance by weakening the enemy troops. Victory meant losing fewer men than the enemy (German supreme command had decided on a threshold) and inflicting losses from which France, being demographically weaker than Germany, would never be able to recover.

Although the battle had no important tactical or strategic outcomes, it left over 500,000 dead and 800,000 wounded, and was a forerunner of planned slaughter on a massive scale. Together with Auschwitz and Hiroshima, Verdun symbolises the 20th century use of modern technology to perpetrate mass destruction.

The war was not only a historical and political event, but was also a cultural event in the anthropological sense. Collective psychology was transformed by the violence of military action and the pitiful living conditions of the troops, who were crowded into the trenches like rats and subjected to weeks of bombardment or gas attacks. Pioneering medical research by doctors at the front found soldiers venerating irrational, codified gestures and rituals that had saved their lives on occasions, placing their trust in lucky charms, or in the cult of saints, of sacred images and miracles if they were Roman Catholics. While the politicians who had led their countries into the war were increasingly discredited, there was growing trust in the military commanders, lower officers or commanders, who attempted not to waste lives in futile actions and tried to guarantee a minimum level of comfort for their troops. The myth of the commander was born on the battlefield, where it gained strength, idealised and exalted in the post-war years by the totalitarian regimes (and not only): leaders whose charisma and rhetoric exerted a religious fascination over the masses. This would have a decisive influence over the new style of politics and parties.

The conflict also marked a sharp discontinuity in art, culture and public sensitivity to the *avant-garde*: Joyce and Faulkner, German expressionism and the Bauhaus, scientific recognition of Freudian and Jungian psychoanalysis, are just some of the many examples confirming the new artistic and cultural vision of the West.

While the war was experienced as a catastrophic rebirth heralding a new world, the post-war period dashed these expectations, generating increasing levels of insecurity that dulled faith in democracy and favoured the rise of totalitarian regimes. However, what Stefan Zweig called "the world of yesterday"[1] vanished even in countries like Great Britain and France,

---

[1] S. Zweig, *Die Welt von Gestern. Erinnerungen eines Europäers*, Stockholm, 1944.

where the political systems were more resistant. Inflation and downward social mobility eroded the credibility and consensus of the middle-class political parties, and faith in parliamentary systems and their ability to handle the crisis effectively collapsed. Soldiers demobbed at the end of the war demanded economic and social recognition in compensation for the years spent at the front, but governments embroiled in the post-war crisis were unable to maintain the promises made during the war. Thousands of ex-servicemen joined organisations like the *Stahlhelm* in Germany or the *American Legion* in the States, interested not only in public commemoration ceremonies or in helping members and their families, but often exerting a strong influence on politics by supporting right-wing parties. To paraphrase José Ortega y Gasset,[2] the eruption of the masses into history radically changed political competition. Opposing ideologies created a climate of civil war in the different countries, aggravated by the violence to which people had become accustomed during the war. Influenced by the Bolshevik revolution, politics became ideological, the object of totalising and religious devotion, with myths and symbols prevailing over rational programmes. The new mass movements formed: firstly the socialist and Catholic parties, then the communists and revolutionary right-wing groups. The new totalitarian movements formed in reaction to the aftermath of the war, and were more successful than the traditional parties in attracting consensus, with their charismatic leaders, simple direct slogan and mass rituals anticipating national harmony in a classless society. The Soviet Union, Italy and Germany were the political laboratories between the two wars, creating the concept of a totalitarian state and the new man. The success of European totalitarian regimes was helped considerably by the mass movements associated with them, fundamentally important in creating consensus for the German and Italian dictatorships. Adult movements like Italy's *Opera nazionale dopolavoro* and Germany's *Kraft durch Freude*, or the *Gioventù italiana del Littorio* and *Hitlerjugend* for young people, spread propaganda among their members and provided them with leisure activities. Radio and cinema became vital means of spreading ideas, principles and news reports by using the most innovative and sophisticated publicity techniques to sell political ideology. These were the same methods used by psychologists working for the army during the war to convince soldiers to their countries' objectives were justified, encouraging them to resist the enemy and fight for final victory. In 1917, the German government, High Command and Deutsche Bank promoted the creation of *Universum-Film AG* (UFA) to produce propaganda films for the troops fighting at the front. It went on to

---

[2] J. Ortega y Gasset, *La rebelión de las masas*, Barcelona, 1929.

become the country's most important film company, occupying a central position in the media empire under the control of Joseph Goebbels, the Third Reich's Minister of Propaganda from 1933 to 1945.

Figure 10.1. British trench during the Battle of the Somme

10.2. Total war: industrial planning and mobilization

No one has ever been able to demonstrate that the Great War was the inevitable outcome of the imperialistic and economic rivalries between the major European powers. At the end of the 19th century, liberals like Gladstone and Pareto[3] actually believed that the growth of international trade and the globalization of financial investments would bring peace. None of the possible causes of the war really demonstrates the origin of the conflict, apart from the political and diplomatic intrigue enveloping the European courts and chancelleries between the assassination of Archduke Franz Ferdinand in Sarajevo on 28th June 1914 and early August, when all governments accepted that war had now become inevitable. The causes were ac-

---

[3] William Ewart Gladstone, a liberal politician and several times Prime Minister of the United Kingdom; Vilfredo Pareto, Italian economist and sociologist, emigrated to Switzerland, where he held the chair of Political Economy at the University of Lausanne.

tually much less important than the economic effects of resource management during the war and the political consequences in the post-war years.

It was generally agreed that the war would soon be over, and economists also agreed that the states involved would not have the material and capital resources to conduct a long modern conflict. The German General Staff based its strategy on the "Schlieffen Plan": the German army planned to crush France in less than eight weeks, before Russia could mobilise its troops, then the German army would move rapidly to the Eastern Front, where it would defeat Russia. The success of the plan depended on a sudden surprise attack. The French General Staff, influenced by French military tradition (from the Gauls to the Jacobins) and Henri Bergson's concept of *élan vital* (vital impetus), held that the attitude of the French troops was not defensive, but that they should be systematically launched in attack. Accordingly, General Foch's "Plan XVII" was that France would respond to a German attack with an immediate counter-offensive in Alsace-Lorraine. What actually happened was very different: Belgium resisted for longer than the Germans had imagined, Great Britain rapidly organised an expeditionary force it sent to France, and – most importantly – Russia attacked East Prussia before mobilization was completed. After the Battle of the Marne, the armies halted and settled down into defensive positions along a line of opposing trenches from the Swiss border to the English Channel.

Subsequent history showed that defensive tactics supported by machine-guns, barbed wire and trenches prevailed over offensive actions. The conflict was more mobile on the Eastern Front, but turned into a gigantic siege on the Western Front, a war of attrition between the two opposing coalitions.

To meet the colossal needs of the armies, governments and supreme commands had to obtain raw materials, in addition to planning the manufacture of armaments and rationing of food supplies. This was more important for Germany, which did not possess the colonial empires and resources of France and Great Britain. By autumn 1914, Germany had finished its stocks of munitions, and the members of the *Entente* imposed an economic blockade to prevent Germany from trading with neutral states. Even after conquering eastern territories, the German Empire encountered constant difficulties caused by the scarcity of food supplies. The civilian population bore the brunt of the shortages, since their rations were reduced to ensure adequate supplies for the troops at the front.

Germany reacted to the blockade by using its U-boats to weaken Great Britain and launching an indiscriminate submarine offensive.

The British suffered considerable losses: over 500,000 tonnes of shipping in April 1917 alone. If German attacks had continued at the same rate, the British merchant navy would have shrunk rapidly, leading to shortages of arms, raw materials and food supplies in the country. The crisis was resolved by giving shipping convoys an escort of battleships, and the shipyards increased their output.

At the same time, the merchant navy was placed under centralised command, imports were rationed and reduced, and the domestic output of agricultural products was increased. The decisive event came, however, when the United States declared war on the central European empires in April 1917. The USA had no army ready for immediate deployment on the French front, and it took about a year to train Pershing's expeditionary force, but it made its financial and industrial resources available to the members of the *Entente*. The German commanders had underestimated the resistance of a modern industrial nation, and the Allies had overestimated the effects of their economic blockade of Germany. Although the industrial capacity and food supplies of the Central Empires were always unstable and continually on the brink of disaster, the lands conquered in Eastern Europe (Poland, Romania and the Ukraine) enabled them to continue their war efforts until autumn 1918. Following the Russian surrender, they were even able to launch a series of offensives on the Western and Italian fronts in the summer of 1918, creating serious problems for the opposing forces.

The supply of raw materials was a delicate aspect of the German arms industry. Before the war, Germany had imported 43% of its raw materials from abroad, and this was the first sector to come under state control. August 1914 saw the creation of the *Kriegsrohstoffabteilung* (War Raw Materials Department), headed by industrialist Walther Rathenau (president of AEG).[4] The idea actually came from another high-level manager of his

---

[4] Walther Rathenau was a convinced "corporatist". In 1918, reflecting on the experience of the war years, he illustrated his personal idea of the relationship between the state and capitalism in *Die neue Wirtschaft*, Berlin, 1918. He favoured a mixed economy, permeated by the principle of social solidarity. It was centred on the large modern industrial company, both public and private, some of whose profits would be directed towards a collective dividend in order to guarantee social harmony. The war had imposed "a new way of thinking" and the new economy should now reflect "morality" and a "sense of responsibility". Rathenau favoured the introduction of worker participation in company management (co-management). He envisaged new "self-administered" aggregations of private companies, guaranteed and supported by the state, similar to the mediaeval corporations. He hoped for a new classless society consisting only of workers. Accused of aiming to transform the German economy "into a corporate business", like AEG on a larger scale, Rathenau was not involved in writing the constitution of Weimar. He disagreed with the model that emerged during the Constituent Assembly, believing that there was not sufficient widespread awareness that a new spirit of collaboration between entrepreneurs and workers was the fundamental prerequisite for

company, Wichard von Moellendorff, who was the first to point out the problem, and would become the under-secretary to the *Reichsminister für Wirtschaft* (Minister for Economic Affairs) after the war, and also contributed to the constitution of the Weimar Republic. The department was responsible for registering the availability of raw materials and organizing their assignment to the different industries. Specific agencies controlled by the Department had the task of locating the different products required: minerals, metals, textiles, leather and chemicals.

Until 1915, the arms industry was efficient enough to increase output constantly, guaranteeing an adequate supply of arms and munitions to the front and maintaining slight superiority over the Allied forces of the *Entente*. However, Great Britain's economic mobilization turned the tables. In the battles of Verdun and especially the Somme (July-November 1916), the British had the definite advantage in the number of shots fired, spurring German High Command to redress the disadvantage and produce more arms and munitions by increasing the technological efficiency of German industry. The Hindenburg Plan was an economic policy shaped by the needs of war; it aimed to double industrial output, especially in the arms and munitions sectors. The new *Kriegsamt* (War Office) headed by General Wilhelm Groener took centralised control over all the bodies supervising the arms industries, including Rathenau's department.

The Plan replaced the male workforce fighting at the front by mobilizing women, minors, invalids and prisoners of war, and concentrated industrial production in order to eliminate inefficiency and waste. When Germany gained access to the resources of the Eastern territories annexed under with the Treaty of Brest-Litovsk, imposed on Soviet Russia in March 1918, it appeared possible that the country would obtain the vital resources it needed for the decisive offensive.

The German troops broke through the British front in March and the French front in June, but were driven back at the Second Battle of the Marne, where US troops also fought. Germany now lost the initiative, and the defeat seriously weakened the German army. The government's plan had set impossibly high targets for German industry, which it failed to meet, and German High Command had underestimated the military effectiveness of the new tanks.

Great Britain was completely unprepared to face a long conflict. Lord

---

new forms of economic organisation. Another intellectual affected by the Great War was Ernst Jünger, a voluntary recruit in 1914 who became the German Army's most famous hero, and it is unsurprising that he described "the shift from democracy to the state of labour" in a chapter of his book *Der Arbeiter. Herrschaft und Gestalt*, Hamburg, 1932.

Kitchener was appointed Minister of War in August 1914 and the reforms he introduced included conscription, a departure from tradition in a country that had always relied on a volunteer army. Liberal culture discouraged state intervention in the economy, but the need to support the armies at the front soon imposed interventionist measures. The Defence of the Realm Act allowed the government to direct the arms industries and control the workforce. Centralised planning was introduced in 1915 with the creation of the Ministry of Munitions headed by David Lloyd George.

The German occupation of Northern France deprived the French of raw materials and industries. Arms and munitions production was entrusted to the state arsenals, but these soon proved insufficient to meet the needs of the army, and it became necessary to integrate them with private enterprise. In 1915 an undersecretary for Artillery was appointed in the Ministry of War, and this office then became a ministry in its own right in 1916 under Albert Thomas: the *Ministère de l'Armement*. The war economy was organised into regional groups and consortia, but remained essentially entrusted to private enterprise; iron and steel imports were managed by the *Comité des Forges*, the association of metallurgy industries.

Italy entered the war in 1915 and created an undersecretary for arms and munitions, subsequently creating a specific ministry in 1917. This headed an industrial mobilization system with a central committee and seven (subsequently eleven) regional committees, including politicians, military personnel, entrepreneurs and representatives of the workers. The arms industry was integrated with auxiliary factories, which were given priority assignment of commissions, energy and raw materials.

Russian output remained far below the real needs of its armed forces, despite the creation of specific arms industry committees in 1915. This was due to the country's limited productive capacity, the shortage of specialised workers and poor communications systems. In addition, German occupation of Poland and the Baltic regions deprived Russia of factories and mineral deposits. Industrial output was at its height in 1916 and allowed General Brusilov's army to mount a victorious offensive and break through the Austro-Hungarian front as far as the Carpathians, causing serious difficulties for the armies of the Central Empires in the East.

Arms production was coordinated in the USA from July 1917 by the War Industries Board, which organised supplies for the army, navy and Allied forces, and planned industrial output according to strategic priorities. Other offices were also created in connection with the war economy; members were generally recruited from finance and business, together with officers from the armed forces.

The war drove the growth of mining, heavy industry, steel, chemicals and engineering, which favoured concentration and rationalization of industry and the construction of larger factories. The conflict provided an incentive to technological progress in all sectors involved in the war effort. The British navy's conversion from coal to petrol in 1912 drove fuel consumption and spurred the search for new petroleum deposits worldwide. The use of motor vehicles by the armed forces drove the car industry. The chemical industry expanded with the production of explosives and poison gases (used first by Germany in 1915), tyres, and medicines. There were also constant innovations in aviation, with planes used on reconnaissance missions, for bombing raids and aerial combat. Dutch entrepreneur Anthony Fokker developed machine-gun synchronization gear so that gunners could fire bullets through their own plane's propeller without damaging it, while Italian aviation industrialist Giovanni Battista Caproni designed the war's most efficient strategic bomber. Aviation also drove important advances in metallurgy (providing incentives for lighter alloys and metals like aluminium), engine technology, fuels and lubricants. The innovations introduced during the war contributed to the birth of commercial aviation in the post-war period.

Radio became widespread and popular during the 1920s, and also made important technological progress due to its use by the military forces.

The war dissolved the international monetary system based on the *gold standard* because the central banks of the countries involved suspended convertibility to gold. Formally, the United States remained on the gold standard, but after entering the war it introduced certain restrictions on gold payments and allowed the banks to increase the issue of banknotes in relation to their metal reserves. For the *Entente*, the fundamental monetary problem was to support parity of the sterling with the dollar, given that the British currency supported that of the other Allied states. This was, however, very difficult, because from 1915 Great Britain ceded its foreign investments and accumulated further debts. Only the entry of the USA into the war resolved the monetary issue, because the US Treasury granted credit directly in dollars.

Because it was generally believed that the war would not last long, all those involved underestimated its cost. Until 1917, Great Britain and France supported their minor allies with increasingly high loans. After entering the war, the United States became the principle "lender" of the *Entente*.

Between April 1917 and November 1918, the United States exported arms and goods to European nations worth 10.3 billion dollars and granted another 7.1 billion in credit; the total inter-allied debt amounted to 16.4 billion dollars. Great Britain lent around 7 billion to the Allies, but received 3.7 billion from the United States. The war credits were a burden for Britain, because it paid for US goods in dollars and then had to obtain loans from the United States to finance the other countries. On the other hand, the US Treasury financed US exporters, supporting the domestic economy, and so American supremacy was consolidated also by the war credits.

After the war, the Allies asked the United States to cancel their debts or at least to compensate them with German reparations. Although these debts had enabled the shared victory, and the USA had suffered no material destruction and lost fewer men in the war, the new Republican administration was adamant in demanding repayment.

The question of inter-allied war debts damaged international relations and was an important factor preventing a return to the pre-war situation. The world's economic and financial centre shifted from London to New York, and this would force the USA to take on the central role in the multilateral system. Until 1914, the stability of the international economy was based on Great Britain keeping its own market open to goods from the rest of the world, and exporting long-term capital. However, the USA operated a protectionist policy that was more attentive to the needs of its domestic market, especially of farmers, and US foreign investments were extremely limited and mostly short-term. This scenario prevented a return to the pre-war equilibrium regarding the balance of payments of the single countries and the mechanisms of the *gold standard*.

The Central Empires were excluded from the world markets, and adjusted their balance of payments with balanced bilateral agreements between states, thereby reducing or even eliminating currency payments. Expenditure rose sharply between 1914 and 1918, and fiscal pressure was not applied sufficiently to close the gap between income and expenditure. The cost of the war was mostly financed by increasing the public debt, launching special war loans and by increasing the money supply, which contributed to the rise of inflation and led to a drastic redistribution in wealth that penalised people with a fixed income.

Inflation was higher in the Central Empires, and reached abnormally high levels after the war with the removal of controls introduced during the conflict. Between 1914 and 1919 the wholesale price index (1913 level = 100) rose from 106 to 415 in Germany, from 102 to 357 in France, from 100 to 242 in Great Britain, from 96 to 364 in Italy, and from 98 to 206 in the United States. The neutral states were also affected. State finances in the post-war period also bore the burden of pensions paid to war widows and orphans, and to injured veterans who could not work.

The governments of victorious countries all believed that they would be able to balance their finances with resources taken from the defeated nations.

The Treaty of Versailles in 1919 demonstrated the impossibility of finding shared solutions to construct a European equilibrium between the winners and losers. Germany took all the blame for the conflict. The Great War began as a European "state" war, but quickly became a cultural and ideological conflict, partly because state propaganda campaigns aimed to convince soldiers and civilians alike that the war was just and should continue to the bitter end. As Carl Schmitt wrote,[5] the "punitive" peace terms shattered the *jus publicum Europaeum*, making it impossible to return to the old system of cooperation between states. Versailles therefore betrayed the most important objective of US President Woodrow Wilson's *Fourteen Points* as a programme for a just and lasting peace, and laid the foundations for a second war. Germany was deprived of territories, Danzig and East Prussia were separated from the rest of the country, its colonies were confiscated, and its materials and armaments were requisitioned. Its army was limited to 100,000 men, its navy to six ships, and it was not allowed to have an air force. However, the most humiliating blow was the price Germany had to pay for triggering the conflict: 132 billion gold marks. This colossal sum was more than the country could ever hope to pay, especially since it was isolated from the international economic system and had no possibility of exporting goods to accumulate hard currency.

John Maynard Keynes disagreed with his own government, and left the British delegation at the peace conference. He wrote in *The Economic Consequences of the Peace*[6] that the treaty created the conditions for future turmoil, stressing that Germany was the "central pillar" of the European economy, and that German "prosperity and initiative" were essential to European well-being. He correctly predicted that France and Great Britain would destroy the peace by "demanding the impossible" and sacrificing "substance to appearance".

The system designed by US President Wilson soon lost what should have been its principal guarantor of world harmony and peace. The Republicans won the mid-term elections in 1918, and the US Senate refused to ratify the peace treaty or join the League of Nations. In November 1920, Warren Harding's clear victory over the Democrat candidate for the presidency made him the twenty-ninth US president. The new Republican administration imposed a policy of isolationism.

---

[5] C. Schmitt, *Der Nomos der Erde im Völkerrecht des Jus Publicum Europaeum*, Cologne, 1950.

[6] J.M. Keynes, *The Economic Consequences of the Peace*, London, 1919.

10.3. The geopolitical and economic consequences

The peace treaties ratified the dissolution of the European and Ottoman empires, and the birth of new independent countries. Theoretically, the new borders should have respected the principles of nationality and self-determination contained in Wilson's *Fourteen Points*, but this was not always the case. The integrated economic systems of the Central European Empires were broken up after the war, since sources of raw materials were cut off from industrial centres and communication networks were interrupted. The starkest example of this is Austria, which lost its mines in the Balkans, the port of Trieste, and its industries in Bohemia. The Eastern European states (except for certain regions of Czechoslovakia and Poland) were mainly agricultural, and had low *per capita* levels of income and consumption, together with extremely high rates of inflation, which depreciated their currencies. As a survival measure, their governments reinforced protectionist customs barriers and/or devalued their currency to render exports more competitive, but these economic policies hampered the growth of European trade. In addition, most of these new states were in conflict with their neighbours over borders and ethnic issues.

The Bolshevik Revolution and the long Civil War that followed it meant that Russia left the international economic circuits. The Soviets denounced secret diplomacy; they published the agreements made between the tsar and Allied powers, and repudiated all the country's foreign debts. The government of People's Commissars implemented a policy of "war communism", nationalizing Russian industries and placing them under the control of collectives of workers and experts, nationalizing land and requisitioning agricultural food products. This allowed it to support the Red Army, but plunged the civilian population into poverty and starvation. The famine lasted until the early 1920s, alleviated only by the international aid coordinated by the Red Cross and some US humanitarian organisations.

Demographic losses due to the First World War were extremely severe, amounting to about ten million soldiers and seven million civilians killed by disease, starvation and massacres (including the Russian Civil War and the Armenian genocide by the Turks).[7] The 21 million people wounded often had disabilities making them unfit for work. The younger and more fertile age groups were those most affected, and this created important generation gaps in the 1920s, with economic consequences for levels of consumption

---

[7] J. Winter, *Victimes de la guerre: morts, blessés et invalides*, in S. Audoin-Rouzeau, J.J. Becker (eds.), *Encyclopédie de la Grande Guerre 1914-1918*, Paris, 2004, pp. 1015-1024.

and the labour supply. The worldwide Spanish flu epidemic in 1918-1920 further decimated soldiers and civilians, causing millions of deaths.

Physical destruction was concentrated in the areas of Europe that had been battlegrounds (Northern France, Eastern Europe, Eastern Italy, the Balkans and the Middle East). Agriculture suffered the worst damage, and this was compounded by the lack of fertilizers, labour and machinery.

At the end of the war, the world's economic centre shifted from Europe to North America. Great Britain was no longer the leading foreign investor, and the United States, which had always had a net debt with Europe, became a creditor from 1916. In the space of just five years from 1914 to 1919, the value of US capital abroad rose from 3.5 to 7 billion dollars.

The New York Stock Exchange replaced London as the world's leading financial market. US exports grew just as rapidly, doubling during the country's three years of neutrality until 1917. At the end of the war, the US trade balance registered a 6.4 billion dollar surplus. The decentralization of international trade and production also affected other areas of the world. The needs of the *Entente* drove agricultural production and output of raw materials in Latin America, Africa and Asia. Rising prices increased export profits and the accumulation of hard currency by countries like Argentina and Uruguay. In some cases, industrial development was triggered by the need to substitute imports.

Japanese exports, especially textiles, rose sharply on all Asian and Indian Ocean market, replacing British products even in East Africa. At the end of the conflict, Japan's foreign trade had trebled in comparison with 1913.

Table 10.1. Inter-allied public debt at armistice (millions of dollars)

Debtors	Creditors			
	United States	Great Britain	France	Total
Great Britain	3696	–	–	3789
France	1970	1683	–	3653
Russia	188	2472	955	3614
Italy	1031	1855	75	2961
Belgium	172	434	535	1141
Others	21	570	672	1264
	7077	7014	2238	16423

Source: G. Hardach, *Der Erste Weltkrieg 1914-1918*, cit.

Table 10.2. State finances 1914-1918

		1914	1915	1916	1917	1918	1914-1918
Germany (billion marks)	income	8.8	25.8	27.8	52.2	44.4	159.0
	expensese	2.5	1.8	2.1	8.0	7.4	21.8
	deficit	6.3	24.0	25.7	44.2	37.0	137.2
France (billion francs)	income	10.4	22.1	36.8	44.7	56.6	170.6
	expenses	4.2	4.1	4.9	6.2	6.8	26.2
	deficit	6.2	18.0	31.9	38.5	49.9	144.5
Great Britain (million pounds)	income	560	1560	2200	2700	2580	9590
	expenses	230	340	570	710	890	2730
	deficit	330	1220	1630	1990	1690	6860
Russia (billion rubles)	income	5.7	11.7	18.1	–	–	35.5
	expenses	2.9	2.8	4.0	–	–	9.7
	deficit	2.8	8.9	14.1	–	–	25.8
United States (billion dollars)	income	–	–	0.7	2.1	13.8	16.6
	expenses	–	–	0.7	1.1	4.2	6.0
	deficit	–	–	0	1.0	9.6	10.0

Source: G. Hardach, *Der Erste Weltkrieg 1914-1918*, cit.

Table 10.3. World production and trade by geographical area (1913-1924, %)

	Share of world production mondiale		Share of world trade	
	1913	1923	1913	1925
Europe	43	34	59	50
North America	26	32	14	18
Asia	20	21	12	16
Latin America	7	8	8	9
Africa	2	3	4	4
Australia	2	2	3	3
	100	100	100	100

Source: G. Hardach, *Der Erste Weltkrieg 1914-1918*, cit.

Bibliography

Audoin-Rouzeau S., Becker J.J. (eds.), *Encyclopédie de la Grande Guerre 1914-1918*, Paris, 2004.

Clark C., *The Sleepwalkers. How Europe went to War in 1914*, London, 2012.

Ferguson N., *The Pity of War: Explaining World War One*, London, 1999.

Frieden J.A., *Global Capitalism. Its Fall and Rise in the Twentieth Century*, New York, 2007.

Fussel P., *The Great War and Modern Memory*, Oxford, 1975.

Hardach G., *Der Erste Weltkrieg*, Munich, 1973.

Keegan J., *The First World War*, New York, 1998.

Leed E.J., *No Man's Land. Combat & Identity in World War I*, Cambridge, UK, 1979.

Winter J., *Sites of Memory, Sites of Mourning. The Great War in European Cultural History*, Cambridge, UK, 1995.

Chapter 11
THE POST-WAR YEARS: THE AGE OF INSECURITY

SUMMARY: 11.1. The difficult return to the international monetary system. – 11.2. German hyperinflation. – 11.3. Economic expansion in the 1920s. – 11.4. The Soviet Union. – Bibliography.

11.1. The difficult return to the international monetary system

Some countries experienced a phase of growth in 1919. The United States, Great Britain, France and Japan experienced the biggest boom as demand started to grow again after the end of the war and the capital accumulated during the conflict began to circulate. However, the following year brought recession. Factories reduced their output and unemployment rose, aggravated by the numbers of demobbed troops returning onto the labour market. The decline was accentuated as inflation and the constant depreciation of the exchange rate led many countries to implement austerity policies. During the short-lived phase of expansion it was mistakenly thought that the conversion of the war economy to a peace economy would be relatively quick and straightforward. Political and financial circles concluded that the world economy could be restored to equilibrium by returning as quickly as possible to the *gold standard*.

The gold standard had not actually created pre-war stability, but rather the opposite: it had functioned so excellently due to the economic and social conditions of *la belle époque*. Sterling had been the currency used for international payments, but Great Britain had now lost its financial supremacy to the United States and its currency was in difficulty. The correlation between British investments and foreign trade no longer supported the equilibrium that had disintegrated during the Great War, Russia was isolated, and Germany war reparations to pay. Only the USA would be able to support the system. Social and political conditions had also changed radically. The working class had acquired greater bargaining power in all countries, and this usually reduced possibilities of influencing flexibility and the cost of labour.

Political competition was radicalized by the extension of voting rights, the increased consensus enjoyed by social democrats, and the birth of European communist parties. Governments were often heterogeneous coalitions favouring employment and economic expansion, as in France, Germany, and Italy before fascism. The system lost credibility because there was no longer any certainty about as to the currency readjustments which had restored balance in the past, almost automatically. International financial operators were no longer as sure as they had been in the past that governments would respond to currency devaluation by raising interest rates and introducing austerity policies. After the removal of inter-state control mechanisms and the restrictions on movement of capital introduced at the start of the war, the fluctuations in exchange rates increased speculation and worsened inflation, especially in countries with weaker currencies.

There were two possible ways to restore convertibility to gold: either a simple return to pre-war parity or a realignment to the new conditions. The countries returning most rapidly to convertibility were those like Germany (together with Austria, Hungary and Poland), whose own monetary systems had been destroyed.

Most countries had returned to the *gold standard* by 1927. Where inflation had been very high, convertibility was restored without implementing any real reforms, by simply devaluing the currency and reducing parity with gold to align with the economic changes occurring after the conflict (Belgium, France and Italy). States where prices had risen less dramatically actually returned to the same pre-war values (Sweden, Netherlands, Switzerland and Great Britain). The countries most emblematic of the two different approaches to return were Great Britain and France. The former returned to the *gold standard* in 1925 and adopted pre-war parity because the Conservative government (with Winston Churchill as Chancellor of the Exchequer) aimed to restore London's former position as the world's financial capital. The Federal Reserve (the US central bank) supported this manoeuvre and reduced its own interest rates to favour the movement of capital towards London. The British government adopted a rigid policy to restrict public spending, while the Bank of England increased the interest rate, reducing credit. The economy went into recession: investments fell and unemployment rose. Exports collapsed because the sterling was overvalued and the crisis created severe problems for the coal industry, forced to compete with German and Polish mines. Mine owners cut wages and increased working hours. Stanley Baldwin's government hoped that miners would accept the conditions for the good of the country, but negotiations broke down and the Trade Unions proclaimed a General Strike in support of the miners on 2nd May 1926. This was Britain's most massive strike so far and divided the country, but essentially failed to achieve its aims. The

Unions were forced to call off the strike after ten days, and in 1927 the Conservative government introduced a series of measures limiting the right to strike. The return to pre-war parity meant that the sterling was overvalued, which damaged the export industries and working classes, although it benefitted the financial institutions in the City and rent-seekers, the traditional electorate of the Conservatives, because their foreign credits appreciated.

France was quite a different case; its northern regions had been devastated in the war and it had contracted enormous debts with Great Britain and the United States. French illusions about paying for reconstruction with German reparations vanished after the occupation of the Ruhr.[1] France used its central bank and state bonds to finance its post-war efforts, thus increasing inflation but stimulating investments in industry, which modernised and became competitive on the foreign markets. The *franc* was drastically devalued in comparison with its pre-war value. French politics was torn between the left-wing favouring a heavy property tax, and the right-wing favouring an increase in indirect taxation. Political fragmentation and the proportional electoral system made parliamentary majorities unstable and conflictual; governments were short-lived. Depreciation of the exchange rate discouraged French governments from implementing the austerity policies that would create stability. Finally, Raymond Poincaré returned as head of the government in 1926, and also took control of the Ministry of Finance. He put an end to all projects involving a wealth tax, reduced public spending and raised indirect taxes. This meant that capital secretly exported abroad now returned to France, and the *franc* stabilised. The experience of these years led France to accept a return to gold convertibility at a level compatible with the changes due to the war. French currency returned to the *gold standard* at just 1/5 of its value in 1913. The low value of the franc stimulated exports. Together with the international operators' expectations of a revaluation of the franc, this encouraged the entry of capital. According to the model belonging to pre-war theory, the automatic adjustment mechanisms should have restored balance, but this no longer happened. Great Britain's weak currency and constantly negative balance of payments meant that both gold and currency left the country, whereas France had a strong currency and a constantly positive balance. The movements of trade and capital were no longer able to restore balance in the international financial system. The Bank of France could prevent appreciation of the franc only by using tools that restricted freedom to oper-

---

[1] In 1923, France and Belgium occupied the Ruhr area in reaction to Germany's failure to make war reparation payments.

ate on the market. Otherwise, it would never have managed to accumulate such an enormous quantity of gold in its reserves, which actually doubled between 1926 and 1929. Another evident anomaly, compared with the pre-war situation, was that gold mainly entered the United States and France, so that the two countries came to possess approximately 60% of the world's gold reserves between them.

A new element of the system's fragility was gold's limited availability worldwide. The response to the shortage was the *gold exchange standard*, i.e. the possibility of holding short-term credits in currencies like the dollar and sterling as reserves.

This was, however, a further element of weakness because it jeopardized the most vulnerable link in the system, Great Britain, with its negative balance of payments, small gold reserves and the greatest financial liabilities. There was a danger that France might sell off its reserves of foreign currency to convert them to gold. In 1927, the *Banque de France* wanted the Bank of England to convert 20% of the British currency it had accumulated into gold, but the British refused on the grounds that this would make it difficult to maintain sterling's parity with gold, and the French considerably reduced the scale of their demand.

The most serious problem was the almost total lack of cooperation between the governments and central banks of the various countries, which gave priority to national interests. The other states were generally forced to keep interest rates high, restricting credit in order to preserve their own gold reserves. The United States possessed the world's most substantial gold reserves (45% of the total in 1926) and should have exported capital abroad to ensure the fluidity of the international payments system, but did this intermittently and only until 1927. Although the volume of US investments towards the rest of the world was equal to around 2/3 of the total, these were unevenly distributed, and since the majority were short-term ventures, their overall effect was destabilizing. In 1919-1920, the volume of US investment was substantial and mostly directed towards Europe, but it contracted immediately after the end of post-war recovery until 1923; then there was a period of growth until 1926, followed by another abrupt interruption; the final period of consistent recovery occurred in 1927 and 1928. The disinvestment of US capital after the 1929 Wall Street Crash plunged the entire system into crisis.

In the second half of the 1920s, the debtor states survived only because of the entry of new short-term capital. The creditors were partly responsible for their vulnerability because they had failed to exercise control over the use of loans and had then suddenly interrupted them, making it materially impossible for their debtors to honour their obligations. The system's collapse was inevitable when US investments stopped. The lack of cooperation between the major powers prevented the correct alignment of the international monetary system, and currency policies directed towards ensuring convertibility and safeguarding gold reserves contributed to deflation.

11.2. German hyperinflation

At the end of the war, the German mark was worth just a tenth of its pre-war value, and in early 1922 it fell even further, to a value of around 0.02%. In 1923 it collapsed completely, becoming practically worthless. The crisis was accelerated by the French and Belgian occupation of the Ruhr, despite the disapproval of Great Britain and the United States.

In the midst of this economic turmoil (a communist uprising was attempted in Hamburg), the Weimar government paid for the passive resistance of the workers by printing banknotes to pay wages and salaries for workers and office staff. Inflation spiralled out of control. When the crisis peaked with Adolf Hitler's attempted *coup* in November 1923, the German government took steps to stabilize the currency.

It introduced a new currency, the *Rentenmark*, the value of which was guaranteed by an international loan secured by real assets: land, buildings and factories. The new currency issue was limited to 2,400 billion marks. The initial objective was to restore public confidence. The German government also undertook to introduce more rigorous fiscal legislation. The situation improved in 1924 with the Dawes Plan,[2] which recognized that Germany would never be able to pay its debts unless enabled to do so. Annual reparation payments were reduced and Germany was given more time to pay. A substantial international loan was granted to the German government, which in turn promised to introduce more severe restrictions on public spending. Germany returned to the gold standard. Its new currency was known as the *Reichsmark* and had the same value as the previous *Goldmark*. The economic situation improved as the political climate in Europe relaxed. In 1925, Germany signed the Treaty of Locarno, which also provided the opportunity to improve relations with France. Aristide Briand and Gustav Stresemann headed their respective delegations at the conference, receiving the Nobel Peace Prize for their commitment to creating peaceful relations between the two countries. In 1926, Germany was admitted to the League of Nations.

---

[2] Charles G. Dawes, politican and head of the Commission reviewing German reparations German, United States vice-president from 1925 to 1929 and Nobel Peace Prize winner in 1925.

Historians have attempted to explain the origins of German hyperinflation. In the absence of a shared interpretation, the doubt remains that the German political authorities – whatever their political allegiance (social democrats, Catholics and liberals) – had no alternatives, since they were trapped by reparations, the economic crisis, and the eversive actions of the radical movements on the Right and Left. Evaluation of the effect this has had on modern Germany is equally complex, compared with the obvious and immediate downward mobility of the classes with fixed incomes (especially office workers and pensioners, while trade unions were able to obtain pay rises for factory workers to compensate the erosion of their real salaries). As Wolfgang Schivelbusch has written,[3] some German historians have stressed that the population perceived military collapse in the autumn of 1918 and the total disintegration of the mark in 1923 as a single "shock defeat": hyperinflation aggravated the trauma even more than defeat on the battlefields. The short-lived economic euphoria of 1920-1921 (the depreciation of the mark increased exports) gave Germans the illusion that they had escaped from war-time poverty, similar in some ways to the enthusiasm following the Russian defeat and the great Western offensive in spring 1918. Public expectations of success were fanned by the military in the first case and by politicians in the second. On both occasions, however, German citizens were devastated when their illusions were shattered. Hyperinflation came as another devastating blow to German society, a dizzying feeling that everything was spiralling out of control and that previous stability was completely and utterly lost. An entire generation would lose all its moral sense, ready a few years later to abandon any kind of rational attitude and embrace the myths launched by Adolf Hitler if this would ensure a national revival. Hyperinflation therefore generated widespread nihilism and facilitated mass consensus for Nazism (National Socialism) in every social class and across the generations, along with enthusiastic support (or at least silent indifference) for its anti-Semitism.

Following the Second World War, the new democratic Germany was aware of the moral disgregation into which hyperinflation had plunged the country during the Weimar period. The German Federal Republic was proclaimed on 23rd May 1949, and Article 88 of its constitution defined it as a priority of the Bundesbank to guarantee stable prices; the same principle was also fully embraced by the new European Central Bank.

---

[3] W. Schivelbusch, *Die Kultur der Niederlage*, Berlin, 2001, p. 253.

Figure 11.1. German children playing with devalued marks

11.3. Economic expansion in the 1920s

After the 1921 recession, world industrial output recovered and overtook pre-war levels in 1925, but some significant differences existed between Europe and the rest of the world. Some countries made outstanding progress, like the United States, Japan and the British Dominions, while Central and Eastern Europe returned to the pre-war levels more slowly. European states saw their share of international trade contract: before the Great War, US imports accounted for 50% of the total, but its share had risen to a third in the first half of the 1920s. From 1925 until 1928, expansion was robust and involved Europe more, although the process was not homogeneous everywhere. Industrial output increased by 20% and primary sector output by 10%.[4] Technological innovations contributed greatly to increasing output, despite reductions in working hours due to union pressure and to greater government concern for the living conditions of the workforce.

The industries driving growth were those of the Second Industrial Revolution, especially electricity and the car industry, which stimulated production in other sectors (fuels, metals, chemicals, rubber, electrical components, leather, road building). The chemical industry was another sector in

---

[4] D.H. Aldcroft, *From Versailles to Wall Street*, Princeton 1981, p. 127.

rapid development (artificial fibres, fertilizers, tyres, pharmaceuticals). Vertically-integrated multi-functional companies grew in size and were organized in specific divisions; they became multinational, creating branches and building new plants abroad in order to avoid customs barriers and keep their products' final costs low. They also developed marketing techniques and devised advertising campaigns to launch new products.

There were increasing numbers of bicycles and sewing machines. Electricity made it possible to sell goods that became widespread during the 1920s, including radios, gramophones and telephones (plus washing machines and fridges in the USA). Radio sets became popular due to the creation of public broadcasting companies like the BBC and CBS. Totalitarian regimes used radio as a fundamental means of spreading propaganda to the masses. In Italy, for example, the Fascist regime created the *Ente italiano per le audizioni radiofoniche* (Italian Radio Company), which was granted the broadcasting monopoly. In order to ensure that families had a radio, the regime agreed with a consortium of producers on the manufacture of the simple and inexpensive *Radio Balilla*, which could be paid for in instalments through Fascist institutions like the Party or its recreational associations.

Reduced working hours and growing urbanization contributed to the emergence of new lifestyles and new leisure pursuits; the modern *entertainment* industry appeared. Cinemas sprang up everywhere, and Europeans tried to imitate the big Hollywood film companies with their colossal film studios and cinema chains. European governments encouraged the concentration of activity (UFA in Germany and *Svensk Filmindustri* in Sweden) in order to contrast the US film industry's overwhelming effect on trade and culture. Record companies also formed during this period, like RCA in the United States and Pathé in France. The publishing industry grew, diversifying production and selecting authors according to genre (novels, adventure, travel, detective stories, history). National and local newspapers increased their circulation, helped by cheaper paper and the higher output achieved with the new printing presses, and also increased their earnings through the sale of advertising space, like the magazines with their photographic services. Radio made big sporting events like the world boxing championships into mass events; the volume of betting also made sports like horse racing commercially important. More people took holidays by the sea or in the mountains, driving the tourism industry and development at tourist destinations. The growth of foreign travel and cruises brought hard currency into the most popular countries and led to the use of prepaid financial tools like *travellers cheques*. Some US telephone companies experimented with a metal card allowing their customers to differ payment for services, the forerunner of the modern credit card. Charles Lindbergh's pioneering 1927 trans-atlantic flight paved the way for intercontinental plane flights.

Unlike the United States, and despite growth in the most innovative industrial sectors, unemployment in Europe's more traditional industries (textiles, coal mining, steel and shipyards) continued to be higher than before the war. This was due to the growth in output capacity generated by the war and by the industrialization of other continents. Difficulties in agriculture also prevented employment growth. After the boom during the war and immediate post-war years, prices gradually fell. The primary sector (land and mining) was the main source of income for almost all countries of the world, and their economies were almost exclusively based on exports to the industrialised countries. The demand for raw materials drove production, but also increased the risks of excessive dependence on an export trade based mostly on a single product. With food prices already falling, there was the danger of an abrupt contraction in the demand for products required by industry (such as cotton, palm oil or rubber) and minerals; this would cause a sharp contraction in national income, leading to a fall in consumption and reduced capacity to import manufactured goods from developed countries. Falling agricultural prices and contracting farm incomes generated conditions of uncertainty and instability in the global economy, just like the flow of short-term capital. Historians tend to claim that the fall in prices was due to the weak growth of demand rather than to an excess of supply.[5] Uneven income distribution impeded more extensive growth of consumption. Even the increase in *per capita* income disguised a growing divide between financial and company profits and those generated by labour. The statistics support this theory. The most important US companies increased their profits by over 40% between 1925 and 1928, while salaries increased by less than 5%. In most European countries, as in Britain, policies directed towards restoring the gold standard used the leverage of reducing labour costs.

After 1925, while Europe slowly recovered from the losses it had suffered during the war, the United States experienced an unprecedented boom. Between 1920 and 1928, its GDP grew by 43% and real national income increased by 3.4% per year between 1923 and 1929, industrial production increased by 45% between 1922 and 1929, and productivity rose by 5.3% per year between 1919 and 1929.

US exports increased rapidly between 1923 and 1928, financed by the flow of capital invested in the rest of the world, and the balance of trade

---

[5] D.H. Aldcroft, *From Versailles to Wall Street*, cit., pp. 220-230.

was consistently positive. Growth was spectacular, driven especially by the car industry, electricity and real estate. The US achieved "interconnected development", with about ten years during which entrepreneurs' positive expectations were regularly fulfilled without any abrupt downturns in the economic cycle. This fueled the illusion of having created a self-propelling model, due to the enormous potential of capital and resources. Nevertheless, as President Calvin Coolidge proclaimed in his last official address, "the main source of these unexampled blessings lies in the integrity and character of the American people".[6]

Most importantly, the building industry also boomed as it worked to meet the growing demand for urban accommodation, although it was also driven by speculation. For example, the Florida land boom saw land values soar in 1925 and then plummet in the next year. Capital was constantly drained from the primary sector towards industry and financial activities. The boom was driven by the exceptional growth of producer goods and consumer durables. Modern consumer society developed in the United States much earlier than in Western Europe, where it took hold only after the Second World War. The war stimulated innovations and the manufacture of new products for civilian use. Costs fell progressively due to economies of scale and increased productivity, and also to the spread of large-scale retail distribution, allowing companies to increase their profits without raising their prices. Company growth and the increasing complexity of management problems encouraged the separation of ownership and management. The expansion of the middle class, rising salaries and the spread of consumer credit, which made it possible to pay for purchases in instalments, guaranteed such large sales volumes that company investments were amply repaid, and a considerable share of profits could be used for research and development. DuPont, for example, became the world's leading producer of artificial fibres like rayon, a completely new product that could replace natural fibres. The electricity industry grew extremely rapidly, doubling energy production between 1923 and 1929. Big companies like General Electric[7] diversified their activities, which ranged from radio sets to locomotives, from household appliances like toasters, hotplates and fridges to industrial plants, and from lightbulbs to telecommunications. Radio sets (400,000 in 1922 and 8 million in 1928) and household appliances spread rapidly and earlier in the US than elsewhere, helping to modify the lifestyles of millions of American families. The electric fridge is em-

---

[6] J.K. Galbraith, *The Great Crash 1929*, New York, 1954, p. 1.

[7] J.A. Frieden, *Global Capitalism. Its Fall and Rise in the Twentieth Century*, New York, 2007, pp. 160-165.

blematic. The first fridges were extremely expensive at $900, which was double the price of a Model T Ford, but by the end of the 1920s prices had fallen to just a third, so that a fridge was now cheaper than the new Ford Model A. While film was still seen as more of an art form in Europe, the big Hollywood production companies (Metro-Goldwyn-Mayer, Paramount, RKO, 20th Century Fox and Warner) exploited economies of scale by making several films at the same in their giant studios. They employed dozens of screenwriters and directors (many were European) to create stories designed for different types of audience, and kept the most famous actors and actresses under exclusive contract to ensure the loyalty of their fans, constructing myths and fame around the famous *star system*. However, the most typical and representative sector was the car industry, which from now on was to become a critical factor in the modern industrial economies of the 20th century. By the end of the 1920s, there were 26 million cars on the road (almost one for every five inhabitants), and around half of these were paid for in instalments. The car industry provided incentives to many other sectors: steel, petroleum, tyres, electricity, mechanical engineering, leather and textiles. It accelerated the mobility of the population, offering total independence and much greater flexibility than the traditional means of transport, and stimulated the development of new lifestyles. The spread of mechanized vehicles mobilized the resources for the construction of an extensive motorway network and elegant new suburbs for the middle class, consolidating growth in the building industry. The car industry was also fundamentally important in improving the management and organizational networks of the big modern corporations. Concentration and vertical integration processes were accelerated by the need to overcome inefficiencies and delays caused by suppliers, and also by the need to reduce waste and internal transaction costs between the various internal divisions. Henry Ford pioneered this approach, but General Motors under Alfred P. Sloan rapidly took the lead, introducing innovations in management, organization, finance, marketing, and research and development. The company's diversified production included various brands, like Buick, Cadillac, Chevrolet, Oldsmobile and Pontiac, which differed in prestige, performance and price, and were aimed at the needs, tastes and wallets of different kinds of target customer.

Innovative industries like the car industry paid higher salaries than the traditional industries, and attitudes towards the trade unions were less hostile, because companies needed a stable and reliant workforce.[8] On the

---

[8] The mental and physical reliability of workers on the production line had to be totally controlled. After his medical degree, Louis-Ferdinand Céline visited the Ford fac-

other hand, the increased productivity achieved every year made increased labour costs marginal, so that they did not lead to increased production costs or reduced profit margins. As Werner Sombart had already written in 1906, after a trip to the United States,[9] the standards of working class housing and services in the USA were much better than in Europe, more similar to those enjoyed by Europe's lower middle class.

The US economy slowed down at the start of 1929. The market was saturated, and the pronounced income divide in US society prevented a further rise in consumption. The agricultural sector was afflicted by falling incomes and high debts. Only the stock market seemed to follow its own course, although there were signs in late 1928 and early 1929 which seemed to indicate that the bubble was about to burst. The economy contracted drastically at the end of 1929, and the stock exchange effectively collapsed. The factors that had sustained growth for so long were now in decline, ending the illusion of "a new era of permanent prosperity" and the presumption of the *American way of life* – at least for a time.

11.4. The Soviet Union

The Russian Civil War ended in 1920 with the evacuation of Baron Pyotr Vrangel's White troops from their last stronghold in Crimea, and the last resistance in the Ukraine was crushed in 1921. The Union of Soviet Socialist Republics was proclaimed on 30th December 1922. The economic situation was tragic, since "War Communism" had destroyed an economy already crippled by the Great War. In 1921, Russian industrial production stood at just 12% of the pre-war level, while iron and pig iron ouput had dropped to 2.5% of pre-war levels.[10] The centralized State Planning Committe (Gosplan) created in 1920 proved ineffective, while the nationalisation of businesses was mostly incomplete and did not, in any case, improve the situation. The state was unable to manage or control the manufacturing industries. Many companies continued to operate independently, facing shortages of raw materials and worn-out machinery, and attempted to sell

---

tories in Detroit as part of a League of Nations mission to study occupational safety and health. He used this experience in a chapter of *Voyage au bout de la nuit*, where he painted a grotesque picture of the alienation and total de-personalisation of car workers on the assembly line. L.F. Céline, *Voyage au bout de la nuit*, Paris, 1932.

[9] W. Sombart, *Warum gibt es in den Vereinigten Staaten keinen Sozialismus?* Tübingen, 1906.

[10] N. Werth, *Histoire de l'Union soviétique. De l'Empire russe a la Communauté des Etats indépendants 1900-1991*, Paris, 1992 (it. translation: *Storia dell'Unione Sovietica. Dall'Impero russo alla Comunità degli stati indipendenti 1900-1991*, Bologna, 1993, p. 190).

their products directly on the black market. This meant that the central administration had the monopoly of trade, but actually possessed very few goods that could have been bartered for agricultural products. The rouble was worthless, and the circulation of money had dissolved.

The Red Army's violent requisitions of peasant property discouraged the rural population from cultivating the land, and provoked hundreds of revolts in country areas. Agricultural production fell to less than half of pre-war levels, while the percentage of produce marketed was now only 8% of the 1913 total. Land expropriation and the sub-division of the es-tates belonging to the tsar and the great landowners, egalitarianism im-posed by rural communes, the breakdown of communications and inter-ruption of the normal trading circuits combined to make the USSR revert to the natural economy. Only state requisitions ensured basic supplies for citizens, and around two million people migrated from towns and cities to the country between 1917 and 1921. In 1921, a terrible famine in the Low-er Volga region aggravated a situation that was already desperate. Despite international aid, around 1.5 million died, adding to the losses caused by war and epidemics.

As early as spring 1920, a Peasant Congress convened in Tambov and recruited a militia to fight the Bolsheviks and liberate the region. The in-surrection was crushed by one of the Red Army's most brilliant officers, Mikhail Nikolaevich Tukhachevsky. However, the most tragic revolt, which caused the Soviet government to change its economic policy, was led by the soldiers and sailors of the of Kronstadt naval base on Kotlin Island opposite Petrograd, in March 1920. These were the same troops who had been at the forefront of the Soviet revolutionary forces in 1917. The rebels constituted a Provisional Committee that immediately de-manded freedom of expression, new elections, fairer and more generous food rations, the end of armed requisitioning, and the possibility to oper-ate independently for artisans and peasants who did not employ salaried workers. Repression was brutal: thousands of rebels were killed and the survivors were deported to concentration camps (*gulag*) controlled by the political police (*Cheka*).

Nonetheless, the uprisings accelerated a review of the requisition poli-cy, convincing even Lenin of the need for a radical change. The New Economic Policy (NEP) adopted at the 10th Congress of the Russian Communist Party in spring 1921 partially restored the market economy. Payment in kind replaced the obligation to consign almost all produce to the state; domestic trade was liberalized and peasants were allowed to sell their surplus produce on the market; small businesses was permitted, and those with fewer than twenty employees were privatized in exchange for giving the state a share of total output (10-15%). Mixed companies were formed with the participation of foreign capital; workers could change workplace, and technicians enjoyed greater prestige. The NEP marked a return, albeit partial, to capitalism. Nikolai Ivanovich Bucharin, the Bolshevik party's most brilliant theoretician, realigned the economic policy decisions taken in 1921 to the fundamental principles of marxism, maintaining that they signaled a transition towards the agrarian revolution, an essential pre-condition for industrialization, and therefore of the proletarian uprising and future socialist society. This justification was also accepted by Lenin, who talked of an "alliance of workers and peasants". The aim was to set up a virtuous cycle between agriculture and industry. The growth of agricultural production would ensure food supplies for towns and cities, together with a surplus for export. This would then accumulate currency, which could be used to buy technology and accumulate capital to drive the recovery of the big companies that would produce goods for the domestic market: machinery, tools and chemicals for the primary sector.

The NEP was actually designed as a sort of truce after the terrible suffering caused by the Civil War: the aim was to attract those middle-class technicians who had not emigrated and to increase public consensus towards the government and party.

Although the NEP effectively represented a brief truce offered by the communist regime, and constituted a short-lived *liaison* between intellectuals and political authorities, its more ambitious economic objectives were not achieved. In 1927, industrial output was worth around 18% more than in 1913, and primary sector production was about 10% higher. However, agricultural output figures were inflated by the increase in industrial crops. Cereal production was still less than before the war, hampered by the liquidation of the large estates and excessive fragmentation of peasant plots. In 1926, the amount of cereals effectively marketed was lower than in 1913. Aside from systematically falsified official statistics, cereal production in the Soviet Union never actually reached the levels of the tsarist era. Low state-imposed prices obstructed food supplies to the cities, as did the fact that industry produced goods that the peasants either did not want, or else could not afford to buy. In addition, the NEP limited investments in some strategic sectors like infrastructures and arms. However, when the USSR signed the Treaty of Rapallo in 1922, it also made a secret agreement with Germany, which allowed the new arms banned by the peace treaty to be tested on Russian territory, and the USSR also enjoyed some of the technological benefits. Aside from the ideological divergences and discussions within the party, the NEP was totally incompatible with the war economy model that was typical of totalitarian regimes: rigid centralized planning and a definite bias towards investments in heavy industry and armaments rather than towards mass consumer goods.

Lenin, who was already ill in 1922, hoped for gradual progress marked by the collaboration between working class and peasantry set out in the NEP, advancing without any unforeseen rifts towards the construction of socialist society.

His death in January 1924 was followed by a succession battle, with Stalin firstly supporting Bucharin's defence of the NEP against Trotsky, who advocated launching a rapid process of industrialization and subtracting resources from agriculture to invest in the secondary sector.

In 1928, after finally gaining control of the Party, Stalin criticized the inadequacy of the NEP and proclaimed the need to plan the stages of economic development for the USSR, thus launching agricultural collectivization and imposing industrialization.

Figure 11.2. Poster celebrating achievement of the objectives of the first five-year plan in four years

Table 11.1. Distribution of world income and population by region (1860, 1913, 1929 %)

	1860		1913		1929	
	income	population	income	population	income	population
North America	14.8	0.1	32.9	6.3	38.3	7.4
Oceania	0.5	3.1	1.4	0.4	1.3	0.4
North-west Europe	29.3	11.1	27.6	11.5	24.0	10.7
Soviet Union	7.2	6.7	7.3	8.7	6.6	8.4
South-east Europe	9.8	7.9	8.5	8.2	8.4	8.9
Latin America	3.8	3.4	4.0	5.0	4.7	6.0
Japan	1.4	2.9	1.5	3.3	2.1	3.5
Far East	1.4	2.4	1.9	3.8	2.0	4.4
Southwest Asia	11.8	22.3	6.9	20.3	6.0	19.9
China	20.0	40.1	8.0	32.5	6.6	30.4
Total	100.0	100.0	100.0	100.0	100.0	100.0

Source: D.H. Aldcroft, *From Versailles to Wall Street 1919-1929*, cit., p. 304.

Bibliography

Aldcroft D.H., *From Versailles to Wall Street 1919-1929*, Berkeley, 1971.

Eichengreen B., *Golden Fetters. The Gold Standard and the Great Depression 1919-1939*, Oxford, 1992.

Eichengreen B., *Globalizing Capital. A History of the International Monetary System*, Princeton, 1996.

Frieden J.A., *Global Capitalism. Its Fall and Rise in the Twentieth Century*, New York, 2007.

Graziosi A., *L'Urss di Lenin e Stalin. Storia dell'Unione Sovietica 1914-1945*, Bologna, 2007.

Kindleberger C.P., *A Financial History of Western Europe*, London, 1984.

Schulze H., *Weimar. Deutschland 1918-1933*, Berlin, 1982.

Zaslavsky V., *Storia del sistema sovietico. L'ascesa, la stabilità, il crollo*, Rome, 1998.

Chapter 12
THE CRISIS OF CAPITALISM

12.1. The Wall Street Crash

The Wall Street Crash caused the world recession, but although the crash marked the start of an economic crisis, it was not actually the most important cause. It firstly affected the financial system; brokers unable to pay their debts to the banks went bankrupt. The value of shares given as collateral plummeted, undermining the stability of the banks, which then reduced the volume of credit granted to their own customers in order to strengthen reserves. While prices plunged and took company profits with them, loan instalments remained unchanged, thus worsening the conditions of debtors. The first bank failures in 1930 triggered a massive run on the banks, which further aggravated the situation of their assets. To ensure survival, the banks stopped supplying money to business. The financial crisis rapidly reverberated across the real economy, producing a downward spiral of deflation (reduction of the money supply, collapse of demand and prices), also because the monetary authorities and government refrained from intervention. Industry entered a phase of depression. Overproduction then led to a drop in the value of goods, stock and investments. Bankruptcies rose and growing numbers of jobs were lost. As unemployment grew and consumption plunged, demand fell even further, thus completing the cycle of recession. Furthermore, maintenance of the gold standard imposed a restrictive monetary policy, aggravating the liquidity crisis.

The US stock exchange had already suffered two strong contractions in December 1928 and March 1929, and when a fresh crisis broke out in October, there were hopes that it was just a beneficial deflation of the bubble. While the Dow Jones (the share index indicating the New York Stock Exchange trend based on share values of the 30 most important companies) at the time was not exceptionally high in comparison with peaks registered in the second half of the 20th century, the system's fragility lay in the weaknesses of the credit sector, which should have supported it. The banking system was unhealthy. Unlike Europe, many small US banks were not under the control of the Federal Reserve; operating with their own meagre resources, they had a limited range of action and inadequate management. On the other hand, the stock exchange system leapt forward, driven by three factors: a) the speculative actions of some big operators; b) easy credit policies; c) new money management systems, like *investment trusts,* a British innovation of the late 19th century. US citizens bought the shares of an investment company, which then used the capital to speculate on the stock exchange. In this way, even small savers could use the services of a professional operator with a share portfolio of several hundred companies, who could therefore diversify the risk much better than a single company. A hundred of these trusts formed in the US towards the end of the 1920s. Financial promoters were initially bound by strict regulations to operate transparently, but caution was cast aside as the market spiralled rapidly upwards. This meant that savers acquired the trust's shares and essentially gave it *carte blanche* to operate on their behalf. This entailed a high risk, especially when it is considered that these shares often came without any voting rights. Investment trust shares were admitted to trading only in 1929, but the New York Stock Exchange obliged them to provide information and act transparently and so the trusts preferred to be listed on the stock exchanges of minor cities to avoid advertising their management practices. Their justification was that this avoided triggering a rush to acquire the shares they had selected, and they promised to provide information in the future.

Many *investment trusts* generated others, thus multiplying their shares. The same brokers lent to their own customers or created new companies. The illusion of a healthy economy was fed only by the extraordinary vitality of the stock exchange and share values were not correlated with a company's ability to make profits. Sales were driven by the fact that it was enough to deposit a percentage and leave the shares as collateral. Nobody would keep the shares in any case, because everybody wanted shares just in order to sell them again.

The Federal Reserve knew of the speculative bubble from 1928, and was aware that it ought to be reduced. However, no action was taken because there was a risk of incurring the hostility of the market or influencing the imminent presidential elections. When prices eventually collapsed, euphoria gave way to panic. The Wall Street Crash entered its most dramatic phase on 10th October, culminating on 13th November when the Dow Jones registered a loss of 43% in a single month. This was followed by a reaction, but it was impossible to recover more than 50% of the autumn's losses. Then came another fall, which reached its lowest point in summer 1932. The great economic depression was now in full swing, and the stock exchange would climb back to the minimum 1929 level only at the beginning of the 1950s. Liquidity dried up and the course of events changed radically. The collapse of share prices deprived the banks of their margins on assets under warranty, and debtors preferred to lose their deposit rather than pay the sum agreed. The stock exchange crisis spread to the credit market, which began to shrink; prices plummeted and debt deflation began, since the reduced value of collateral increases the level of debt because the run on liquidity by private citizens and companies leads to the progressive collapse of share values, with the consequent depreciation of assets ceded to support loan payments. The recession spread to the real economy, causing investments, employment and consumption to collapse. The recovery market during Calvin Coolidge's presidency had been extraordinary, and so was its collapse. Speculation requires a feeling of security and widespread optimism; "blind faith" in the institutions is an essential condition for a boom.[1] There must also be an abundant accumulation of capital because it is fed by loans, and savers are more likely to risk investing a share of their savings when savings are higher. Speculation is usually triggered by prosperity, and not after a depression. Some economists, like Milton Friedman, have emphasized the mistakes made by the Federal Reserve in tackling monetary policy before and after the bubble burst.[2]

Figure 12.1. New York share prices (1926-1938, according to the Standard Statistics index, 1926 = 100)

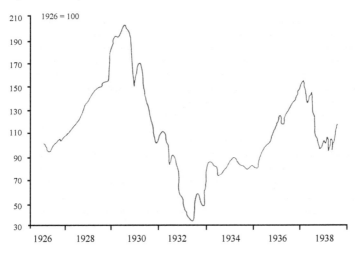

---

[1] J.K. Galbraith, *The Great Crash 1929*, cit.

[2] M. Friedman, A.J. Schwarz, *A Monetary History of United States 1867-1960*, Princeton, 1963 and M. Friedman, A.J. Schwarz, *The Great Contraction (1929-1933)*, Princeton, 1965.

12.2. The Depression

The withdrawal of capital from the New York stock exchange by foreign investors, minor US credit institutions and companies created gigantic losses for single investors. Everyone stopped using their capital. The companies using the stock exchange to trade shares and bonds plunged into a frenetic rush to liquidity, trying to end their exposure and reduce costs. The property sector saw increasing insolvencies and repossessions, depreciating the value of land and houses. The industrial production index declined rapidly. The car industry suffered a sharp downturn, although it was mostly the small companies that shut down or were absorbed by the giants. Ford was the hardest hit of the big car companies, while General Motors reacted by concentrating on public transport vehicles and diversifying into aviation and diesel engines for locomotives, increasing the profitability of its foreign subsidiaries. Opel acted similarly in Germany and benefitted from supplying the Nazi regime. Prices and imports plummeted. Agricultural produce was so devalued that it was no longer profitable to grow or harvest crops. In the Midwest states, many farmers left their wheat in the fields because sale prices did not cover production costs. Livestock farmers slaughtered their herds because they could no longer feed them. Farmers were increasingly indebted, and many lost their farms because they were no longer able to meet their loan payments.

Foreign exports contracted by over 20%, damaging the economies of other countries, especially those whose exports mostly consisted of just one raw material or agricultural product. Coffee was the most visible example; the price collapsed and demolished the economy of Brazil, where it was used to fuel steam locomotives in a bid to stop the price falling. Deflation increased rapidly in two stages: the first was from the collapse of the stock exchange to contraction of manufacturing and the consequent reduction of stocks; the second was from the fall in share prices to the fall in the prices of goods and in the value of imports.

The correlation between the stock exchange and the real economy was partially of a psycologic nature[3] and partly caused by the abrupt contraction of credit when banks and businesses competed to achieve the maximum level of liquidity. World trade was swept into a spiral of contraction, diminishing by almost 70% between 1929 and 1933. In 1930, the US Senate passed the Smoot-Hawley Tariff Act imposing customs duties on imports. This immediately triggered a series of tit-for-tat measures by other countries, thus aggravating the collapse of international trade. Even Great

---

[3] J.K. Galbraith, *The Great Crash 1929*, cit.

Britain abandoned its traditional free trade stance and adopted a preferential tariff for its dominions and colonies. The hyperprotectionist policy of the United States closed its domestic market to the rest of the world, generating a backlash from the other nations. Countries producing raw materials and agricultural products saw their own exports drop sharply, and then reduced their imports from industrialized states. Consequently, US foreign trade contracted rapidly. There was a global downturn in trade, income and consumption. The United States continued to demand payment of war debts, at the same time refusing to act as a last resort credit provider, while the Smoot-Hawley Act made it more difficult for debtors to make repayments. When Great Britain and 25 other countries came off the gold standard in 1931, followed by the United States in 1933, the international economic system disintegrated.

Those countries belonging to the "gold bloc" (including France, Belgium, the Netherlands, Switzerland, Poland and Italy) remained on the gold standard, but they tackled the fall in exports by raising import duties, implementing strict controls over currency exchange and the movement of capital to prevent gold from leaving the country. Protectionism marked the decline of world trade and ushered in a new phase of mutual relations regulated by bilateral *clearing* agreements, which compensated imports and exports to ensure that currency did not leave the country. The onset of depression after the Wall Street Crash was accelerated by internal contradictions in the United States, and by the fragility of the international relations reconstructed after the Great War. Imbalances were already evident in 1928 during Herbert Hoover's presidential campaign, when he promised to end poverty. US farmers were badly hit by the collapse of world demand for their agricultural products; prices and land values fell, but the farmers' level of debt increased.

In the 1920s, cars symbolized growth. Henry Ford brought production and consumption together in a virtuous cycle. However, despite Ford and the sales mechanism of payment in instalments, millions of people were excluded from prosperity. The gap between offer and demand gradually expanded on the domestic market, while international trade was restricted by the new protectionist tariffs, and remained vital only as long as the United States was able to ensure a constant flow of loans. The world economic system was inevitably oriented towards instability, unless one great world power could implement policies to consolidate its mechanisms. Great Britain had done this until 1913 but was now unable to, while the United States simply refused. The US should have opened up the market, started a series "of long-term anti-cyclical loans" and supported the credit system "during the crisis". The lack of a global "lender of last resort" meant the overall impact of the world depression.[4] Many observers believed they were witnessing the end of capitalism. Interviewed in 1932 by writer and journalist Emil Ludwig, Benito Mussolini answered a question about the world economic situation by stating that he considered it not as a crisis "in the system", but rather "as a crisis of the capitalist system".[5] Mussolini confided an even more damning judgement to Yvon De Begnac, a young fascist biographer of *il Duce*, when he proclaimed that "liberalism is dying, capitalism is in its death throes".[6] His evaluations were reinforced by the the US government's incapacity to relaunch the economy. In contrast, Russia's first five-year plan launched by Stalin was a complete success, enabling the industrialisation of the Soviet Union. This made an extremely positive impression on many US intellectuals, including the New York Times Moscow correspondent, Walter Duranty, who made no attempt to hide his admiration in articles informing the US public about the enormous progress made by the Russian economy, defining it as "stroke of genius".[7]

The most pressing problem was unemployment, given the lack of state support. In spring 1931 over ten million were jobless, but only 20% had access to any form of aid. Almost 30 million US citizens had no income. Two million were vagrants , mostly young people riding illegally on goods trains in search of occasional jobs to allow them to survive. A quarter of all schoolchildren were malnourished, although the percentage was much higher in the more depressed areas. Average salaries fell by a fifth compared with 1929 levels. Millions of US citizens fled famine and emigrated to the country areas. On the other hand, thousands of Midwest farmers lost their farms to the banks and then emigrated towards California in search of a better future. This situation inspired John Steinbeck's 1939 novel, *The Grapes of Wrath*,[8] which rapidly became a best seller.

Herbert Hoover never wavered in his attitude to paying unemployment benefit. As a *self-made man*, he viewed *self-government* and individual responsibility as the kingpins of US culture and society. The President had no desire to establish an organized welfare system. He was patron of the President's Organization for Unemployment Relief, but the organization had no state funding and was revealed to be propaganda exercise.[9] Even Al Capone funded a soup kitchen for Chicago's homeless. According to Hoo-

---

[4] C.P. Kindleberger, *The World in Depression 1919-1939*, Berkeley, 1973.

[5] *Mussolinis Gespräche mit Emil Ludwig*, Berlin, 1932.

[6] Y. De Begnac, *Taccuini mussoliniani*, Bologna, 1990, p. 532.

[7] P. Brendon, *The Dark Valley. A Panorama of the 1930s*, London, 2000.

[8] J. Steinbeck, *The Grapes of Wrath*, New York, 1939.

[9] P. Brendon, *The Dark Valley*, cit.

ver, the "depression" was psychological. Aid for the unemployed and their families was left to the actions of private charitable bodies or local administrations, which did not have the resources needed to deal with extreme poverty.

Franklin D. Roosevelt, the governor of New York state, was initially opposed to state welfare benefits, but the scale of poverty led him to increase taxation on the highest incomes and create a committee to tackle the emergency. However, with no help from federal government, local administrations could not continue helping the poor without risking bankruptcy. The most effective intervention was by Huey Long, populist leader of Louisiana, who multiplied the state's debt and pressurized the most important banks to finance those in most difficulty in order to prevent their failure.

The situation worsened: at the start of 1933, over 12 million were unemployed, while industrial production and farming incomes halved and the value of exports fell by 70%. The liquidity crisis was aggravated as worried citizens withdrew their money from the banks to avoid losing their saving, and stockpiled supplies in their homes. Four hundred banks failed in the months immediately preceding Roosevelt's entry to the White House (the final total was over 5,000).

In January 1932, Hoover tried to increase the availability of credit by creating the Reconstruction Finance Corporation and giving it a federal fund of two million dollars to help the biggest banks. However, this intervention was too limited to turn the situation around, and the more solid banks refused credit to the more fragile banks or to businesses.

The President did not believe that the state should take strong steps to revive the national economy. He swore by the virtuous behaviour of the market and did not consider it possible to increase national wealth by wasting public money. Nevertheless, even Herbert Hoover made certain attempts to contrast deflation. He encouraged agricultural cooperatives, in order to give farmers some sort of control over prices; the Federal Reserve reduced the bank rate from 6 to 5% and bought up state bonds. However, the banks with money did not use it to expand credit, because they needed to re-balance their own crisis-hit budgets and did not trust their customers. Hoover announced tax cuts and asked companies to limit lay-offs. Subsequently, he attempted to limit government expenditure by demanding a balanced budget. The result was that federal spending could not be increased to support purchases of goods and services, while re-balancing the budget would have implied increasing taxes, or else reducing expenditure, or choosing both options, thus further depressing the economy. The other factor that aggravated deflation was loyalty adherence to the gold standard. The aim of balancing the budget was driven by fear of inflation and the desire to maintain and defend a solid currency for national prestige. For this reason, no measures were taken to arrest deflation or to reduce unemployment for two years.

It was only in 1931 that Hoover tried to react to the crisis, alarmed by the scale of the depression in Central Europe. He took the unilateral decision to grant a moratorium on the debts of European countries, including Germany's war reparations; in 1930, the Young Plan had already offered Germany easier terms for paying its debts by creating the Bank for International Settlements. Hoover also provided funds for banks and work began to build the Golden Gate Bridge across San Francisco Bay. Nonetheless, confidence did not return.

In 1931, the Empire State Building was inaugurated in New York City, but the construction company was able to rent out only 20% of the total and was losing a million dollars a year on it by 1934.

The police dealt summarily with protests and strikes, arresting and beating union activists and agitators, and industrialists formed their own private armies to protect their factories. One of the most violent episodes occurred in Washington DC, just a few yards from seat of government. In summer 1932, a crowd of 20,000 unemployed Great War veterans arrived in the capital to demand early payment of their insurance, which was not due until 1945. They set up camp on the edge of the city, refusing to leave unless the government met their demands.

The recession was a harsh blow to Germany. The failure of a great Viennese bank, the Credit Anstalt, had a domino effect in 1931. Withdrawal of foreign capital and the contraction of its exports proved fatal for the German economy. The situation was aggravated by the nature of the banking sector; it was based on the universal banks with their close links to industrial companies, which were therefore more exposed to the risks created by a liquidity crisis. Hundreds of businesses failed, and in July the government attempted to stop savers withdrawing their money by closing the banks. To save the banks in difficulty, the state took over their shares and became owner of 60% of the sector. Chancellor Heinrich Bruning enjoyed the trust of President Hindenburg and governed by issuing a series of decrees, supported also by Article 48 of the Weimar constitution, which gave the government full power in an emergency. He persevered with deflationary policies up to the end of his mandate (March 1930-May 1932), aiming to maintain a balanced budget and control inflation by reducing public spending and salaries, to reduce the value of Germany's foreign debt in relation to the currencies of its creditors. Bruning was convinced that the Allies would eventually cancel reparation payments; in 1930, Germany's debts amounted to 24,000 million gold marks, but the Reichsbank had just 5,000 in its reserves. In any case, Bruning's reasoning followed the prevalent economic ideas of the time, and he was convinced that deflation would relaunch the economy. In his memoirs, he insisted that his decisions had been correct, accusing the political parties of ousting him as head of the government just before he was able to achieve his objective.[10] In actual fact, foreign prices fell more rapidly than domestic prices, exports collapsed, and the Chancellor tightened his deflationary policies in the attempt to reduce the balance of payments deficit and Germany's foreign debt. This meant that the money shrank by over 40% in just two years, leading to the same fall in incomes and industrial production.

Consequently, unemployment rates soared and by 1932 over 6 million were jobless.

Bruning was a technocrat, totally unable to perceive the seriousness of the crisis or understand the looming political disaster. It was as if he were operating in a vacuum, while German streets were the scene of conflicts between groups of communists and national socialists, and the traditional parties lost credibility by supporting his government in the Reichstag. The increasing failures of banks and businesses and growing unemployment correlated with the exponential growth of the consensus enjoyed by the National Socialist movement (NSADP), which rapidly became Germany's leading party. In the 1928 elections, the Nazi Party obtained only 2.6% of votes and 12 seats in the Reichstag, but in the first elections after the crisis, in September 1930, they obtained 18.3% and 107 seats, while in July 1932 they obtained 37.8% and 230 seats in parliament to become Germany's leading party. Only one other anti-establishment party – the Communist Party (KPD) – succeeded in increasing its share of the vote, although not as spectacularly, coming third in November 1932 (when the Nazi Party lost ground for the first time), just behind the Social Democrats. The two anti-democratic movements (KPD and NSADP) together obtained 50% of the vote and held over half the seats in the Reichstag (292 out of 584).

Economic insecurity and unemployment rocked democratic systems everywhere. In 1930, 2.5 million lost their jobs in Great Britain, and in 1931 Ramsay MacDonald headed a National Government similar to the wartime coalition, made up of Conservatives, Liberals and Labour MPs who had left their own parties. The British Union of Fascists (BUF) was founded in 1932 by Oswald Mosley, a former Conservative and then Labour MP, in open imitation of Italian fascism. At the start of 1933, French industrial production had fallen sharply compared with 1929, while exports dropped by 64% between 1930 and 1935 due to revaluation of the franc.

---

[10] H. Bruning, *Memoiren 1918-1934*, Stuttgart, 1970.

The agricultural sector still employed a third of the population and was hard hit by the drop in prices. The numbers of jobless were actually quite low compared with other countries (500,000 at the start of 1935), because around one million North African and foreign workers had to leave the country, but France was weakened by political instability and financial scandals. On 6th February 1934 thousands of protesters belonging to extreme right-wing movements, like *Action Française*, gathered in Place de la Concorde to storm the National Assembly as it met to approve a new government. At the same time, communists and unemployed militants gathered to attack the parliament. The clashes between police and demonstrators were extremely violent. Paris had not witnessed such a dramatic day since the Commune of 1870.

The crisis of capitalism seemed irreversible. In 1933, it was decided to organize a great meeting of all nations in an attempt to rebuild the international economy. The world conference opened in London on 12th June 1933, but all efforts to achieve any form of cooperation were shattered from the outset by the US decision to come off the *gold standard* and devalue the dollar to boost prices on the domestic market without any international agreement about the fluctuating exchange rate. As Roosevelt proclaimed, the United States had the right to give priority to its own national interests. Charles Kindleberger reports the reaction of Ramsay MacDonald: the British Prime Minister objected that Europe had no desire to interfere with the domestic US policies but that it would have been useful to seek a solution which avoided a chaotic situation in Europe generated by the American success.[11] From this moment, each country sought its own way out of the depression, independently of the others.

12.3. The Keynesian revolution

Traditional economic doctrine proved incapable of explaining the crisis, and application of orthodox remedies generated the global depression. In 1929, the law formulated by French economist Jean-Baptiste Say at the start of the 19th century (also known as the "law of markets") was still considered a valid part of economic theory. Say claimed that offer always creates its own demand in a free trade system, so that the production of goods generates an aggregate demand of equal dimension, given that salaries and profits are used to buy what is produced. If people saved, prices would drop and people would then start buying again; "the invisible hand" of the market would restore balance.

---

[11] C.P. Kindleberger, *The World in Depression*, cit., p. 202.

Nonetheless, John Maynard Keynes tried to understand and interpret the new situation. His theories were decisive because they offered remedies for restarting the economy. According to Keynes, rational behaviour in conditions of uncertainty makes consumers express a choice about the occurrence of an event – about which they possess limited information – and they must therefore reason in terms of probability and/or trust. In this way, he showed that there could actually be a lack of demand for which there were no automatic adjustment mechanisms; consequently, corrective intervention was necessary.[12]

The demise of Say's Law imposed a new order of importance for economic issues: value and distribution (i.e. the formation of the price and distribution of wealth) lost importance when faced with the problem of demand and the extent to which banks and governments were obliged to act to bolster purchasing power. This marked the birth of the macroeconomy and attention to aggregated data (aggregate supply and aggregate demand for consumption and investments). Keynes reversed cause and effect: it is demand that determines offer, and not *vice versa*. Investment decisions depend on the expectations of profit; in a situation of great uncertainty, expectations may shift from optimism to pessimism, causing a sudden dramatic collapse of investments. Keynes aimed to contest mainstream economics, which held that in the long term the invisible hand of the market would ensure equilibrium and full use of all factors of production on condition that there prices and salaries were suitably flexible. This was a strong conviction of the British Treasury and Bank of England, but an opinion which Keynes had already tried to demolish in 1925.

There was however the problem that the long term could be politically intolerable for democracies, as shown by the development of the various dictatorships after the crisis. Moreover, Keynes aimed to propose measures compatible with economic freedom.

Totalitarian states made ample use of *deficit spending*, but Keynes' approach highlighted the desire to create economic mechanisms that would allow recovery without compromising democracy or capitalism.

Keynes was long considered a radical in the United States, and his ideas were consequently rejected by the economic and financial community. Many, including Roosevelt, held that his suggestions about an anti-cyclical effect of public spending were a rationalization of the unavoidable.[13]

---

[12] J.M. Keynes, *The General Theory of Employment, Interest and Money*, London, 1936.

[13] J.K. Galbraith. *Economics in Perspective*, Boston, 1987.

Table 12.1. Variations in industrial production and GDP (1929-1938, %)

Country	1929-32		1932/33-1937/38		1929-1937/38	
	Ind. prod.	GDP	Ind. prod.	GDP	Ind. prod.	GDP
Austria	− 34.3	− 22.5	53.8	18.6	1.0	− 4.8
Belgium	− 27.1	− 7.1	42.3	9.8	3.7	2.0
Denmark	− 5.6	4.0	47.1	15.1	38.9	19.7
Finland	− 20.0	− 5.9	96.2	48.7	56.9	39.9
France	− 25.6	− 11.0	20.0	7.9	− 11.8	− 4.0
Germany	− 40.8	− 15.7	122.2	67.5	31.6	41.1
Italy	− 22.7	− 6.1	48.5	20.8	14.8	13.5
Luxemburg	− 32.0	n.a.	40.2	n.a.	4.7	n.a.
Netherlands	− 9.8	− 8.2	35.1	12.2	22.0	3.1
Norway	− 7.9	− 0.9	40.8	29.2	29.9	28.0
Spain	− 11.6	− 8.0	3.0	9.0	− 13.1	0.4
Sweden	− 11.8	− 8.9	72.4	38.3	53.8	26.0
United Kingdom	− 11.4	− 5.8	52.9	25.7	35.4	18.4
Bulgaria	n.a.	26.8	n.a.	17.7	n.a.	49.2
Czechoslovakia	− 26.5	− 18.2	51.5	20.3	− 3.9	− 1.6
Hungary	− 19.2	11.5	58.7	24.5	29.9	10.2
Poland	− 37.0	n.a.	86.2	n.a.	17.4	n.a.
Romania	− 11.8	n.a.	49.3	n.a.	31.6	n.a.
Yugoslavia	n.a.	−11.9	n.d.	28.0	n.a.	12.8
USSR	66.7	6.9	164.7	59.3	311.1	70.2
USA	− 44.7	− 28.0	86.8	46.6	3.3	5.6

Bibliography

Chancellor E., *Devil Take the Hindmost. A History of Financial Speculation*, London, 1999.

Eichengreen B., *Golden Fetters. The Gold Standard and the Great Depression 1919-1939*, Oxford, 1992.

Evans R.J., *The Coming of the Third Reich*, London, 2003.

Frieden J.A., *Global Capitalism. Its Fall and Rise in the Twentieth Century*, New York, 2007.

Friedman M., Schwarz A.J., *The Great Contraction (1929-1933)*, Princeton, 1965.

Galbraith J.K., *The Great Crash 1929*, London, 1955.

Ingham G., *Capitalism*, Cambridge, UK, 2008.

Chapter 13
STATE INTERVENTION

SUMMARY: 13.1. The New Deal. – 13.2. Germany. – 13.3. Italy. – 13.4. The Soviet Union. – Bibliography.

13.1. The New Deal

The financial crash of 1929 ended an exceptional period of prosperity, and the consequences were not only social and economic, but also political, cultural and psychological. The *American Way of Life* was threatened. While many feared authoritarianism and the end of democracy, this crisis created the conditions for the implementation of radical reforms.

In November 1932, the Democrat candidate Franklin Delano Roosevelt won the US presidential elections and took on the task of reviving the country. His election victory was overwhelming. During his campaign, he promised a new approach but never actually specified what this meant. He had no ideological line to follow, but took a completely pragmatic approach, also due to the worsening of conditions between his election and entry to the White House, as hundreds of banks failed. His task was not just to revitalize the economy but also to revive the morale of the US people, which he did by speaking to them regularly on the radio from the start of his presidency.

The principal novelties of Roosevelt's early presidency were 1) the "Brain Trust" of university professors and financial experts, whose "strategic line" was directed at acting effectively and rapidly; 2) the collection of an impressive quantity of data to form an empirical basis for intervention; 3) the determination to depart from mainstream approaches.

The new administration produced an unprecedented amout of new legislation in its first 100 days of government. The New Deal can be seen in two stages: economic policy from 1933 to 1935, and more attention to social policies from 1935 to 1938.

The first objective was to inject liquidity into the economic system, which was essential, since little money was in circulation and Americans were forced to use foreign coins, stamps and so on. Roosevelt declared a Bank Holiday, closing all US banks for several days, a measure he had actually opposed during Herbert Hoover's presidency. This made it possible to evaluate the solvency of the banks, as the state would aid only those that passed inspection. The financially sound banks were given liquidity and re-admitted onto the market, while the others were closed down permanently. At the same time, Congress took only four hours to pass the Emergency Banking Act giving full financial powers to the president.

Roosevelt also used the Reconstruction Finance Corporation created by the previous administration to purchase bank shares and bonds. This body would later provide support for businesses and local administrations. The most important regulatory measure adopted in relation to the banking system was the 1933 Glass-Steagall Banking Act separating commercial banks from investment banks; the former were to provide only short-term credit, while the latter were to specialize in medium- to long-term credit and stock exchange operations. The Act also prevented the banks from holding, placing, selling or buying shares in private companies; a Senate commission had found that certain banks had sold weak shares to savers, using profits to pay off company debts. The Act also introduced an obligatory guarantee on deposits, with federal insurance for sums up to $2,500.

The Securities Exchange Act of 1934 was directed towards greater transparency against speculation, and prevented insider trading and manipulation of the securities market.

The Securities and Exchange Commission (SEC) was set up at the same time to oversee the activity of the stock exchange. It had the task of evaluating all new stock applying to be listed on the New York Stock Exchange. Although its evaluations were not initially binding, it effectively deterred fraudulent operations and companies that did not have sufficient real guarantees from the market. Subsequently, the commission obtained the right to control and also liquidate holdings that did not respect the new legislation.

Naturally, Roosevelt believed that US economic recovery also required suspension of the gold standard and devaluation of the dollar to boost domestic prices and exports. The USA came off the gold standard in spring 1933. Gold was withdrawn from the market, exports were banned, and owners of gold bullion were obliged to sell to the Federal Reserve at a fixed price. Up to $3,000 million of currency went into circulation unsupported by gold reserves, while silver coins were issued for up to 25% of the total. This last measure was intended to stimulate the recovery of silver mining in the western USA, but it also led to a rise in silver prices, and this created problems for countries like Mexico and China, whose monetary systems were based on silver. Their circulating currency shrank as a result of the price rise caused by the US policy, while the US dollar lost around half of its value in less than a year.

The two most ambitious projects of the Roosevelt presidency were the Agricultural Adjustement Act (AAA) and the National Industrial Recovery Act (NIRA). State intervention in agriculture had two objectives: to artificially bolster internal prices and to detach them from current world market prices. The government also supported exports at prices lower than production costs. Subsidies were given to farmers who reduced the amount of land they worked, and high tariffs protected the US market. Although the Agricultural Adjustment Act was strongly criticized because it led to a contraction of around 25% of cotton output and involved the slaughter of six million pigs, it was generally successful in achieving its objectives.

The NIRA aimed to regulate prices and industrial production, guarantee pay levels for workers, set a limit on working hours, and ensure trade union rights. Its most ambitious objective was to eliminate competition and launch the growth of investments and consumption. Nonetheless, the project proved unpopular with factory owners, trade unions and consumers alike. Factory owners rejected the limitations it imposed on their business activities, and unions and consumers suffered as a result of artificially triggered price rises. No significant growth in production or employment occurred where the NIRA was applied.

Roosevelt's administration also launched a massive series of public works. The most famous of these involved the creation of the Tennessee Valley Authority (TVA) in 1933. The project aimed to transform an economically depressed area by improving land use and providing needed infrastructures, like a series of dams along the Tennessee River to produce cheap energy (at a fixed price) for industrial development. Roosevelt saw this as a way of bringing progress to a rural population that had remained largely excluded from the benefits of economic growth. The public works were organized by federal agencies, of which the most famous was the Public Works Administration (PWA), and provided employment to around a third of the jobless. The programme also included the construction of roads and other civilian infrastructures, such as bridges, airports and public buildings.

In 1935 and 1936, the Supreme Court ruled that the NIRA and AAA were unconstitutional in that they limited economic freedom. The NRA was abandoned, while the AAA was modified so that it could achieve the same objectives while avoiding the risk of further sanctions from the Supreme Court.

The New Deal lends itself to ambiguous interpretations. There is no doubt that Roosevelt's administration revived the spirit of the nation and inverted the decline of its economy. He was the 20th century's most popular president, with the same legendary stature as Washington and Lincoln, and was re-elected in 1936, 1940 and 1944 before the two-mandate limit was introduced after the war. Nevertheless, the economic results of the New Deal did not live up to expectations. In 1937, when public spending was reduced in order to limit the federal budget deficit, a new recession began, and prices in 1939 were still below 1929 levels.

The US economy recovered its vitality only with the Second World War.

The New Deal's most significant legacy was taken up by Western countries after the Second World War; it had shown that state regulation and democracy were compatible (although Republicans considered Roosevelt a dictator and the New Deal as totalitarianism).

The New Deal created a third way, an alternative to competitive capitalism and the communist and fascist systems of centralized economic control. The State took a leading role in stimulating aggregate demand, intervened with income support measures, and abandoned the dogma of a balanced budget in favour of *deficit spending.* Public spending was the system regulator, and the State discovered how to use an expansionary monetary policy to stabilize the economy and achieve full employment.

Figure 13.1. President Roosevelt and the New Deal

13.2. Germany

The November 1932 elections returned Germany's National Socialists (NSDAP) as the country's strongest party (33%), although its consensus actually contracted for the first time (– 4%). When General Kurt von Schleicher was asked by President Hindenburg to form a government, he attempted to provoke a rift in the NSDAP by including Gregor Strasser, the head of its anticapitalist faction. Schleicher seems also to have been conspiring with Ernst Röhm, head of the *Sturmabteilungen* (SA), who contested the support Hitler received from industrialists. However, Schleicher's attempts failed and Adolf Hitler became Chancellor on 30th January 1933. The situation evolved rapidly. Following the burning of the *Reichstag* building, the Communist Party was banned. Elections held on 5th March were a victory for the National Socialists, who obtained 43.9% of the votes. At the end of March, the parliament passed the Enabling Act that made Hitler a dictator to all effects. The Chancellor became the *Führer* of the German nation.[1]

Political parties and trade unions were rapidly suppressed, together with all political rights and freedom of expression. On 30th June 1934 Hitler purged the National Socialist movement of its revolutionary elements, eliminating both Röhm and Strasser.

The regime's priority was employment. As Hitler announced via radio on 1st February 1933, the government would act "with steely determination and the most tenacious perseverance" to rescue German peasants from poverty and eliminate unemployment "within four years".[2] This was to be achieved with a Four-Year Plan involving a massive increase in State investments, paying little attention to the growing public debt. The regime designed a vast series of public works, giving more importance to ideology than to economics.

Hundreds of thousands of workers belonging to the *Deutsche Arbeitsfront* (German Labour Front) built motorways, airports, public buildings and military installations, and were employed in reclamation programmes. Companies were helped, especially in the car industry, and the renovation of private homes was encouraged. The Nazi organization *Kraft durch Freude* (Strength through Joy) provided leisure activities and holidays for workers and their families.

---

[1] Jurist Carl Schmitt justified the juridical validity of the measure by presenting it as an evident case of his theory of "state of exception". Another German intellectual, philosopher Martin Heidegger, initially welcomed the rise of Hitler.

[2] H.U. Thamer, *Verführung und Gewalt. Deutschland 1933-1945*, Berlin, 1986.

Thousands of the jobless enrolled in the *Schutzstaffeln* (SS) and SA. The need for manpower was increased by limiting the use of machinery in public works projects. By 1934, the National Socialist government had spent almost five billion Reichsmarks on job creation. One effective economic and ideological instrument was the "marriage loans" to couples who were about to marry. The only condition was that the bride should leave her work immediately, demonstrating Hitler's traditionalist ideas of woman's role in the family.

In 1933 200,000 more weddings took place than in 1932 and almost 400,000 loans had been granted at the end of 1934.

The campaign to reduce unemployment was supported by the institution of National Labour Service (compulsory from 1935) and by military conscription after Germany's rejection of the Treaty of Versailles. The policy achieved a success unrivalled elsewhere in the world; by 1936 unemployment had been drastically reduced and there were actually manpower shortages.

Naturally, the ultimate aim of the Third Reich's economic policy was German rearmament with a view to launching another war, but in its early years the military budget increased less than spending on job creation and rebuilding national confidence. However, the second Four-Year Plan (1936) directed by Hermann Göring gave more importance to preparations for war than to civilian infrastructures, and the percentage of the national budget assigned to the *Wehrmacht* gradually increased from 4% in 1933 to 50% in 1938.

The Plan encouraged industrial concentration to increase the efficiency of the manufacturing system, and investments were directed towards mining, the chemical industry, producer goods manufacturers, and the arms industry. Considerable efforts were made to increase the degree of autarky, especially involving the raw materials like rubber, fuels and lubricants, wool and cotton that were essential to support the war effort. German companies were encouraged and funded to seek alternatives, and devised some innovative manufacturing processes, such as the synthetic rubber (buna) patented by IG-Farben, and synthetic petrol. But these products were extremely expensive and were never able to satisfy the needs of the armed forces.

Despite all the efforts to increase and improve the output of certain products (cereals, pulses, eggs and fats), agriculture never became completely self-sufficient, and Germany continued to rely on foreign imports, so the regime directed food consumption towards the most plentiful domestic produce (cabbages and potatoes). Only by brutally plundering the countries it occupied (especially in Eastern Europe) was Germany able to feed its soldiers and civilians during the war.

The centralized control exercised by the National Socialist regime did not take over the private sector (unlike the Soviet Union, and to some extent Italy). From 1934, the *Gesetz zur Vorbereitung des organischen Aufbaus der deutschen Wirtschaft* (Law for Organization of the German Economy) organized a system of regional offices to supervise industry.

Their inital task of regulating imports was subsequently delegated to the Reichsbank, which supervised currency controls. Entrepreneurs and workers were brought together in the *Deutsche Arbeitsfront*. Pay and production procedures were regulated by the *Treuhänder der Arbeit* (Labour Trustees), while disputes between capital and labour came under the jurisdiction of specific social courts.

The government managed to direct the big industrial corporations and the banks towards achievement of Hitler's objectives, leaving the structure of private capitalism intact, although harsh conflicts sometimes occurred, as in the case of iron ore. Hitler established that imports from Sweden would gradually be reduced and replaced with German products, regardless of quality or of the production costs involved.

The iron and steel industry contested this decision, because it was unwilling to pay for the operation supported by Hjalmar Schacht, Reichsbank governor and Minister of the Economy from 1934. However, Hitler gave precedence to organization of the war economy over any considerations of profitability or unprofitability regarding State projects, stating that economic problems were first and foremost problems of "willpower?"[3] The establishment of the Salzgitter "Hermann Göring" state steelworks demonstrated the regime's intention to control the steel industry. The company was given priority in the assignment of manpower and raw materials, together with considerable amounts of hard currency to buy machinery in the USA.

Volkswagen was founded in 1937 to produce the low cost family car Ferdinand Porsche designed to Hitler's orders. The new model was intended as Germany's equivalent of the Ford Model T in the USA.

During the war, Heinrich Himmler's idea of creating an industrial empire under the SS culminated in the IG-Farben synthetic rubber factory attached to the Auschwitz death camp.

The regime's investment programme required an exceptional financial outlay. In 1938 only about 60% of public spending (30 billion Reichsmarks) was compensated by fiscal revenues. The cost of rearmament could be met only by increasing the size of the public debt, but military spending had to be concealed from foreign powers. The regime resorted to domestic debt, but not only for currency reasons. One of the most important tools

---

[3] H.U. Thamer, *Il terzo Reich*, cit., p. 604.

used was the MEFO (Metallurgical Research Society) promissory note, the brainchild of Hjalmar Schacht. Four of the most important German companies (Gutehoffnungshütte, Krupp, Rheinmetall and Siemens) contributed to the creation of the *Metallurgische Forschungsgemeischaft* (MEFO). Companies receiving government commissions were paid with MEFO promissory notes; with an interest rate of 4% and discounted by the Reichsbank, these became a real means of payment. The MEFO system enabled the state to prolong its payments indefinitely and in this way to finance rearmament. This operation also concealed military spending, because the promissory notes were commercial and did not figure among State commissions. However, the risk was that of generating high inflation. The regime also used other forms of finance, obliging the banks and the insurance companies to cede their resources to the State. In this way, savings and insurance funds were converted into short-term and long-term State bonds. The conflict between Schacht and Göring, who enjoyed Hitler's suport, was precisely about the sustainability of the debt and the risks of inflation. Military spending was now out of control, but bankers and conservatives failed to understand that the Führer's priorities were to launch a war aimed at acquiring vital space in the East (*Lebensraum*). The cost of the Nazi "war and conquest economy" would be paid by the countries Germany occupied. During the Second World War, this involved systematically plundering their resources and unscrupulously manipulating the exchange rate of the mark against the local currencies. Hitler's voluntaristic vision of policy meant constant fresh starts: only victory would definitively resolve all the Reich's economic problems. In November 1937 Schacht resigned from the government, and in 1939 he was removed from the Reichsbank.

Schacht was equally decisive in modelling the State monopoly of foreign trade. His objective was that Germany should "not purchase more than can be paid for" and buy only "what was actually needed". Imports were essentially limited to what could not be produced in Germany, because it was vital to exercise rigid control over spending in hard currency. Schacht used the clearing houses so that the purchase of raw materials from producer countries was compensated with German exports of the same value. This system based on specific bilateral agreements not only limited the outflow of gold abroad, but also made it possible to pay for imports indirectly and created a market for German goods, giving Germany a strong influence over the producer states. The choice of trading partners was the outcome of a farsighted strategy. These countries in Latin American or Southern Europe needed to export raw materials and agricultural products, thus Germany overcame its own shortages and the producer countries received industrial goods in return. The centre of German trade gradually shifted towards the Balkans, which had the effect of limiting overseas imports and expanding Germany's sphere of political influence over this area.

Paradoxically, Hitler was not in favour of state intervention and centralized planning at all costs. At a private meeting in November 1937 with some military commanders, Göring, and Foreign Minister von Neurath, he firstly stated that Germany's "need for land" made war essential, which should be launched as soon as possible by accelerating the preparations without considering the cost involved. He then told those present that the future would bring "a great improvement in the living conditions of all Western countries", and that progress would be generated by "close integration of the world market, once the Soviet Union had been eliminated".[4] Hitler also proclaimed that the re-armament policy should not be seen as a "feasible basis for long-term economic stability". In February 1940, during a conversation with Goebbels, Hitler expressed severe criticism of ministerialcentralism, blaming Goebbels for the failure of a large number of valid projects. In March 1941, speaking about the arms industry, Hitler praised rivalry between the various companies because it stimulated "competitiveness".[5] In effect, despite preparing for war well in advance, Germany was actually behind the Allies in terms of total mobilization. This was not merely because the Führer wanted to protect the home front from the sacrifices of the Great War and held that women should stay at home in the family rather than work in the factories. The choice of a *Blitzkrieg* (lightning war) strategy resulted in abandoning "deep rearmament" in favour of "broad re-armament". (For example, Germany abandoned development of strategic bombers for its airforce and initially wasted resources on surface shipping, which proved to be completely useless in terms of military objectives, instead of developing submarines).

It was only during the war – thanks at first to Fritz, Todt and then from 1942 to Albert Speer – that the country launched a great effort towards the total mobilization of its resources and manpower. Concentration, rationalization and standardization of manufacturing plants and arms allowed Germany's munitions industry to achieve its maximum output in 1944 despite intense Allied bombing; innovative new weapons were rapidly designed and put into production: V1 and V2 missiles, Messerschmitt Me-262 jet fighter planes, and sub-marines powered by a combination of diesel and electricity.

---

[4] G. Sereny, *Albert Speer. His Battle with the Truth*, London, 1995.

[5] F. Taylor (ed.), *The Goebbels Diaries 1939-1941*, New York, 1982.

13.3. Italy

The Italian economy was on the brink of collapse towards the end of 1932. The universal banks were overburdened by their shareholding in industrial companies and by their loans to help industry deal with the crisis. This took them into a serious liquidity crisis (in comparison with 12 billion *lire* in financial assets, bank deposits and current accounts amounted to only 4.5), just when all economic indices were plummeting. The banks were now in imminent danger of failure, and liquidation of the public's savings. The *Banca d'Italia* itself was unable to deal with the situation adequately. Most corporate credit was impossible to recover and there were no short-term prospects of economic recovery. Only the State could save the banks and Italy's entire industrial system with them. January 1933 saw the creation of the *Istituto per la ricostruzione industriale* (IRI – Institute for Industrial reconstruction). The State gave it the capital required to bail out the banks, but at the same time IRI acquired their shares and industrial holdings, managing them independently, and subsequently disinvesting. The three most important banks were nationalized.

The new Institute was defined as "provisional" and consisted of two sections: the Finance section would evaluate company assets and earnings, liquidating those without concrete possibilities of recovery, or re-launching them when market prospects were more encouraging; the Disinvestment section would provide for privatization after restructuring.

In October 1935, Mussolini decided to attack Ethiopia. The League of Nations imposed sanctions on Italy for an attack against another member state. In March 1936, the *Duce* launched the policy of self-sufficiency with the *"Piano regolatore della economia italiana del prossimo tempo fascista"* (Regulatory Plan for the Italian Economy in the next Fascist Period). This heralded a new phase in which the country would need to expand its "economic autonomy" in order to conduct "an independent foreign policy" Mussolini also hinted at greater State intervention in industry. The most important novelties particularly involved heavy industry. Since the largest joint-stock companies were "capitalistic or super-capitalistic" and therefore represented "an economic and social" problem, those directly or indirectly connected with defence would be organized into *grandi unità* (large units) definined as "key industries", with "special" status "within the State sphere" (this development was facilitated since the regime already controlled most of the arms industry through IRI).[6]

---

[6] B. Mussolini, *Opera Omnia*, edited by E. and D. Susmel, *Dall'inaugurazione della provincia di Littoria alla proclamazione dell'Impero (19 dicembre 1934-9 maggio 1936)*, Vol. XXVII, Florence, 1959, p. 244.

Therefore, the autarky programme originated from awareness that it was inevitable because the entire nation was being prepared for a future war. There were four reasons why autarky was also a political tool for national mobilization: 1) it accelerated exploitation of Italy's domestic and imperial resources; 2) it consolidated the State's economic intervention and control over foreign relations; 3) the general population learned to be frugal, seen by the *Duce* as essential for teaching Italians the Fascist ideal of self-sacrifice for the benefit of the community (from the "Day of the Wedding Rings" to countless campaigns to collect iron and copper); 4) it permanently (apparently, at least) mobilized the entire national community towards the idea of war; Mussolini saw this as the highest calling of the State and its citizens, which exalted the moral and spiritual qualities of single communities.

In this context, it is possible to see that an organized plan gradually took form between 1936 and 1945, whose origins lay in the *Carta del Lavoro* or Labour Charter (the manifesto of Fascist corporativism written in 1927). It consisted of three converging plans to create a new corporative economy of the totalitarian state. The first two were achieved immediately, whereas the third was partly achieved only at the end of the war: 1) centralized planning of resources, investments and production; 2) strategic use of IRI to consolidate heavy industry and increase state control in the vital sectors of the Italian economy; 3) socialization of companies, i.e. the participation of technicians and workers in company management, the distinguishing feature of Fascism's original mixed model, which combined private and state initiative and represented a "third way" in alternative to the capitalist or Soviet systems.

The reform of the banking system, published on 12th March 1936, established the separation of banks and industry, the specialization of banks as providers of short- or of medium- and long-term credit, and finally transformed the Banca d'Italia into the central bank with powers of control. Medium- and long-term credit would be the exclusive prerogative of "special merchant banks" (*istituti di credito speciali*). IRI became a permanent body in June 1937, with a two-fold function: it acted as the fundamental organ of socialization, and also formulated industrial policy.

The experience acquired by IRI and its organization in combining public interest with private efficiency and operating with market principles made it the ideal body to manage the companies that the regime decided to maintain. It became a holding that managed the shares held by the State. It used bank bonds to finance its activities (less of a risk than using shares). In order to provide rational supervision of the companies IRI controlled, sectorial sub-holdings were created (STET, Finmare, Finsider, and Finmeccanica and Fincantieri after the war). In 1939 IRI possessed 44% of Italy's share capital. The State held substantia shares in the steel, electricity, construction, shipping, mining, heavy engineering and arms industries.

The war in Ethiopia revived the Italian economy. Public spending on the military campaign and enhancement of the Empire stimulated recovery in all sectors. Between 1935 and 1939 over 53 billion *lire* (over 10% of GDP in 1936/1937) was spent in Italian East Africa (IEA). Approximately 1/5 of Italian exports were directed towards IEA (24% in 1936), even if this did not mean earnings in hard currency. The regime had previously launched a vast programme of public works, culminating in the land reclamation projects carried out in Italy's Lazio Region. At the same time, it began demographic colonization of Libya and construction of the coastal road. In March 1939, Italy also occupied Albania. In this way, Mussolini conceived the idea of creating a "living space" for Italy in parallel to the German "*Lebensraum*".

Figure 13.2. Self-sufficiency in a poster for La Rinascente

13.4. The Soviet Union

Agricultural collectivization in the *kolchoz* was the pre-condition for forced industrialization. The State intended to seize an important share of agricultural production, partly to feed the working class in urban centres, and partly to export in return for the technology required by the USSR. Also, by finally eliminating the free market encouraged by the NEP, the regime itself formed prices. It kept prices artificially low and obtained the surplus to use for industrial investments, while the peasants were obliged to pay higher prices for tools and manufactured goods. Stalin played constantly on the range of prices and increases in government quotas, forcing the collective farms to perform superhuman efforts to meet State orders. They also had to pay set prices to use machinery provided by machinery stations and tractors supplied by the State. In theory, families had small individual plots to cultivate as they wished, but the regime's continual demands for them to make up the deficit meant that they were actually unable to exploit their own land.

Stalin used the 1927 food crisis as a pretext to start forcing families into the collective farms. The *kulaks* (defined by the Soviet authorities as wealthy agricultural capitalists) were accused of sabotaging the programme and depriving the people of resources. In reality, the myth of the *kulaks* (a difficult class to define) was cunningly created by Stalin in order to have an "objective" enemy to attack and to imtimidate all peasants into spontaneously joining the *kolchoz*. Tens of thousands of Cheka members and party activists in country areas were mobilized against presumed rebels and the hesitant, and used to incite others. The peasants preferred to slaughter their livestock rather than deliver their animals to the State farms, or simply did not sow crops. The Soviet regime blamed the resulting food shortage once more on the *kulaks* to justify their cruel treatment in a campaign of unprecedented violence. Hundreds of thousands of families were deported to the prison camps (*gulags*), and thousands of peasants were slaughtered. Resistance was strongest in Ukraine, the Caucasus and Donbass. Other families had no choice but to enter the *kolchoz*. By spring 1930, about 60% of agricultural land had been collectivized and Stalin re-launched the programme continually. Initially, there should have been 8 million peasants by the end of 1930, but in December of the same year there were already 30 million. The peasants were effectively confined to the farms, because the regime imposed an internal passport for travel, which they were unable to obtain. Managers of the *kolchoz* were frequently dismissed and deported when unable to meet the quotas imposed.

The early 1930s in Ukraine saw a famine that killed millions of people. In 1935 Stalin was able to announce that 98% of the programme had been completed. The first Five-Year Plan was launched in 1928, with extremely ambitious objectives: it estimated that industrial production would grow by 136% and productivity by 110%, correlated with a 35% reduction in costs.[7] Priority was given to the growth of heavy industry, which was supposed to increase from 8% to 16% of GDP. Estimates were comtinually revised and increased. In fact, Stalin himself systematically inflated the figures provided by *Gosplan*. His "determination", according to which all obstacles could be overcome by the force of willpower and by the Soviet spirit, led to anomalies. In the attempt to achieve impossible objectives, companies came into conflict with each other, trying to seize raw materials and capital available over and above the levels set by central planning, because if they did not deliver the predicted results, this would create difficulties for others to achieve their quotas. This was the origin of the short-term emergency management that was a constant feature of Soviet history, involving resources distributed according to the different priorities. In practice, all managers fought hard to obtain recognition that theirs was a "priority project", even resorting to corruption, otherwise they would find themselves accused of sabotage and anti-Soviet activity.

In reality, planning was often replaced by anarchy and improvisation. The first Five-Year Plan was considered complete already in its fourth year. The following Plan was intended to consolidate growth in producer goods, armaments and energy output. Professional courses for workers were increased, and engineering academies for the young communist elites were promoted in order to replace bourgeois technicians.

It is difficult to formulate an unequivocal judgement about the Soviet economy in the 1930s, also because the economic statistics were always systematically manipulated. It is possible to state that the heavy industry, mining and energy sectors developed a great deal, and that the volume of investments was extremely high. On the contrary, however, consumer goods production was systematically neglected. Productivity did not grow as forecast. Forced industrialisation was more intensive than qualitative, and caused enormous waste and irreversible environmental damage in the medium to long terms. Stalin ordered construction of the White Sea-Baltic Sea canal (using political prisoners), which proved to be a perfectly useless undertaking. The lack of capital and technology led to an emphasis on labour, exemplified by the myth the Soviet regime created around the figure of miner Aleksei Grigoryevich Stachanov, and the indiscriminate use of deportees in the concentration camps. Soviet citizens had very few resources available to them (unless they were Party members); they lived with other families in modest homes and in constant terror of arrest by the political police. In those same years, Stalin began a new round of purges, firstly eliminating the old Bolsheviks and then progressively re-

---

[7] N. Werth, *Storia dell'Unione Sovietica*, cit., p. 271.

moving the younger generations of Soviets. In 1937, Red Army commander Mikhail Nikolayevich Tukhachevsky was accused of spying for Germany and executed together with many of the most high-ranking and competent Russian officers.

In the long term, the defects and dysfunctions connected with forced industrialization and the dirigism of the State administration would contribute to the dissolution of the USSR. However, if Soviet planning is evaluated for what it actually was, i.e. the typical war economy of a totalitarian state aiming to increase the country's military capacity to become a great power, there is no doubt that evaluation of the short term effects must be positive. German troops were greatly impressed by the Russian T-34 tank, whose armour was merely scratched by their ammunition and could be penetrated only by 88 mm anti-aircraft shells. In order to win the military contest, Germany had to rapidly design the new Panzer VI Tiger. This was proof that the Soviet steel industry had made huge progress in just a few years.

Table 13.1. Military expenditure during the Second World War (1933-1938, £ million)

Germany	2,868
USSR	2,808
Japan	1,266
United Kingdom Unito	1,200
United States	1,175
France	1,088
Italy	930

Source: A.S. Milward, *Der Zweite Weltkrieg. Krieg, Wirtschaft und Gesellschaft*, cit.

Table 13.2. Increase in real value of military spending (1934-1938, %)

Germany	470
Japan	455
Italy	56
USSR	370
United Kingdom	250
France	41
Czechoslovakia	130
Austria	112
Denmark	115

(follows)

Sweden	98
Netherlands	92
Switzerland	86
Poland	56
Hungary	47
Egypt	280
New Zealand	172
South Africa	140
Australia	123
Argentina	57
Canada	55

Source: A.S. Milward, *Der Zweite Weltkrieg. Krieg, Wirtschaft und Gesellschaft*, cit., p. 48.

Bibliography

Castronovo V. (a cura di), *Storia dell'Iri, 1. Dalle origini al dopoguerra*, Rome-Bari, 2012.

Evans R.J., *The Third Reich in Power*, New York, 2005.

Graziosi A., *L'Urss di Lenin e Stalin. Storia dell'Unione Sovietica 1914-1945*, Bologna, 2007.

Kershaw I., *Hitler. 1889-1936. Hubris*, London, 1998.

Milward A.S., *Der Zweite Weltkrieg. Krieg, Wirtschaft und Gesellschaft 1939-1945*, Munich, 1977.

Picker H., *Tischgespräche im Führerhauptquartier 1941-1942*, Bonn, 1951.

Speer A., *Erinnerungen*, Frankfurt/M-Berlin, 1969.

Zaslavsky V., *Storia del sistema sovietico. L'ascesa, la stabilità, il crollo*, Rome, 1998.

Chapter 14

THE SECOND WORLD WAR: "CREATIVE DESTRUCTION"

SUMMARY: 14.1. Destruction and creation. – 14.2. War and growth. – 14.3. Investments and foreign trade. – 14.4. The sectors in war: agriculture and raw materials. – 14.5. Growth of the arms industry. – 14.6. Planning for combat. – 14.7. War and big science. – Bibliography.

14.1. Destruction and creation

If the First World War was the first real occasion when the new technologies and sectors of the Second Industrial Revolution were available to military forces, the technological transformation of warfare culminated with the Second World War.

The second conflict was truly global, both in the range of destruction and in the geographical area affected; very few areas of the world were spared the direct or indirect effects of war. The countries involved in the conflict emerged with their human and economic resources depleted, although to differing degrees. Once again, the war overturned the political order established after the First World War, removing dictatorships and military regimes, accelerating decolonization, and at the same time creating a new geopolitical situation based on constant confrontation (and under the threat of a potential conflict) between the Western Capitalist bloc and the Eastern Communist bloc (the "Cold War").

For all these reasons, the Second World War marked an undeniable historic break with the past. It was an apocalypse (in real terms for some places like Hiroshima), that reduced the living conditions and life expectancy of many people to the lowest levels, but it also contained some elements of "positive revival". The war brought destruction that would create a new world equilibrium and a new technological and productive model, as the title of this chapter underlines.

Firstly, the war brought a tragic end to the long stagnation caused by the crisis afflicting capitalism from the early 1930s, for which public spending on armaments had proved a powerful antidote. Military spending soared in the years preceding the war, growing by almost 500% in

Germany, 370% in the Soviet Union and 250% in Great Britain (to mention the most evident cases).[1]

The conflict imposed a radical solution, based on the mobilization of an enormous quantity of resources by the states involved, and on the introduction of sophisticated programming and planning policies. The war created full employment, it sustained investments and in some countries it intensified an accumulation of capital goods. Although a large share of this capital was soon destroyed, the knowledge and skills that had sustained its formation were much more difficult to disperse.

Secondly, the industrial nature of the war was the basis for a series of technological opportunities that would radically transform entire sectors in the following decades. The impacts would be wide-ranging, from "micro" effects on companies to "macro" effects on economic systems, directly affecting also the daily lives of ordinary people.

14.2. War and growth

Although it may appear paradoxical, the large-scale destruction of the Second World War coincided with overall expansion of the global economy.

In the first place, the war mobilized extremely vast economic and productive complexes. Including their colonies, the Allied powers could count on a population of over 700 million people, while their respective GDPs amounted to a total of approximately a thousand billion dollars at present prices. The population of the Axis powers – Germany, Italy, Japan and their respective colonies – amounted to around 250 million people, with a total GDP of around $750 billion. This meant that, the economic potential was enormous, even in its destructive potential, considering the size of the population the warring powers could use directly in battle (the Allies deployed around 25.5 million troops and the Axis 17 million at the height of the war), and also the importance of the *assets* involved in the general mobilization. In effect, the war years saw the belligerents' economies working at full capacity, successfully exploiting their own economic potential.

According to some estimates, during the war years total world production increased by about 20%. In a borderline case like that of the USA, its GDP almost doubled and industrial output trebled. Even in the

---

[1] The data on increases in military spending, their impact on the GDP of the various countries, involved in the war and those relative to war damage, are mostly taken from the book by Alan Milward cited in the bibliography for this chapter. The data on per capita GDP are from the statistics published by A. Maddison, *The World Economy. A Millennial Perspective*, Paris, 2003.

case of the other warring nations, growth rates remained strong, falling only in 1945.

Overall, almost everywhere (with the predictable exceptions of Germany and Japan), per capita GDP (at constant prices) recorded in 1950 was greater than in 1938, and the US registered the greatest increase – from a little over $6,000 to $9,500. It should also be noted that plenty of neutral states (like Sweden and Switzerland) or state well outside the war zones (like Australia, South Africa and Canada) increased their industrial output and experienced general improvements in their economic conditions.

However, other countries became impoverished during the course of the war, as they lost their production capacity and resources. Apart from the areas of Western Europe occupied by Germany (Belgium and France – where per capita income in 1945 was half what it had been in 1938 – and the Netherlands), the most dramatic effects were felt in Central and Eastern Europe. Some simple figures convey the extent of the contraction. Between 1938 and the end of the 1940s, *per capita* GDP (at constant prices) in Romania fell from $1200 to less than $900, in Hungary from $2600 to $1700 and in Greece from $2600 to just under $900; Poland, Czechoslovakia and Bulgaria also suffered considerably, although the contraction was less dramatic.

This means that the economic growth generated by the conflict was badly distributed among just a few winning powers (led by the USA), while some countries emerged at roughly their pre-war level but plenty were losers, some in dramatic conditions. In addition to this, the growth in production involved the most scientifically advanced sectors, those subsequently characterizing the world's leading economic (and political) powers.

As to be expected, the resources needed to increase armament production were mobilized at the expense of private consumption. This was because military spending had an increasing incidence on the GDP, and because spending on armaments was financed to a large extent by taxing family incomes. The available data agree in emphasizing the constant rise in military spending during the early 1940s, both in absolute terms and also as a percentage of national revenue, although depression of domestic consumption varied in intensity among the different countries. In 1940, Germany and Great Britain destined over 40% of national revenue to military spending, Japan 22%, the USSR 17% and Italy 12%, while the USA, which participated directly in the war only from 1942, dedicated just 2% of its revenue to its armed forces. In 1943, military spending had risen to 70% in Germany, over 60% in the USSR, 55% in Britain, and over 40% in the USA and Japan, while Italy spent "only" a fifth of its national revenue on its armed forces.

Expansion of the public sector therefore took place via the compression of private consumption (and investments in the private sector). In the final years of the conflict, consumption of consumer durables and non-durables unconnected with the military sector fell; this varied, but was never less than a third of the pre-1939 levels. All governments of states at war introduced measures to control inflation, rationing systems and voluntary limitation of investments and production for private consumption. For example, the data available for Britain show a decline of almost 40% in the clothing production during the war, and a decline of 57% in the output of goods for private consumption.

The increase and the quantity of resources dedicated to "global mobilization" depended on the specific country's intrinsic policy, and on previous industrial policies to sustain heavy industry and the sectors most closely connected with the arms industry. This was evident, for example, in the cases of Germany and Japan, which had both intensified their military spending in the second half of the 1930s and entered the war with over a fifth of their national income already invested in the arms industry. The first two years of the war clearly demonstrated the success of their armament policies, although a series of errors in military strategy (plus the unexpected and underestimated Allied resistance) redressed the initial weight of this advantage, prolonging the conflict and probably changing the final outcome. The USSR benefitted in the same way from the policy Stalin had launched in the early 1930s to sustain heavy industry.

14.3. Investments and foreign trade

The war generally depressed international trade and foreign investments, although the effects differed from one country to another. The overall and undeniable fact is that there was a continuation of the negative trend marking the years of the Great Depression and the isolation caused by the self-sufficiency policies of different countries (Chapter 12). At current prices (and therefore affected by wartime inflation), the volume of foreign trade and investments fell from a total of $3 billion in 1929 to less than $1 billion in 1933 and around $500 million at the end of the war. Some neutral states benefited to a certain degree from the increased demand for imports by the warring states (e.g. over 40% of Sweden's total exports went to Germany), but international trade was affected by the shift from private to public consumption, the reduction in families' purchasing power, and also by the objective increase in the risks associated with transport. The submarine and naval war affected shipping worldwide, from the Atlantic and

North Sea to the Pacific. The data available are unequivocal: hundreds of merchant ships were sunk each year, even those flying neutral colours, and so insurance premiums increased to as much as a quarter of the value of the cargo itself. One exception to this generally negative trend was the US Lend-Lease programme, which began in 1941 and essentially provided food and supplies to the Allied nations, especially those in Europe, in order to help their resistance against the Axis. Before the programme ended in August 1945, the USA transferred goods worth a total of approximately $50 billion (at current prices) to their Allies; two-thirds went just to the UK. Although the beneficiaries paid no interest on the money they owed for goods, which were generally estimated at just 10% of their actual value, the programme was still an important element in the US position as a net creditor when hostilities ended.

Not only did international trade contract, but it also became "regionalized" as it fragmented into geographical blocs. The Anglo-Saxon bloc included the USA and Canada, plus the UK across the Atlantic. The European continental bloc, occupied by the Axis, essentially included the entire continent, except for a few neutral states like Ireland, Spain, Sweden, Portugal and Switzerland. The Soviet bloc was largely autonomous and self-sufficient. The Oriental bloc was headed by Japan, which had extended its control over Chinese Manchuria, and then over Korea.

A limited amount of international trade tended to be conducted within these blocs, although it is not easy to provide reliable estimates. One reason for this is that official statistics include an amount of forced exports, in the form of expropriations and requisitions, which are not always easy to identify and are even more difficult to quantify. According to some data, the occupied territories in Western Europe supplied Germany with a fifth of the coke and heavy vehicles it needed, a quarter of the steel, and as much as 40% of its clothing requirement.[2]

In a similar way to foreign trade, the war also blocked foreign investment by entrepreneurs and companies. As during the First World War, companies belonging to citizens of enemy states were requisitioned. Production either stopped or else continued after nationalization, and international business initiatives came to a halt during the war due to the general uncertainty and the impossibility of transferring capital abroad.

---

[2] The data on the economies of the Eastern European countries are taken from I.T. Berend, *An Economic History of Twentieth-Century Europe. Economic Regimes from Laissez-Faire to Globalization*, Cambridge, 2006.

14.4. The sectors in war: agriculture and raw materials

No sector was spared by the war effort. Agriculture had to contend with reduced manpower caused by conscription, and the policies implemented to contrast the Great Depression had caused a drop in food production almost everywhere during the 1930s, which already produced serious discrepancies between demand and supply as the war began.

The devastation, occupations and requisitions of war added to this initial handicap and the situation was aggravated not only by the lack of manpower, but also by the fact that the arms industry saturated the productive capacity of the engineering and chemical companies. This reduced the availability of fundamental components of the agricultural production process such as farm machinery and fertilizers. In general terms, total world agricultural output immediately after the war was less than a tenth of the pre-war level.

On the other hand, driven by necessity and where it was unaffected by the geography of the war, agriculture achieved good results. The US Midwest rapidly acquired a central role in supplying food to the other Allied nations, followed by Australia and Argentina. This also coincided with improved cultivation methods, and with generally improved average output. However, with regard to global equilibria, it must be stressed that most areas untouched or only partly affected by the war (in particular in Africa, South America and the Middle East) generally had subsistence level agriculture or low productivity and could not easily have replaced the output of the more advanced countries, which were almost all involved in the war.

Raw materials were a second component of the primary sector greatly affected by the war, especially the materials most directly connected with the arms industry. The geography of the conflict and its outcomes determined the destinies of entire sectors (and the economies of producer countries). For example, in the case of natural rubber Japanese control of the producer countries in Southeast Asia seriously damaged imports to the Allied countries, stimulating investments in research to develop synthetic rubber. The USA benefitted greatly from its geographical proximity to Latin America and the friendly behaviour of many Latin American countries with rich natural resources, including Chile (copper), Colombia (which supplied the platinum required for the arms industry), Peru (cotton) and Mexico (petroleum). In short, the war drove mining output to the maximum, but natural and war-related shortages also drove the search for alternative technologies to create valid substitutes.

14.5. Growth of the arms industry

The arms industry grew at an unprecedented rate during the war years, and absorbing an increasing percentage of national income in the nations directly involved in the hostilities. In the USA, for example, the percentage rose from 1% in 1939 to 42% in 1944. During the last years of the war, the incidence of military expenditure on GNP was over 50% in Britain, over 20% in Italy, and over 70% in Germany and Japan.

Massive efforts were made everywhere to increase production, but once Germany's "lightning war" strategy had failed the economic superiority of the Allies became evident, at least in quantitative terms. The nations at war were impressively capable of increasing their overall output extremely rapidly, especially in certain sectors. Germany tripled its total arms production in under three years, and the USSR increased output by two and a half times between 1940 and 1944. In the UK, production of aluminium – an increasingly common material in the arms industry – increased by 50% during the war, while output of gearbox transmission valves tripled in volume. The British aviation industry increased its output by ten times. A total of 700 tanks were manufactured per year in 1939, but this had risen to 9,000 in 1942. Just under 300,000 armoured vehicles were turned out between 1939 and 1945 (a third just in the USA), and 450,000 fighter planes. Lastly, the USA made the overwhelming majority (almost 9,000) of the 11,000 large ships built during the war.

This enormous increase in output was made possible by applying the most advanced mass production methods to the arms industry and also by the increasing industrial concentration, which was the logical continuation of the process launched decades previously with the Second Industrial Revolution (Chapter 7). Everywhere, the leading players in the conflict were the large companies in the capital- and energy-intensive sectors, using continuous production processes to manufacture enormous quantities. During the war, companies that were already world leaders in their respective sectors between the wars now took a central role in the steel and chemical industries, the light and heavy engineering sectors, the oil refineries and fuel industry, the pharmaceutical and electronics industries and other specialized sectors of all nations involved in the hostilities.

Perhaps the most emblematic and important case is the aviation industry, whose leading national companies worked at full capacity during the war. In the USA, Boeing mostly manufactured bombers and increased output from 60 aircraft per month in 1942 to 360 in 1944. Between 1942 and 1945, Douglas Aircraft produced 30,000 planes with a workforce of almost 150,000, while McDonnell mainly manufactured components and employed a staff of 5,000. Mitsubishi and Kawasaki in Japan, Messerschmitt in Germany, and Tupolev in the USSR are well-known companies with similar production capacities, and Britain's Supermarine Aviation Works turned out over 35,000 Hurricane and Spitfire fighter planes during the war.

14.6. Planning for combat

The kind of productive effort described above could only be implemented given essential conditions. The first was obviously the presence of an adequate productive organization, i.e. an articulated industrial system with companies of different sizes cooperating in an efficient productive organization that could meet the needs of the arms industry. Returning to the aviation industry, the production peaks achieved more or less everywhere in the first half of the 1940s were thanks to the efforts of many small and medium-sized engineering firms and car manufacturers, efficiently coordinated by the big companies.

The second condition was the temporary suspension of the traditional mechanisms allocating production factors via market prices in favour of markedly more regulated systems. Everywhere, the war brought the imposition of regulated prices, controls and other measures aimed at compressing private consumption in favour of military spending, including a substantial increase in taxation. Inflation was kept under strict control everywhere, also in view of the enormous amount of money released into circulation to pay for the war effort.

However, market control and price regulation were just the surface of a much more radical and pervasive government intervention in countries directly or indirectly at war, which involved the economic/productive structure supporting the arms industry. One legacy of the Great War firstly and then of the Great Crisis (Chapter 13) had been the intensification of State interference in the economy. Levels of pervasiveness and intensity differed, but after the experience of "war socialism" introduced by the First World War "economic *dirigisme*" – i.e. coordination of the private production system by the "hand of the state"– had become an important element in the vocabulary of rulers and dictators across Europe. The Second World War built on these previous experiences and constituted the logical fulfilment of a philosophy that saw "plans" implemented by direct government intervention as an important ingredient in the process of catching-up and of anticyclical intervention to support development. In some cases, the intensity of State coordination was particularly spectacular, especially when it was grafted onto a tradition of liberalism as in the case of Britain. According to economic historian Alan Milward, the system that took hold in Britain during the war was as distant from democracy as the regimes in Italy and Germany, where, however, direct state intervention and *planning* had already existed from the mid-1930s.[3]

The planning and coordination of the public and private production systems during the war effort certainly produced valuable *know-how* for governments in the post-war years as they launched interventionist economic policies that would make consolidated Western capitalist systems resemble "mixed economies" (Chapter 15).

14.7. War and big science

However, it was not just a case of consistently increased output achieved via the state's coordination capacity or planning methods. The most purely qualitative component (technological and scientific) of the armaments used played an equally important role to that of the "great volumes" and to the courage shown by the troops in the field.

Japan and Germany were both well aware of their own inferior productive capacity and aimed explicitly at the qualitative excellence of their weaponry. Germany specialized in designing and manufacturing U-boats for the submarine war to contrast the superiority of the Allied naval fleet. There was a kind of "parallel war" involving Germany, the USSR, and the USA in a competition to produce tanks that were faster, more resistant and had greater firepower.

The Second World War was even more technological than the previous war, and brought to fruition a series of innovations already the object of companies' research and development departments before war broke out. As during the First World War, there was such a great need for development that almost all financial constraints were eventually removed, making it possible to work on extremely sophisticated projects.

Many innovations studied and achieved during the war would then go on to become fundamental components of the Third Industrial Revolution, a new technological model and the process of globalization that began towards the end of the 20th century.

In many cases, these innovations were incremental and of limited importance, like the Philips dynamo-powered torch, which helped revolutionize night combat strategy; in other cases, however, the technological shift radically transformed products, together with their use and potential for

---

[3] A. Milward, *War, Economy and Society, 1939-1945*, Berkeley, 1979, p. 111.

future applications. The innovations aimed at developing more effective aerial bombing represent a spectacular case. During the First World War aircraft had been mostly used for reconnaissance, observation and fighting, but aerial bombing raids played a fundamental strategic role in the Second World War, used not only to destroy infrastructures but also against the civilian population. For example, from the 13th to 15th February 1945, hundreds of British and US bombers dropped around 4,000 tonnes of explosives on Dresden, a city that would become a symbol of airborne destruction. Planes large and powerful enough to carry unprecedented loads were needed to launch tonnes of explosives on civilian and military targets. Aerial combat methods soon imposed two needs: the ability to fly out of the range of enemy anti-aircraft batteries and the ability to carry out air-raids at night to maximize the surprise factor. This spurred the development of two fundamentally important technologies: pressurization and electronic flight control instruments, including the "automatic pilot". There were benefits in terms of improved targeting systems, and radar and other new technologies also eliminated the need for eyesight recognition, allowing defence forces to give advance warning of air-raids. Radar is an effective example of how the demands of war accelerated the development of an existent innovation (experimented from the mid-1930s).

However, bomber aircraft did not eliminate fighter plans, which actually became more important in heading off the bombers. The need for increasingly fast planes to face the challenges of air-borne combat led to the "application" of an invention from the late 1930s – the reaction engine. The first jet fighters were the German Messerschmitts, which appeared in 1944 and immediately proved to be more effective and efficient than the best propeller-driven fighter planes.

The aviation technology developed during the war then formed the basis for modern commercial aviation and civilian aircraft in the post-war period. In the same way, the sophisticated sighting and guidance systems, reaction motors and the massive potential for destruction – as symbolized by the German armament programme, which culminated in the V2 (long-distance missiles) – laid the groundwork for the aerospace industry and for the successive space launches involving people, and especially for observation and telecommunications satellites.

The development of fighter and bomber planes also required innovations in fuel refinery and chemical processes to obtain high-performance aircraft fuel. In order to cope with the shortage of fuels and other materials, Allied and Axis powers invested considerable amounts in the production of synthetic petrol and additives to improve the performances of existing fuels.

Other sectors were also affected by equally radical innovations with un-expected ramifications such as the chemical and pharmaceutical industries, and of course the energy sector with projects to exploit nuclear energy for military use and then for civilian use. Alongside the aviation industry, the other sector that perhaps benefitted most from the development imposed by military requirements – and would revolutionize business activity and daily life – was the electronics, computers and communications sector. The Second World War immediately proved to be much more *information-intensive* than the Great War. The technological nature of the conflict, the use of long-distance weapons, and the objective improvements in commu-nications systems during the first half of the 20th century had made infor-mation a strategic component of the conflict. However, important infor-mation was provided by increasingly complex calculations, requiring the use of mathematical models that exceeded human capacity. The design and use of machines able to carry out thousands of operations and analyses at the same time was driven by the need to forecast the weather for large-scale air and sea attacks, by complex long-distance electronic sighting systems, and by the race to break the enemy's complex codes used for communica-tions and information.

Between 1943 and 1945, two big projects involving the development of complex data elaboration systems – ENIAC and Colossus – were launched respectively in the USA and Britain, while Germany and Japan were still relatively behind in this sector. In the years after the war, particularly in the USA, there was a further acceleration in research and construction of mac-ro-computers and *mainframes* in connection with space programmes and also driven by the strategic needs arising from the new international con-text created by the Cold War.

Table 14.1. GDP of the great powers during the Second World War (1939-1945, $ billion and 1990 prices)

	1938	1939	1940	1941	1942	1943	1944	1945
Allies								
USA	800	869	943	1094	1235	1399	1499	1474
UK	284	287	316	344	353	361	346	331
France	186	199	82	–	–	–	–	101
Italy	–	–	–	–	–	–	117	92
USSR	359	366	417	359	274	305	362	343
Allies total	1629	1721	1757	1798	1862	2064	2325	2342

(follows)

	1938	1939	1940	1941	1942	1943	1944	1945
Axis								
Germany	351	384	387	412	417	426	437	310
France	–	–	82	130	116	110	93	–
Austria	24	27	27	29	27	28	29	12
Italy	141	151	147	144	145	137	–	–
Japan	169	184	192	196	197	194	189	144
Axis total	686	747	835	911	903	895	748	466
Allies/Axis								
Total	2.4	2.3	2.1	2.0	2.1	2.3	3.1	5.0
USSR/Germany	1.0	1.0	1.1	0.9	0.7	0.7	0.8	1.1

Source: M. Harrison, *The Economics of World War II*, cit.

Table 14.2. GDP and per capita GDP in Europe and in the world (1900-1950)

	Europe				Mondo				
Year	GDP	1913 = 100%	Per capita capita GDP	1913 = 100%	GDP	1913 = 100%	Per GNP pro Capita GDP	1913 = 100%	GDP Europe to world GDP (%)
1990	908,455	73	2,012	85	1,976,876	73	1,263	82	159
1913	1,241,635	100	2,381	100	2,726,065	100	1,539	100	155
1929	1,514,923	122	2,757	116	3,696,156	136	1,806	117	153
1950	2,116,057	170	3,259	137	5,372,330	197	2,138	139	152

Source: Table uses data taken from A. Maddison, *Monitoring the World Economy*, 1995, pp. 227-228.

Bibliography

Berend I.T., *An Economic History of Twentieth-Century Europe. Economic Regimes from Laissez-Faire to Globalization*, Cambridge, UK, 2006.

Harrison M. (ed.), *The Economics of World War II: Six Great Powers in International Comparison*, Cambridge, 1998.

Milward A., *War, Economy and Society, 1939-1945*, Berkeley, 1979.

Pollard S. (ed.), *Wealth and Poverty. An Economic History of the 20th Century*, London, 1990.

Pollard S., *The International Economy since 1945*, London, 1945.

Chapter 15
PROSPERITY AT LAST

15.1. "Greenhouse with cyclamens"

Between November 1945 and October 1946 the Allied powers put captured Nazi leaders on trial at Nuremberg. The trials ended with some of the Nazi regime's chief exponents sentenced to hanging or life imprisonment, and was attended by the New Yorker correspondent, eclectic British writer Cicely Fairfield better known as Rebecca West. Obliged to spend a lengthy stay with other journalists in a large house on the outskirts of the city, West gradually shifted her attention from a rather boring trial – with an obviously foregone conclusion – to what was actually happening around her. Germany was economically and politically destroyed, but even with the smell of the dead beneath bombed-out ruins hanging in the air, continual and increasing signs of a revival were emerging. The paragraphs she wrote about the trial alternate with wide-ranging descriptions of a re-emerging civilian life in cities that she had effectively defined as "dead as gutted animals". Many factors contributed to this vitality, but one appeared to be essential: "The itch to industry, the lech for work, that forced the Germans to make things, and sell them". One of the most significant episodes recounted by West involves the greenhouse of the house where the journalists stayed. A greenhouse where an old one-legged gardener on crutches, painstakingly cultivated cyclamens to sell at Christmas. "Greenhouse with Cyclamens" is the title Rebecca West chose for her account, in which the anguishing trails of the Nazi war criminals alternate with her enthusiastic account of the country's return to life after the devastation of war.[1]

The German revival, in turn, symbolizes the more general process of the revival involving the whole of Europe; although hope for by many, the process took place with an intensity unforeseen at the time.

---

[1] *Greenhouse with Cyclamens I, II* and *III:* the title is repeated in three sections of *A Train of Powder*, published in 1955 in New York.

In 1960, just fifteen years after the end of the war, Europe had recovered and was growing at such a pace that it was defined by many as an "economic miracle". As this chapter will show, the miracle was the result of many smaller "miracles" at the level of the single national economies, fundamentally enabled by the exogenous impulse from the USA's specifically targeted post-war aid policies and the successive economic integration processes of the 1950s. Of course, an additional factor was the complex of Keynesian economic policies adopted by national governments within the framework of the "mixed economy" systems that emerged from the experience of war.

15.2. Europe destroyed

Despite having sown important seeds that would soon come to fruition in the peacetime economy, the war had left much of Europe under a mound of rubble. In neorealist director Roberto Rossellini's acclaimed film *Germany Year Zero*, which he courageously filmed in Berlin in 1948, the leading role is played by destruction, not only of physical spaces, but also of the spaces occupied by civilian and social life. Although so painfully evident, the destruction of towns and cities was just one element of the devastation Europe had inflicted upon itself.

The loss of life had been extremely heavy. According to the most recent estimates, there were between 70 and 85 million military and civilian deaths directly or indirectly caused by war, the equivalent of 3% of the world's total population in 1940. In some countries – like Japan, Poland, the USSR, Germany and Greece – the situation was even worse, with losses ranging from 10 to 15% of the total population. Thirty million people had also been deported and forcibly transferred; many had simply nowhere they could return to.

From the economic point of view, the loss of human capital added to the loss of resources, infrastructures, housing and factories. Industrial capital goods had been destroyed or so severely weakened by the war effort that they were no longer usable. In Axis nations, a fifth of industrial investments were useless at the end of the war. In the Soviet Union, roughly 70% of industrial plants had been damaged or destroyed. In other countries, there had been less devastation of the industrial system, but the damage was still significant, as was the damage to towns and cities, which peaked at 20% in Germany, Poland and Greece.[2]

---

[2] The data regarding physical destruction are taken from A. Milward, *The Reconstruction of Western Europe 1945-1951*, London, 1984.

International trade languished and so did the primary sector, which had largely been overlooked, apart from the mining of essential resources for the arms industry. The principal roads had been destroyed, and special care had been taken to destroy roads connecting the major industrial and urban centres. Bombing and the voluntary destruction of defence forces trying to halt the enemy advance had struck the key infrastructures especially hard, and those that were most valuable like bridges and viaducts. The railway system had collapsed and so had shipping, with the merchant navy reduced to less than two-thirds of its pre-war level.

Overall, whatever indicator is considered, Europe, the Soviet Union and Japan were in the worst of conditions after the war, although it is worth re-iterating that the war had created skills and practices that were clearly important, and had also in many cases contributed to expansion of the industrial base in the warring nations. However, between 1945 and 1946 simple industrial output was half the pre-war level and the same was true for agriculture. Per capita GNP in the major European countries had fallen from over $5,000 to under $4,000 at constant 1990 prices, in the Soviet Union from $2,200 to $1,900, and in Japan it had fallen to less than half the pre-war level. The situation naturally differed from one country to another. If industrial output in 1938 is taken as being 100, comparison with 1947 shows that of the nations involved in the war, only Britain and Belgium were still above the 1938 level. France was at 99, the Netherlands at 94, Italy at 93, Greece at 69, Austria at 55, and Germany at 34.

Japan remained under US occupation until 1952, and began an independent course of economic growth under the aegis of American aid, also helped by its particular geographical position in the new equilibria produced by the Cold War. However, the real problem for the Allies (especially the United States and Britain) was undoubtedly Europe, particularly continental Europe. Relations between the USA and USSR began to cool immediately (between 1946 and 1947) and would soon lead to the creation of two opposing geopolitical blocs, which made it necessary to drive the rapid acceleration of Europe's economic recovery to overcome stagnation and redress the widespread problem of poverty.

Europe's state of prostration and economic inertia was of no benefit to anyone, as shown for example by the fate of the "Morgenthau Plan" (proposed by US Treasury Secretary Henry Morgenthau in 1944) for the almost total de-industrialization of Germany and its transformation to an economy based on the primary sector. The idea of completely dismantling German industry was soon replaced with the intention to construct the more general revival of Western European economies around German recovery.

15.3. The European Recovery Program[3]

Between 1947 and 1951, the growth of GDP and industrial output in most European countries was in double or even treble figures. Industrial output grew in Belgium and Britain by 33%, in France by almost 40%, in Italy and the Netherlands by 55%, in Greece by around 90%, in Austria and Germany by almost 300%. Overall, this meant an average increase of almost 55% in five years.

The growth of industrial production was accompanied by an increase in foreign trade by Western European countries: total exports by Austria, Denmark, Germany, Ireland, Italy, the Netherlands, Norway, Portugal, Sweden and Britain increased by 60-70% between 1948 and 1951.

Between 1938 and 1950, with the understandable exception of Germany, labour productivity also increased almost everywhere at rates ranging from 10 to 30%.

Increased industrial output, labour productivity and foreign trade (also supported by a series of devaluations involving national currencies that were encouraged by the US from the late 1940s) were accompanied by improvements in living conditions (and consumption) for European citizens, as shown by indicators related to housing conditions, food consumption and health status.

The rapid and substantial change in economic conditions was due to a combination of different factors, one of which was certainly the strong desire for recovery in the countries devastated by war and the wish for a return to normality after years of deprivation. A series of economic and institutional factors made it possible to achieve this with a rapid and lasting recovery.

Post-war European governments shared the understanding that recovery should be a) rapid, b) centred on manufacturing and industry, and c) continental, in order to avoid the fragmentation and dislocation characterizing the period after the First World War.

The general objective of the rapid economic recovery, however, came into conflict with a potential *lock-in* situation: in order to revive its productive potential, Europe would need to import everything that was required and which the war had destroyed, from raw materials to capital goods. However, it could not pay for these imports with its own exports, nor were there even the minimum conditions for obtaining credit on the international financial market. The only way to overcome this situation was through ex-

---

[3] The data on the impact of the ERP on European growth are taken from D.H. Aldcroft, *The European Economy 1914-1990*, London, 1993.

ternal intervention, which the USA decided to provide as a massive programme of development aid. The nation that had emerged from the war as
the undisputed economic and political leader adopted a radically different
way from its approach immediately after the First World War.

In the four years between 1948 and 1951, the USA transferred around
$13.5 to Europe, which was a substantial share (about 2%) of its GNP.
This gigantic programme for economic recovery in Europe was known as
the European Recovery Program (ERP) or Marshall Plan after its promo-
tor, US Secretary of State George Marshall. Aid was distributed mostly as
industrial machinery and raw materials needed for industrial production,
and it provided for close coordination between companies requiring these
goods and the ERP offices in the different countries. Goods advanced to
companies were paid for in devalued local currency, and the money was
accumulated in "counterpart" funds, which almost all remained available to
the governments of the nations deciding (voluntarily) to take part in the
Plan. The composition of the vast aid programme clearly shows its aim to
stimulate economic recovery: a third consisted of raw materials; another
third consisted of food and fertilizers; 15% consisted of coal and fuels, and
17% was machinery and other investment goods. All European countries
benefitted substantially from the Plan, especially France and Great Britain
(each with over 20% of the funds), Italy and West Germany (10% each).

The transfer of resources was made more effective in terms of potential
increases in productivity by the fact that the destruction caused by the war
had resolved the problem of *sunk costs* in many countries. The goods that
arrived, and which the USA largely purchased on its own domestic markets,
were technologically advanced and required rapid improvements in workers'
skills. Nor should the political value of the Plan be neglected. On the one
hand, it represented the clear re-establishment of US economic and political
leadership and on the other hand, it revolved around re-establishment of the
fundamental mechanisms of the capitalist market economy, albeit with
some specifically European features. In principle, the Plan was also offered
to the USSR and the countries of Eastern Europe like Hungary and Poland
Poland, where destruction had been widespread; unsurprisingly, neither
the USSR nor the other states now in its sphere of influence accepted the
American offer. In addition, in every country where Marshall Plan aid was
distributed there was a shift towards more politically moderate or "cen-
trist" governments, rapidly abandoned by politicians more directly connected with Communist parties linked to Moscow.

The ERP was also the broad framework for a series of other initiatives
aimed at the consolidation and development of European capitalism: many
European entrpreneurs and managers took advantage of "educational vis-

its" and trips to the USA, which played a fundamental role in modernizing organizational models and technological, strategic and commercial approaches of European companies. When the Program ended in 1952, it had achieved undeniable and wide-ranging success, especially regarding the formation of high-technology industrial fixed capital and transfer of the most advanced technologies and organizational practices.

15.4. Trade and international agreements

Europe's economic recovery was essentially based on the reconstitution of its production capacity, but was also based on the revival of trade, *in primis* between the countries taking part in the reconstruction programme. Taking the 1948 level as 100, the export index among countries benefitting from the ERP stood at 175 in 1952. There was a need to focus not only on domestic markets but also on a wider geographical area – which inevitably meant all of Western Europe – and this drove European countries to implement initiatives to increase economic cooperation.

1947 saw the creation of the Committee for European Economic Cooperation, which soon became the Organization for European Economic Cooperation (OEEC).[4] Another example of cooperation, based on the creation of a shared trade area and the removal of customs duties and barriers, involves two specific sectors of heavy industry – coal and steel – that had also been a crucial point in the past, especially for Franco-German relations. In 1951, France, Germany, Belgium, Luxembourg, the Netherlands and Italy formed the European Coal and Steel Community, in order to regulate the European market of these two important basic industries with a central role to play in the recovery process.

Cooperation was in turn based upon a fundamental prerequisite, i.e. a significant reduction in customs tariffs. These had been lowered considerably everywhere, and were even below the average level of the early 1930s, i.e. before autarky became stricter and before the economic isolation due to the crisis. There was widespread international agreement on the need for restoration of the favourable international trade conditions encouraging global development before the long "European civil war" triggered with the outbreak of the First World War. Negotiations began immediately after the end of the war, leading in 1947 to a general agreement on international trade (General Agreement on Tariffs and Trade – GATT). By the early

---

[4] Other developed countries (Canada, Australia and Japan) joined the OEEC in the early 1970s, and the organization changed its name once more to become the Organization for Economic Cooperation and Development, or OECD.

1950s GATT had gradually come to include many Western capitalist economies and played a fundamental role in the general recovery of the international economy.

GATT was just one component of a broader effort to reconstruct the bases of an international economy violently weakened in the crisis generated by the two wars. Just a few years previously, two institutions essential to the regeneration of an international economic system had been created: the International Monetary Fund (IMF) and the International Bank for Reconstruction and Development (IBRD), more commonly known as the World Bank, which initially financed the countries engaged in reconstruction. The IMF was, in turn, essential to support the regime of fixed exchange rates (against the US dollar or gold) and full convertibility of the currencies introduced in 1944 at the same Bretton Woods Conference that formed the two institutions. The IMF was also assigned the crucial task of providing short-term loans to compensate temporary external payment imbalances in the member countries, which implicitly gave it a central role in the complex process of reconstructing international trade.

Therefore, the general process taking place in the post-war period was an ambitious modernization of the international capitalistic system, now based on cooperation and on the activities of surveillance and intervention implemented by the regulatory organizations. This system assigned the key role of coordination to the nation that had emerged from the war as the undeniable economic, political and military leader of the West: the United States.

In any case, there was no question of attempting to re-establish the exceptional conditions in the first decades of the first phase of globalization, which had then fallen apart in First World War trenches. A series of exogenous factors made this impossible. Firstly, the rapidly cooling relations between the two opposing blocs made it unimaginable. Nor was it possible to forecast immediate re-launch of a positive economic cycle without overcoming the isolation that had marked the 1930s as nations reacted to the crisis. International trade areas formed gradually, although they were limited in size, which meant a regionalization of the world economy rather than re-globalization.

Two important examples of this are the Council for Mutual Economic Assistance (Comecon, formed in 1948 to facilitate trade between the Communist bloc states) and the European Union (founded in 1957 by Italy, France, Germany, Belgium, the Netherlands and Luxembourg).

Comecon initially consisted of Bulgaria, Hungary, Czechoslovakia, Poland, and Romania, naturally with the USSR. It was formed to coordinate the complex relations between the planned economies of the Eastern Bloc whose prices were established outside market mechanisms, which then created problems with the shift from self-sufficiency to international trade.

On the other hand, the European Union (EU) – originally created as the European Common Market, then the European Economic Community – was the logical outcome of cooperation process launched during the Marshall Plan and then followed by agreements on coal and steel. The underlying idea was to gradually remove restrictions on the free circulation of goods, people and capital within the area of the Union and the process was completed in 1992 (Chapter 21).

15.5. Mixed economy, nationalizations and development policies

The renaissance of international trade and cooperation was an essential component of the post-war recovery process, for both capitalist and communist blocs. In many ways, this was an "exogenous" factor not directly controlled by the individual national governments, although they could use tools designed to enhance their capacity for economic intervention, as they did with increasing determination. The war had taught European governments the need for planning and the benefits of a mixed economy, and the West was well aware of the achievements obtained with a "purely" planned system in the Communist bloc. It was therefore natural that many European governments adopted forms of political-economic and industrial intervention, with the State playing a greater or lesser role in coordination and intervention through state companies and nationalized agencies administering natural monopolies.

In Europe, state-owned companies were widespread and sometimes monopolistic in capital-intensive sectors and those involving a high level of technological research like telecommunications, electricity generation and supply, refineries, coal and steel, the car industry, aviation and shipyards, and played an essential role in decisions regarding policy and territorial economic development in the different states. Additionally, the State presence in the natural monopolies and in the base industries contributed to another pillar of the post-war economic recovery: the creation of a *welfare* system in almost every country. This meant extending welfare benefits to almost all citizens, mostly related to health insurance and pensions, and had an important anti-cyclical effect on the labour market and investment dynamics.

Between 1950 and 1965, public spending across Europe rose from an average of around 25% of GDP to around 35%; a fifth of the total was dedicated to health and social security programmes. This all contributed to the creation of an original and "continental" variant of capitalism in a Europe that was rapidly completing its own reconstruction. European capitalism was marked by the presence of big companies partly (or totally) controlled by the state alongside a vast private sector, and by the tendency to redistribute the benefits from industrialization by means of welfare policies. A fair degree of social harmony was achieved via the implicit acceptance of relative salary moderation, which was, however, compensated by a high level of investment. Allowing for the inevitable differences between the different states, this was a form of market capitalism that tempered the excesses of profit-seeking by taking care of broader social needs: a "social market economy".

15.6. Miracle, miracles

The "lech for work" described by Rebecca West had crystallized into an extraordinary economic outcome, and not only in Germany. Between 1950 and 1973 per capita GDP in Western European countries grew by an average of 4% (at constant prices); Austria, France, Finland, West Germany, Italy, Greece, Portugal and Spain actually had higher growth levels. Japan (which was in a state of dramatic prostration at the war's end) actually grew at an average rate of 8%, which was extraordinary in comparison with a US growth rate of 2.5%. After a destructive and catastrophic war, the principal world economies became "economic miracles" at almost the same time. In the countries mentioned, national wealth was generally increased by a rapid rise in productivity of all factors, especially in the industrial manufacturing sector (given the general decline of the primary sector, which accounted for a quarter to a fifth of total national income in all Western European countries). The increase in disposable income largely went to finance a considerable rise in private consumption, which was finally able to grow after the end of wartime austerity, also aided by the spread of modern mass distribution systems. At the start of the 1970s, food accounted for 27% of total family spending. In 1950, just twenty years before this, families expenditure had been 45% in Britain, France and Germany, and 60% in Greece and Italy. What was soon defined as "consumerism" spread across Europe: the numbers of cars grew constantly, roads and infrastructures were built, thousands of telephones were installed each day, and radio and television subscribers increased exponentially. The housing market was an important catalyst in the process, also due to the large-scale urban development programmes implemented, and it actually absorbed a quarter of total investments between 1950 and the early 1970s.

In the meantime, the Communist bloc did not fall behind. The socialist economies tended to pay little attention to private consumption as a driving force of economic growth and concentrated on public consumption directed towards increasing industrial investment, but increased their GDP and productivity even more than the West. According to available estimates for the period 1950-1970, the total GDP of the Eastern European economies and the USSR registered annual increments of 7-8%.

The combined effect of the "economic miracles" in Eastern and Western Europe and Japan was the gradual narrowing of the divide between GNP in these economic macro-regions and that of the USA with its benchmark economy. Taking US per capita income as 100, the Western European average was about 49 in 1950, Japan's average was about 20, and the USSR average was 26. By 1973, the respective percentages had risen to 84, 69 and 37.

In conclusion, by the start of the 1970s – after two decades of continuous sustained growth – the countries that had invested vast resources in reconstruction had returned to good levels of competitiveness. Their citizens now enjoyed much better living conditions than between the two world wars, and their economies had become highly industrialized, technologically advanced, and generally stronger.

The world economy was still a long way from the level of integration achieved during the decades of the first globalization, but international agreements and a general spirit of cooperation meant that the slow process of re-establishing world trade had begun.

However, these were not the only areas where important transformations were taking place. A similar fermentation was taking place in other areas of the world that had until then been only marginal players in the world economy.

Table 15.1. Customs duties in several countries (1913-1952, %)

	1913	1925	1927	1931	1952
Belgium	6	7	11	17	–
France	14	9	23	38	19
Germany	12	15	24	40	16
Italy	17	16	27	48	24
Netherlands	2	4	–	–	–
United Kingdom	–	4	–	17	17
United States	32	26	–	–	16

Source: D.A. Irwin, *The Gatt's Contribution to Economic Recovery, in Post-War Western Europe, Board of Governors of the Federal Reserve System*, International Discussion Papers, Finance 442, 1993.

Bibliography

Aldcroft D.H., *The European Economy 1914-1990*, London, 1993.

Eichengreen B., *The European Economy since 1945. Coordinated Capitalism and Beyond*, Princeton, 2007.

Foreman-Peck J., Federico G., *European Industrial Policy. The Twentieth Century Experience*, Oxford, 2009.

Milward A., *The Reconstruction of Western Europe 1945-1951*, London, 1984.

Chapter 16

DECOLONIZATION: LIGHTS AND (MANY) SHADOWS

SUMMARY: 16.1. Rich and poor. – 16.2. The nature of underdevelopment. – 16.3. Decolonization. – 16.4. Political instability. – 16.5. Asian destinies. – Bibliography.

16.1. Rich and poor

The years of "great prosperity" had started a process of convergence between the economies destoyed by the war and the United States, which had become the stable economic and political leader of the capitalist world. This gradually shrinking *gap* involved more than just per capita GDP, because it also concerned technology, productivity, and above all "life styles".[1]

The consumerism that spread throughout European societies in the post-war decades was the most evident sign that well-being had returned after the austerity of war and rationing. The desire for well-being was expressed by the general spread of consumption and life style models already consolidated in the USA, which was described as "Americanization". The new prosperity was also enjoyed to a lesser extent by the Communist bloc countries, and even extended to Japan as it emerged from US occupation into an intense growth phase that involved whole-hearted adoption of Western life styles.

Prosperity was therefore widespread and macroscopic, appearing as a "miracle": an economic revolution bringing radical changes to social structures and daily life in the countries it benefitted.

However, it also had the effect of dramatically increasing the gap separating the reviving and recovering industrialized economies from other countries, which enjoyed only marginal benefits of the positive global economic cycle that began in the early 1950s.

Alongside the "rich" nations or those rapidly becoming rich there were

---

[1] The data used in this chapter are taken from the website containing decades of research by Angus Maddison: *http://www.ggdc.net/maddison/oriindex.htm*.

also a great many "poor" nations, some of which were becoming even more impoverished. This was so widespread that it was impossible for the newly prosperous West to ignore when it observed what were defined as the "underdeveloped countries", a term normally accompanied by the further definition of "non-industrialized".

The underdeveloped countries definitely covered more of the globe. According to statistics provided by Angus Maddison, world average per capita GDP in 1960 was just under $3,000 (at 1990 prices). Taking this as a hypothetical dividing line between wealth and poverty, all the Western industrialized countries were of course above this level, as were the more dynamic centralized economies (Czechoslovakia, Bulgaria, Hungary and Poland), Japan, some Arab principalities, and Latin American countries like Peru, Mexico, Uruguay, Argentina and Chile. Only two African countries were above the line: Gabon and South Africa. The Indian sub-continent and Southeast Asia were completely absent from the group of rich nations, while Australia and New Zealand were the only countries in Oceania among the wealthy. China's per capita income was just a fifth of the world average, making it one of the least developed countries.

The vast group of poor countries (where underdevelopment involved low education levels and precarious living conditions) differed in terms of geographical size, political regime, institutional structure, culture and religion but they shared three characteristics. Firstly, almost all these countries were in the southern hemisphere or equatorial regions, with economies based on the primary sector population growth rates well above the world average.[2] Secondly, many were still colonies, ex-colonies or protectorates. Lastly, almost all had extremely unstable political regimes, although of different types.

16.2. The nature of underdevelopment

Underdevelopment was caused by a number of interconnected factors. Firstly, without exception the economic structure of all the poor countries depended heavily on the primary sector. For some, ranging from China to almost all the African states, much of South America and Indochina (French colonies in Southeast Asia), this was mostly subsistence-level agriculture, involving nomadic forms of farming in some extreme cases. Other countries were able to use exports from the mining industry to compensate for imports of a minimum quantity of industrial and consumer goods, needed mainly for agriculture.

---

[2] A. Maddison, *The World Economy. Historical Statistics*, Paris, 2003.

The recent war had corrected some of these macroscopic imbalances, given the warring states' need for food imports, but the return to normality had cancelled these benefits. The exceptions were the countries whose natural resources were in constant demand by the West as its economy boomed. Petroleum was the first of these resources, which explains why in 1960 some non-industialized countries (e.g. Qatar, Kuwait and the Arab Emirates – all British protectorates at the time) already boasted a per capita income (very unequally distributed) much higher than many of the most industrialized countries.

Dependence on agriculture and its fluctuations linked to climatic factors like drought or flooding and to international market price trends also influenced the fate of the secondary sector in these countries.

India is an important example of this dynamic interdependence, a country where agriculture accounted for over 50% of national income and employed 70% of the population. The underdeveloped primary sector dramatically reduced the capacity of the vast rural population to save and accumulate, also limiting their tendency towards consumption. This made India and many other countries in similar conditions unattractive towards foreign investors, whose predatory strategies mostly focused on subtracting natural resources instead of "fertilizing" domestic industry.

In the underdeveloped countries, the small incomes from an agricultural sector with low yields coexisted with a population growth rate that had begun to soar in the years after the war.

Before the war, population growth rates were similar worldwide (0.8% per year), but the developed countries experienced an increase to 1.3% from the 1950s, while the the underdeveloped countries began to grow at a rate of over 2%. Much of the responsibility for this growth was connected with Western aid designed to fight poverty and increase a life expectancy that rarely exceeded 50 years, while life expectancy in the more advanced countries was 70. Demographic pressure combined with extremely low per capita income so that living conditions immediately worsened. This damaged the prospects of economic growth, and poor countries that found themselves almost completely dependent on international aid, with no way to escape from the poverty trap.

16.3. Decolonization

Although the First World War had directly or indirectly eliminated the Austro-Hungarian, Ottoman and Russian Empires, much of the planet was still subject to some form of "imperial" domination of the colonial type when the Second World War broke out.

British *dominions* included protectorates, ports, directly governed colonies and countries of the Commonwealth, reaching from Canada to Central, Eastern and Southern Africa, from Palestine to Suez and from the Arabian Peninsula to India, Australia and New Zealand.

France was the dominant power in North Africa and Central West Africa, Madagascar, Syria, southeast Asia, and Indochina (now Cambodia and Vietnam). The Netherlands still had colonies in Indonesia, Italy in Libya and the Horn of Africa, and Japan in Chinese Manchuria, Taiwan and Korea, while the Soviet Union essentially covered the same areas as the former Russian Empire.

In some respects, it is no exaggeration to state that the Second World War was the last "great war" between the empires created in the first phase of globalization. Therefore the colonies were called on to take part in a conflict that – unlike the previous war – was also widely and bitterly fought in the dominions. Half a million soldiers from the colonies of the vast British Empire lost their lives in battle, and civilian casualties were even higher: some estimates are that around 5% of the population died in the Dutch East Indies and up to 8% in French Indochina. In other cases, the percentages were far lower, but still represented hundreds of thousands of deaths.

The British Empire appeared to demonstrate considerable unity, symbolized by its Eighth Army consisting mainly of soldiers from the *dominions*, including South Africa, New Zealand and India. However, this unity already showed signs of strain – almost everywhere – between the two wars, in connection with growing anti-colonial and independence movements that often culminated in open revolt. None of Europe's colonies were immune to anti-colonial pressure, and the reactions of the ruling powers had included violent repression.

In short, the war had accelerated a process of disintegration that had already begun.

Japanese conquest of Southeast Asia coincided with expulsion of the Dutch from Indonesia, the British from Singapore and the French from Indochina, and also with the attempt to create independent states (although these were of course linked with Tokyo). However, the USA was emerging from the war as the real victor, with the power to dominate the world and set the international agenda, and openly opposed any form of colonial rule in Asia. The US approach was based on ideological respect for the principles of self-determination, and also on the very pragmatic observation that in many cases colonial rule had aided the consolidation of communist revolutionary ideologies. The USA therefore opposed the re-establishment of French colonial rule over Indochina, considering it as leading to intolerable instability in what was becoming a region of key importance in international politics.

More than a war fought on the battlefield, another type of war actually dealt the final blow to Western imperialism. The Cold War and the strategic moves of the two opponents on the international chessboard formed the base for a new attitude to colonial policy. Three "approaches" emerged after the war: concession of independence to colonies, progressive decentralization of power, and maintenance of the status quo. The first of these represented the US position and was the approach that prevailed.

One event effectively incapsulates this radical shift: the "Suez Crisis" of October 1956. The specific episode was triggered when the Egyptian government policy of strengthening the country's geopolitical position led it to nationalize the international Suez Canal Company, which had built and administered the Canal. Israeli opposition to Eygptian plans was supported by France and Britain, which both decided to re-assert their control over one of world trade's most important infrastructures. The reaction of the USSR in support of Egypt then provoked US intervention against its two allies, with the consequent withdrawal of British and French troops from the Canal area in 1957. Resolution of the Suez Crisis essentially represented a defeat for Britain and France – the two major colonial powers – caused by an anti-Soviet decision of the USA, effectively marking the end of colonialism in Africa, but not only in Africa. The colonial empires had a politically unacceptable anachronism in the new post-war world.

The "de-colonization" process (and the birth of new independent states) that had begun immediately after the war accelerated during the late 1950s and early 1960s. India became independent in 1947, Libya in 1951, Cambodia in 1953, and then Sudan, Tunisia and Morocco in 1956. French West Africa was decolonized in 1960 and Belgian rule ended in the Congo. The process was not always peaceful: 1962 saw the end of the war between France and Algeria, the most dramatic and bloody colonial independence struggle, which lasted seven years and cost almost 200,000 lives. In Asia, the French attempt to re-establish control over Indochina ended in a serious military defeat by Vietnam in 1954, leading to the independence of Vietnam, Laos and Cambodia in the same year.

16.4. Political instability

On 11th July 1960, *Life* magazine published a report on the independence of the Belgian Congo (subsequently Zaire), introduced by Larry Burrows' famous photograph of King Baudoin of Belgium during his official visit to Leopoldville (subsequently renamed Kinshasa). The European monarch represents an outdated world and is seen saluting the crowd from an open-top car, oblivious to the African youth behind him who has seized the royal sword, the symbol of command. The photograph is considered a symbol of the colonies' right to self-determination, but it also raised an important question: how would the young African use that sword?

In general, the independence achieved by the ex-colonies in Africa and Southeast Asia did not usher in a phase of prosperity and wealth for the peoples now freed from foreign control.

Firstly, a signed declaration of independence did not mean that a pen stroke immediately cancelled the structural problems shared by the economies of former colonies. These included both the reliance of domestic consumption and foreign trade on a primary sector subject to strong fluctuations, and the backwardness of the manufacturing sector. Further problems were high levels of demographic pressure and poverty, together with a dramatic shortage of human capital. The situation was aggravated by the lack of a true ruling class. The leaders of the ex-colonies, who had studied abroad, conspired and struggled in the years between the two wars, who had often become charismatic revolutionary leaders and had courageously fought in the wars to liberate their own countries, did not prove to be equally capable of rapidly constructing the administrative and institutional structures needed for modernization. Apart from a few cases, the colonial powers had more or less deliberately kept their overseas possessions in dramatic conditions of backwardness. Almost everywhere in Africa and Asia, independence was followed by extreme political instability marked by the emergence of military dictatorships.

The existence of two opposing blocs during the Cold War also influenced both US behaviour towards the colonial powers, and the domestic policy of many ex-colonies after achieving independence. The United States and Soviet Union used strategies designed to attract the new states into their respective spheres of influence, offering vital economic aid in return for political alignment.

Nevertheless, the laborious decolonization process also saw the emergence of the interests and political projects of these new players, who were determined to contrast the influence of the two super-powers. In April 1955, a summit held at Bandung in Indonesia was attended by 29 African and Asian nations, including many newly independent former European colonies. The Bandung Conference was organized by ex-Dutch colony Indonesia, and by India, Ceylon (Sri Lanka), Pakistan and Burma (Myanmar), which had recently gained their independence from British rule. The Conference aimed to promote cooperation; its concluding declarations contained opposition to any forms of colonialism, constituting an implicit condemnation of Soviet and Western interference in the enfranchisement of newly independent and developing states, and also promoted the idea that countries might deliberately choose to be independent of the two major blocs. After Bandung, the idea of "non-alignment", meaning political independence from the two opposing USA/USSR blocs became an explicit doctrine, which was repeated at conferences in Cairo (1957) and finally in Belgrade (1961), when the Non-Aligned Movement was officially formed.

Figure 16.1. King gives up a colony and his sword

EXCITEMENT CARRIES AWAY BOTH CELEBRATOR AND KING BAUDOUIN'S SWORD. KING, UNAWARE OF LESE MAJESTY, MAINTAINS SALUTE AS SNATCHER DASHES OFF

16.5. Asian destinies

The countries represented at Bandung included both India, which played a leading role among the organizers of the event, and China.

In the pre-industrial period, the two countries had possessed most of the world's wealth between them (Chapters 1 and 2), but in 1955, the year of the Conference, their economic role had become even less than marginal. In terms of per capita GDP, both were well below the world average; China's was a fifth of the world average, i.e. 20 times less than the United

States, and India's was only slightly ahead of China. Together, their populations numbered one billion, out of a total world population of approximately 2.700 billion. Life expectancy was 48 years in China and 38 in India – just half that of the capitalist West. In both countries, the primary sector accounted for around 40% of GDP, and the percentage of the population living in urban centres was between a quarter and a fifth the percentage of the most developed countries.

Besides being two overpopulated giants, both with overwhelmingly rural populations living in more or less marked conditions of poverty, China and India also shared other characteristics. The first and most evident of these was a long history of decline from a position of world economic, political and cultural leadership to a state of permanent backwardness and marginalization. In the case of India, this had also coincided with formal subjection to British imperial rule for around a century. Although China had been spared colonial status, the two Opium Wars (1839 and 1856) left it with weakened national sovereignty and dependent on the decisions of Western international policy, and it had endured a ferocious Japanese invasion and occupation between the two world wars.

The Second World War brought profound changes for both countries. India obtained its independence from Britain peacefully in 1947, while China's Civil War between Mao Zedong's Communist forces and the Nationalist Kuomintang ended in 1949 with the Nationalist flight to Formosa (now Taiwan). In this way, both countries had re-established a solid national identity and developed a governing class that could concentrate on policies aimed at sustaining economic growth and development.

To achieve this, both countries did what was very common among many ex-colonies and underdeveloped Third World nations: the ruling class concentrated on "invasive" economic intervention and centralized coordination of the economic stakeholders.

China's Communist Party had gradually consolidated its control over the country's economic system. From 1953 it began to collectivize the means of production; lands and businesses were gradually nationalized and the first Five-Year Plan was launched. In this phase, the USSR exercised an influence that was not only ideological: it supplied China with concrete aid in the form of steel, electricity and engineering technology, together with technical advice and training for thousands of young people. Centralized coordination was very successful during this first phase: industrial output doubled and agricultural yields rose. China's GDP grew and average living conditions improved. Once again, Angus Maddison's data show that per capita GDP grew on average by 8-9% per year between 1953 and 1958, with outstanding peaks in 1956 (13%) and 1958 (18%). However, the progress made with the first Five-Year Plan was soon cancelled by a series of planning blunders. The ambitious development programme (especially for industry) launched in 1958 and known as the "Great Leap Forward" was a failure; it caused famine in rural areas, forced to use their resources to sustain the process of forced industrialization and urbanization. China's GDP in the early 1970s was negative; according to some estimates, 20-30 million peasants died from the poverty and starvation generated by these failed attempts at economic reform.

India's new ruling elite also tackled the problem of underdevelopment with centralized planning and direct state intervention, but adopted less of an "extremist" approach than China. Its first Five-Year Plan was launched in 1951, and mostly involved the primary sector. However, it was clear from the outset that the governing class of the new democracy gave more importance to state intervention in order to achieve the aims of its planning policy. From 1956, public enterprise was explicitly inserted into a socialist style "mixed" economy system, with the fundamental and strategic sectors (steel, energy, *utilities*, transport and communications) mostly managed by state-owned companies. In these sectors, private companies were allowed only a marginal and regulated presence, and were in any case subordinated to the public sector, although they enjoyed freedom of action in all other sectors. State companies were explicitly assigned objectives to prevent an excessive concentration of economic power under private control, as well as supporting employment and – importantly – reducing the economic inequalities between the different regions of the new state. Overall, the direct economic intervention of the Indian government did not obtain the same success as that demonstrated by China's economic indicators. India's fluctuating GDP meant that growth was generally quite low, and it contributed to the persistence of all the typical problems of underdevelopment, including those related to the drainage of internal resources caused by importing more than it exported.

Nevertheless, not all policies implemented in the developing countries and ex-colonies were doomed to failure. In 1955, the year of Bandung, Taiwan and South Korea – a state formed after forced separation from the northern part of Korea following a bloody civil war lasting over three years – already boasted per capita income levels double those of India and China. By 1970, the divide had grown even wider: the two "tigers" (as the booming economies of Southeast Asia were known) now boasted a per capita income three times that of India and China. In 1980, the year after China's liberalization, the divide with Taiwan and South Korea had grown to 4.5: something had unleashed a new growth energy in these countries.

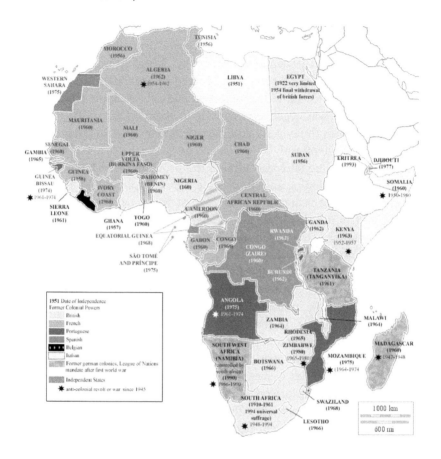

Table 16.1. Growth of the developing countries (1913-1987, per capita GDP in dollars and position)

Country	1913		1950		1987	
	GDP per capita	Position	GDP per capita	Position	GDP per capita	Position
Argentina	1,770	1	2,324	2	3,302	5
Chile	1,255	2	2,350	1	3,393	3
Philippines	985	3	898	7	1,519	11
Mexico	822	4	1,169	5	2,667	7
Peru	819	5	1,349	4	2,380	8
Colombia	801	6	1,395	3	3,027	6
Thailand	652	7	653	8	2,294	9
South Korea	610	8	564	9	4,143	2

(follows)

Indonesia	529	9	484	11	1,200	12
Brazil	521	10	1,073	6	3,417	4
Taiwan	453	11	526	10	4,744	1
Pakistan	438	12	390	12	885	13
China	415	13	338	14	1,748	10
India	399	14	359	13	662	14
Bangladesh	371	15	331	15	375	15

Source: T. Hikino, A.H Asmden, *Staying Behind, Stumbling Back, Sneaking Up, Soaring Ahead. Late Industrialization in Historical Perspective* (1992).

Table 16.2. Distribution of the major industrial companies in developing countries (1985, grouped by area and by sector)

Country	Industrial sector groups				
	High-tech	**Mid-tech**	**Low-tech**	**Petrol**	**Total**
Asia	23	40	36	19	118
South Korea	11	13	11	0	35
India	7	15	10	7	39
Taiwan	5	7	5	1	18
Malaysia	0	2	3	1	6
Philippines	0	0	3	3	6
Others	0	3	4	7	14
Latin America	4	15	20	12	51
Brazil	3	5	7	3	18
Argentina	0	4	6	2	12
Mexico	0	2	3	1	6
Venezuela	1	1	3	1	6
Chile	0	3	1	1	5
Others	0	0	0	4	4
Middle East	2	3	2	6	13
Turkey	1	2	2	1	6
Others	1	1	0	5	7
Africa	0	2	10	6	18
Total	29	60	68	43	200

Source: Table from "South 600", in *South*, August 1987, pp. 14-24.

High-tech sectors: chemicals, pharmaceuticals, computers, electrical and electronic products, scientific and aerospace equipment.
Mid-tech sectors: rubber, stone, clay and glass products, metals, engineering, transport vehicles and car industry.
Low-tech sectors: food, textiles and clothing, wood and paper, various products.

Bibliography

Betts R.F., *Decolonization*, London, 1998.
Gauthier A., *L'économie mondiale depuis la fin du XIX siècle*, Paris, 1995.
Levine P., *The British Empire. Sunrise to Sunset*, Harlow, 2007.
Reinhard W., *Kleine Geschichte des Kolonialismus*, Stuttgart, 1996.

Chapter 17
FROM KEYNES TO NEOLIBERALISM

SUMMARY: 17.1. The end of Keynesian economics. – 17.2. The 1970s recession. – 17.3. Retreat of the public sector in the West. – 17.4. Privatizations in Europe. – 17.5. Why privatize, how to privatize. – 17.6. Privatization and development. – Bibliography.

17.1. The end of Keynesian economics

Towards the end of the 1970s, the world's top 500 companies included Brazil's Petrobras, Argentina's YPF and Mexico's Pemex – world leaders in the petroleum industry – together with Italy's Eni and France's Elf-Aquitaine; Renault and Alfa Romeo in the car industry; Saint Gobain; Rhône-Poulenc (giant French chemical company), British Steel and Italsider, Italy's leading steel company; Norway's Norsk Hydro (aluminium), Belgium's Cockerill and a series of other very large companies in different sectors.[1] Despite their differences, these companies shared one very important characteristic: all were controlled by the governments of their respective countries. The top 500 *ranking* included around fifty of these state-controlled companies, evidence of their importance among the world's largest corporations. Yet this was also the moment when Britain's Conservative government led by Margaret Thatcher embarked on a vast privatization programme involving a large number of state-controlled companies, and the British example was soon followed by many other industrialized Western nations.

In fact, while the early 1980s marked the period when the public sector was at its peak of expansion in the advanced capitalist economies, it also marked the beginnings of the process to dismantle the state's direct role in the economy, which had been built up during the previous century using public companies and strongly interventionist economic policies.

For several decades, both the industrialized countries and those attempting to launch a development process had relied on the "mixed" economy to accelerate and sustain growth (Chapters 15 and 16), and now

---

[1] J.H. Dunning, R.D. Pearce, *The World's Largest Industrial Enterprises 1962-1983*, Aldershot, 1985.

the "pendulum" began to swing back gradually towards reducing state interference in the economy.

Aside from the single and specific measures marking this phase (liberalizations, decommissioning, privatizations involving vast industrial complexes owned by the State, intense de-regulation of public services and "natural monopolies"), it is important to stress the radical shift in the general economic philosophy that had dominated most of the capitalist economies since the Great Crisis of the 1930s (Chapters 12 and 13). This had revolved around various forms of public intervention aimed at achieving full employment as the essential pre-condition for maintaining high levels of economic growth and development.

The generation that experienced the Great Depression had also seen how war generated full employment (Chapter 14), and then witnessed one of the greatest Keynesian operations ever put into practice – the Marshall Plan (Chapter 15). Even the wave of nationalizations marking the years of "great prosperity" belonged to this scenario, while the excesses of late 18th century liberalism were now just a memory. After the Second World War, stable growth was often achieved within a framework where the state's direct and indirect intervention had an anti-cyclical function but also stimulated growth, as illustrated by the experience of the developing countries (Chapter 16). Demand was the driving force in this scenario. This meant private demand, but also – and above all – public demand, which was financed via substantial taxation and by structural deficit spending. None of the most advanced economies was immune to this tendency, including the USA; during the Kennedy presidency in the 1960s, federal support was been given to civilian and military programmes, including an ambitious aerospace programme.

Keynsian growth policies had been implemented at different levels of intensity using different tools in the different nations, but were a constant during all the years of great prosperity in the post-war period and gave excellent results. Now the 1970s brought a set of serious problems into what had been a relatively calm context, provoking a vast revolution that would threaten the entire structure of post-war economic and industrial policies.

17.2. The 1970s recession

Although intensity levels differed, the 1970s were a time of general recession when all the industrialized countries experienced the same difficulties: high inflation and a stagnating GDP, plus the unusual problem of rising unemployment. In the USA, for example, unemployment rose from around 4.5% in the 1970s to almost 10%, while inflation rose into double figures after 1975. Other countries were in an even more dramatic situation: unemployment in Britain and Italy climbed to 12% and inflation to over 20%. The impact on France and Germany was less, but the scale of the problem was nevertheless vast, especially when compared with the levels of almost full employment and minimum inflation in the previous decades. To those used to growth rates of 5% and over, GDP now appeared to stagnate, growing slowly at roughly 1-1.5% in almost every country. The capitalist countries were once again pervaded by the dramatic feelings of uncertainty and instability that had marked the 1930s.

Two dramatic petrol crises in 1973 and 1979 were triggered by a rise in petrol prices following a decision taken by the international producers' cartel OPEC. The daily lives of Western Europeans were once again affected by shortages, a return to the stress of wartime after thirty years.

The ensuing desperate attempts by Western governments to recover competitiveness through systematic currency devaluations definitively swept away another pillar underpinning the recovery of the world economy in the post war decades: the system of fixed exchange rates introduced with the Bretton Woods Conference in 1944.

The downturn followed years of uninterrupted growth, representing an undeniable contradiction for an economic philosophy based on the Keynesian principles that demand was the driving force. In this climate of uncertainty, liberal principles now began to re-surface in the universities – after going underground for decades – and especially in government departments and ministries. The first to speak out against the Keynsian thought dominating Western economic policy were "monetarist" economists, who held that the gradual and controlled expansion of money in circulation was an essential ingredient of growth, and would have short-term effects on gross domestic product that would contain inflation in the medium to long term.

The Keynesian idea of demand as the driving force was radically opposed by economists who believed that it was an essential objective of economic policy. In this case "supply" was intended as the mass of "producers", particularly in the private sector, whose implicit dynamism had been too long compressed by the fiscal and regulatory constraints of the postwar decades. According to *supply-side economics,* liberalizations, decreased regulation and lower tax pressure on citizens and businesses would contain inflation by stimulating demand, reducing unemployment and allowing free price competition. According to this view, a reduction in fiscal pressure would actually lead to an increase in total government revenue through economic growth. The prerequisite for success of the solutions offered by *supply-side economics* was therefore a climate of whole-hearted liberalism.

Towards the end of the 1970s this was implemented by conservative governments in Great Britain (under Margaret Thatcher from 1979) and in the United States (under Republican president Ronald Reagan from 1981).

17.3. Retreat of the public sector in the West

The public sector – intended in the broad sense of state economic intervention via fiscal policy, public spending and partial or total state control over public bodies and companies – had expanded continually in the West, a process that had already started between the two world wars in some cases. The establishment of organized *welfare* systems in Western Europe (Chapter 15) had also contributed to giving governments absolute leadership in economic affairs via their spending capacity and unprecedented control of resources.

In the case of Italy, the State's entrepreneurial activity was systematized after the war in an organizational pyramid reaching from the government to a Ministry for State Shareholdings (*Partecipazioni statali* – 1956), to a series of public institutions controlling various private-law companies in the most disparate sectors (including banks).

France and Britain experienced parallel expansion of the "state intervention" through an intense process of nationalization, mainly involving transport, communications, energy and utilities in general. A similar process took place also in Germany and Scandinavia, but to a lesser extent.

In the countries where public enterprise was most intense, the outcome of these processes was that the State played a central role in the formation of gross capital and investments (in the most evident cases, like Italy, France and Britain, it accounted for a fifth to a quarter of the total). The state enterprise system achieved undeniable successes in the regulation of natural monopolies, rationalization of the offer in the extremely capital-intensive sectors, and investment in the sectors with the highest rates of research and development. In many cases, like Italy for example, the "state enterprise system" played a decisive role in completing modernization of the country's infrastructures, in the development of transport, and of telephone and motorway networks.

The public sector and state enterprise were not however immune to problems, which became particularly pressing just when the State sector reached its point of maximum expansion at the end of the 1970s. The general crisis of the Keynesian model did not spare public enterprise, which came in for heavy criticism. In the general climate of liberalism, the weaknesses of the Keynesian model were stressed and the inability of *dirigisme* to tackle the crisis brought a rediscovery of "the benefits of the market" and of the principal unit generating wealth and development: private enterprise. The fact that state-owned companies destroyed more resources than they actually created – straining state budgets already in difficulty – no longer worked in their favour, despite the redistribution they objectively performed. In some countries like Great Britain and Italy, public opinion also became increasingly critical of public sector workers' privileges; it was easy to accuse the public sector of being less efficient than the private sector. The image of the public sector was damaged even further by political parties that "took over" the "state enterprise system", resulting in inefficient allocation of investments and resources, and by the discovery of widespread clientelism and corruption. Even the traditional arguments in favour of state enterprise were weakened by technological progress, which allowed and actually encouraged the presence of several operators on the same market. The growing hostility in Western countries towards the idea of the "entrepreneur state" eventually created a bipartisan ideological movement that stressed the benefits of *deregulation*, meaning gradual reduction in government regulation of the economy. Deregulation proceeded alongside privatization; it was important to privatize within a framework providing an actual increase in competition, not simply to transfer to private ownership the benefits of a monopolistic status previously enjoyed by state-owned companies.

17.4. Privatizations in Europe

Starting in the 1970s and continuing throughout the 1990s, a vast privatization process transformed the economic structure of almost every European country. The dynamic process unfolding in Western Europe was essentially following the contraction of the public sector (whose course was already traced). On top of this came the radical transition occurring in Eastern European countries and the former Soviet Union, where the entire centrally directed economic system began to be dismantled from 1989, the symbolic year the Berlin Wall "fell". This resulted in an unprecedented wave of dismissions, which continued until at least the end of the century.

Nevertheless, privatization did not involve only Western and Eastern Europe, where there were historical reasons for the concentration of a larger share of State-owned companies and those operating within planned economies. Nor were Asian and Latin American countries immune, although around 30% of the over 4,000 privatizations registered from the end of the 1970s and the early years of the 21st century involved large companies in Western Europe. The decommissioned companies had provided about 50% of total revenues, demonstrating the absolute importance of the public sector in mixed economy systems.

The United Kingdom's Conservative government led by Margaret Thatcher launched the great movement in 1979 with the sale of British Petroleum, followed by British Aerospace and Cable & Wireless in 1981, and the process went ahead rapidly during the 1980s. The British programme was by the far the most wide-ranging due to the number of privatizations (around 180) and revenue involved (over 145 billion 1995 dollars), accounting for more than 10% of Britain's GDP in 1995.

Scarcely a decade later it was the turn of France, which had one of the world's largest public sectors; it began with the nationalizations carried out after the Second World War and continued during the "economic miracle" until the 1980s, when Socialist governments nationalized important companies like Paribas and Saint-Gobain. Between 1986 and 1990, the conservative government of Jacques Chirac privatized some of France's largest companies in strategic sectors like radio and television, banking and insurance, electricity and *utilities*, for a total of almost 100 billion francs of the time. The following governments were no less determined: the sale of Rhône-Poulenc, Elf, BNP, Total, Pechiney, Air France and France Telecom brought the French state at least another 350 billion francs, with a vast programme involving every sector and worth almost 3% of Britain's GDP.

Italy was the third European country – given the importance and pervasiveness of its public sector – to implement an unprecedented privatization policy second only to Great Britain: in ten years it privatized around a hundred companies, to the value of around $100 billion, equal to 8% of its GNP in 1995.

In total, Western European privatizations were worth $650 billion, corresponding to 7% of the Western Europe's GDP in the mid-1990s.

17.5. Why privatize, how to privatize

In just a couple of decades privatization gradually dismantled a structure that had been built up over fifty years, beginning with gradual State intervention in the economy during the Great Crisis. The governments involved in the privatization process based their decisions to sell on a range of reasons presented to the public. A first series of reasons related to economic efficiency: according to this viewpoint, privatized companies would increase their capacity to produce income and profits, while also improving the services offered to customers. The idea that state-owned companies had a determining role in eliminating monopolistic rents – obtained by the private sector to the detriment of products and services it offered – was now opposed by an evidently neoliberal school of thought seeing efficiency as inseparably connected with private enterprise.

A second series of reasons concerned structural aspects connected to the efficiency and transparency of the financial markets. In many cases, privatizations of vast companies possible only by attracting foreign investors and institutional investors, who were willing to finance this kind of operation only if there was a guarantee of trasparency and equity in the ownership structure of companies run with the exclusive aim of generating "value" for their shareholders. Furthermore, much decommissioning took the form of public offers, which required more efficiency in the stock markets. Not without reason, the first country to privatize was the United Kingdom, which had Europe's most advanced securities market.

A third set of reasons was more contingent, but had more influence on public opinion and the political debate. The State stood to make substantial amounts of money from privatizations, and – more importantly privatization would put an end to what was was seen as the drainage of public resources used to cover the losses caused by poor management.

Lastly – although this involved only certain countries that had begun to decommission following the Treaty of Maastricht, which from 1993 fixed the economic parameters and behaviour of the European Community member states – privatization was essential to obtain full citizenship rights in Europe. During the 1990s, this aim was pursued by Western Europe, and increasingly also by Eastern and Central European countries after the fall of the Berlin Wall (Chapter 19).

In the last decade of the century, privatizations went ahead rapidly in Hungary, Romania, Czech Republic, Slovakia, Slovenia and the Baltic states of Estonia, Latvia and Lithuania. In total, the private sector in these *transition economies* leapt from about 20% of GDP in the early 1990s to over 60% just ten years later. Revenues were very substantial: over 10% of GDP in Bulgaria, Croatia, the Czech Republic, Lithuania and Poland, over 30% in Hungary and Slovakia.

Everywhere, privatization meant mobilizing a vast complex of financial resources, making it necessary to find adequate tools and methods to manage a process that would profoundly change the nature of capitalism in Europe and the world.

There were three basic ways in which the public sector's contribution to total world GDP fell from an average of 10% to just 5%.

The first of these was prevalent in economies like that of Great Britain, which already had efficient, transparent and advanced stock markets, and was based on substantial public offers.

Elsewhere, for example in France, the State wanted to ensure that the controlling majority of shares remained in French hands in the case of companies in the strategic sectors – energy, banking, and utilities. This produced a version of privatization that included the creation of a "hard core" of stable shareholders, while the rest of the company shares were put on the market. In many cases, the government chose to remain present by issuing *golden shares*, in other words shares conferring special powers to veto shareholder decisions. In other cases, privatizations took place when companies were ceded via auction or private negotiations to national or foreign investors judged capable of restructuring and re-launching the companies considered important, also in terms of employment.

A third and widespread method – especially involving the previously planned economies – was based on the public distribution of *vouchers*, which could then be converted into shares. The aim was to create a vast group of shareholders among the general population, and at the same time start up financial markets in countries where none existed. These policies were successful in the Baltic republics, but in other cases they merely accentuated inequalities and allowed the concentration of enormous wealth in the hands of just a few indidviduals, as happened in Russia at the end of the century. Starting in 1992, Boris Yeltsin's government embarked on an intense process of "economic westernization" based on liberalization and privatization, which resulted in the rapid formation of an aggressive class of private investors via dynamics that were less than transparent. These "oligarchs" enjoyed considerable wealth and had excellent political relations. In a short time, they were became owners of gigantic industrial organizations, especially in the energy and mining sectors. By doing this, they became an alternative centre of power to the State, and exerted extremely strong influence over Russian domestic and international economic policy.

17.6. Privatization and development

During the 1990s some developing economies in Latin America (Mexico, Argentina and Brazil, in particular) began privatizations in fundamental sectors (energy, telecommunications, mining) as did China, India and Russia; this rapidly brought them in line with the process taking place in Western countries, at least in terms of the capital mobilized. The movement also affected Sub-Saharan Africa and Southeast Asia, where substantial privatizations were implemented in Thailand, Indonesia and Malaysia.

Foreign private capital was involved in these processes, and it was directly invested in purchasing ownership of companies in countries considered to be developing or industrializing. Foreign investments were often as important as domestic investments throughout the 1990s, and played an important role in the technological modernization and convergence of the most marginal economies. The two Asian giants – China and India – accelerated "selective" privatization of companies in all sectors considered non-strategic. In China, the public sector's contribution to GDP shrank from 80% in the early 1980s to 20% at the end of the millenium, and the dynamics of the Indian economy were similar, although less marked.

During the last three decades of the 20th century, the role of the State in the economy changed radically in both developed and developing countries.

The mixed economy that had the years of prosperity in the West and the Keynesian principles that had inspired the mixed economy were now under attack. At the same time, the collapse of the communist regimes and the great changes taking place in Asia and Latin America moved in the same direction, driving the marginalization of the State's economic role and increasing the role of liberal principles in political and economic policy decisions.

This created a global economic system in which governments left increasing space for the private sector, limiting their own role to that of outlining and regulating the general framework of action for foreign and national companies and entrepreneurs. Privatization, liberalization and deregulation were now the widespread features of the world economy as it entered the new millennium. It is not yet possible to formulate a historical evaluation of this period, but contemporary views seem to tend cautiously towards registering positive tendencies in terms of increased efficiency and opportunities of development and technological modernization for the most backward countries.

Table 17.1. Shares of GDP and private sector employment in Eastern Europe (1989-1994)

	GDP			Employment		
	1991	1995	2002	1991	1995	2001
Albania	24	60	75	–	74	82
Armenia	–	45	70	29	49	–
Azerbaijan	–	25	60	–	43	–
Belarus	7	15	25	2	7	–
Bosnia Herzegovina	–	–	45	–	–	–
Bulgaria	17	50	75	10	41	81
Croatia	25	40	60	22	48	
Czech Republic	17	70	80	19	57	70
Estonia	18	65	80	11	–	–
Macedonia	–	40	60	–	–	–

(follows)

Georgia	27	30	65	25	–	–
Hungary	33	60	80	–	71	–
Kazakhstan	12	25	65	5	–	75
Kirgizstan	–	40	65	–	69	79
Latvia	–	55	70	12	60	73
Lithuania	15	65	75	16	–	–
Moldavia	–	30	50	36		
Poland	45	60	75	51	61	72
Romania	24	45	65	34	51	75
Russia	10	55	70	5	–	–
Serbia and Montenegro	–	–	45	–	–	–
Slovakia	–	60	80	13	60	75
Slovenia	16	50	65	18	48	
Tajikistan	–	25	50	–	53	63
Turkmenistan	–	15	25	–	–	–
Ukraine	8	45	65	–	–	–
Uzbekistan	–	30	45	–	–	–
Average	**20**	**44**	**62**			

Source: S. Estrin, J. Hanousek, E. Kocenda, J. Svejnar, *The Effects of Privatization and Ownership in Transition Economies*, in *Journal of Economic Literature*, Vol. XLVII, September 2009, pp. 1-30.

Table 17.2. Public sector share (1978-1991, % of GDP)

	Production		Gross domestic investments	
	1978-85	**1986-91**	**1978-85**	**1986-91**
Argentina	4.7	4.7	11.4	8.5
Austria	6.5	13.9	–	6.2
Bolivia	13.0	13.7	26.9	26.9
Brazil	5.0	8.6	26.3	15.2
Chile	13.6	12.9	16.2	12.0
France	10.7	10.0	15.2	11.6
India	10.8	13.8	42.5	39.0
Indonesia	15.4	14.1	14.7	10.3
Italy	6.7	5.6	12.2	12.9
Japan	–	–	10.2	5.5
Korea	9.6	10.3	26.2	15.3

(follows)

Mexico	12.0	11.0	26.8	14.3
Peru	8.5	5.3	14.4	7.7
Taiwan	–	–	29.5	17.7
Thailand	–	–	15.6	13.5
United Kingdom	5.9	3.0	15.1	5.6
Venezuela	23.1	23.0	40.7	53.6

Source: World Bank, *Bureaucrats in Business: The Economics and Politics of Government Ownership*, Washington, DC, 1995.

Table 17.3. Privatizations in developing countries (1988-2003)

	Number of transactions	Revenue (million dollars)
Latin America and Caribbean	1,270	90,274.96
Eastern Europe and Central Asia	5,634	78,132.05
Eastern Asia and Pacific area	417	40,398.46
Southern Asia	399	14,440.00
Middle East and North Africa	307	10,049.88
Sub-Saharan Africa	979	8,238.46
Total	9,006	241,533.81

Source: World Bank, *Privatizations 1988 to 2003 – Sectors. Infrastructure, Energy, Primary, Financial, Manufacturing and Services*, 2003.

Bibliography

Kikeri S., Kolo A.F., *Privatization. Trends and Recent Developments*, in *World Bank Policy Research Working Paper 3765*, 2005.

Thomas J.-P., *Les politiques economiques au XXe siecle*, Paris, 1994.

Toninelli P.A. (ed.), *The Rise and Fall of State-Owned Enterprise in the Western World*, New York, 2000.

Vickers J., Wright V. (eds.), *The Politics of Privatisation in Western Europe*, London, 1989.

Chapter 18
THIRD WORLD, "THIRD WORLDS"

SUMMARY: 18.1. Fragmentation of the Third World. – 18.2. A legacy of the past. – 18.3. The disadvantages of the latecomers . – 18.4. Sectors and companies. – 18.5. Developmental states. – Bibliography.

18.1. Fragmentation of the Third World

In the mid-1960s only two countries in East Asia could boast a per capita income above the world average: Japan and Hong Kong.[1] The latter enjoyed privileged status as a commercial port city and British concession, while the former had successfully completed its reconstruction process and was rapidly recovering the positions it had lost. Japan was reactivating a powerful productive system in the base sectors through its large integrated and diversified corporations (*keiretsu*), supported by small supplier businesses. Having recovered the organizational capacities that years of war and occupation had not eliminated, Japan was now on a par with many of the Western countries at the "economic miracle" stage, at least in terms of the apparent prosperity demonstrated by its citizens' gross disposable income.

However, Japan's success could not conceal the fact that the wealth generated by petrol – the resource essential for industry – stopped at the Arabian Peninsula. The world east of Arabia was largely underdeveloped, a condition that included ancient giants like China and India and more recently formed nations like Pakistan, Bangladesh, Cambodia and Vietnam.

Ten years later during the great crisis that hit the West in the 1970s, there were signs of change in the Far East. In 1975, Japan and Hong Kong were joined by Singapore, a small city-state that had gained its independence in 1965. Another ten years later two more counties in this area joined the "club" of developed countries in 1985: South Korea and Taiwan. Each of these economies had experienced a period of dramatically rapid growth: taking per capita GDP in 1965 as 100, South Korea rose to 220 in 1975

---

[1] The data used in this chapter are taken from: *http://www.ggdc.net/maddison/oriindex.htm*.

and almost 400 in 1985. At the same time, Taiwan moved up from 100 to 374, and Singapore went over 400.

This unprecedented success was unequalled by the other countries in the area, like Vietnam and Bangladesh, which either stagnated or had much lower growth rates, and unequalled also by developing countries in other parts of the world.

Even among the more dynamic South American countries, it was impossible to find growth rates similar to Asia. Between 1965 and 1985, Argentina had moved up from 100 to 107, while others were more successful, like Mexico (from 100 to 167) and Brazil, which doubled its per capita GDP at constant prices.

In short, while the Third World had been an indistinct area of general underdevelopment, a different and fragmented picture began to emerge in the 1970s and 1980s. Despite their attempts to launch growth, some countries were still emerging from the stagnation trap or even showing signs of regression. Others, however, proved capable of starting rapid processes of convergence, which soon aligned them with the development standards of the more advanced countries.

In an important piece of comparative research on late-industrializing economies, business historians and economists Alice Amsden and Takashi Hikino identify several categories of developing countries, based on the characteristics of their industrial development and maturation processes, and on their dynamics of *catching up* (i.e. convergence) with the most advanced economies.[2] Although the dividing line between the different groups is flexible, there is no doubt that for some economies – especially the "little Asian tigers", i.e. Taiwan, Singapore, Hong Kong and South Korea, plus a couple of cases in South America – the outcome of late access to industrialization was successful, a kind of *sneaking up* process that resulted in a convergence demonstrated by per capita income and life styles.

However, other countries (even those with a minimum level of industrialization in labour-intensive sectors, like Pakistan and the Philippines) seemed unable to avoid lagging behind, while some were even stumbling back, as in the case of Argentina.

Historical and economic research has identified a series of elements explaining the origins of the different development paths. These explanations include various institutional and cultural aspects, which eventually influence not only the prevalent models of managing economic activity and

---

[2] T. Hikino, A.H. Amsden, *Staying Behind, Stumbling Back, Sneaking Up, Soaring Ahead. Late Industrialization in Historical Perspective*, in W.J. Baumol, R.R. Nelson, E.N. Wolff (eds.), *Convergence of Productivity. Cross-Country Studies and Historical Evidence*, New York, 1994.

forms of company organization, but also influence – perhaps more decisively – the ways in which the State conducts its relations with the economic system. These dynamics are generally valid and are worth examining in more detail.

18.2. A legacy of the past

Many of the so-called Third World countries, both non-industrialized and industrializing, shared a history of colonial domination but had also experienced a substantial permanent transfer of resources and knowhow from continental Europe. In some cases, like many of the African nations, colonial rule had not affected the traditional economic structure based on subsistence agriculture with little dynamism and artisanal manufacturing at a very low level of capital intensity. In this case, the base for constructing an eventual process of convergence was fragile and unstable, often non-existent. For this reason, the economic formula remained for a long time based on stagnation, poverty, expropriation of natural resources and exploitation of the population by the political and military elite; the possibility of accumulating and mobilizing enough capital resources to launch a process of growth remained remote.

Elsewhere, however, the decade preceding the Second World War had created a different set of opportunities. In many Central and South American countries, including Argentina, Brazil, Chile and Mexico, immigrants mostly from continental Europe had brought a substantial core of experience into the manufacturing sector; many immigrants were non-specialized workers, but there were also large percentages of experts, artisans and plenty who were ready to set up their own independent businesses.

In Asia, manufacturing knowhow had been transferred via migration (for example, many businesses operating in Indonesia, Malaysia, Taiwan and Thailand were owned by Chinese and Indians), via the colonial legacy, and from Europe (to Indonesia, China and India, Malaysia) or Japan (to Korea, China and Taiwan).

There were also many foreign businesses from North America and Europe operating in both areas; attracted by the natural resources and by promising consumer markets, they transferred modern technology and brought a fresh input of entrepreneurship.

Given these pre-conditions, however, during the 1950s and 1960s, a difference also emerged between those able to use this technological base to construct their own development model, and those unable to escape the trap of foreign dependence.

It is easy to understand that what was simplistically defined as the Third

World was actually very varied and contained a variety of different potentials, although the starting point for all these nations was underdevelopment and economic stagnation. Above all, there was a difference between the countries with previous experience of manufacturing and those without any, which appeared to be doomed to inevitable stagnation. In the first group, it is possible to distinguish between the countries that successfully broke with the past and began a process of industrialization according to their own original "formula", and those which remained tied to the "colonial" dynamics of the pre-war period.

18.3. The disadvantages of the latecomers

Even for the countries with a minimal industrial base, *catching up* was far from being a simple process. According to some estimates, at the end of the 19th century per capita GDP of the economic leader Great Britain was two to three times higher than that of the more backward continental European economies. For the backward *latecomers* of the 1970s, the distance to catch up had become enormous: the development frontier was (still in terms of per capita GDP) twenty-five times higher than the level registered in the most underdeveloped countries.

It seemed that the traditional "recipes" for convergence between the end of the 19th century and the Second World War was now in increasing difficulty, or had stopped functioning. What needed eliminating were the age-old accumulation mechanisms of the primary sector (they were too slow and gave insufficient results), which had accompanied the growth paths of backward continental European countries, like Italy. It was equally impossible to promote rapid development based on *labour intensive* sectors and on low salaries; these would not allow sufficient accumulation and were not sustainable in the medium to long term because salaries tend naturally to rise, and also because of the need to encourage demand and domestic consumption to sustain the development process.

Recent and past experiences also showed that it was impossible to use devaluation to create a lasting process of growth and alignment with international standards. In the short term this might actually facilitate exports in base sectors, allowing accumulation to start, but in the medium to long term devaluation generated instability, affecting imports of needed inputs, together with salaries and workers' living conditions, as well as the more general conditions of macro-economic stability of any country choosing to implement measures of this kind.

Lastly, the general extreme backwardness of 20th century *latecomers* advised against waiting for foreign companies to provide the final impulse towards economic and technological convergence; there was little incentive for foreign investors to move into unpromising markets, and any interest they might have was limited to natural resources or cheap labour.

Given these conditions, it was extremely difficult to imagine a return to the technological *catching-up mechanism* once reconstructed and analyzed by Alexander Gerschenkron (Chapters 6 and 7). According to his analysis, during the second half of the 19th century, *latecomer* countries like Germany and the USA had successfully caught up with Britain in the cutting-edge sectors, which Britain had not been able to control adequately. A century later this was no longer possible: the technology *gap* had become too wide, and the capital and knowhow required to catch up rapidly were just too great.

Historians who have most recently analyzed economies that were most successful in catching up and becoming world leaders have identified three ingredients giving an adequate explanation of their success. The first involves the sectors with a leading role in the successful process; the second is related to the peculiar forms of company present in the country, and the third – although not in order of importance – is the role of the State in the promotion, management and coordination of industrialization.

18.4. Sectors and companies

As noted by Amsden and Hikino, one common feature of the development paths taken by the successful countries in launching their "upward spiral" of growth consists of a deliberate and definite concentration on sectors that can be defined as technologically "average" or mature. It was therefore a question of achieving and maintaining stable leadership in industries using easily available technology, because the sector was already consolidated and did not require excessively specialized human capital. Furthermore, there were none of the difficulties encountered by the countries which focused their efforts on cheap labour, which was difficult to sustain. In the historical period examined here, the sectors of interest were steel, basic chemicals, cars, consumer electronic goods, and standard computer industry components, such as semi-conductors. The result of this strategy was that in the mid-1980s, two-thirds of the top 200 companies in developing countries (excluding the petrol industry) were operating in medium to low technology sectors, and only thirty in sectors defined as *high tech*.

Within these circumscribed sectors of activity, the companies in rapidly industrializing countries aimed to obtain competitive advantages through increased output and by constantly improving the efficiency of organization and production management; they focused their best talents and biggest investments in human resources on efficiency.

Precise sectoral specialization, which also focused on sectors in constant growth on the international market and therefore on maximizing potential export trades and the entry of foreign currency, naturally implied the presence of large companies capable of adequate economies of scale for productions that were already markedly standardized. In the case of modern *latecomers*, however, the leading companies had some peculiar strategies and organizational structures.

In the first place, their prevalent strategies included a high degree of diversification for several reasons. The first was a quite evident desire to reduce the risks connected with performing a single activity without having exclusive control of the technology, which was now relatively easy to obtain. The second reason was that the small size of the domestic market not only encouraged export trade, but also drove diversification in different sectors. Lastly, but not in importance, came a further element, which was the relative ease for these companies in acquiring production technologies in the low and medium technology sectors, together with the absence of *core technology* able to foster diversification in neighbouring sectors.

In all the late-industrializing countries – in Asia and South America alike – the diversification strategies used by the major companies were accompanied by organizational structures very different from those leading growth of the big integrated corporations during the second Industrial Revolution (Chapter 7). In a way that was more similar to the situation of the first *latecomers* like Japan, the dominating structure was the "group", a legal unit on which a series of other legal units depended through share ownership; the latter operated in the sectors of interest to the company's "conglomerated" diversification strategy. Despite having different names (*chaebol* in Korea, *grupos* in Brazil and Argentina) these organizations shared (and continue to share) a set of characteristics: in addition to their marked diversification and considerable size, they are generally under the close control by a family and have close and privileged relations with the political authority. Almost all these "groups" included *trading companies*, whose essential task was to connect with the international markets.

The diffusion of these conglomerates in the latecomer economies of Southeast Asia, Latin America, and in some Mediterranean countries (for example, Turkey) is also due to their objective importance in the respective economies. As in Japan between the two wars, these peculiar "structures" accounted for substantial proportions of GDP, of production in their respective sectors, of stock market capitalization and of the total manufacturing exports of their country's manufacturing sector. According to some estimates for the early 1990s, the total turnover of the first ten groups amounted to around 6% in India, 8% in Brazil, and over 10% in Argentina and Mexico. In Taiwan and Indonesia their share rose beyond 20%, while it was close to 50% in South Korea, where over 70% of major companies were affiliated to one of the leading *chaebols*. Lastly, the dynamic presence of the "groups" was important to ensure effectiveness of the third pillar supporting the rapid emergence of the economic late comers in the second half of the 20th century: state intervention in order to accelerate development.

18.5. Developmental states

Nowadays, the role of governments in convergence is effectively described by the term *developmental state:* this summarizes the idea that state initiative took a direct and important role in creating the conditions for private companies to operate, and was also responsible for defining and directing the action of private capital towards maximum efficiency within a general and combined development strategy. The governments that deliberately acted as development "accelerators" did not reject the use of planning policies or the creation of state-owned companies in strategic sectors, because these could bring in large amounts of foreign currency (the petrol industry was the leading sector in this respect). However, the real essence of the developmental state was its sophisticated capacity to interact with the private sector, which was required to pursue its own aims of profitability within a framework provided by an overall policy of regulated production.

The developmental states governing the rise of late comer and non-industrialized economies operated in very different contexts and their initial conditions were very different. Nonetheless, they shared some strategic functions and were guided by the basic principle that the efficiency of the manufacturing sector (to be enhanced and increased by an accurate subsidy policy) would have positive economic effects on the entire population. These functions included the fundamentally important creation of an efficient banking system to channel financial resources towards selected investment objectives. New *development banks* founded in Asia and South America were the principal channels for financing infrastructures and industrial plants in the state and private sectors alike.

The development banks – directly controlled by governments – offered medium- and long-term credit at extremely low interest rates. One significant example of this is the Korean Development Bank, which in the early 1970s provided over 40% of the total funding granted to private industry by the Korean banking sector. During the same period, the percentage was over 35% in Mexico. When credit was granted, it often involved bank ownership of share quotas in the companies funded, which gave the development banks great influence in companies' strategic decisions and in encouraging their organizational efficiency.

Bank credit decisions in every country were shaped by the need to sustain investments aimed at reducing imports and maximizing exports. The general plan consisted of initial support for the sectors where it was possible to accumulate foreign currency reserves. This currency was then used to finance development in neighbouring sectors that used domestic raw materials and could attract new technology and advanced knowhow from abroad once the development process was under way. This meant that the development banks themselves had to be capable of understanding global tendencies in order to favour the sectors offering the most promising prospects on each occasion. For example, the Korean Development Bank invested mainly in the textile industry in the 1960s, but supported the steel and metalworking sector during the following decade.

In return for providing advantageous credit terms, the banks required companies to respect fixed standards in technology and in strategic aims and objectives regarding international competition. All operations were accurately monitored, and it is fair to say that the development banks drove the spread of a management and efficiency culture in the countries where they operated.

International competitiveness measured in relation to company exports was one of the *targets* that *developmental states* pursued with the greatest determination. One particularly significant example is the Taiwanese government; at the end of the 1970s it not only provided subsidies to companies based on the quantity of their exports, but also allowed domestic sales only to companies able to demonstrate that substantial amounts of their production were exported.

Other methods often used by the *developmental states* included fiscal incentives, and price control in the base sectors that supplied inputs to other manufacturing industries. Government interventions obviously required accurate planning in order to maximize the aggregate effects of these incentive policies.

Within the variegated global panorama of development paths attempted and documented in the second half of the 20th century, in many cases it was possible to avoid the underdevelopment trap. Some countries belonged to the vast category of underdeveloped and non-industrialized economies immediately after the war, but then rapidly implemented modernizing growth processes that placed them firmly in the "club" of the most advanced nations. This huge success was due to the combination of government action to develop the national manufacturing sector and independent entrepreneurial impulses in the private sector. In its most successful forms, the action of the *developmental states* can be likened to a gigantic effort to harmonize collective interests with private initiative in order to regulate capital and – naturally – labour.

Alongside the many success stories of small city-states like Hong Kong and Singapore, and of larger states like Indonesia, Malaysia, South Korea, Brazil, Mexico and Turkey, there were also failures, confirming the fundamentally "institutional" nature of these struggles to combat underdevelopment. Argentina is an example: during the same decades, this great South American country was unable to activate the virtuous circle connecting state coordination and private initiative, and it wasted entrepreneurial energy on short-term industrial policies that did not create any stable development pattern.

Table 18.1. Relative backwardness by country groups (1800-1970, per capita GDP in 1960 dollars)

	Year				
	1800	**1860**	**1913**	**1950**	**1970**
Developed countries					
(A) Average	198	324	662	1,054	2,229
(B) More developed	240	580	1,350	2,420	3,600
Underdeveloped regions					
(C) Average	188	174	192	203	308
(D) Less developed	130	130	130	135	140
Relative backwardness					
B/A	1.2	1.8	2.0	2.3	1.6
A/C	1.1	1.9	3.4	5.2	7.2
Historical examples	**Distance from world development frontier**[a]				
Backward Europe, late 19th century (e.g.: Nordic countries)	from 1.8 to 3.3				
Underdeveloped world, end 19th-start 20th century (e.g. Japan)	from 3.3 to 7.0				
Developing countries after Second World War, average	11.9				
Recently developed countries, average 1970s	25.7				

[a] The distance from the world development frontier is measured as the proportion of the per capita GDP of the most developed economies.

Source: T. Hikino, A.H. Amsden, *Staying Behind*, cit., 1994.

Table 18.2. Types of business groups in the world

Country	Conglomerates	Vertically integrated groups	Assets of groups in financial sector
Brazil	1.4	0.04	–
Chile	5.1	0.06	0.24
India	4.2	0.04	0.05
Indonesia	2.1	0.04	0.45
Korea	1.7	0.04	–
Mexico	2.7	0.02	0.05
Philippines	3.1	0.08	0.60
Taiwan	1.6	0.02	0.01
Thailand	3.5	0.04	0.35

Source: T. Khanna, Y. Yafeh, *Business Groups in Emerging Markets. Paragons or Parasites?,* in *Journal of Economic Literature,* 45, 2 (June 2007), pp. 331-372.

Bibliography

Amsden A.H., *The Rise of "The Rest". Challenges to the West from Late-Industrializing Economies*, Oxford, 2001.

Guillén M.F., *The Limits of Convergence. Globalization and Organizational Change in Argentina, South Korea and Spain*, Princeton, 2001.

Hikino T., Amsden A.H., *Staying Behind, Stumbling Back, Sneaking Up, Soaring Ahead. Late Industrialization in Historical Perspective*, in W.J. Baumol, R.R. Nelson, E.N. Wolff (eds.), *Convergence of Productivity. Cross-Country Studies and Historical Evidence*, New York, 1994.

Musacchio A., Lazzarini S.G., *Reinventing State Capitalism. Leviathan in Business, Brazil and Beyond*, Cambridge, Mass., 2014.

Chapter 19
THE END OF A GREAT DREAM

SUMMARY: 19.1. A crisis with deep roots. – 19.2. Gorbachev's impossible dream. – 19.3. The difficult return to the market economy. – 19.4. Towards a new State capitalism. – Bibliography.

19.1. A crisis with deep roots

Although the first half of the 1970s was a period of severe crisis for all the world's economies, mainly due to soaring petrol prices, the USSR appeared unaffected by the shockwave hitting the rest of the world. GDP fell by 6% between 1973 and 1975 in the USA, while unemployment doubled to 9%. The situation was even worse in Western Europe, which depended more heavily on petrol imports from the Middle East; hundreds of thousands lost their jobs in the great industrial regions of Great Britain, the Ruhr and Italy's northwest. For the first time, since the Second World War and the subsequent years of record growth, Japan experienced a contraction in the wealth it produced.[1]

In 1978, two American economists had produced data showing that the USSR's economy did not present the same regular and repeated cyclical fluctuations as the Western economies. This meant that its influence on the world economy and its capacity to create economic turbulence was practically zero. However, this apparent stability concealed some extremely serious and widespread criticalities. The GDP growth rates of the 1950s, not to mention those of the first Five-Year Plans, were just a distant memory. The reforms of the 1960s and 1970s bore fruit slowly. Economic development rates had dropped from a level of 6% in the decade after the Second World War to 3.8% in 1971-1975, and had fallen to extremely low levels (0.8 and 1.4%) by 1979-1980. Agriculture was in the same state as the economy in general. The growth of per capita consumption had fallen from an average of 5% in the 1960s to just over 2% towards the end of the following decade. Nevertheless, these figures cannot describe the relatively low quality of most goods, or the long queues to buy even basic consumer

---

[1] S. Kotkin, *Armageddon Collapse 1970-2000*, Oxford, 2001, pp. 10-13.

goods, nor do they depict the dramatic worsening of the physical and mental problems of many Soviet citizens: alcoholism, abortion, infant mortality and – for men – a reduction in life expectancy.

Although the "visible hand" of Stalinist planners had transformed what had once been an extremely poor country into one of the world's major industrial economies over a couple of decades, it did not have the same scope or power to impose the economic reforms introduced after Stalin's death. Without abandonng the fundamental principles of the centralized economic model, Krushchev began to open towards private consumption, allowing a glimpse of a kind of "socialist consumerism". This then spread in different ways and to different degrees among the other Eastern bloc countries during the second late 1960s. However, while the planned economy had been able to generate "extensive development", it was less capable of shifting towards "intensive development" via interventions to improve the quality of both fixed and human capital. The GDP growth rate of 6% in the 1960s was no longer comparable to the rates of the 1930s or 1950s, so that total productivity increased by just 1.4%.

Once the fundamental problems of Russian economic backwardness immediately after the October Revolution had been solved, centralized planning became much more complex. As time passed, the level of bureaucratization in the Soviet economy rose considerably. At the start of the 1980s, the Soviet industrial system was based on forty sectors or groups of industries, each coordinated by a ministry. Before the 1973 reform, these ministries interacted directly with the hundreds – and sometimes thousands – of companies under their direct control.

In addition, while the fall-out from military technologies nearly always benefitted adjacent civilian sectors in the Western countries, increased military spending in the USSR actually had a negative effect on the rest of its economic system. The USSR concentrated so many technical and human resources on its defence sector that it deprived all the other sectors, making them much less dynamic.

The reforms introduced by Premier Kosygin in the 1960s had very little effect on changing this mechanism, but merely increased the level of decentralization; their impact was limited given that the fixed price system continued. Talk of company profits had little real meaning if prices remained "artificial". On the other hand, managers had few opportunities to improve company performance to any substantial extent when both supply and prices were subject to centralized control. In conclusion, despite a slight initial improvement, the reforms of the 1960s had no real effect on the overall situation of the Soviet economy, but merely increased the level of centralized control.

The problems of agriculture and the limited impact of reforms meant that GDP growth was much slower in the 1970s. Although per capita consumption had increased during the two decades after the war, growth rates now began to slow. Moreover, aside from the purely statistical aspects of the situation, widespread dissatisfaction with mass consumer products became increasingly evident.[2]

Another crisis factor was the petrol question. Between the end of the 1950s and the early 1960s, the USSR had initially derived political benefit from selling its petrol abroad and thus creating divisions in the West. Subsequently, helped by rising prices after the crisis in 1973-74, petrol export became the only means for the government to obtain the dollars to buy the technology it needed in order to reduce the *gap* with the West. Some of the profits derived from OPEC's price policy would finance sales of petrol to the Comecon countries at fixed prices. However, towards the end of the 1970s and early the 1980s petrol production no longer grew as it once had, and attempts to locate new petrol fields, especially in Eastern Siberia, were slow to fulfil expectations, partly due to the use of poor technologies. The solution was to find alternative sources of energy, especially natural gas, so that GDP could grow without an increase in petrol production. In the early 1980s, the West was already aware that the USSR possessed all the potential to become the world's leading producer of natural gas. Here again, the technological constraints could only be overcome by exporting petrol or other materials to the West.[3]

The situation even more fragile from a structural point of view. Falling birth rates in the early 1980s were due not only to the economic crisis, but also to the extremely high abortion rate (estimated as an average of approximately ten per woman of childbearing age). This meant that while Russia's population had traditionally had the highest fertility levels in Europe, it was now unable to reproduce itself for the first time in history, so that each year, more Russians died than were born.[4]

Thus, the crisis leading to the dissolution of the USSR was deeply rooted in the central planning system. However, it also had political causes, es-

---

[2] J. Adam, *Economic Reforms in the Soviet Union and Eastern Europe since the 1960s*, Hong Kong, 1989; R.N. Cooper, *Economic Aspects of the Cold War, 1962-1975*, in M. Leffler, O.A. Westad (eds.), *The Cambridge History of the Cold War*, Vol. 2, Cambridge, UK, 2010.

[3] T. Gustafson, *Crisis and Plenty. The Politics of Soviet Energy under Brezhnev and Gorbachev*, Princeton, 1989.

[4] F. Lutz, S. Scherbov, *Survey of Fertility Trends in the Republics of Soviet Union: 1959-1990*, in W. Lutz-S. Scherbov-A. Volkov (eds.), *Demographic Trends and Patterns in the Soviet Union Before 1991*, London, 1994, pp. 19-40.

pecially the enormous discrepancy between the programmes established by Communist Party leaders and the human and material resources used to implement them.

The political component of the crisis concerned only the Communist Party *establishment*. Initially designed as a flexible tool that would allow the leadership to move a reluctant population towards a utopian vision of society (Communism), the Party had become a self-referential structure for a privileged class, and its highest levels (the *nomenklatura*) had become a parasitic social caste.

19.2. Gorbachev's impossible dream

According to Richard Pipes, when Mikhail Gorbachev was elected head of the Communist Party in 1985, the USSR presented what Lenin would have defined as "revolutionary conditions"; in other words, there was a stalemate between the country's dominant elites and the general population. The former were no longer able to govern and the latter were no longer willing to be governed as they had been in the past. Nonetheless, according to Lenin, there are also subjective conditions required for a revolution to break out: the population's ability and will to take action. Without these conditions, a revolutionary situation may slowly lose force even at a time of serious crisis.[5]

The political and generational changes that brought Mikhail Gorbachev to the leadership of the Politburo represented an attempt to revive the socialist dream in a profoundly changed society. Despite all its weaknesses, the USSR was a country where the urban population was now double the rural population. It had mass holiday accommodation for over 30 million people; 93% of families owned a television set, 90% a fridge and 60% a washing machine; 3% of the population was enrolled in university, and Western tv series were as popular as they were in other countries like France, Britain and Germany. On the other hand, less than 10% of the population owned a telephone, and citizens were obliged to inform the police if they wanted to own a typewriter. In spite of everything, Gorbachev was seen as the only real and eagerly awaited heir of Krushchev's reformism, and was totally convinced that it was still possible to revive a form of "socialism with a human face".[6]

In November 1987, on the 70th anniversary of the October Revolution, Gorbachev reiterated his conviction that the Soviet system would remain

---

[5] R. Pipes, *Can the Soviet Union Reform?*, in *Foreign Affairs*, Fall, 1984.

[6] S. Kotkin, *Armageddon Averted*, cit., pp. 39-43.

solid and projected towards the future by adhering to the measures approved after his nomination as General Secretary of the Party.[7] This meant eliminating "habitual formulas and schemes" and reducing "the gap between word and deed". His intended reforms would achieve the transition from a centralized command system to a democratic system in the space of two to three years. The new system would be based principally on economic methods and on an "optimal combination of centralism and self-management", which required "a more businesslike and more democratic attitude", together with improved organization and greater discipline. Gorbachev's reforms were symbolized by the word *perestroika* (restructuring), which would give a new impulse to the development of socialism.

Many in the USSR, especially Gorbachev's enemies, believed that the system could not be reformed; the Soviet Union was not Hungary, and what had been achieved there would be impossible in a large country with a large economy. Gorbachev needed to give greater responsibility to those capable of following him. This is also why he concentrated power in several "super ministries" for the manufacturing and agri-food sectors, and introduced a reform to strengthen the powers of the USSR president, elected by the 2,500 members of the Congress of People's Deputies (750 designated by the Party and unions, 1500 elected by universal suffrage).

However, the Party Secretary rapidly ran out of political capital. His promises of reforms and improved living standards were shattered by low growth rates, falling private consumption (according to a 1988 report, only 23 of the 211 official food products were available in food shops) and even inflation (20% in 1990), which was officially impossible in a planned economy.

He was also plagued by a series of disasters, a personal version of "Murphy's Law"[8] ("Gorbachev's Law"), involving the Chernobyl nuclear disaster, earthquakes in Central Asia and Armenia, and a series of bad harvests due to extremely cold winters and hot summers. Lastly came a fall in the price of petrol, which had provided the USSR with 60% of the currency it used for imports, especially of technology. However, what most weakened Gorbachev was the victory of nationalist independence movements in the Baltic States (Estonia, Latvia and Lithuania), and he was overwhelmed by the events of summer and autumn 1991. In August, a self-proclaimed State Committee on the State of Emergency deposed the president and attempted to take power. The popular reaction across the country was im-

---

[7] M.S. Gorbachev, *Document. The 70th Anniversary Address*, in *Foreign Affairs*, Winter 1987/88 issue.

[8] *Soviet Union, Murphy's Law in Moscow*, in *Time*, 9.10.1989.

mediate, especially in Moscow where crowds flocked to support the President of the Russian Parliament, Boris Yeltsin, and the mayors of Moscow and Leningrad. Yeltsin suspended Party activities and dismantled the KGB. Soon afterwards, the presidents of Russia, the Ukraine and Belarus decreed the dissolution of the Soviet Union. In the following months, eight more former Soviet republics joined them to form the Commonwealth of Independent States. In December, Gorbachev resigned from the presidency of a state that no longer existed.[9]

19.3. The difficult return to the market economy

Yeltsin faced some extremely difficult challenges, including four that were absolute priorities. One concerned the need to construct a democratic state based on free elections and the adoption of a new constitution. Another was the creation of a market, which required fiscal and monetary stabilization to prevent rising prices from causing inflation. A third priority to tackle was an enormous programme of privatization. In addition, the country required a new legal system, and this would inevitably take longer to implement, since it involved introducing laws, creating courts, and training thousands of lawyers.

Yeltsin announced his economic reforms in October 1991. The greatest and most rapid transformation of a centralized economy into a market economy took just three years. The Russian government chose a very similar policy to the *shock therapy* of Polish Deputy Prime Minister and Finance Minister Leszek Balcerowicz, adopted by Warsaw's first non-communist government after free elections in June 1989. In Poland, timely policy decisions made it possible to halt hyperinflation rapidly and put many goods back in shops, while absenteeism in factories was reduced by 50% at the same time. On the other hand, many state-owned companies were forced to close, and unemployment climbed from the official figure of 0.3% in January 1990 to 6.5% by the end of the same year. In the next two years, GDP fell by 9.78% and 7.02%. In Russia, the Gaidar government (an ineffective combination of economists with the reforming zeal of "Young Turks", "mediocre politicians from Yeltsin's home town" and "competent ex-ministers of the USSR")[10] attempted to emulate the Polish

---

[9] F. Halliday, *A singular Collapse. The Soviet Union, Market Pressure and Inter-State Competition*, in *Contention*, 1-2, 1992, pp. 121-141; A. Dallin, *Causes of the Collapse of the USSR*, in *Post-Soviet Affairs*, 8/2, 1992, pp 279-302; A. Åslund, *Revisiting the End of the Soviet Union*, in *Problems of Post-Communism*, 2011, pp. 46-55.

[10] S. Kotkin, *Armageddon Averted*, cit., p. 118.

success, but the Yeltsin himself admitted later that the country was in a situation where "theory was powerless". The state deficit was estimated at 20% of GDP in 1991 and continued rising. The country's gold reserves had effectively vanished. Industrial output was plummeting. Official statistics registered a 6% fall in GDP at the start of 1991 and 17% by the end of the year, while inflation was estimated at 250% a month, i.e. an annual rate of almost 3,000%. Prices of some commodities, such as bread and milk, were protected from this shock therapy in order to protect the weakest elements of the population; other pressure groups linked to industry obtained a delay in the liberalization of the energy industry and fuel prices.[11]

The monetary and financial situation was even worse. The Soviet central bank was replaced by central banks in each of the fifteen former Soviet republics. However, while the Russian central bank was authorized to print money, the other fourteen could issue credit in roubles, and the big companies did the same, issuing credit to each other to obtain the supplies they needed. Inflation had appeared to be under control at 7-8% in July 1992, but soared again to 25% per month in autumn. The pensions of millions of citizens became worthless, and the salaries of those with higher level qualifications suddenly lost much of their purchasing power.

It was only in July 1993 that Russia obtained the suspension of credit emission in roubles by the other former Soviet republics. This was the sign that shock therapy had ended, as had Gaidar's leadership. His replacement was Viktor Chernomyrdin, who succeeded in bringing inflation under control where his predecessor had failed; it now fell from 2,250% in 1992 to 840% in 1993, 223% in 1994, 131% in 1995, and was 11% in 1997.

The privatization policy was launched at the beginning of 1992, when about 150 million Russians received a *voucher* with the nominal value of 10,000 roubles ($25, soon devalued to just $2) to participate in the IPOs for all types of privatization. The vouchers could be sold and often ended up in the hands of extremely powerful Russians (foreign investors were excluded from this stage of the process), which paved the way for new centres of power, without any benefit to the State. For example, car manufacturer Avtovaz (which managed the Togliattigrad car factory built with FIAT) was privatized for just $45 million. FIAT had previously made an offer of $2 billion dollars for the company, but was excluded because – it was said – the government did not want foreign ownership of Russian property. In this case, as with the collettive farms, the workers had precedence, and were

---

[11] Z. Medvedev, *Post-Soviet Russia. A Journey Through the Yeltsin Era*, New York, 2000.

authorized to buy 51% of shares. The State continued to hold substantial shares in many companies, ready to cede them to selected investors, all of whom were Russian.

Although around 80% of companies were privatized during this period, the true and most important privatization season was in 1995 and 1998 and involved 29 big groups. The government's financial and fiscal problems had led it to seek loans from the new private banks, known as *loans for shares*, i.e. credit guaranteed by government shares in the petrol industry and other sectors. The shares could be sold by auction if the government did not repay its debt, which is what actually happened. The problem was that the same creditor banks were authorized to manage the auctions. These included Oneximbank, which benefitted the most from this operation, and whose president – Vladimir Potanin – had created the scheme. The outcome was inevitable: the State received much less than the real value of the companies put up for sale, while certain people managed to build up enormous personal fortunes. When Mikhail Khodorkovsky bought 78% of Yukos shares, worth around $5 billion, he paid just $310 million; Sibneft, another giant in the same sector was worth $3 billion, but was bought by Boris Berezovsky and Roman Abramovich for just $100 million.[12]

The Russian government did not make enough effort to contrast this perverse mechanism, which contributed to the formation of a new oligarchy of powerful businessmen. Their origins were essentially of three kinds. One group consisted of high-level former Party officials, and another of managers of big companies with solid personal connections to political power, the former KGB and the industrial establishment. In addition, there were figures connected with the criminal activities that had sprung up in large and small towns and cities immediately after the end of the USSR, involving both the first private businesses and larger scale international trafficking of drugs, arms and people. In *Russia's Capitalist Revolution*, Åslund recalls a conversation in 1999 with a Russian oligarch, who said: "There are three kinds of business men in Russia. One group is murderers. Anther group steals from the private individuals. And then you have honest business men like us who only steal from the state".[13] All the elements existed for what one researcher has called – with a play on words – the "piratization" of the Russian economy. Like true "pirates", these individuals

---

[12] A. Åslund, *How Russia Became a Market Economy*, Washington, 1995; M. Boycko, A. Shleifer, R. Vishny, *Privatizing Russia*, Cambridge, 1995.

[13] A. Åslund, *Russia's Capitalist Revolution. Why Market Reform Succeeded and Democracy Failed*, Washington, 200, p. 160.

became extremely wealthy. According to the 2004 ranking by US magazine *Forbes*, 36 of the world's billionaires were Russian.[14]

The economy had been privatized, but had the country become a democracy? According to Kotkin, Russia had become a democracy without liberalism; in 2008 Åslund explicitly highlighted the failure of the transition to democracy, while other authors speak of "capitalism without capitalists" or "market Bolshevism" without democracy or, yet again of the 1990s in Russia as a *lost decade*, an expression used to define Japan's economic stagnation during the same decade.[15]

In a country that saw a return to forms of barter (increasing from 5 to 50% of sales in industry from 1992 to 1998), the new Russia formed its society and economy around these enormous personal fortunes, and on a "real" power that was able to influence official power. From a strictly economic point of view, Russia essentially re-formed around the energy industry. Gas and petrol accounted for 25% of GDP in the mid-1990s, when the Russian economy began to grow rapidly before it was halted by a short but violent crisis in 1997-1998 caused by a speculative attack on the rouble. The central bank lost a large share of its foreign currency reserves, while the prices of petrol and gas fell. The situation was aggravated by the crisis in Asia and by the fears of those who had invested in the government bonds of emerging and transitional economies. Things worsened in summer 1998 with the collapse of the Moscow Stock Exchange; the government was forced to devalue the rouble and declare debt default, and the Russian economy lost 4.9% of its GDP in one year.[16]

19.4. Towards a new State capitalism

Although economic recovery coincided with the passage of power from Yeltsin to Putin, it would be a mistake to say that the new president was responsible for economic growth. Initially, Putin benefitted from the country's new economic development rather than driving it. Between 1999 and 2001, the economy grew an average of 8-10%; it then settled to levels that were more modest – but still high (5-8%) – before the 2007-2008 crisis.

Putin's achievement was that he managed to redefine the balance of

---

[14] M.I. Goldman, *The Piratization of Russia. Russian Reform Goes Awry*, London, 2003.

[15] S. Kotkin, *Armageddon Averted*, cit., pp. 142-170; P. Reddaway, D. Glin, *Tragedy of Russia's Reforms. Market Bolshevism Against Democracy*, Washington, 2000; A. Åslund, *Russia's Capitalist Revolution*, cit.

[16] A. Åslund, *How Russia Became a Market Economy*, cit.

power between the State and oligarchs, introducing a new fiscal system to reduce the problem of corruption. In addition, the popular support he enjoyed during his first mandate helped Putin to adopt a different attitude to the oligarchs and impose laws that they had never accepted in the past. In February 2000, just two months after becoming President, Putin made it clear that the oligarchs would be treated no differently from any other small or large businessman. This was a sign that the Russian *tycoons* would no longer be able to flout government regulations or enjoy the privilege of direct access to the Kremlin. Putin promised not to interfere in the oligarchs' business, but in return they were required to keep their distance from politics and not challenge or criticize the president. Putin's political power was shifting towards authoritarianism, which was no novelty in Russia, while the oligarchs developed the relational capital essential for them to achieve "institutionalization of the informal" and obtain political protection, in a Muscovite *quid pro quo* between politics and the economy.[17]

Whoever disagreed with these rules spent a short time in prison (Gusinsky) or went into exile (Berezovsky). The most striking example is Khodorkovsky, whose spectacular rise to economic and financial power was followed by an equally dramatic fall. He was reputed to control a hundred Duma deputies, and attacked Putin over the misdeeds of a state-owned petrol company. Khodorkovsky's Yukos went bankrupt in 2003, and he was sentenced to nine years in prison for tax fraud. In 2010, with less than two years of his prison term left to serve, he was charged and found guilty of embezzlement and money laundering. Khodorkovsky should have stayed in prison until 2017, but received a pardon from Putin in 2013 and was allowed to leave the country.[18]

During much of the first decade of the 21st century, internal demand was strong. Despite relying greatly on exports of raw materials for the energy industry, it continued after 2004 despite the fall in petrol prices. Inflation fell from 18.6% in 2001 to 10-11% in 2007-2008, while official unemployment figures fell by 9% to 6-7%; the proportion of the population living in poverty halved between 2001 and 2007, decreasing from 27.5% to 13.4%.

The industrial sector has experienced important changes. It is not always easy to invert the tendency of machinery and tools towards obsolescence, except in the sectors with strategic importance in the new national and international economic situation (energy and energy products). Above

---

[17] S. Guriev, A. Rachinsy, *The Role of Oligarchs in Russian Capitalism*, in *Journal of Economic Perspectives*, 19, 1, 2005, pp. 131-150.

[18] R. Sakwa, *Putin and the Oligarch. The Khodorkovsky-Yukos Affair*, London, 2014.

all, light manufacturing suffers most from what economists call the "Dutch disease": international competition makes it impossible to maintain positions when the rouble appreciates and competitiveness is reduced. It was better to downscale the production system and return to importing light industrial goods from Asia, especially from China.[19]

Given all these tendencies, the State's presence in the economy is increasingly powerful and pervasive, seen as new "state capitalism". This is particularly evident in the energy sector. Gazprom (the world's biggest energy company), Rosoboronexport and Rosnet are the leaders in the energy sector, which accounts for the largest share of GDP and attracts vast amounts of money from abroad, but they also own other enormous industrial groups (Rosoboronexport controls Avtovaz, Russia's leading car manufacturer), and have extremely important interests in television and the press. Gazprom, for example, owns two of Russia's major dailies, *Komsomolskaya Pravda* and *Izvestia*, and the NTV television network.

The Russian economy and consumption levels improved regularly thanks to petrol, but at a certain point the drive from energy products was no longer sufficient. In 2007, the price of petrol was $72 a barrel and the economy grew by 8.5%; in 2012 the price was $111 dollars, but growth was only 3.4%, although the government had raised salaries and pensions and increasing its military spending, in a way that was not unlike the Soviet approach.

The crisis that began in 2007-2008 had few negative effects in Russia, except in 2009. Between 2010 and 2013, when the price of crude oil remained high, net capital exports amounted to $232 billion, which was twenty times more than in 2004-2008. At the beginning of 2014, the rouble began to fall alongside falling petrol prices, which meant that the amount of money imported remained the same. Imports became more expensive and inflation began to rise. Devaluation of the rouble also effected foreign debt, having less of an impact on sovereign debt (which stood at $57 billion in 2013) than on the debt of state-owned and private companies, which was ten times higher.[20]

In January 2012, Putin launched a new privatization programme to revive the economy. However, he did not abandon the State's role in designing the project to transform the structure of the productive system, concentrating more on high-tech sectors and creating economic conditions to encourage foreign investments. Putin re-launched the programme halfway

---

[19] N. Oomes, K. Kalcheva, *Diagnosing Dutch Disease: Does Russia Have the Symptoms?*, in *Imf Working Paper*, April 2007.

[20] *The Russian Economy. The End of the Line*, in *The Economist*, 20.11.2014.

through the year, just after he was re-elected president for the third time, but in June 2013 Prime Minister Medvedev reduced it to about half of the financial objectives for 2014-2016.

This meant that the situation was already difficult when the US and EU imposed sanctions on Russia for its support of pro-Russian rebels in the eastern Ukraine, although the sanctions did not have all the desired effects. Despite the relentless fall in the price of petrol, the Russian economy reacted in a way that all observers found surprising to a certain extent. Between June 2014 and June 2015, the economy contracted by 4.6% (the rouble fell by 37% against the dollar), which was the most dramatic contraction since the 2008-2009 crisis; real incomes dropped for the first time in the fifteen years since Putin first became president. Nevertheless, the economic system also presented positive elements, according to a classical textbook model of economics. The substitution of imported goods with Russian products allowed 78% of the companies quoted on the Moscow Stock Exchange (MICEX) to earn more than their foreign competitors during the first half of 2015 (for example, Rosneft earnings increased by 17%, whereas those of competitors increased by just 1%). On the other hand, the sanctions imposed on the oligarchs closest to Putin seem to have been much more effective, since Western companies prefer not to have their names associated with figures belonging to the Russian president's inner circle.[21]

Many things have changed since the end of the Soviet Union. In 1992, the year after the USSR ceased to exist, the ratio between Russia's GDP and the USA was 1:14; by 2014 the gap had narrowed to 1:9.3, and was actually 1:4.9 at purchasing power parity.[22] These numbers are useful, but do not paint the full picture. As seen, modernization of the Russian economy is not yet complete, nor is privatization. In addition, so many doubts surround the quality of Russia's democratic system that the term often used to describe its political and economic system is "authoritarian capitalism"; this is a concept Russia has in common with China, but also with other countries like Singapore, although their histories and development paths are quite different from Russia's.

---

[21] *Russia's Economy. Phase Two. Russia's Economic Problems Move From the Acute to the Chronic*, in *The Economist*, 21.1.2016.

[22] *http://www.tradingeconomics.com.*

Figure 19.1. USSR GNI growth (1928-1987)

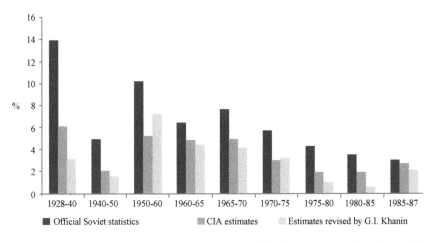

Source: M. Harrison, *Soviet Economic Growth since 1928. The Alternative Statistics of G.I. Khanin*, in *Europe-Asian Studies*, 1993, 45, 1.

Figure 19.2. Russian GDP (at purchasing power parity, $ billion 2013, 1989-2016)

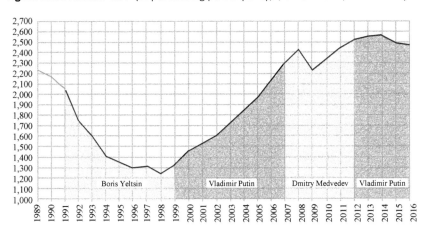

Figure 19.3. Russian rouble (rouble/dollar exchange rate, semilogarithmic scale, 1997-2015)

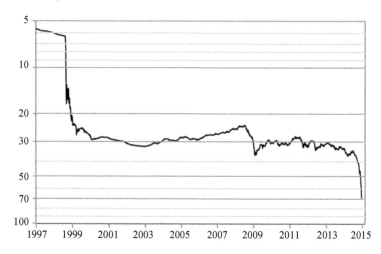

Source: Bloomberg.

Bibliography

Benvenuti F., *Russia oggi. Dalla caduta dell'Unione Sovietica ai nostri giorni*, Rome, 2013.
Goldmann M.I., *The Piratization of Russia. Russian Reform Goes Awry*, New York, 2003.
Gudkov L., Zaslavsky V., *La Russia da Gorbaciov a Putin*, Bologna, 2010.
Kotkin S., *Armageddon Averted. The Soviet Collapse, 1970-2000*, Oxford, 2001.

Chapter 20
UNSTABLE LEADERSHIP

20.1. Reagan's America: reviving the economy and reducing the role of the state

At the start of the 1980s, US society faced far-reaching problems. The end of dollar convertibility in 1971 and soaring petrol prices after the Yom Kippur War (1973) had created imbalances that were difficult to correct. The stagflation of the 1970s led to a rise in unemployment, falling profits and the stagnation of earned income, thus casting doubts on the traditional solutions used to overcoming this type of crisis. The degree of confusion and uncertainty afflicting US society provided the basis for the changes imposed by President Ronald Reagan, elected in November 1980.

In January 1981, the new president's inaugural address launched the key phrase that would mark a substantial proportion of his two mandates: less state intervention in the economy. With these words, Reagan launched what was essentially a set of measures to re-start the economy based on a *supply side* approach: tax cuts for medium to high incomes and companies in order to stimulate consumption and investments, reduced spending on social services, and less state intervention in the labour market. The cuts in social spending were used to increase military spending, in a move with obvious strategic implications (a more assertive containment strategy towards the expansionist ambitions of the USSR, engaged since 1979 in the Afghanistan War and also very active in Africa). This measure had also the purpose of obtaining typically Keynesian effects, both direct (maintaining or increasing employment in a strategic sector that provided jobs for tens of thousands) and indirect (through investments in research and development with positive effects on many sectors). Between 1980 and 1987 *welfare* spending fell from 25.5 to 18.3% of the federal budget, while military spending rose from 29.7 to 35.2%. However, the cuts were linear, because a reduction in spending on certain areas (pensions and medical care for the elderly, tax deductions for mortgages) would have lost Reagan and his Republicans too many votes. Economic deregulation was simpler to implement, creating fewer social and economic problems, and even fewer political problems.[1]

However, the results did not live up to expectations, and in many cases were the opposite of what was intended by a president who based his political activity on containing public spending. The reduction in fiscal revenues drove the federal deficit to over 5%, which meant a substantial rise in the public debt, and this would influence many of the decisions made during subsequent administrations.

Nevertheless, the dollar appreciated, helped by the Federal Reserve's rigorous monetary policy. It had already raised interest rates in 1979, when they were around 11.5%, increased them gradually to 21.5% in December 1980 and then down to below 10%, which had been the 1978 level), allowing the US economy to take maximum advantage of the falling prices of raw materials in the first half of the 1980s. Unemployment reached 10% in 1982-83, and gradually decreased to below 6% by the end of the decade. Inflation was once again under control: it fell from 11 to 13% in 1979-80, 3.6% in 1985, and went below 5% in 1989-1990. This indicated the growing confidence of consumers and investors. From this perspective, Reagan's policy appeared successful, but other figures gave no cause for euphoria. Average GDP growth during the decade was below 3%, which was less than the 1970s, and old fears re-surfaced when Wall Street fell by 25% in October 1987. This was especially true for the middle classes, who had been more convinced than others by Reagan's promises of a new boom.[2]

It is no surprise that Reagan's presidency saw the first fears of a possible end to the "American century". This feeling intensified during the second half of the 1980s with the panic caused by the collapse of the stock exchange. Some observers talked of the relative decline of the USA,[3] although academics were unable to agree on this judgement.[4] Pentagon officials were concerned that defence production was falling in many base industries,

---

[1] W.C. Berman, *America's Right Turn. From Nixon to Clinton*, Baltimore, 1998.

[2] F. Romero, *Il modello americano*, in V. Castronovo (ed.), *Storia dell'economia mondiale, 6. Nuovi equilibri in un mondo globale*, Rome-Bari, 2002, pp. 184-187.

[3] The best-known and most influential academic in this field at the time was British historian P. Kennedy, *The Rise and Fall of the Great Powers. Economic Change and Military Conflict from 1500 to 2000*, New York, 1987.

[4] The best-known and most influential critic of the "decline" theory was political scientist Samuel P. Huntington, director of Harvard University's Center for International Affairs. His article contained the harshest attack on this theory (*The US – Decline or renewal?*, in *Foreign Affairs*, Winter 1988-1989).

putting the production capacity of the entire US industrial system at risk.[5]

During the 1980s, semiconductors became increasingly important worldwide due to their strategic role in the development of the electronics industry, seen in the USA as symbolizing the country's industrial competitiveness and its national security. The US had until then controlled the world market, although it encountered difficulties from the second half of the 1970s with competition from a powerful Japanese industry that was determined to penetrate the US industrial system. For example, Fujitsu attempted to take over Fairchild Semiconductor owned by the French Schlumberger group. Defense Secretary Caspar Weinberger's veto was decisive in preventing this, but perhaps even more so in allowing Fairchild's sale a few months later for $122 million to a US company, National Semiconductor.[6] This was just one of many aspects of a real trade war between the US and Japan. Tensions between the two countries grew alongside the increasing US trade deficit (it rose from below $7 billion to almost $40 billion between 1980 and 1985), blamed by American manufacturers and Washington on the yen, which they considered to be greatly undervalued.

20.2. Japan's lost challenge

The Reagan administration transformed these tensions into a kind of battle, initially for survival and then for US economic recovery from the serious difficulties it faced during the early 1980s. Washington won the contest by using every means it could – especially its political and strategic role – reminding Tokyo that Japan was sheltered under the US nuclear umbrella. The Plaza Accord (called after a famous Fifth Avenue hotel in the heart of Manhattan) was signed in September 1985 by the USA and Japan, and also by Great Britain, France and Germany, and allowed the US dollar to depreciate against the yen by 51% over two years (1985-1987), taking it down from about 262 to 130 yen.

The immediate effect was a slight contraction in Japanese exports. Japan's central bank attempted to contrast this by cutting interest rates and pursuing a strong expansive monetary policy, which had already been launched at the start of the decade. The Japanese central bank dropped its official interest rate from 9% in 1980 to 4.6% in 1986 and to 2.5% in 1987.

---

[5] Department of Defense, *Bolstering Defense Industrial Competitiveness*, Washington, July 1988.

[6] D.K.H. Walters, *Deal to Sell Fairchild Semiconductor to Fujitsu Cancelled*, in *Los Angeles Times*, 17.3.1987; A.L. Friedberg, *The Strategic Implications of Relative Economic Decline*, in *Political Science Quarterly*, 104, 3, Fall 1989, pp. 401-431.

Japan's economic solidity allowed the country's investors to buy some of the historic symbols of American industry. In 1988, Bridgestone was able to buy Firestone, winning the contest with Pirelli. In September 1989, Sony bought one of the Hollywood giants, Columbia Pictures, for $4.4 billion from Coca Cola, its owner since 1982. One month later, the Mitsubishi group paid over $846 million for 51% of the company owning the Rockefeller Center, one of New York's most famous skyscrapers.[7]

Despite the gaps between US and Japanese GDPs and their per capita GDPs, many took it almost for granted that Japan would become the world's leading economic power in the 21st century. In the first half of the the 1980s, while the US economy struggled with a difficult recovery, Japanese GDP grew at an average of 4%, remaining over 3% despite slower growth in the second half of the decade. The liquidity injected into the system drove companies, especially manufacturers, to increase their fixed investments; these rose to around 20% of GDP, which was a similar level to the 1960s. These investments increased the competitiveness of Japanese industry and compensated for appreciation of the yen, while certain markets, especially the US market, were now "used" to products *made in Japan* and price elasticity was much lower.[8]

Liquidity meant that huge amounts of capital were directed towards foreign investments, whereas the influx of short-term capital was much lower (20-30 billion *vs.* 120-130 billion dollars). During this period, Tokyo became one of the world's most dynamic financial markets and rapidly gained a leading international position. The Tokyo stock exchange experienced a period of euphoria as the Nikkei index climbed from 12.598 in September 1985 to 38.915 in December 1989. At the same time, a huge property bubble formed. Land prices in urban residential areas soared, especially after 1985; in real terms, the national increase was 61.6%, but prices in the country's six biggest cities increased by 196.4%

The political authorities also appeared to have caught the growing mood of optimism, convinced that the property boom and rising stock exchange confirmed the solidity of the system. However, the first hints of concern were starting to circulate in the central bank, although it was unable to provide the government with concrete grounds for a change of direc-

---

[7] C. Rappaport, *Japanese Tyre Maker Aims to Become World's Largest*, in *Financial Times*, 14.5.1988; P. Richter, *Sony to Pay $3.4 Billion for Columbia Pictures. Japanese Firm Willing to Offer High Price to Get Film, TV Software for Video Equipment It Makes*, in *Los Angeles Time*s, 28.9.1989; R.J. Cole, *Japanese Buy New York Cachet With Deal for Rockefeller Center*, in *The New York Times*, 31.10 1989.

[8] K. van Wolferen, *The Enigma of Japanese Power*, London, 1989; S. Tsuru, *Japan's Capitalism*, Cambridge, UK, 1993.

tion. Consequently, the banking system continued to pump money into the property sector above all, favouring big and small operators whose only collateral for their debts was the land they possessed or were in the process of buying, on the assumption that prices would either remain stable or rise even higher. The official interest rate was raised for the first time from 2.5 a 3.25% in May 1989, and three more times in the following 14 months until it stood at 6% in summer 1990, the highest level since 1981. However, the Bank of Japan's actions did not bring an immediate halt to the property bubble, which peaked in September 1990 when urban land prices were four times those of 1985.[9]

The stock exchange fell rapidly: at the end of 1990, the Nikkei index fell to 23,848, losing 15,000 points in a year, continuing to drop until it stood at 16,924 by the end of 1992. One year later, the property market also began to fall – as rapidly as it had risen. At the same time, some banks were already in a critical situation; bad debt amounted to around $1,000 billion at the end of 1991, and the figure would continue to grow in the following years. A series of bankruptcies began, hitting a banking system that just a few years earlier had seemed one of the world's most solid and vigorous (in 1987, US magazine *Fortune* reported that nine of the world's leading non-US banks were Japanese): six banks failed in 1992, and dozens more in 1993 and 1994.[10]

The consequences damaged the entire economic system. The banks made less credit available to business, creating difficulties mostly for small and medium companies, increasing numbers of which went bankrupt between 1991 and 1995. The big companies began a far-reaching reorganization process, which meant concentrating on their *core business*, reviewing their diversification strategies; in the case of the biggest *keiretsu* it meant eliminating entire sectors. This obviously involved a huge reduction in employment, restrictions on salaries, and gradual relocation of their activities; in the manufacturing industry, outsourcing rose from 4% to around 14% during the 1990s.[11]

This was the start of the *lost decade* of the 1990s. The Japanese economy fell into deep stagnation, with a GDP growth rate of around 0% and a level of inflation that also gradually dropped towards zero, and then became

---

[9] *http://www.tradingeconomics.com/japan/interest-rate*; Y. Noguchi, *Land Prices and House Prices in Japan, in Housing Markets in the U.S. and Japan*, Chicago, 1994, pp. 11-28.

[10] T. Hoshi, A. Kashyap, *The Japanese Banking Crisis. Where Did it Come From and How Will it End*, Nber Working Paper, 7250.

[11] H. Miyoshi, Y. Nakata (eds.), *Have Japanese Firms Changed? The Lost Decade*, London, 2010.

negative from 1999 to 2003. The central bank gradually reduced the official interest rate down to 0.5% by 1995. Before this, the government had essentially used only fiscal leverage, increasing taxes on consumption and thus helping to depress internal demand even further. This was more of a political and social policy than an economic policy, aimed at obtaining resources to finance the growing cost of social welfare for Japan's rapidly ageing population. Only in the second half of the decade did the government launch expansive policies as it attempted to avert an increasingly dangerous economic trend. Public spending grew in the form of public investments financed with deficit spending, and the deficit rose from 3.4% of GDP in 1995 to 7.6% in 1999, while the public debt increased from 105% to 130% of GDP. However, as in many Western countries two decades previously, despite the abundant financial resures used, the results of this economic policy fell far short of expectations.[12]

20.3. The dynamic recovery of the United States

At the end of the 1990s, Japan was no longer seen as challenging the United States. The Japanese economy was still the second in the world, but the gap with the United States was wider than in the previous decade. The US economy began to grow from the end of the Gulf War until 2001, much more than any other G7 member state. Once again, the United States proved the ideal environment to apply the Schumpeterian idea of "creative destruction"; in the last 20 years of the century, it lost around 44 million jobs during the reorganization of the economy but gained 73 million jobs in the private sector, meaning that there were actually 29 million new jobs. To give an idea of the scale of the phenomenon, 4 million jobs were created in Europe during the same period, but almost all were in the public sector. In the 1990s alone, the US economy created over 14 million new jobs, while Europe lost almost 5 million. US economic growth was relatively limited between 1990 and 1995 and remained on average below 2.5%, but between 1996 and 2001 it grew more than in any other period of history except the 1950s, and was permanently over 4%.[13]

Many factors made this decade the "roaring" 1990s. Slow growth in the late 1980s continued during George Bush's presidency and led to a psycho-

---

[12] F. Hayashi, E.C. Prescott, *The 1990s in Japan. A Lost Decade*, in *Review of Economic Dynamics*, 5, 1, January 2002, pp. 206-235; W.R. Garside, *Japan's Great Stagnation. Forging Ahead, Falling Behind*, Chaltenham, 2012.

[13] J.A. Franke, P.R. Orszag, *American Economic Policy in the 1990s,* Cambridge, Mass., 2002.

logical crisis. Despite the rapid and – in some ways – spectacular victory in the first Gulf War, the US political system seemed unable to offer an outlet for the various demands generated by industry and society's most diverse groups. Bush's limits on public spending continued the policy implemented by Reagan (whose vice president Bush had been for 8 years), but now encountered both old and new social and political constraints. An ageing population (mostly Republican voters) was unwilling to forego any traditional welfare policies. The immigrant population, which had increased greatly during the 1980s, was bringing radical changes to the composition of the US working class. This involved the manufacturing sector, where the salary gap widened once more, overturning a key component of the *American dream*, in which *blue collar* workers were central to the growth of internal demand for consumer durables. It also involved the composite tertiary sector, where many of the new jobs were concentrated, and the middle class felt increasingly insecure. However, the country's economic and financial difficulties obliged Bush to abandon one of his solemn electoral promises in 1990, when he allowed the Democrat dominated Congress to increase taxes without using his power of veto.[14]

Together with the feelings of unease and frustration afflicting different social classes to varying degrees, this decision to increase taxes proved fatal to Bush's hopes of re-election in November 1992. The participation of a third candidate, businessman Ross Perot, was a rare event in US presidential elections, and Perot's success in obtaining 19% of the vote played a decisive role in the victory of Bill Clinton. However, the new presidency did not bring a return to the welfarism of previous Democrat administrations, partly because the trade unions no longer linked the Democrat Party to its traditional electoral base; the profound restructuring of the US economy during the 1980s had eroded much of the unions' influence, leading to a sharp fall in membership.

Clinton's programme was aimed at modernization of the US economy. Aged 46 when elected (Bush was 68), Clinton belonged to a culture that was more open to innovations, and he seemed more capable of accompanying the country into the new world that had begun to develop rapidly in the early 1990s: the world of electronics, with its countless aspects affecting the economy and the lives of millions of people. Clinton's programme also contained a reform of the health system, fiscal incentives in favour of education, and a reduction in the *welfare state* aimed at making certain protected categories return to work.

---

[14] R. Valletta, *Job Loss during the 1990s*, Frbsd Economic Letter, 97-05, February 21, 1997.

It was not simple to implement this programme. The public deficit inherited from the Reagan and Bush administrations prevented new expenditure. On the other hand, Federal Reserve head Alan Greenspan (nominated by Reagan in 1987) had introduced low interest rates to take the US economy out of recession. Clinton devoted a great deal of energy and some of his political capital to eliminating the deficit, an essential condition for general economic recovery, and his policy came to seem more Republican than "classically" Democrat. The same could also be said for Clinton's wholehearted support for the NAFTA free trade agreement, which eliminated many trade barriers between the United States, Canada and Mexico.[15]

However, US society continued to fear the changes taking place. This partly explains how the Republicans gained a majority in both Congress and the Senate, and they were also helped by Clinton's inability to implement many of the reforms promised in 1992. The following two years were much more successful for Clinton who returned to areas that were traditionally Democrat terrain, and his re-election in 1996 was helped by the substantial recovery now taking place, with unemployment down to around 5%.[16]

Ten years after Japanese economic euphoria, US society now appeared in a similar psychological state, and the difficulties of the 1980s seemed distant. Since the USSR no longer existed, the USA was now the only great power, and it seemed set on a course towards the "American century". Company restructuring in the 1980s involved not only the composition of the workforce, but touched on all aspects of organization from technology to shop floor layout. The US industrial system entered the 1990s with renewed efficiency, and no other developed country could rival its competitiveness. Massive investments in the high-tech and computing sector opened up a new divide between US companies and their European and Japanese competitors. US company spending accounted for around 40% of total world spending in this field, i.e. roughly double the amount European companies invested in information technology, and eight times the world average.[17] However, the 1990s were also the period when new names appeared on the world scene (Bill Gates, Paul Allen, Ted Turner, Craig McGraw, Larry Ellison, Andrew Grove, Jeff Bezos and others), inheriting and continuing the limitless capacity of US society to produce absolute excellence in the different economic sectors.

---

[15] A. Grenspan, *The Age of Turbulence. Adventures in a New World*, New York, 2007.

[16] J.A. Franke, P.R. Orszag, *American Economic Policy in the 1990s*, cit.

[17] R.J. Gordon, *Technology and Economic Performance in the American Economy*, Nber Working Paper, 8771, February 2002.

Some operated in high-tech and information technology; together with biotechnology, these were the cutting edge of technology and were also the sectors that attracted most interest from private and institutional investors (e.g. *mutual funds* or pension funds) as the economic situation gradually consolidated. With regard to the state, the federal deficit gradually disappeared and actually became a surplus in 1997. Wall Street appeared unstoppable; between December 1991 and January 1992, the Dow Jones index recovered to the level preceding the October 1987 crash, soaring to 16,302 in December 1999.

The boom of this *new economy* was short-lived, and the Dow Jones index dropped around 3,000 points in August 2001. The first signs of economic difficulty were already felt in early 2000. New investments fell sharply. The economic growth rate dropped from 6.44% at the end of 1999 to 5.50% at the end of 2000, and then declined during the first eight months of 2001. Greenspan had just raised the interest rate from 5% to 6.25%, but hurriedly dropped it again, fearing a new phase of economic decline.[18]

20.4. China in the global economy: political repression and economic reform

Neither Greenspan nor others could foresee the events of September 11th. The terrorist attack was a severe psychological blow to the United States. The government and Federal Reserve responded immediately with economic and monetary interventions, in addition to the political and military interventions in Afghanistan and Iraq. Wall Street had climbed back to its September levels by December 2001. Many people wondered if – and to what extent – Al Qaeda might be the USA's real challenger. The immediate consequences of the attack meant that public opinion was less interested when China joined the WTO in December 2001 following years of difficult negotiations.[19] On the other hand, as Larry Summers said in 1995, when he was Undersecretary at the Treasury during Clinton's presidency, the United States could not afford to repeat the mistakes made a century before by the international political and economic system still centred on Great Brit-

---

[18] *http://www.macrotrends.net/1319/dow-jones-100-year-historical-chart*; *https://www.federalreserve.gov/datadownload/Review.aspx?rel=H15&series=bf17364827e38702b42a58 cf8eaa3f78&lastobs=&from=&to=&filetype=csv&label=include&layout=seriescolumn&type =package.*

[19] *China's Economy and the Wto. All Change*, in *The Economist*, 10.12.2001.

ain, which had underestimated the importance of German and Japanese achievements.[20]

At a G20 summit in 2010, the international press reported the existence of an informal but immensely powerful G2, although this was immediately denied by the two parties concerned, the USA and China. Less than two years later, when China became the world's leading export nation in 2012, reducing the ten-point gap with the United States, Japan and Germany in under ten years, the situation was very different. In 2012, many people wondered if the 21st century would be the Chinese century, and a sinologist suggested that China was "buying the world". This shows just how much China had achieved since the start of the reforms introduced by Deng Xiaoping (1978), and since the sanctions imposed by the international community in reaction to Tienanmen Square (1989), or even since it had joined the WTO (2001). During the 1990s, China's GDP grew at an average annual rate of over 10%, and GDP growth rates never fell below 8% during the following decade, despite the 2007-2008 crisis.[21]

So many books have been written about the transformations to China's economy and society between the late 1970s and the present. However, perhaps the well-known Chinese writer Yu Hua best summarizes the dramatic and epic developments of just a few decades: "The last forty years have been for China what the last four hundred years have been for Europeans".[22]

The changes launched in 1978 have profoundly reformed the Chinese economy. From agriculture to industry and banking, all sectors have been thoroughly changed: the foundations were laid first in the primary sector, with new land management and the creation of *township and village enterprises*, the closure of the collective farms (abolished in 1983), and partial liberalization of prices of agricultural products to create internal demand in rural areas. Immediately after this came changes to the banking system with the creation of four state banks: the Bank of China (BOC), the People's Bank of China for Industry and Commerce (PBOC), the China Construction Bank (CCOB) and the Agricultural Bank of China (SBC).

In 1979 China introduced laws to attract foreign investments in designated "special economic zones" (SEZ)[23] and launched its "one-child poli-

---

[20] L.H. Summers, *An Assessment of American Economic Thinking and Policy Towards China*, in *United States-China Relations*, 2, 23, 1995, pp. 1-8.

[21] Z. Brzezinski, *The Group of Two That Could Change the World*, in *Financial Times*, 13.1.2009; A. Kroeber, *Vast Gulf Ensures a G2-Dominated World Order is Kept at Bay, ibid.*, 2.6.2009; P. Nolan, *Is China Buying the World?*, Cambridge, 2012.

[22] Yu Hua, *La Cina in dieci parole*, Milan, 2012.

[23] R. Coase, N. Wang, *How China Became Capitalist*, New York, 2012, pp. 59-64.

cy" to control population growth. In 1980, China joined the World Bank, and state-owned companies were allowed to keep a share of their profits to finance investments and productivity bonuses. The BOC became the central bank in fact and in law. In 1985, the number of SEZs rose to 14, and internal migrants flocked to these areas along the Chinese coast where foreign companies paid much higher wages. In 1986 China applied to join GATT, the first step towards its subsequent entry of the WTO.

Concerns in the Chinese Communist Party (CCP) and in society in general became more acute among those worried about the changes taking place and those who wanted to accelerate change. These tensions culminated dramatically in government repression of the Tienanmen Square protests, when around a thousand protesters were killed and about 30,000 arrested.

Deng, the architect of the reforms, ordered the shift to repression out of concern for social stability. The CCP General Secretary, riformist Zhao Zyiang (a supporter of President Hu Yaobang, who was disgraced in 1987 and replaced by the more conservative Li Peng, then died suddenly in April 1989), was discharged and replaced by Jiang Zemin, the Mayor of Shanghai. In 1993, Jiang also became President of the People's Republic of China and remained in office for ten years. He was actually in power for a total of fourteen or even sixteen years (since he continued to serve as Chairman of the Party's powerful Central Military Commission for two more years).

The collapse of the USSR and the transition beginning in Eastern Europe dealt a hard blow to the conservative wing of the CCP, which remained hostile to the economic changes taking in place in China during the last fifteen years or so. Consequently, after just over two years of stagnation, Deng was finally able to relaunch his reforms in 1992 during his southern tour of China. In the following autumn the CCP Congress defined the course outlined by Deng as aiming to develop a "socialist market economy".

State-owned companies were the first to experience the new situation; 1993 saw the start of a radical restructuring policy that reduced the number of jobs in these companies from 76 to 50 million by 2000. At the same time, business legislation introduced different forms of ownership; in this way, the *state owned enterprises* (SOE) became public limited companies. The following year saw the first privatizations of the smaller SOE, which were sold firstly to employees and managers, but also to foreign investors. In the year Deng died, 1997, the CCP Congress decided to limit state intervention in the economy to certain strategic sectors (defence, communications, elettricity, petrol, aviation and railways).

In 2002, the year after China entered the WTO, the CCP recognized the role of the private sector in China's economy and allowed businessmen to join the Party. This involved changing the CCP statute, amending an article to state that the CCP represented "the vanguard of Chinese society" instead of "the vanguard of the working class", as in the previous text, which had remained unaltered since the Party's foundation in 1921. The new generation of leaders who rose to power in 2003, President Hu Jintao and Premier Wen Jiabao, completed reform of the SOEs, and concentrated on the 196 most important companies with the aim of creating around thirty internationally important groups. For this purpose, state owned companies were placed under the control of a new organization, the State Owned Assett Supervision and Administration Commission (SASAC).[24]

China appeared almost unaffected by the 2008-2009 crisis, and actually turned itself into one of the emerging economies driving world economic growth, also helped by the package of measures implemented by the Chinese government (worth 4 trillion RMB, i.e. over $586 billion). While developed economies saw their GDP fall, and the overall growth of the world economy remained extremely limited, China's GDP still grew at an impressive rate: 9.0% in 2008, 8.7 % in 2009, 9.9% in 2010, 8.8% in 2011 and 7.3% in 2012.[25]

On 30th April 2014 the first page of the *Financial Times* quoted a source close to the World Bank, which said that China would become the world's leading economy by the end of the year, ahead of even the most optimistic forecasts made just a couple of years before. China's official statistics agency expressed its reserves about the methodology used to draw these conclusions and commented – with a remarkable degree of understatement – that it "could not confirm these data as official statistics".[26] Nevertheless, world public opinion swung between highlighting concerns over the world economy's growing reliance on the Chinese economy and focussing on the old and new weaknesses of China's social and economic system. In the first case, it was pointed out that China had become the "workshop of the world", the same expression used to describe mid-18th century England, although a large share of Chinese manufacturing output was produced for foreign companies and much was exported, providing a

---

[24] B. Naughton, *The Transformation of the State Sector. Sasac, the Market Economy, and the New National Champions*, in B. Naughton, K.S. Tsai (eds.), *State Capitalism, Institutional Adaption, and the Chinese Miracle*, Cambridge, 2015, pp. 46-71.

[25] *http://data.worldbank.org/indicator/NY.GDP.MKTP.KD.ZG?locations=CN*.

[26] C. Gilles, *China Overtakes US as the Top Economic Power This Year*, in *Financial Times*, 30.4.2014; M. Wolf, *On the Top of the World*, *ibid.*, 3-4.5.2014.

growing trade surplus that was in part used by China's monetary authorities to buy US Treasury bonds; this was said to represent a kind of security investment for the Chinese, or to indicate a new element in US dependence. In the second case, attention was focused on China's excessive investments in fixed assets as opposed to consumption, its booming property investments that would sooner or later become a bubble, a higher public debt than was officially declared (due to the difficulties of estimating provincial and local government debt), higher unemployment than indicated by official figures, a largely incomplete liberalization process that penalized foreign investors, a financial system concealing dangerous weaknesses, and the growing level of debt among Chinese businesses.

China's economic growth rate began to fall; between late 2014 and early 2015 it dropped firstly below 8% and then below 7%. Despite government reassurances that these figures agreed with its forecasts, there were increasing concerns in the developed countries about the effects this slower growth might have on their own economies. At the same time, the slipping growth rate confirmed the opinions of those who saw a Chinese return to "normality", with a future of much lower growth rates, closer to the best performances of the developed countries led by the USA.

The country is still in the midst of extremely important and difficult changes. At the end of 2013 there was a new impulse towards the liberalization of China's economic system (the market no longer has a "fundamental" role, but has "a "decisive" role in the allocation of resources). Moreover, despite recognizing the SOEs guiding role, the Chinese government intends to strip them of the privileges they have enjoyed and of their access to economic and financial resources at fixed prices. The situation is not without its difficulties. During an annual session of the National People's Congress in March 2015, premier Li admitted that "deep problems with the country's economy are becoming increasingly evident".[27] The measures concerning the SOE were accompanied in summer 2015 by a considerable move towards convertibility of China's currency, the renminbi, allowing it to fluctuate in relation to market pressures and the actual state of the economy. This decision was applauded by the International Monetary Fund, but the consequent depreciation of the renminbi gave rise to worldwide concern. When the Shanghai stock exchange began to fall – and then to plummet – in July and August 2015, the effects on the world's other stock exchanges were immediate. Besides demonstrating increasingly deep-seated world integration – at least at the financial level – this also highlights the

---

[27] T. Branigan, *China Lowers Growth Target to 7% as It Fights 'Deep-seated' Economic Problems*, in *The Guardian*, 8.3.2015.

weakness of a stock exchange system buoyed up by the chronic insufficiency of supply in comparison with the demand for shares. At first the Chinese government preferred to let the market forces act, but was then compelled to intervene decisively to support the stock exchange by buying up shares worth $200 billion.[28] The question cannot evidently be limited just to the stock exchange. Stating a half-truth, "The stock market sell-off is not the problem," says Chinese economist, David Daukoi Lee, who continues, "The problem – not a huge one, but a problem nonetheless – is the Chinese economy itself. It requires corrective action from Chinese authorities – not surgery, but acupuncture".[29] The issue involves not only the reforms already implemented but even the credibility of a power that once seemed absolutely unassailable. At the same time, the severe battle against corruption that was launched several years ago is perhaps achieving some results at the political level, but has also partly slowed private enterprise.

Today, many wonder about the future of China, no longer seen as the new challenger to the USA; some even suggest the Chinese model may be nearing its end. They underline that China's present rulers have an even more difficult task than Deng, who had to deal with a poor and still partly preindustrial society, with no middle class, and extremely variegated media, which, although strictly controlled by the authorities, represented a new form of expression for Chinese society. Power was not concentrated in one single person, but in an articulated and complex structure that required efforts to achieve agreement. Perhaps the time is approaching when Chinese political power and society will have to find a new balance between more modest economic growth and the growing pressures from the relatively wealthier classes and also from those who are still relatively poor. As a McKinsey analyst wrote in 2016, the reality is that the Chinese economy now consists of "multiple subeconomies, each more than a trillion dollars in size. Some are booming, some declining. Some are globally competitive, others fit for the scrap heap".[30] This is perfectly consistent with the words of Justin Yifu Lin, ex-chief economist and former vice-president of the World Bank, who issued an invitation to "demystify the Chinese economy".[31]

---

[28] *Stock Sell-off Highlights Beijing's Dilemma*, in *Financial Times*, 25.8.2015; J. Anderlini, *Credibility on the Line, ibid.*, 30.8.2015.

[29] D. Daokui Li, *China's Problem Is the Economy Itself, Not the Market sell-off*, in *Financial Times*, 31.8.2015.

[30] G. Orr, *What Might Happen in China in 2016?*, in *http://www.mckinsey.com/business-functions/strategy-and-corporate-finance/our-insights/what-might-happen-in-china-in-2016*.

[31] J. Yifu Lin, *Demistifying the Chinese Economy*, Cambridge, Mass., 2012.

Figure 20.1. China GDP growth rate (1990-2016, %)

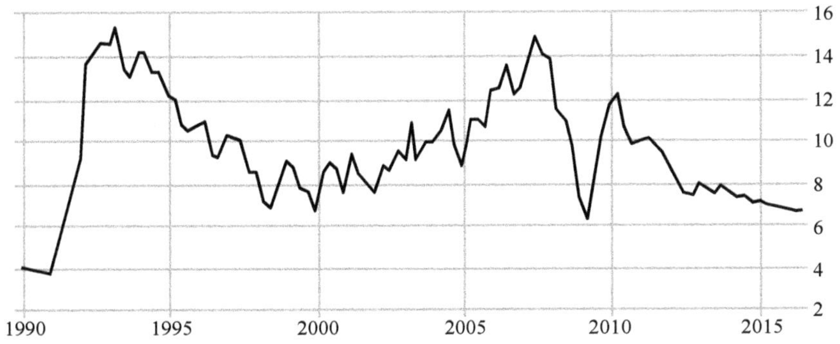

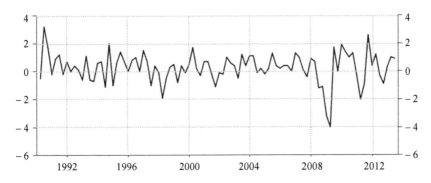

Source: www.tradingeconomics.com.

Figure 20.2. Japan GDP growth rate (1991-2013, %)

Source: *www.tradingeconomics.com.*

Bibliography

Chiarlone S., Amighini A., *L'economia della Cina. Dalla pianificazione al mer-cato*, Rome, 2007.

Galambos L., *The Creative Society – And the Price Americans Paid for It*, Cambridge, Mass., 2012.

Lemoine F., *L'économie de la Chine*, Paris, 1990.

Stiglitz J.E., *The Roaring Nineties. A New History of the World's Most Prosperous Decade*, New York, 2003.

Vogel S.K.J., *Japan Remodeled. How Government and Industry Are Reforming Japanese Capitalism*, Ithaca, 2006.

Chapter 21
EUROPE IN SEARCH OF AN IDENTITY

21.1. The end of the Cold War and German Reunification

The crisis in the Soviet system and the fall of the Berlin Wall allowed the USA to emerge victorious in political/military terms, while another power appeared victorious in a way that was more richly symbolic in political/cultural terms – Europe. The end of the Cold War and the reunification of Germany represented the fulfilment of a dream that belonged not only to the "old" and "new" citizens of the German Federal Republic. The foundations were laid for completion of a project that some of the best and most passionate minds in European politics had cultivated for four decades, albeit not always in a precise and linear fashion. However, aside from the evident jubilation expressed, the reality of the situation was much more complex, and the new European balances were the result of a complex interconnected system of political and economic interests.

At the institutional level, the course to follow was more or less obligatory following the decisions of the European Council taken in June 1988, which recalled that the Single European Act (1986) signed by the European countries had confirmed their intention to continue moving towards and Economic and Monetary Union. The task of studying the procedures required to actually achieve Economic and Monetary Union was given by member states and their heads of state to Jacques Delors, President of the European Commission. The Delors Report was examined in late June 1989, when East German citizens were beginning to make their first "journeys of hope", entering Federal Germany via Hungary. The Report was to form the basis for the Treaty of Maastricht, signed in February 1992 and implemented from the start of 1993. However, the concrete sense of the new Treaty's provisions was now evaluated and expressed in relation to the changes affecting Central-eastern Europe since the summer of 1989, particularly following the fall of the Berlin Wall on 9th November 1989.[1]

During the second half of the 1980s, the project of a single European currency was seen as a useful way to consolidate rigorous policies and control inflation, but the EU member states were divided on this very issue. There was an even stronger divergence of opinion between the central banks and politicians. The latter were led by the German Bundesbank, stalwart in their defence of rigorous monetary and economic measures and the inflation control; they welcomed the idea of a single currency, but only for those countries that were able to fulfil criteria regarding debt, deficit and inflation. On the other hand, the politicians, led by Germany's Chancellor, Helmut Kohl, did not share this severe approach, and were therefore less convinced in their support for a single European currency. In addition, the United Kingdom remained tenaciously opposed to the idea of a single currency, seen as a kind of "Trojan horse" for the creation of increasingly strong EU supernational institutions, which Prime Minister Margaret Thatcher believed would damage British national interests. She was convinced that the Bundesbank – strenuous in its defence of the Deutschmark – was her most important ally. Nonetheless, for political reasons once again it was impossible to stop the course indicated by Delors: at the most, it might be adjusted or delayed. Then in summer 1989, the crisis in Eastern Europe and German reunification had a completely unpredictable impact on the situation.

The Western European economies had never completely recovered from the crisis of the mid-1970s, despite improvements made to structural conditions in the following decades, a period marked by an overvalued dollar and falling prices of petrol and major raw materials. The growth rates of the 1960s were just a distant memory: the rather modest rate of 4.6% in 1965-1974 fell to 2.9% in 1975-1984, sliding towards 2% in the second half of the decade. On the other hand, the neo-liberalism of the USA and UK had triggered a revision of European policies, leading to the progressive commitment to reduce state intervention in the various economic sectors. The EU mechanisms to compensate the discrepancies between wealthier and less prosperous areas began to suffer increasing bureaucratic and administrative delays, usually resolved through political mediation during late-night meetings of heads of government. As the world economy was starting out on an extremely deep-seated transformation leading to the emergence

---

[1] B. Eichengreen, *The European Economy Since 1945*, Princeton, 2006, pp. 353-354; J. Gillingham, *European Integration, 1950-2003. Superstate or New Market Economy?*, Cambridge, UK, 2003, pp. 157-163; V. Castronovo, *L'avventura dell'unità europea. Una sfida con la storia e il futuro*, Turin, 2004, pp. 78-131.

of new countries, and the USA and Japan appeared to compete for economic supremacy in the 21st century, Brussels increased EU funding for the weaker regions and training for the jobless by about 40%. Nevertheless, the share allocated to its agricultural policy remained extremely high (ca. 50% of the total budget). This left little EU funding for research and development or for scientific and applied research, less even than some of the major US and Japanese multi-national companies dedicated to their own projects.[2]

The first effect of the prospect of German reunification was to reunite the leading Western European countries – France, Great Britain and Italy – in the conviction (for different reasons) that European stability could be guaranteed by the existence of two Germanies and not by a single great Germany. A reunified Germany would of course have problems at the outset, but it would recover in the long term and inevitably become more internationally important. Some decisions were made for emotional reasons that involved political calculation (like the equal exchange rate between the West German and East German marks). The enormous financial efforts Germany faced to achieve true unification (modernization of its infrastructures, elimination of obsolete industrial plants, immediate social interventions, and so on) led to a complete reorientation of the decisions made by the principal European partners regarding creation of the Economic and Monetary Union. On the one hand, those who had previously been cautious towards it now became favourable (if not wholehearted supporters of the single currency). On the other one, those who had supported it (even their support depended on certain conditions) now became even more rigorous. They were demanding – and foreseeing – what actually occurred until the final months before the single currency was introduced in 1998: an "inner circle" and an "outer circle" – a core of countries already prepared for this step, with a second group of countries that would eventually adopt the single currency at a future stage.[3]

This began a debate that marked the entire period after the adoption of the single currency, practically until now, between those viewing the single currency as a tool – albeit imperfect – for strengthening the process of European unification, and those who believed its adoption should depend on achievement of effective convergence by fulfilling definite criteria that were uninfluenced by political interests.

---

[2] S. Tarditi, G. Zanias, *Agriculture*, in A. Smith, L. Tsoukalis (eds.), *The Impact of the Community Policies on Economic and Social Cohesion*, Bruges, 1997.

[3] M. Marshall, *The Bank. The Birth of Europe's Central Bank and the Rebirth of Europe's Power*, London, 1999, pp. 78-89.

The European Community agenda before the fall of the Berlin Wall contained a series of steps towards Economic and Monetary Union, and this formed the basis for the Treaty of Maastricht (February 1992), which defined the phases of this process. Given this calendar of rapid and complex stages, the economic and monetary crisis that struck the United Kingdom and Italy in 1992-93 was even more dramatic. The two countries were attacked by international speculation and forced to abandon the exchange rate agreements and devalue their currencies shortly after all EC countries had agreed to limit the fluctuation of exchange rates; Spain and Portugal were in the same situation just a few months later. Despite the enormous financial efforts involved in its unification process, Germany with its Deutschmark appeared as a pillar of stability.[4]

21.2. The terms imposed by the Treaty of Maastricht

In the following years, especially in the phase that began in 1994, EU member states intensified their efforts to achieve the economic convergence that would lead them into a closer union. A special European Monetary Institute (EMI) was created for this purpose (the direct predecessor of the European Central Bank), to work with the Commission on a final report indicating the countries that fulfilled the criteria for voluntary entry into the Economic and Monetary Union. They included: 1) an inflation rate no more than 1.5% higher than the average of the three best performing (lowest inflation) member states of the EU (when the report was drawn up, the maximum rate in question was 2.7%); 2) a deficit no more than 3% of GDP; 3) a stable exchange rate, attested by membership of the European monetary system for at least two years before the final inspection; 4) stable interest rates, therefore interest rates on long-term government bonds that were no more than 200 base points above those of the countries with the least inflation; 5) a national debt amounting to no more than 60% of GDP or else "subject to substantial and continual reduction".[5]

The technical and institutional framework was at risk several times due to the economic problems afflicting all European Union countries. From the outset, the enormous cost of German reunification was much greater than expected. However, France was unable to present itself as a true alternative to Germany (also in economic terms), and actually pursued the

---

[4] K. Torbiörn, *Destination Europe. The Political and Economic Growth of a Continent*, Manchester, 2003, pp. 190-220.

[5] T. Padoa Schioppa, *Engeneering the Single Currency*, in P. Gowan, P. Anderson (eds.), *The Question of Europe*, London, 1997, pp. 162-177.

German "Rhineland model" of capitalism at the theoretical level as an intrinsically essential component of the French economic/social model. Symbolically, the Rhine was finally uniting France and Germany instead of separating them. At the same time, Italy was in the grip of a political and institutional crisis, and its economy began to decline. This all meant that the phase launched by the Treaty of Maastricht was a troubled period for the EU. The single market created in 1993 offered new opportunities to all economic stakeholders and Europe did not turn into the impregnable "fortress" that some had feared and others had hoped to see. In any case, the liberalization and privatization movement had been particularly strong in Europe, achieving results that often exceeded government expectations.[6]

The EU's fragile boundaries were certainly unable to halt the globalization processes taking place. The continent's economy was affected by deep-seated sub-movements also involving big business in real *mega-mergers* along the same lines as in the USA, especially in telecommunications (with the advent of mobile phones), pharmaceuticals and financial services.

However, it was the institutional sphere that saw greatest efforts made during this period. The Delors Report, which had lead to the Treaty of Maastricht, provided for the creation of a European Central Bank (ECB) and a three-stage process leading to monetary union in 1997, or in 1999 at the latest. However, the timing of these procedures was partly dictated by political timing, especially by the Danish referendum in which the electorate rejected the Treaty. On the following day, the Danish decision was commented with extreme arrogance by Director General of the French treasury and future ECB President Jean-Claude Trichet ("Denmark should be punished for its foolishness", according to some sources, and "an 'insignificant country' should not be allowed to delay the European intregration process", according to others), showing little respect for the will of the Danish people.[7]

Debates in the following years often focused on the flexibility or inflexibility of the Maastricht criteria. Several times both Germany and the Netherlands talked about the possibility of a "two-speed" Europe, with an advanced core of countries already prepared for entry into the Economic and Monetary Union (EMU) followed by a second group of countries that were not yet in a condition to enter. Between 1996 and 1998, the debate

---

[6] C. Jackson, *The European Community and the Challenges of the 1990's*, in P.M. Lützeler (ed.), *Europe After Maastricht. American and European Perspective*, Oxford, 1994, pp. 41-52.

[7] J. van Overtveldt, *The End of the Euro. The Uneasy Future of the European Union*, Chicago, 2011 p. 36; J. Nordvig, *The Fall of the Euro. Reinventing the Eurozone and the Future of Global Investing*, New York, 2014, p. 26.

focused on the real ability of various countries to fulfil all the conditions of Maastricht, especially in the cases of Italy and Spain. Ultimately, the decision was a political one: Italy (or Spain) outside the euro would be too dangerous a rival in many sectors, and the exclusion of these states from the euro might also have given a signal to the less open and vigorous part of the business sector and those who intended to take advantage of Italy's weakness in comparison with its principal EU partners.[8]

21.3. Arrival of the euro

The agreement reached by heads of state and government allowed a fairly large first core of participating countries to enter the EMU; although none of the first participants actually failed to meet the Maastricht criteria, these were interpreted more as a guideline than as a rigid requirement for EMU entry.

On 2nd May 1998 an extraordinary meeting of the European Council decreed that eleven countries met the Maastricht criteria and could enter the EMU (Austria, Belgium, Finland, France, Germany, Ireland, Italy, Luxembourg, the Netherlands, Portugal and Spain). Two others (Denmark and the United Kingdom) actually met the criteria, but had decided not to join the EMU (the Treaty envisaged this possibility, known as *opt-out*). Greece and Sweden wanted to enter but were not considered to be ready. Extenuating negotiations were required to set the euro conversion rates for the national currencies of the countries admitted to the EMU. The phase preceding this decision was beset by difficulties and clashes between those advocating a more rigid interpretation of the criteria (Germany, strongly supported by the Netherlands and Luxembourg) and those wanting to see a more "tendential" and therefore more political interpretation (especially the countries like Italy and Spain, which had difficulties fulfilling all five criteria).

From January 1999, the euro replaced the ecu (used as the internal unit of account by the European Community since the creation of the European Monetary System), while the next two years saw completion of all the banking and monetary procedures required before coins and banknotes in the new euro appeared came into use on 1st January 2002. The operation was successful from a strictly monetary point of view, but contained the seeds of a disease that would be difficult to cure. The fiscal aspects of the monetary union were underestimated and this created problems for its stability from the outset, although many countries in the following years registered

---

[8] H. James, *Making the European Monetary Union*, Cambridge, Mass., 2012, pp. 168-174.

interest rates that were lower than before or than they would have been if they had not joined the EMU. At the same time, the banking boom noted by some acute observers represented a further challenge to Europe's (old and new) monetary policy makers.

The two structural weaknesses (lack of common fiscal policies and the *banking glut*, i.e. the excessive quantity of international loans between banks) were not exclusively European, but the complexity of European governmental mechanisms made them particularly dangerous, given that the rules and institutional fabric on which the EU was based had not been adapted. Some basic questions (about what a single market meant in this new context, and the standardization levels required to make it function effectively) were avoided, partly due to the negotiations to include former communist states in the EU.

The political and symbolic importance of the completion – or near-completion – of the European unification dream took precedence over all other considerations. On the other hand, the entry of the new countries made all the recommendations about more careful and rigorous behaviour less important; their much weaker economies still required great changes, and their transition to a market economy had given varying results.

Years later, on 19th May 2010 in a speech to the Bundestag during a discussion about the Greek bailout, the message from German Chancellor Angela Merkel was that "the rules mustn't be written to suit the weakest but to suit the strongest" and the others must adapt.[9] However, no one was able or willing to deliver this harsh message in the first years of the new century; when it became a subject of public debate, particularly during the most acute phase of the Greek crisis in 2013-2015, it took on other meanings.

In 2002, twelve of the fifteen EU member states adopted the euro (in the following years the group expanded to nineteen out of twenty-eight countries) and in just a few years, the European currency appeared to acquire a strength and international status not unlike that of the US dollar. However, even in its best periods, the euro never exceeded 25-30% of world currency reserves.

Adoption of the single currency was not without difficulties, less at the technical level than for the perverse effects it had on prices in the various countries. It provoked a dramatic and almost general rise in the prices of symbolic products that varied from one country to another (the impact of inflation on the consumer price index has been estimated for only 0.2%).

---

[9] Plenarprotokoll 17/42, Deutscher Bundestag Stenografischer Bericht, 42. Sitzung, Berlin, Mittwoch, den 19. Mai 2010, p. 4128; H. Thompson, *The Crisis of the Euro. The Problem of German Power Revisited*, Sheffield Political Economy Research Institute, Paper 8, 2013.

This meant an initial tide of disaffection, which politicians in many countries were able to exploit for electoral purposes. Nonetheless, European citizens appeared very satisfied after only a few years, as shown by the Eurobarometer, which rose from 53% in 2000 to 62% in 2004 and 65% one year later.[10]

However, even before the 2007-2008 crisis began, it became quite "normal" to criticize the single currency in various European countries – including those in the group of six founding members and even members of various governments – who attributed the euro with the worst defects. In France, Sarkozy partly based his 2007 presidential election campaign on the impossibility of using the euro to aid employment policies, while Italian Premier Berlusconi stated that his unwillingness to impose further limits on economic growth beyond the limits introduced with adoption of the euro. Although the European Central Bank did not perhaps become what the Frankfurt correspondent of the *Wall Street Journal* had envisaged – an independent centre of power without parallel in the world – it demonstrated definite powers of resistance under heavy pressure. In the words of the first ECB president, Wim Duisenberg, at a press conference, referring to requests by the Belgian premier to reduce interest rates: "I hear, but I don't listen".[11]

Two years after the introduction of the euro, ten central and eastern European countries entered the EU. The per capita GDP of these new members ranged from 79% of the EU average in the best case (Slovenia) to 30.5% in the worst case (Bulgaria). The "driving force" of transition from the planned economy to the market economy started to weaken, although foreign investments (from Western Europe, the USA, South Korea and Japan) did not decline, since they were attracted by encouraging market prospects and a plentiful supply of cheaper and generally well-educated labour. In these countries, as in several southern European countries already in the EU, the efficiency of their economic systems depended on reforms to the labour market, public administration and tax system.[12]

There was a very different climate after 2003, when the labour market reforms desired by Germany's Chancellor Schröder were approved. Until then, Germany had been paying for its unification, and its slowed economic growth rate temporarily prevented it from being the "European powerhouse" it had always been. Although the reforms introduced by the Social Democrat premier met with strong opposition from trade unions and the left wing of his own party, costing him an election defeat in 2005 and beginning Angela Merkel's rise to power, they were actually an economic turning

---

[10] *http://ec.europa.eu/COMMFrontOffice/publicopinion/index.cfm.*

[11] *https://www.ecb.europa.eu/press/pressconf/2001/html/is010411.en.html.*

[12] *A Survey of EU Enlargement. In The Nick of Time,* in *The Economist,* 29.5.2008.

point for the country. Germany was no longer just an efficient country with too many rigid social and economic constraints; it now made flexibility a means of regaining the competitiveness it was losing. Working hours that adapted to market needs, the introduction of *mini jobs*, and limits on welfare spending were the foundations for the grand recovery of German exports. Just when the crisis was approaching, and even more so in its most difficult years, the German economy was able to recover its competitiveness as the basis for repeated and growing surpluses in trade (making Germany the world's greatest exporter from 2005 to 2009) and its current account balance. Given that the exact opposite was happening in southern Europe, the European Commission and many neutral observers saw these German achievements as a destabilizing factor for the continent.[13]

21.4. The origins of the European crisis

On the other hand, the first successes of the euro actually created situations subsequently seen as paradoxical, and would lead to a crisis it is still difficult to overcome. Interest rates in Spain and Greece were much lower than in Germany, and this had many consequences: in Spain the principal effect was a property bubble, which allowed the country to maintain its average GDP growth rates above the European average in 2007-2008, but more generally it meant that banks and other investors invested more in southern Europe. Up until the 1990s, most of the national debt of the various countries was in the hands of private and institutional investors of the same country, but monetary union brought a radical change: in 2008 three-quarters of the Portuguese national debt was in foreign hands, half of the Spanish and Greek debts and over 40% of Italy's debt.

According to the Bank for International Settlements, in 2010 the German banks held €610 billion in government bonds of the so-called "PIIGS" (Portugal, Ireland, Italy, Greece and Spain), while the French banks actually held €778 billion. A second aspect of this general "euro-euphoria" was that some truly gigantic financial corporations emerged in Europe. Santander merged with Abbey National in 2004, later acquiring also the Royal Bank of Scotland; Unicredit merged with Hypovereinsbank, acquiring a strong position in many central and eastern European countries; HSBC Holdings merged with Crédit Commercial de France and ABN merged with AMRO. Many other mergers took place, including consolidation in the Italian financial sector, where Intesa San Paolo and Unicredit became

---

[13] *Dissecting the Miracle. The Ingredients of German Economic Success Are More Complex Than They Seem*, in *The Economist*, 15.6.2013.

much stronger.[14] However, the dangers of "financialization" of the economy can also be seen in this process: financial organizations became excessively strong, but regulations and international control systems were relatively inconsistent. Consolidated national interests and powerful pressure groups combined with the weaknesses of European institutional structures, thus helping – even involuntarily – to create a fertile terrain for a crisis that would arrive from the USA, as in 1929.

The crisis hit Europe in 2008. To begin with, there was no awareness of its seriousness. UK Prime Minister Gordon Brown later reported what took place in Paris at an extraordinary summit of heads of state and government in October 2008, when many of those present stated that it was a crisis for the USA to resolve. Few at the time understood that at least half the toxic assets issued by the US banks were "in the belly" of Europe's major banks. A year later, Germany's SDP Finance Minister Peer Steinbrück repeated: "Our system is healthy; it is the American system which is sick", criticizing the USA and UK for their lack of interest in measures to regulate the financial markets.[15]

EU citizens appeared to have clearer ideas. By 2009, the number of Europeans who distrusted Europe had risen dramatically. During the following years, there was a gradually widening divide between north and south, between rich and poor, instead of hopes of balanced growth and real unification in a climate of solidarity. At the same time, Eurosceptic and anti-EU movements gained ground, and dissenting voices became increasingly louder, even within European institutions.[16]

The crisis first affected countries like Ireland and Spain; their deficits had been kept under control in previous years, but the property bubble had been particularly important and had contributed greatly to the growth of GDP. Then came Portugal and Italy, the EU's third economy, with a national debt second only Greece as a percentage of its GDP. However, the risks appeared more limited because Italy had an economy with high asset values and high savings rates, Italian citizens held a large proportion of the debt, and its institutions functioned (*in primis* the presidency, Foreign Min-

---

[14] *http://intermarketandmore.finanza.com/piigs-non-solo-italia-badate-bene-31347.html/bank-holding-piigs*; *http://bruegel.org/2013/11/mergers-and-acquisitions-of-banks-in-the-euro-area-where-are-the-borders*, Mergers and acquisitions of Banks in the Euro Area: where are the borders?

[15] *http://www.handelsblatt.com/politik/deutschland/regulierung-finanzmaerkte-steinbrueckknoepft-sich-briten-vor/3210678.htm*, *Finanzmärkte. Steinbrück knöpft sich die Briten vor*, July 1st, 2009; International Monetary and Financial Committee, Twentieth Meeting October 4, 2009, Istanbul, Statement by Mr. Peer Steinbrück, Minister of Finance On behalf of Germany.

[16] L. Topaloff, *Political Parties and Euroscepticism*, London, 2012.

istry and security forces). Nonetheless, the fragility of the Italian political system and its management by Premier Silvio Berlusconi created a climate of extreme distrust. Italy was in a state of crisis; after shrinking for years, its public debt now began to rise again and the country's credibility was seriously endangered.

The crisis became much more dramatic in 2009 and 2010, when Greece showed the first signs of being unable to meet its debt obligations. German, French and British banks were heavily exposed to the Greek debt. During the following years, the most delicate point – and also the most socially and politically dramatic point – involved implementation of the correct measures to save the banks and safeguard Europe's entire financial system, protecting this strategy under the label of "Greek bailout".

The governments of all these countries encountered enormous difficulties, but perhaps the most spectacular case was Italy. At the Cannes summit in early November 2011, Italy and Spain were invited to ask the IMF for financial aid. The refusal of Spanish Premier Zapatero (defeated at the polls a month later) triggered a series of very similar declarations. Italy's Finance Minister Tremonti commented at the time: "I can think of better ways to commit suicide"[17] (i.e. financial aid, although he accepted monitoring by the IMF). Merkel's reply to the request for an increased German contribution to the *firewall* around the Eurozone was: "None of this is *fair*, but I won't commit suicide" (although she demanded that Italy and Greece implement economic reforms). Berlusconi was forced to resign a few weeks later, despite having a sufficient majority in the Italian parliament: the international markets were said to have passed a vote of no confidence. Berlusconi's government was followed by a technocratic government led by Mario Monti, President of Bocconi University and former EU Commissioner with responsibility for Competition (hastily nominated a Senator for Life before being called upon to form a government).[18]

According to Joschka Fischer, the Schröder government's Foreign Minister, the turning point came well before this, in October 2008; Germany refused to participate in a European bailout fund, fearing that France might use it to pay off its own debts, thus giving national governments the responsibility for managing the crisis. In his words, this decision indicated a "a rupture with the entire German policy on Europe until that moment (...) and the beginning of the re-nationalization of the European Union.[19]

---

[17] *http://it.reuters.com/article/topNews/idITMIE9AO01D20131125, Zapatero rivela: a summit Cannes 2011 pressioni su Italia per richiesta bailout*, 25.11.2013.

[18] *How the Euro Was Saved*, in *Financial Times*, 11.5.2014; H. Thompson, *The Crisis of the Euro*, cit., pp. 10-14.

[19] J. Fischer, *Se l'Europa fallisce*, Milan, 2015, p. 39.

Despite Germany's contradictory and limiting condition of being too big for Europe and too small for the world, its leadership in understanding the crisis and how to recover has sown the seeds of new long-term difficulties for the entire continent.

These new approaches were even more evident during the interminable handling of the Greek crisis, passing through various phases at national and EU levels between 2010 and 2015. However, it became more evident that many measures formally directed towards bailing out Greece (to put its "creative" national accounting in order and force it to eliminate the culpable ommissions of its fiscal policy) were directed towards rescuing the banks exposed to the Greek debt: austerity was difficult to manage and difficult to digest for economies already badly affected by the crisis. However, it seemed increasingly evident that certain reforms (clear regulations about economic competitiveness, the labour market, taxation and the public administration) could no longer be postponed, also due to the different economic approaches of the principal EU countries. Furthermore, the prevailing idea – and not only in Germany – was that agreement on severe measures to contain public spending would make it possible to recover from the crisis without falling into deflation; this has been known in Europe since 2012 as the *fiscal compact*.[20]

However, the figures showed a different reality, which could only be changed – and in part – by the ECB's belated *quantitative easing* policy. Draghi's declaration in 2012 – "Within our mandate the ECB is ready to do whatever it takes to preserve the euro. And believe me, it will be enough"[21] – was the strongest signal directed at the markets since the start of the crisis, and it also meant that Frankfurt's policies now diverged from the line of the Bundesbank, which caused some unrest in the Eurotower.

The issue still under discussion is the ability/willingness of Eurozone member states to surrender their own sovereignty over fiscal policy. Until now, it has seemed that the continuation of national fiscal policies has compensated for their loss of sovereignty over monetary policy. However, the contradiction of a currency unsupported by a sovereign state remains unresolved, especially in moments of crisis.

Although debt reduction is actually foreseen as a medium- to long-term process, it has still had deeply lacerating and wounding effects, with extremely negative social and political consequences in many European coun-

---

[20] *A Fiscal Compact For A Stronger Economic And Monetary Union*, in *ECB Monthly Bulletin*, May 2012, pp. 79-94.

[21] *https://www.ecb.europa.eu/press/key/date/2012/html/sp120726.en.html*. Speech by Mario Draghi, President of the European Central Bank at the Global Investment Conference in London 26 July 2012.

tries. Unemployment figures have risen to almost 25% in Spain and Greece, 15-20% in Portugal and Ireland; social and economic inequalities have increased throughout the EU. Nevertheless, in 2015, the Eurozone as a whole had not yet recovered its pre-crisis GDP: while it was still an average of 2% below the level of the first trimester of 2008, it was actually much lower than this in some countries. However, in a certain sense more damage has been done by the widespread clichés regarding the corruption and inefficiency of southern Europe, generally contrasted with the sobriety and efficiency of northern Europe, although this is hardly evident in the decisions taken by the banking sector in these northern countries.

A divided and confused Europe has long debated the pros and cons of Grexit (Greece's exit from the euro and perhaps also from the EU) to save the entire system, and not only as a possibility but almost – among certain European politicians – as an event to be hoped for; on the other hand, avoidance of Grexit would confirm the solidity of the European model's basic values. This discussion has long seemed like a pantomime, and those involved appear unable to see the forest for the trees. There was a brusque awakening in late June 2016, when another country, the United Kingdom, traditionally seen as a *reluctant European,* democratically decided to abandon what it seemed possible to criticize, hate, even ridicule, but not to abandon – the European Union.

The Brexit vote has split the United Kingdom along generational and cultural divides, causing a political upheaval of a kind unusual in a country that is generally politically stable, despite the alternation of power between Conservative and Labour. The repercussions of this decision are still unclear, although its first effects appear to confirm predictions of new difficulties and the beginnings of a recession in Great Britain. It is certain, however, that the consequences will affect not only Britain but the entire continent, but perhaps not only in a negative way. It seems inevitable that some of the financial activities now concentrated in London will move to other European capitals, together with the headquarters of US and Japanese multinationals. The economic effects will be quantifiable only with time. The political effects are increasingly immediate, but take different forms. On the one hand, a taboo has been broken. Implosion no longer appears impossible for the institution forming the basis of seventy years without war, Europe's longest period of peace, although the fate of Yugoslavia has left a dramatic and indelible mark on this period. On the other hand, the most widespread reaction has been a renewed willingness to recreate the construction of a united Europe on different bases, with less centralization and bureaucracy. It is still too early to understand which of these two paths will be pursued with greater determination.

Figure 21.1. Manufacturing output in Europe and USA (1997-2010, % of GDP)

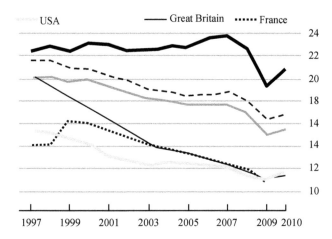

Source: US Bureau of Economic Analysis; Eurostat.

Figure 21.2. Per capita GDP of EU countries (1,000 euro, 2015)

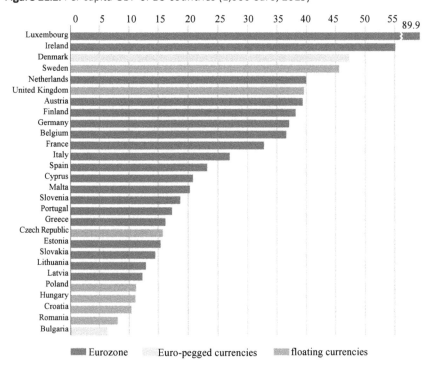

Source: *The Economist*.

Figure 21.3. Economic indicators of Greece, Ireland and Portugal (2008-2015)

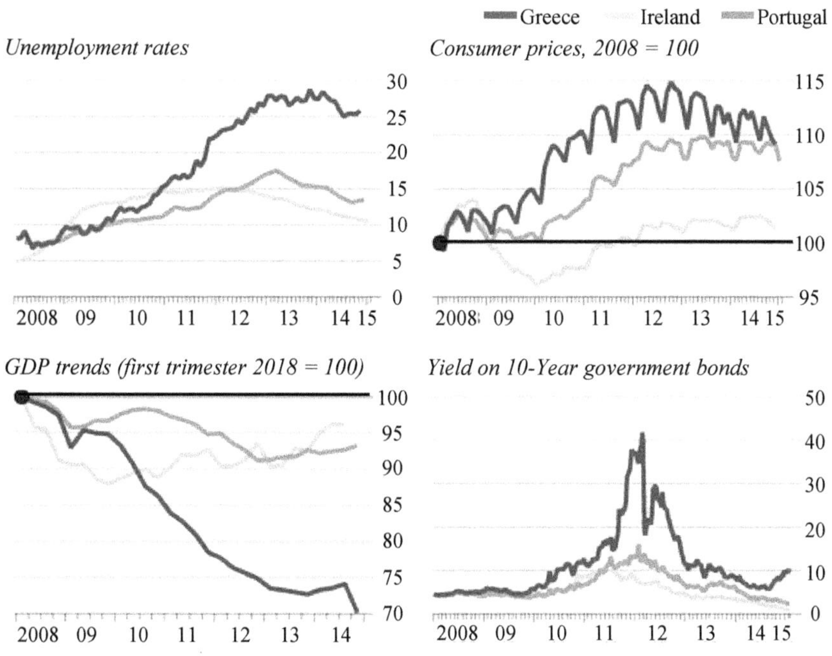

Source: *Thomson Reuters.*

Bibliography

Castronovo V., *L'avventura dell'unità europea. Una sfida con la storia e il futuro*, Turin, 2004.

Fauri F., *L'integrazione economica europea 1947-2006*, Bologna, 2006.

James H., *Making the European Monetary Union. The role of the Committee of central Bank Governors and the Origins of the European Central Bank*, Cambridge, Mass., and London, 2012.

Stiglitz J.E., *The Euro. How a Common Currency Threatens the Future of Europe*, London, 2016.

Varoufakis Y., *And the Weak Suffer What They Must? Europe's Crisis and America's Economic Future*, London, 2016.

Chapter 22

THE GLOBALIZED WORLD

SUMMARY: 22.1. BRICS. – 22.2. The success of the market and state intervention in Asia. – 22.3. The commodities boom and development of south-south economic relations. – Bibliography.

22.1. BRICS

The most important outcome of globalization has been to spread economic development to areas previously almost unaffected by this process. In some ways, economic growth has been spectacular in what were once known as "developing countries" and are now called "emerging economies". Their total contribution to world economic growth has risen from 31% in the 1980s to 46% in the 1990s, to a dominant 67% in the early years of the 21st century, and then to over 70% in the first half of the following decade. Researchers and commentators agree that the driving force of the world economy has shifted decisively to the economies of these emerging countries.

This situation has many aspects, and not all allow one single interpretation. The most striking aspect certainly concerns the extraordinary changes affecting China's economy and society. China has now become the "world's factory", even more so than England in the mid-19th century. It has also been the world's biggest exporter since 2011, joining the *mega traders*, the group of countries with a large share of world trade and whose export trade accounts for at least 50% of GDP. China is the first country after 19th century Great Britain to achieve this kind of position.[1] Even more outstandingly, China is now an extremely important economic and commercial partner for over a hundred countries, giving it an enormous influence on the present world economy. In other words, China is a true *dual hub*, a revolving door for a constant flow of imports and exports.

The existence of a real economic system centred on China demonstrates the country's role and importance in the world economy. The complex in-

---

[1] A. Subramanian, M. Kessler, *The Hyperglobalization of Trade and Its Future*, Peterson Institute of International Economics, Working Paper 3, Global Citizen Foundation, June 2013.

ternational division of labour implemented by Beijing now includes practically every continent. China's global presence is based on the identification and exploitation of raw materials, importation of industrial and other *commodities*, collaboration along the production system, and exports of mid- and low-tech goods to its partners.

Observers perceived these processes at the time, particularly after China entered the WTO in December 2001 after 15 years of difficult negotiations. The effect was immediate: Chinese exports rose sharply: from 3.9% of GDP in 2000 to 6% in 2003. As the Chinese economy gradually opened up to foreign investors, the country soon became the principal destination for foreign investments.

However, the rise of China must be seen within the context of the general transformation affecting the entire world economy since the 1990s. The rapidly changing world situation and the company's need to offer long-term prospects to its big investors led Goldman Sachs to set up a research group. Headed by James O'Neil, it worked to identify underlying dynamics that might be of interest to the bank and its most important clients. The result was the report *Dreaming with BRICS: The Path to 2050,* a reaction to 9/11 and the debate it triggered about the pros and cons of globalization. The report set out the case for changing the image of a process entirely centred on the USA to show that there were many reasons for urging a wider vision of the world economy; sheer force of numbers and geopolitics meant the gradual emergence of the countries making up the new world of "bricks" (BRICs): Brazil, Russia, India and China.[2]

These four countries had many things in common and many differences, but the former prevailed. The BRICs are the only countries in the world apart from the USA with a GDP over $600 billion, more than 100 million inhabitants, and a surface area of over 2 million sq. km. In the first years of the 21st century their economic growth rates ranged from 4% for Brazil to 11% for China, which they were generally able to maintain (Brazil had some difficulties) until the crisis hit at the end of 2008.[3]

Starting in 2010, the BRICs began to meet annually. Here was an evident political reaction to the ineffective decisions taken at the London G20 meeting in April 2009, which attempted to deal with the crisis. In 2011, for purely political reasons, South Africa was invited to join as representing Africa, and the BRICs became the BRICS.

During the worst years of the crisis, the BRICS cooperated very closely

---

[2] J. O'Neil, *Dreaming with BRICS. The Path to 2050*, London, 2003.

[3] *Follow the Yellow Bric Road. Welcome to Tomorrow's Economic Giants*, in *The Economist*, 9.10.2003.

with each other, even creating a bank. The Shanghai-based New Development Bank BRICS was established at the 2014 summit in Brazil to enable economic-financial and commercial transactions between member states; it also represents a real challenge to the IMF and its regulations, traditionally weighted towards developed countries. Economist Joseph Stiglitz has defined the creation of this bank as "a fundamental change in global economic and political power".[4]

Because these countries had high growth rates during the worst years of the crisis, especially China and India (GDP + 60% and + 40% approximately, 2008-2013), the Goldman Sachs forecasts seemed about to come true ahead of time. Apparently there was no need to wait for 2040-2050 in order to confirm that these four or five economies had become more important for the world economy. In 2012, the BRICS produced a quarter of the world's wealth, and it was predicted that they would account for a third of the world's GDP by 2020. However, 2013 brought the first signs that the era of the BRICS was already ending.

The situation varied greatly from one country to another. China's GDP began to slow, falling gradually from 8-9 % to around 6%. According to the Chinese government, this meant that growth was now becoming more "normal" after years of growth rates around 10-12%. China was not the only country feeling a need to restore balance to an economy too heavily weighted towards investments in fixed assets. It also needed to increase domestic consumption by the middle class (a market of 350-400 million people in China, similar in size to the European market) and the weaker classes, who were still largely concentrated in the country areas. Salaries rose more quickly than expected, thus confirming Premier Wen Jiao Bao's forecast in February 2012 that China would soon cease to have the lowest labour costs. In effect, the Chinese value chain adapted by moving the most *labour intensive* activities to Vietnam, Malaysia and India.

Even before the crisis, Russia's GDP growth rate began to slow in comparison with the first years of the new century, but the collapse it suffered in 2009-2010 was worse than other countries; GDP dropped ten points in a year and then fell below zero. Economic recovery pushed the growth rate back up to around 5% in 2011, but at the end of the year it began to fall rapidly again. Growth was negative once more in 2014 under the combined effect of falling petrol prices and the sanctions the West imposed on Moscow for supporting the civil war in the Ukraine. Government programmes for further privatization of the Russian economy were launched in 2012-

---

[4] *Nobel Economist Joseph Stiglitz Hails New Brics Bank Challenging US-Dominated World Bank & Imf*, in *Democracy Now*, 17.7.2014.

2013 to attract foreign capital, but had very little effect. In fact, the most visible outcome of the country's increasing difficulties after 2014 was actually a massive exodus of capital during the second half of the year, accompanied by devaluation of the rouble, which lost approximately 50% of its value.[5]

Brazil's growth rate fell equally sharply; at the beginning of 2010 it was still 8%, but dropped to 1% in the second trimester of 2012. This wiped away the Brazilian "difference" on which the country had based almost a decade of hopes fuelled by the fast-growing internal demand (also driven by possibly over-generous consumer credit), together with its solid industrial system that interacted with all of South America. Brazil had generally been able to control inflation and its state finances, despite a tendency to concentrate on welfare spending, especially pensions, for political/electoral reasons during the presidencies of both Lula and Roussef. Brazil's new *middle class* felt both economically empowered and held political hostage by a system that had created too many expectations, which no one – and certainly not the government – was capable of satisfying.[6] Its GDP continued to fall, dipping below zero in the last trimester of 2013. It was difficult to invert this trend, at least in the short term, and another contributing factor was the political instability connected to Roussef's impeachment for her role in the scandal regarding the state petrol company Petrobras and its funding for the 2010 and 2014 election campaigns.[7]

The situation was somewhat different for India, which had been competing with China since 2009 for the highest GDP growth rate and had actually managed to draw slightly ahead of its rival, with a stable growth rate of over 7% according to the previous two years' data. India had always been distant from China's extremely successful development model based on exports, and its growth was uneven and asymmetrical. India's economy had been 20% larger than China's in the 1970s, but by 2015 it was just a fifth the size of the Chinese economy. India was trapped in its many contradictions and risked remaining "a great unfinished work" of globalization.[8]

Indian agriculture lacks efficiency, but nonetheless succeeds in supplying resources to the world's second largest population. The country also

[5] K. Hille, *Moscow Expects Recession in 2015*, in *Financial Times*, 2.12.2014.

[6] J.P. Rathborne, *Economic Slowdown Puts Latin America's Aspirations at Risk*, in *Financial Times*, 16.4.2014.

[7] J. Leahy, *Roussef's Campaign Aides Face Arrest in Petrobras Investigation*, in *Financial Times*, 22.2.2016; *Lessons of the Fall. Impeachment May Give the Brazilian Workers' Party a Brighter Future*, in *The Economist*, 22.5.2016.

[8] G. Rachman, *Richer than Great Britain and Poorer than Africa*, in *Financial Times*, 25.9.2012; V. Mallet, J. Crabtree, *Industrial Evolution*, *ibid.*, 6.5.2014.

has an industrial sector that includes state-owned companies, together with large private corporations permanently at the centre of the Indian economic establishment (Tata, Aditya Birla Group, Infosys), and big foreign electronics multinationals (Microsoft, Oracle, Digital/Compaq, Hewlett Packard, Fujitsu, Siemens, Cisco Systems, Ericcson, Sony and others). These companies have made the Karnataka State capital Bangalore an Indian version of Silicon Valley, the ideal location for *business process outsourcing*, especially *back office* services for finance and the major world airlines. Nonetheless, India's total manufacturing output remained at around 15% of GDP from the 1970s, and the crisis has driven it to an even lower level for several years. India's infrastructures are extremely poor and inadequate; per capita investment in infrastructures rose from around $500 to $1,500 between 2000 and 2015, whereas Chinese investments during the same period rose from $1,000 to just under $6,000 at purchasing power parity. A 2015 World Bank study estimated that India needed investments of $1.7 trillion in order to provide the country with a modern infrastructure system by 2020. This is a very difficult objective, given that only the state can finance these huge investments and that the ten biggest companies in this sector have bank debts of over $125 billion.[9] Despite his 2014 election slogan promising "minimum government maximum governance", India's Prime Minister Narendra Modi has encountered unexpected difficulties in attempts to carry out a drastic overhaul of India's economic model. He has preferred to adopt a fragmentary strategy, slowly eliminating the many constraints on private enterprise that have impeded the country's economic development. Modi is just one of the many who are discovering that India is actually a very difficult country to change.[10]

22.2. The success of the market and state intervention in Asia

However, these real difficulties cannot cancel the deeper changes affecting the entire planet in the last thirty or so years. Most have taken place in Asia, but then gradually extended to the other southern hemisphere continents; even sub-Saharan Africa has been involved in this since the 1990s, and even more intensely since the first years of the 21st century.

The most striking case is South Korea, one of Asia's poorest and most destitute countries immediately after the Second World War, which divid-

---

[9] H. Sender, *If You Built It, Can They Come?*, in *Financial Times*, 21.6.2015.

[10] V. Mallet, J. Crabtree, *One Direction*, in *Financial Times*, 18.5.2015; M. Vaishnav, *Modinomics at Two. The Indian Economy Under the Bjb*, in *Foreign Affairs*, 8.3.2016.

ed the Korean peninsula. Nevertheless, it was already seen as successful by 1960, and many countries have attempted to imitate the Korean model of economic development, particularly in Asia.[11] This model was based on the following elements: priority given to structural factors, above all education and health policies; the leading role played by Korean technocrats, trained on the lines of Japan's Miti model, but with more elements of American culture; authoritarian governments within an outwardly democratic institutional framework; strong protectionist policies and incentives to Korean company's competing on the international markets; the influential role of the big private corporations, the *chaebol*. These factors allowed South Korea to carry out a process of industrialization with nothing to fear from the world's economic giants, particularly the USA.[12] South Korea initially built up its industry based on the more mature sectors: steel, cars, shipbuilding and chemicals. However, development was accelerated by Korea's ability to acquire the most advanced technologies. The speed and success of its growth are illustrated by just a few figures. In 1970, per capita wealth in South Korea was just $295, about a fifth more than the Asian and African average, but less than half the South American average of $650. By 2008, when the crisis began, South Korea's per capita wealth had risen to almost $19,300: three times the level of South America, five times the average of Asia (excluding Japan), six times the level of China, and thirteen times that of Africa. Even more striking was the way South Korea closed the gap with Japan. In 2000 its *per capita* wealth at purchasing power parity was less than half that of Japan ($16,500 *vs.* $32,000), but this had increased to $34,386 by the end of 2015, only slightly behind Japan's $35,8045.[13]

The government began a cautious liberalization policy in the 1980s, slowly dismantling the protectionist model of the previous two to three decades. Within this context, however, it has been unable to make any changes regarding the big groups (*chaebols*) that dominate South Korea's economy and form the core of the country's industrial system. Their influential role has not diminished, given that the top ten *chaebols* actually controlled around 75% of South Korea's GDP in 2014-2015.[14] It is no surprise that the country has risen rapidly in the world ranking, from 36th place in

---

[11] S.E. Chapin, *Success Story in South Korea*, in *Foreign Affairs*, April 1969.

[12] World Bank, *Korea, Managing the Industrial Transition*, Vol. I, *The Conduct of Indus- trial Policy*, Washington, 1987.

[13] UN, National account, database; *http://it.tradingeconomics.com/country-list/gdp-per-capita-ppp*.

[14] P. Dicken, *Global Shift. Mapping the Changing Contours of the World Economy*, New York-London, 2011, pp. 194-195.

1970 to 16th in 1990, 14th in 2010, and 11th in 2016. Close collaboration between universities and the big private companies has meant enormous investments in research and development and allowed South Korea to become a world leader in electronics and telecommunications. Its best known company is Samsung, but there are now 17 South Korean companies among the first world's top 500 manufacturers, compared with just 10 in 1990.[15]

South Korean growth has been accompanied by the development of other Asian countries, particularly Singapore, Taiwan and Hong Kong (known as "the four Asian tigers"), whose success has become increasingly evident since the 1980s. Their political histories are very different. Singapore is a former British colony, and Taiwan was the last refuge of the Kuomintang after its defeat in the Chinese Civil War; Hong Kong was a British colony until 1997, but enjoyed a special economic statute also after its return to China. These countries can (and must) be considered as confirming a successful Asian development model launched in the 1970s. In the 1980s, when the World Bank was still influenced by the prevailing viewpoint of the time and too inclined to observe only what happened in the financial centres of Singapore and Hong Kong, it had difficulty in accepting that the progress made by these countries was not the result of liberal policies. Only in 1993 did a new World Bank study admit that the success of Hong Kong, Singapore, and of Taiwan, Malaysia, Indonesia and Thailand, should be considered a real "economic miracle" based on specific industrial policies, and in certain cases also on state protection for nascent industries. Confirmation arrived a few years later, following the short but serious Asian crisis of 1997-1998: China, Korea and Taiwan were affected only in part and continued to grow, since their industrial development was more advanced, whereas Thailand, Malaysia and Indonesia were held back for a time because their development was still too weak to withstand the impact of the crisis.[16]

Of the first four Asian tigers, Singapore had some very peculiar features. As a small city-state, its size set it apart from the other Asian states, except for Hong Kong, which it resembled in some ways. Singapore has also been important as a model for China. During his 1978 visit, Deng Xiaoping was impressed by the economic model of Singapore's much-loved Prime Minister Lee Kuan Yew, its paternalistic ruler for several decades. In the space of

---

[15] D.S. Zagoria, *Is Korea The Next Japan*, in *Foreign Affairs*, Summer 1989.

[16] World Bank, *The East Asia Miracle. Economic Growth and Public Policy*, New York- Oxford, 1993; J. Studwell, *How Asia Works. Success and Failure in the World's Most Dynamic Region*, London, 2013, pp. XIV-XV.

just twenty years or so, Singapore's population of just under 6 million (75% ethnic Chinese) had experienced extraordinary economic and social development, and the reformist Deng saw Lee's combination of state intervention and openness to foreign investment as a path China should follow with care.[17] However, China could never hope to copy Singapore's strategic position, which had allowed it to become one of the world's most dynamic financial centres over the previous two decades. Most importantly, Singapore was now the world's most important port, since around 40% of the world's sea-borne trade passes through the Strait of Malacca every year.[18]

The Asian tigers have grown in number, and the original four have been joined by Thailand, Indonesia, Malaysia and Vietnam. This is also partly due to China's expansion of its value chain, since its manufacturers need partners able produce a share of their goods at even lower costs. In other cases, it involves economic and entrepreneurial development in nearby countries. In short, the "billions of entrepreneurs" in a well-known book, which examines the growth of opportunities and entrepreneurial talents in India and China, do not all live in these two countries. Vast numbers are also present in other Asian countries.[19] This massive growth has made it possible to reduce the number of people in Asia living on less than $2 a day by 50% since the start of the 21st century.[20]

22.3. The commodities boom and development of south-south economic relations

A large share of this undeniable success is connected with the enormous Chinese demand for raw materials. In fifteen years, China has become the world's leading industrial manufacturer and trading power, and its greatest consumer of raw materials. In 2010, China used 20% of the non-renewable energy resources, 23% of the main agricultural products and 40% of the basic metals consumed in the world. To be more precise, it consumed 50% of the cotton, around 40% of the copper and aluminium, less than half the

---

[17] Lee Kuan Yew, *From Third World to First. Singapore and the Asian Economic Boom*, New York, 2011, pp. 595-603; E.F. Vogel, *Deng Xiaoping and the Transformation of China*, Cambridge, Mass., 2011, pp. 290-291.

[18] L.Y.C. Lim, *Singapore's Success. After the Miracle*, in *Handbook of Emerging Economies*, London, 2014, pp. 203-226; J. Grant, *Singapore tests success*, in *Financial Times*, 27.11.2014.

[19] T. Khanna, *Billions of Entrepreneurs. How China and India are reshaping their future and yours*, Harvard, 2011.

[20] J. Noble, *Addicted to Debt*, in *Financial Times*, 14.5.2015.

coal, a fifth of the meat, wheat and soybean (much of the soybean as pig feed).[21] The *commodities* market has experienced a real boom since the start of the new century, entering in 2003 what has been defined as the "super-cycle" of commodity prices, with increases of 100, 200 and even 300-400% in just a few years. The most valid explanation of this trend connects it to the demands for raw materials generated by the BRICS, especially by China.

Prices began rising sharply in 2003; certain products accelerated in 2007-2008, and the trend continued during the crisis, although more slowly. The effects of the crisis in the more developed countries and contraction of the Chinese demand then combined to cause a fall in prices, which for some raw materials was very dramatic (50-70% for petrol, copper and iron ore).[22]

In many Asian countries, not to mention various South American and African states, China's increased demand for raw materials has led to important economic-social changes. The Chinese government has accompanied these operations, nearly always involving state-owned enterprises, in a way that has provided new opportunities to the countries exporting raw materials, particularly in Africa. Since Chinese strategy implies no interference in a country's internal affairs, its companies also do business with dictatorships, and it uses a combination of financial resources, technical expertise and influence on the UN Security Council to protect these countries from international sanctions.[23]

In many cases, this economic-commercial exchange means that Chinese companies build new infrastructures (roads, ports, railways) or improve those already in place, the decadent legacy of the colonial period or the early years of independence. In addition, China needs to maintain a fair balance of trade with its African partners. General improvements in living standards have allowed these countries to achieve better consumption levels, due to the very low cost – even for the poor African markets – of many mid- and low-tech Chinese goods.[24] The economic growth of sub-Saharan

---

[21] S.K. Roache, *China's Impact on World Commodity Markets*, Imf Working Paper, WP/12/115, May 2012.

[22] B. Erten, J.A. Ocampo, *Super-Cycles of Commodity Prices Since the Mid-Nineteenth Nentury*, DESA Working Paper No. 110, ST/ESA/2012/DWP/110, February 2012; *Why the Commodities Super Cycle Was a Myth. Falling Prices Show the World Is Not Running Out of Resources*, in *Financial Times*, 31.8.2015.

[23] S. Halper, *The Beijing Consensus. How China's Authoritarian Model Will Dominate the Twenty-first Century*, New York, 2012, pp. 44-45 e 99-101.

[24] L. Xing, A. Osman Farah (eds.), *China-Africa Relations in an Era of Great Transformations*, New York, 2013.

countries is bringing Africa increasingly into the globalization mechanism, and not only as a passive player. This is confirmed by the GDP growth rate, which has remained steadily 2% to 3% percentage points above the developed economies since 2000. However, it is the striking development of Africa's foreign trade that provides more important confirmation. It has perfectly overlapped the world trade cycle since the first years of the 21st century,[25] although the exports of at least fifteen African countries are excessively reliant on just two or three products for 75% of the total value. Moreover, these products are usually exported unprocessed, so that the greatest share of the value chain remains in the hands of international traders or big consumers.[26]

The unprecedented geographical expansion of economic development is causing profound changes in the world economic equilibrium. The most important new element is the growth of "south-south" trade between emerging countries, which has become increasingly important in the last twenty or so years, at the expense of the traditional north-south trade between developed and developing countries. Between 1990 and 2010, trade in non-petroleum goods between southern hemisphere countries, including the recently industrialized nations, rose from 9% to 21% of the total, trade in mid-tech goods ranged between 28% and 35%, and trade in high-tech goods increased from 21.5% to just under 30%.

In this kind of context, the free trade policies advocated by the WTO are fundamentally important. However, the scale and importance of the process has meant that the major players in the world economy, especially the USA and China, are now developing new political-commercial policies to protect their own national interests, aiming to bring about greater interdependence between the economies of their chief trading partners in the world's most important areas.

This is the background to moves to establish a North American and European free trade area, known as the Transatlantic Trade and Investment Partnership (TTIP). The negotiations have taken years, attracting criticism and causing concern to different economic sectors and public opinion in both Europe and the USA. If the project is successful, it will unite about 50% of the world's GDP and a third of its international trade. However, many doubts about its feasibility remain, at least in the short term. Great

---

[25] *http://www.imf.org/external/np/ds/matrix.htm.*

[26] A. Goldstein, N. Pinaud, H. Reisen, C. Xiaobao, *China and India. What's in It for Africa*, Oecd Development Centre, February 2006; Omotunde E.G Johnson (eds.), *Economic Diversification and Growth in Africa. Critical Policy Making Issues*, Berlin, 2016.

Britain's exit from the EU has greatly weakened the project, also because it has strengthened the positions of states like France and Germany, which are long-term sceptics about some parts of the agreement.[27] In the USA, where both candidates in the 2016 US presidential elections were openly against the agreement, scepticism has always been a constant, and Donald Trump's election victory seems to have put an end to US involvement in a project towards which Barack Obama had worked hard.

Problems have also beset the other great trade agreement, the Trans-Pacific Partnership (TPP), advocated by the USA to re-affirm its role and curb the growing Chinese presence in the Pacific area. Talks began in 2005, concluding in February 2016 with an agreement between twelve countries (Australia, Brunei, Canada, Chile, Japan, Malaysia, Mexico, New Zealand, Peru, Singapore, the USA and Vietnam). Trump's victory in November 2016 had an even greater effect on shelving this other great free trade project than on the TTIP.[28]

US strategy has been rather unconvincing and unclear, even for its closest allies, as confirmed by the surprising success of China's initiative to establish the Asian Infrastructure Investment Bank in 2014. Despite political and diplomatic pressure from the USA, almost sixty countries (including the United Kingdom, France, Germany, Italy, Spain, Brazil, Russia, India, many of the Gulf states, Kazakhstan, Uzbekistan, Indonesia, and many Southeast Asian countries) hurried to join the new bank. Many of these considered the institute as the Chinese regional equivalent (of a "region" as vast as much of Asia) of the World Bank (influenced principally by the USA) and the Asian Development Bank (controlled by Japan).[29]

This is one element of a vast Chinese strategy; it aims to achieve free trading relations and better defend its own interests by offering itself as a partner for far-reaching investments in connection with its One Belt One Road strategic plan, also known as the Silk Road Economic Belt and 21st Century Maritime Silk Road. With an initial fund of €40 billion provided by the China Investment Corporation (the Chinese sovereign wealth fund), China Development Bank, Export-Import Bank of China and the State

---

[27] *US-EU Trade Talks Reach Critical Stage*, in *The Economist*, 21.1.2014; *Trading Places. What the Aversion to Global Trade Says about Europe and America*, ibid., 30.4.2016.

[28] *Trade, Partnership and Politics. With Negotiations Secret, Optimism about a Path-breaking Trade Deal is Hard to Share*, in *The Economist*, 24.9.2013; *Trade, at What Price? America's Economy Benefits Hugely from Trade. But Its Costs Have Been Amplified by Policy Failures*, *ibid.*, 2.4.2016.

[29] *The Infrastructure of Power. Reasons to Be Enthusiastic about China's Answer to the World Bank*, in *The Economist*, 2.7.2016.

Administration of Foreign Exchange, the new bank will provide finance for new infrastructures and for industrial and financial cooperation projects to exploit resources. The first areas it will focus on will very probably be central and southeast Asia.[30] In any case, as shown by the railway line connecting central China since 2014 to the railway hub at Lodz (Poland), trains are faster than ships (14-18 days by rail instead of 30 by sea from China to Hamburg, ideal entry point to the European market). Not only do trains have the advantage of speed, but they also offer better possibilities of forging close political and economic relations with the countries they cross. Moreover, it should be remembered that each far-reaching Chinese initiative envisages so many variants that it appears to form a part of an even broader strategy.[31]

Figure 22.1. GDP growth rates of BRICS (1994-2014)

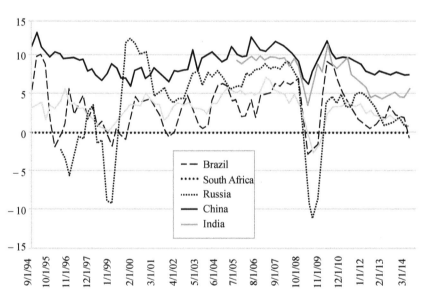

Source: Thomson Reuters.

---

[30] Min Ye, *China's Silk Road Strategy. Xi Jinping's real answer to the Trans-Pacific Partnership*, in *Foreign Policy*, November 2014; The Economist Intelligence Unit, *Prospects and Challenges on China's 'One Belt, One Road'. A Risk Assessment Report*, 2015; J. Stokes, *China's Road Rules. Beijing Looks West Toward Eurasian Integration*, in *Foreign Affairs*, 19.4.2015; C. Clover, L. Hornby, *Road to a New Empire*, in *Financial Times*, 13.10.2015.

[31] *http://www.reuters.com/article/us-china-railway-kemp-idUSKCN0X41U7.*

Figure 22.2. Chinese market share of certain commodities (2009-2010, %)

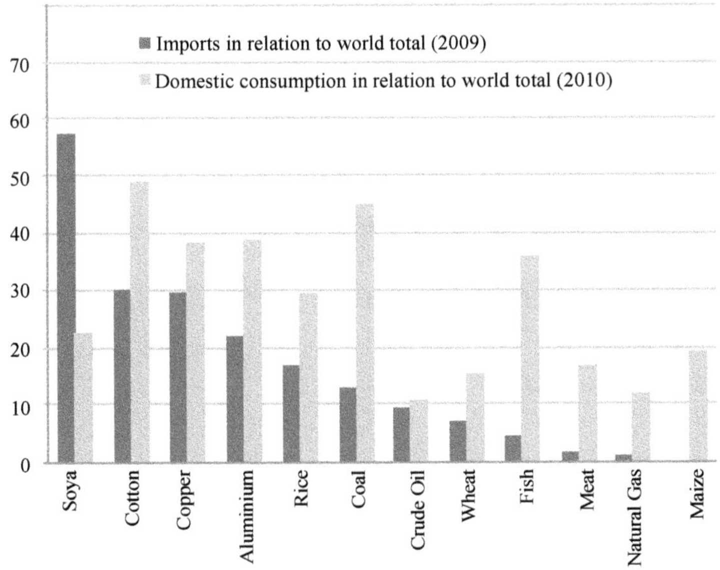

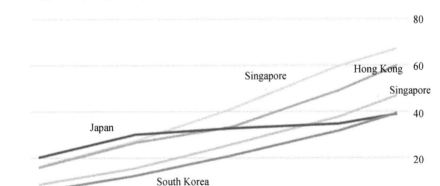

■ Imports in relation to world total (2009)

▨ Domestic consumption in relation to world total (2010)

Source: S.K. Roache, *China's Impact on World Commodity Markets*, IMF Working Papers, 2012, 12, 115.

Figure 22.3. Per capita GDP growth rates of some Asian countries ($1000, at Purchasing power parity, 2011)

Source: International Monetary Fund.

Bibliography

Berger S., *How We Compete. What Companies Around the World Are Doing to Make it in Today's Global Economy*, New York, 2005.

Ferguson N., Kissinger H., Li D., Zakaria F., *Does the 21st Century Belong to China? The Munk Debate on China*, Toronto, 2011.

Goldstein A., *Bric, Brasile, Russia, India, Cina alla guida dell'economia globale*, Bologna, 2011.

Khanna T., *Billions of Entrepreneurs. How China and India are Reshaping Their Future – and Yours*, Harvard, 2011.

Masina P.P., *Il Sud Est asiatico in trappola. Storia di un miracolo mancato*, Milan, 2014.

Yergin D., Stanislaw J., *The Commanding Heights. The Battle for the World Economy*, New York, 1998.

Chapter 23
A DIFFERENT KIND OF CRISIS?

SUMMARY: 23.1. The origins of the financial crisis. – 23.2. Bailing out the banking systems. – 23.3. Uncertainties after the crisis. – Bibliography.

23.1. The origins of the financial crisis

The crisis began in 2007 with the first difficulties in the US property market. It then spread to some European countries before turning into a truly global crisis, which is having a profound effect on the process of globalization. The initial *subprime* crisis appeared to involve only the US mortgage market, where a superficial approach to lending meant that when interest rates rose, many low-income borrowers were actually unable to pay their mortgages and interest; however, it gradually revealed the vast extent to which the world economy was now financialized.

In effect, before exploring the complicated mechanisms leading to the crisis, and its different stages in the following years, it is important to consider the profound transformations to the international financial system during the second half of the 1970s and the early 1980s. The mass of capital in circulation following the rise in petrol prices gradually brought changes with both short-term and mid- to long-term impacts. The first phase of globalization of the financial markets involved the interaction of the Eurodollar market (already in existence for about 15 years) and the petrodollar market; the massive use of petrodollars to finance the economies of the developing countries led to the serious international debt crises of the early 1980s, and again ten years later. This was the multiplying effect of two enormous masses of capital; once combined, they produce results that can be quantified in geometric and not mathematical terms. The international financial system has been compelled to adapt to this growing mass of resources by continually adjusting its productive capacity to the money supply: in other words, it has had to innovate by continually inventing new financial tools for the allocation of these huge amounts of money.[1]

In 1980, the total value of financial *assets* (including bank deposits, pub-

---

[1] G. Mellman, *The Vandal's Crown. How Rebel Currency Traders Overthrew the World's Central Banks*, London, 1995; S. Strange, *Mad Money*, Manchester, 1998

lic debt, private debt securities and equities) was $12 trillion, but their value had risen to $196 trillion by 2007. In 1980, they represented almost 150% of world GDP, and this share had risen to 351% by 2007. However, many changes were taking place within this framework: this mass of financial resources had gradually moved away from bank deposits (down from 45% to 29% of the total) towards institutional investors. The two items with the highest growth rates were equities (from 23% to 29%) and private debt securities (from 14% to 25%), and this growth was also sustained in the following years. In 2007, the total value of *assets* amounted to just over $206 trillion, equal to 351% of world GDP.

This meant that there were plenty of warning signs. In December 2006, *The Economist* used a rather more triumphant tone than usual in its forecast for the following year, announcing that "Market capitalism, the engine that runs most of the world economy, seems to be doing its job well".[2] In mid-February 2007, Federal Reserve head Ben Bernanke presented a relatively rosy situation to Congress, with US economy that was doing well, growing at a more sustainable rate (a new "soft landing", like that described by his predecessor in the mid-1990s). There were no great concerns about the share of the mortgage market that was more at risk, since families' extra-debt was now offset by the fall in long-term interest rates.[3] During the same weeks, the IMF stated that "residential investment was a substantial drag on U.S. GDP in the second half of 2006. Over the past few months, there have been some tentative signs of stabilization at least on the demand side, as sales of existing homes, mortgage applications, and potential homebuyer intentions have generally steadied or improved". However, the same publication affirmed that "there remain risks that the fallout from the housing correction could be amplified, particularly if tightening lending standards in the subprime sector were to lead to a broader reappraisal of credit availability across the economy or if household cash flows were to weaken". Such a development – concluded the IMF – "could imply a deeper and more prolonged slowdown or even a recession in the United States, with potential spillovers to other countries".[4]

Returning to the summer of 2007, which was, in a way, just a long beginning, insiders were not completely unaware of what was happening. In mid-July, the managers of an Australian *hedge fund* disclosed that the fund

---

[2] *Happiness (and How to Measure It). Capitalism Can Make a Society Rich and Keep It Free. Don't Ask It To Make You Happy As Well*, in *The Economist*, 19.12.2006.

[3] *Sunshine and Light, Mostly*, in *The Economist*, 15.2.2007.

[4] International Monetary Fund, *World Economic Outlook April 2007. Spillovers and Cycle in Global economy*, Washington, 2007, pp. 7-8.

was reducing its investments due to the difficulties of the US credit market "following concerns in relation to sub-prime residential mortgages and have made margin calls".[5] Before the end of July, the situation began to affect US banks, which fell several points on Wall Street.[6] On 1st August, the *Financial Times* wrote that "little debt market bombs are starting to explode on the balance sheets of financial institutions around the world".[7]

News arrived thick and fast in August. What at first glance seemed a credit problem was tackled in the usual way; on 17th August the Federal Reserve cut the bank rate by a quarter of a point, an indirect admission that the credit squeeze could cause problems for the US economy. In September 2007, the idea began to spread that the world economy might have reached a turning point. The phase of growth and stability of the last twenty years seemed to have ended, but the economy's greater flexibility gave it more ability to absorb the shock, appearing to produce permanent stability. In that precise moment, it seemed foolish to consider testing this assumption by combining the turbulence of the credit markets with the vulnerability of the property markets. However, the risk remained, related to an excessively generous use of the new financial products, whose *fall-out* was poisoning the short-term credit markets that were vital for the economy to function correctly.[8]

One year later, the situation was completely different. The crisis had become much more serious and threatened the entire international financial system. First came the failure of Fannie Mae and Freddie Mac, two of the USA's biggest providers of mortgage finance. This was followed in September by the bankruptcy of Lehman Brothers, one of the world's most prestigious and important investment banks, and Merrill Lynch was taken over by Bank of America.[9] Bank employees – some in tears – left the skyscraper with their possessions in cardboard boxes, and these images became symbols of a world unexpectedly discovering its hidden weaknesses.

The deeper underlying causes of the crisis gradually became clearer. China's huge trade surplus generated an excessive amount of capital in Asia, used by Beijing to buy US bonds, which pushed interest rates down

---

[5] *Subprime Crisis. The Basis Capital Letter to Investors*, in *Financial Times*, 18.7.2007.

[6] *Banks Burnt by Credit Meltdown*, in *Financial Times*, 27.7.2007.

[7] *Subprime Grenades*, in *Financial Times*, 1.8.2007.

[8] *The Turning Point. Does the Latest Financial Crisis Signal the End of a Golden Age of Stable Growth?*, in *The Economist*, 20.9.2007.

[9] C. Mollenkamp, S. Craig, S. Ng, A. Lucchetti, *Lehman Files for Bankruptcy, Merrill Sold, in AIG Seeks Cash*, 16 settembre 2008; P. Chapman, *The Last of the Imperious Rich. Lehman Brothers, 1844-2008*, London, 2010.

worldwide in the first few years of the 21st century. The European banks obtained finance in the USA and used these funds to buy unstable equities. All these factors combined to drive the debt level upwards in a world that appeared to have become less risky.[10]

Money was unwisely lent to people with a *poor financial story* (no bank account, no credit card). These high-risk debts were passed to financial engineers in the big banks, who packaged them together with low-risk financial products in the mistaken conviction that the US property market behaved differently from one city to another. However, house prices fell across the entire country in 2006. These financial products were used to protect other securities, CDOs (*collateralised debt obligations*), i.e. fixed interest securities protected by a portfolio of obligations, loans and other assets, which were then sliced into portions (tranches) according to the level of risk. Investors bought the more secure *tranches* from banks on the strength of AAA ratings assigned by the *rating* agencies, unaware that banks had paid agencies to give a more generous evaluation of the risk level.

When the US property market began to suffer, a chain reaction revealed all the fragilities of the financial system. The products of financial engineering proved to be insufficiently protected, and the value of mortgages based on these products collapsed, falling in some cases to zero. Previously considered secure, CDOs were now worthless and impossible to sell at any price, despite their rating.

Trust, another fundamental element of the international financial system, had already vanished a year before the end of Lehman Brothers. Short-term credit was either interrupted or else granted at extremely high interest levels to discourage the market. At the same time, the immediate return of short-term credit was demanded. This was the situation causing the problems of Northern Rock, a British bank specializing in mortgage loans.[11] The failure of one small link plunged the entire debt chain into a crisis. Financial tools like *credit default swaps* (agreements in which the seller compensates the buyer in the case of default by a third party) had been created to spread the risk, but were now seen to concentrate it even more. AIG, a major US insurance company, risked bankruptcy under the weight of the vast number of CDOs it had sold.[12]

---

[10] J.E. Stiglitz, *Freefall. America, Free Markets, and the Sinking of the World Economy*, New York, 2010.

[11] B. Walters, *The Fall of Northern Rock. An Insider's Story of Britain's Biggest Banking Disaster*, London, 2008.

[12] R. Boyd, *Fatal Risk. A Cautionary Tale of Aig's Corporate Suicide*, Hoboken N.J., 2011.

23.2. Bailing out the banking systems

The bankruptcy of Lehman Brothers ($639 billion, the biggest in US history) caused panic. Three days before this happened, on 12th September, J.P. Morgan had published its forecasts for the following year, indicating that the GDP of the USA would accelerate in the first half of 2009. It is likely that no economic forecast has ever been more mistaken, as Alan Greenspan recalled some years later.[13] On 22nd September, Morgan Stanley and Goldman Sachs ceased to operate as investment banks, and became traditional commercial banks accepting deposits from private citizens and companies. This began a process of profound change on Wall Street, and was just the first in a series of events disrupting international finance and redefining the relations between the system's principal operators. The Federal Reserve supervised the operation.[14] A week later, on 28th September, the US Congress approved the Troubled Asset Relief Programme (TARP), a $700 billion rescue plan for the banking sector. According to some experts, this was only an estimate, representing a compromise between the $1 trillion requested by Wall Street and the initial figure proposed by Treasury Secretary Henry Paulson.[15]

It was a sign that government intervention was going to play an extremely important role in the development of the crisis. On the next day, the British government nationalized the Bradford & Bingley, assuming over £50 billion in mortgage loans and debts, providing a further £18 billion to allow Santander to take over two hundred Bradford & Bingley branches. In the following days, the Irish government declared that it would guarantee all deposits in the Republic's banks for two years. The governments of France, Belgium and Luxembourg worked together on a bailout package for Dexia, and the German government did the same for Hypo Real Estate. A few days later, the British government announced a £500 billion intervention package, and in mid-October it provided another £37 billion just to recapitalize the Royal Bank of Scotland. The Dutch government intervened with €10 billion to rescue ING, and Sweden's government provided the country's banks with a 1.5 billion *krone* (€205 billion) credit line. In

---

[13] A. Greenspan *Never Saw It Coming. Why the Financial Crisis Took Economists by Surprise*, in *Foreign Affairs*, 2013.

[14] J. Hilsenrath, D. Paletta, A. Lucchetti, *Goldman, Morgan Scrap Wall Street Model, Become Banks in Bid to Ride Out Crisis. End of Traditional Investment Banking, as Storied Firms Face Closer Supervision and Stringent New Capital Requirements*, in *The Wall Street Journal*, 22.9.2008.

[15] A.R. Sorkin, *Too Big to Fail. The Inside Story of How Wall Street and Washington Fought To Save the Financial System and Themselves*, London, 2009, pp. 446-448.

early November, the US government decided to invest $40 billion in AIG preferential shares and another $45 billion to cover its debts, establishing a different approach from the one taken a few months earlier with Lehman Brothers. Although AIG had committed the same sinful mistake ($400 billion in derivative securities, mainly CDOs to protect other investments), its failure would have had a greater impact, bringing down every financial institution that had insured its credit risk.[16]

In the following weeks and months, the crisis hit all the world's stock exchanges, bringing the first signs that the international economic system was in difficulty. The Dow Jones fell by around 50%, from 14,000 in summer 2007 to just over 7,000 in the next two years, as did the S&P500. Between September 2007 and February 2009, the London share index fell from 6,500 to 3,500 points (its lowest point during the crisis).[17]

Barack Obama's victory in the presidential elections on 4th November 2008 was decisive for the outcome of many measures introduced in the last period of the Bush presidency, but the biggest novelties came in the very first months of the new presidency. Several bipartisan measures had already been introduced during the transition period between the two administrations, signalling that a new approach would now prevail. The Fed intervened in mid-November to invest $100 billion in Fannie Mae, Freddie Mac and Federal Home Loan Bank stock, and $500 billion in their mortgage-backed securities. The intention was to restart the mortgage and property market. Without consumer lending, consumption would fall, bringing increased unemployment, more defaults, and further problems for the financial system. The new administration could not afford to let this happen. The Fed added a further $180 billion in loans to *hedge funds* and other investors to enable the consumer credit market to pick up again. In order to overcome creditors' last fears, the Fed also declared its willingness to write off the debt in the case of a large number of consumer defaults.

The government also supported the plan to rescue Citigroup, the biggest US bank, by accepting to absorb 90% of the bank's losses on $300 billion of toxic assets. This move was also symbolic: for years, Citibank had been to the forefront in demanding repeal of the Glass-Steagall Act. There was criticism when the bank's managers were not removed as a condition of its bailout, although Citigroup was effectively under government control, since a former Treasury Undersecretary during Clinton's presidency, Robert Rubin, was a senior adviser. Rubin's protégé, Timothy Geithner, presi-

---

[16] H. James, *The Creation and Destruction of Value. The Globalization Cycle*, Harvard, 2009, pp. 114-115.

[17] *http://www.dowjones.com*; *https://uk.finance.yahoo.com*.

dent of the Fed in New York, was nominated to the Treasury by the new administration. On taking office, Geithner immediately made it clear that he was opposed to nationalization of the banks in difficulty, even on a temporary basis; it would damage the prospects of recovery and create uncertainties about the banks' daily operation, while the international press would see the "spectre of nationalization" as something to avoid.[18]

Consolidation of US finance was entrusted to the Public-Private Investment Program for Legacy Assetts (PPIP) launched in February 2009. This was accompanied by the Fiscal Stimulus or Recovery Act, officially known as the American Recovery and Reinvestment Act of 2009 (ARRA) and worth $785 billion, which was then increased to $831 billion.[19] The new measures were aimed at stimulating US economic recovery by saving existent jobs and creating new ones. Other objectives were to provide temporary relief programs for those most affected by the recession, to invest in infrastructure with prospects of long-term benefits, in education, health, and renewable energy, and to stabilize the finances of local and state governments.[20]

During the 2008 presidential election campaign, some conservatives had criticized Obama as wanting to allow socialists and their ideas into the White House, and these measures appeared to strengthen his enemies' convictions. There were interventions in favour of the US car industry in April 2009, when the government was forced to mount a massive rescue operation to save General Motors and Chrysler, the biggest US car manufacturers, from bankruptcy. This involved temporary purchase of 50% of GM shares, reduction of its workforce, and an injection of liquidity to silence its creditors. Chrysler's recovery was managed in part with FIAT, which was immediately granted a 20% stake in the company in return for its role in the restructuring process; FIAT had the prospect of becoming Chrysler's majority shareholder within a few years, when recovery would be complete and the company would be able to repay the government loan.[21]

---

[18] *The Spectre of Nationalisation. There Are Ways for Governments to Revitalise Banks without Taking Them Over*, in *The Economist*, 22.1.2009.

[19] B. Eichengreen, *Hall of Mirrors. The Great Depression, the Great Recession, and the Uses – and Misuses – of History*, Oxford, 2015, pp. 289-301.

[20] *The Obama Rescue. This Week Marked a Huge Wasted Opportunity in the Economic Crisis*, in *The Economist*, 12.2.2009.

[21] S. Mufson, *Gm's New Escape Route. Partial Nationalization*, in *Washington Post*, 28 aprile 2009; *Chrysler and General Motors End Game*, in *The Economist*, 30.4.2009.

23.3. Uncertainties after the crisis

The 2007-2008 crisis immediately became a case for economists and financial historians to study, and thousands of books, articles, essays and papers about it were soon published. The discussion was not entirely confined to academic circles and became partly public, precisely because the crisis had such dramatic effects on the lives of millions of people in different countries. The debate about the origins of the crisis was not a mere academic exercise, nor was it limited to the financial sector. In March 2009, the *Financial Times* wrote: the "credit crunch has destroyed faith in the free market ideology that has dominated Western economic thinking for a generation. But what can – or should – replace it?" These words then gave rise to a series of articles, and the replies proposed various ways to avoid a repetition of the crisis.[22] Not all the many international interventions were seen as effective. The report from the US government-appointed Commission states very clearly that the crisis could have been avoided. However, this report was not unanimously approved. Four of the Commission's ten members presented a minority report, criticizing its failure to provide an accurate evaluation of the amount of international capital looking for profitable investments in the US mortgage market[23], what upset public opinion the most was the multi-million dollar bonuses paid to the *top executives* who had led the banks into the crisis and – in some cases – into bankruptcy. In the following years, the general worsening of economic conditions meant that public opinion became even more hostile towards the fat salaries of these top managers. On the other hand, few of these top executives were actually accused of criminal action, although their behaviour was heavily cricized and some actually resigned.[24] Galbraith told the Senate Judiciary Committee that those who had made mistakes, even the regulators,

---

[22] *The Future of Capitalism*, in *Financial Times*, 23.3.2009.

[23] The Financial Crisis Inquiry Commission, *The Financial Crisis Inquiry Report. Final Report of The National Commission. The Causes Of The Financial And Economic Crisis In The United States*, Official Government Edition Submitted By Pursuant To Public Law 111-21, Washington, 2011; *The Official Verdict America's Fcic Report is Big, Surprisingly Readable and a Disappointment*, in *The Economist*, 3.2.2011.

[24] *Top 12 CEO Departures of 2009*, in *Forbes*, 15.12.2009; http://ig.ft.com/sites/2015/bank-ceo-compensation-2015/; http://www.reuters.com/article/us-swiss-vote-pay-id USBRE9AN0BW20131124; C. Copley, *Swiss voters reject proposal to limit executives' pay*; http://blogs.worldbank.org/allaboutfinance/executive-pay-and-the-financial-crisis, L. Bebchuk, *Executive Pay and the Financial Crisis*, 31.1.2012; J. Eisinger, *Why Only One Top Banker Went to Jail for the Financial Crisis*, in *The New York Times Magazine*, 30.4.2014.

should be treated so harshly that they would feel "in their bones, the power of the law".[25]

When the report was eventually published, the international financial system was very different from the way it had been a few years earlier; the crisis had shaken its very foundations, and there was even talk of a new world order.[26] Nevertheless, the data on the total value of financial assets show an almost immediate recovery. The 2007 value of $206 trillion dropped to $189 trillion in 2008, but then recovered in 2009 to its level at the start of the crisis in 2007; it rose to $219 trillion in 2010 and to $220 trillion in 2011. The single items most affected by the crisis were shares, which fell from $64 trillion to $47 trillion between 2007 and 2011, government bonds, which rose from $32 trillion to $46 trillion (indirectly due to the cost of the crisis), and non-securitized loans, which rose from $50 trillion to $60 trillion. When the McKinsey Institute published these data (in mid-2012), it was still uncertain about the outlook; it was unclear whether the system was in a phase of contraction or reorganization.[27]

In effect, a far-reaching reorganization of the banking system had been effected through mergers with the banks that were in difficulty. The ownership structures of some of the major world banks had changed when the sovereign investment funds of the Arab Emirates, Singapore, and, most importantly, China began buying shares during the most difficult period of the crisis in 2008-2009. In 2008 alone, their total investments in the financial system amounted to over $75 billion. The major US, Swiss, Italian and German banks were involved in these operations, which did not generally have positive results.[28] The regulatory system was reformed in the aftermath of criticisms related to its loose surveillance of the markets. In Great Britain, the tripartite system established in 1998 (Treasury, Bank of England and Financial Services Authority, FSA) was criticized for its ineffectiveness and slowness to intervene before and during the crisis. In 2012-2013, the FSA was replaced by two bodies: the Financial Conduct Authori-

---

[25] *Utip.gv.utexas.edu/Flyers/GalbraithMay4SubcommitteeCrine.*

[26] P. Coggan, *Paper Promises. Money, Debt and the New World Order*, London, 2011.

[27] McKinsey Global Institute, *Financial Globalization. Retreat or Reset? Global Capital Markets 2012*, New York, 2013.

[28] *The Invasion of the Sovereign-Wealth Funds. The Biggest Worry about Rich Arab and Asian States Buying Up Wall Street is the Potential Backlash*, in *The Economist*, 18.1.2008; J. Willman, *Sovereign Wealth Funds. Yesterday's Bad Guys Ride to the Rescue*, in *Financial Times*, 21.1.2008; L. Anderloni, D. Vandone, *Sovereign Wealth Fund Investments in the Banking Industry*, working paper n. 2012-24, University of Milan, Department of Economics, Management and Quantitative Methods, December 2012.

ty, and the Prudential Regulation Authority, which was directly controlled by the Bank of England.[29]

In general, greater controls were introduced at all levels, obliging the banking system to behave differently and make radical changes to strategy. In any case, while the problem was to avoid the fear voiced in the title of a well-known book – *too big to fail* – the aftermath of the crisis made the problem more acute. The banks were now even bigger and even more interconnected with the entire system (in 2013, the six major US banks were 37% bigger than in 2008-2009). Some new legislation, such as the Dodd-Franck Act, could not be applied immediately, since it required interventions by around a hundred financial institutions. However, the banking system resisted well, although certain limitations contained in the reform (making it more difficult for the Fed to intervene in a liquidity crisis of healthy banks) threatened to greatly reduce the central banks' role as lenders of last resort, one of the cornerstones of the modern banking system.[30]

For this reason, the regulators tried to do what they had always done, and just made the regulations stricter, e.g regarding the *ratios* for banking work, the work inside the banks, and the links between banks. They introduced a far-reaching innovation that has been described in a very simple way: instead of asking all the banks "precisely how their payment system functioned", the question had become "show me how it works". This has allowed – or should allow – entry to much more complex areas of the banking system, which had been (to use a euphemism) somewhat shady. The regulators had obtained a role in decisions; this is the difference between *conduct regulation* and *prudential regulation*, the terms used for the new regulatory bodies created in Great Britain.[31]

At the global level, the most important intervention in this sense came from the Basel Committee on Banking Supervision (BCBS), which in 2001 introduced Basel III, an international regulatory framework to strengthen the regulation, supervision and risk management of the banking sector. The framework is based on the interaction between two approaches, defined as "microprudential" (related to the regulation at the level of single banks) and "macroprudential" (related to the system risks that may build up in the banking sector, and their procyclical amplification over time). The principal points of the framework include the need to make the banking sector more resilient to the impacts of economic and financial tensions, irrespec-

---

[29] *Review of HM Treasury's Management Response to the Financial Crisis*, London, 2012.

[30] B. Eichengreen, *Hall of Mirrors*, cit., pp. 323-324.

[31] *Chained but Untamed*, in *The Economist*, 12.5.2011; *A Dangerous Embrace, ibidem*.

tive of their origins; to improve risk management and *governance*, and last-ly, to make the banking sector more transparent.[32] These regulations form the basis of the European Banking Authority's stress tests on banks.

However, these interventions cannot ensure that history will not repeat itself, and many people are still convinced that the bankers have not yet learned their lesson.[33] The strictest measures to avoid the repetition of certain risks can be adopted only in relation to the banking and financial system. In any case, what emerged during the crisis was that a large share of the operations and products most at risk were actually managed by operators who the financial authorities were juridically unable to control, thus making all attempts at regulation extremely difficult. This is known as the *shadow banking system*. It is estimated to be extremely large, and thus represents a potential danger for the system, also because of its close links to the "official" banking and financial system.[34] The most recent estimates (based on data from 26 countries) of its size range from a minimum of $36 trillion (59% of these countries' GDP and 12% of the total global financial system) to a maximum of $137 trillion (40% of the financial system's total *assets*). If the first estimate were exact, it would indicate a drop of $36 trillion from the 2007 peak while the second figure would indicate an increase of 125%.[35]

The crisis began as an economic and social problem among the weaker sectors of US society. Borrowers were unable to pay the interest on mortgages provided by an over-generous banking system, which then had to pursue its customers in order to increase its volume of business during a period of low interest rates. The crisis firstly affected the US financial sector, and then turned into a global crisis. Attempts made by various governments to inject resources into their countries' economies had little effect.[36]

---

[32] Bank for International Settlements, *Basel III. A Global Regulatory Framework for More Resilient Banks and Banking Systems*, Basel, 2011.

[33] A. Admati, M. Hellwig, *The Bankers' New Clothes, What's Wrong with Banking and What to do about it*, Princeton, 2014.

[34] Financial Stability Board, *Global Shadow Banking Monitoring Report 2015*, Basel, 2015.

[35] Federal Reserve Bank of New York – Staff Reports, T. Adrian, Hyun Song Shin, *The Shadow Banking System. Implications for Financial Regulation*, Staff Report No. 382, July 2009; Brookings Papers on Economic Activity, A. Metrick, G. Gorton, *Regulating the Shadow Banking System*, Fall 2010, *http://www.brookings.edu/about/projects/bpea/papers/2010/regula ting-shadow-banking-system-gorton*.

[36] *China Seeks Stimulation. A Stimulus Plan to Inject $586 Billion into China's Economy. But the Devil Lies in the Detail*, in *The Economist*, 10.11.2008; D. Weinland,

The world economy has now been in a state of crisis for almost a decade. Although global GDP rose from $57.5 trillion in 2007 to $78.1 trillion in 2014, it fell to $73.4 in 2015; GDP growth was around 4% in 2000, fell below 3% after the crisis, and now stands at just a little over 2.5%. GDP in the USA has grown at around 2.5% since 2010, and Japan's economic growth rate has hovered around zero for about 20 years. EU growth rates from 2000 to 2007 ranged between 2% and 4%, but have been between 1% and 2% since 2010 (and slightly lower than this in the Eurozone).[37]

Since emerging countries and markets are also growing more slowly, and aging populations are no longer a problem only for the most advanced economies, there is a risk that the world economy has entered a long – "secular" – phase of stagnation, to quote Larry Summers, Bill Clinton's former Treasury Secretary.[38] The structural changes to the economy caused by globalization have probably brought about a "substantial change" in the natural balance between savings and investments, causing a decline in the balance or in the normal interest rate associated with full use. Imbalances between the countries with large trade surpluses, like China and Germany, and the countries with structural deficits have an increasingly destabilizing effect on the world economy.

The answer many people give today is no different from what Keynes said in the 1930s: the problem lies with demand, not supply. Demand must be revived, but this requires policy makers to understand exactly where the problem lies. This is the only way to overcome the dilemma of knowing whether or not "this time is different".

If they cannot diagnose the problem correctly, there is the risk of confirming the words of those who say that this time is no different.[39]

G. Wildau, *China Financial Regulator Clamps Down on Shadow Banking. Chinese Banks have Disguised Risky Loans as Investment Products*, in *Financial Times*, 2.5.2016.

[37] *http://www.worldbank.org.*

[38] L.H. Summers, *U.S. Economic Prospects. Secular Stagnation, Hysteresis, and the Zero Lower Bound*, in *Business Economics*, 49, 2, pp. 65-73; Id., *The Age of Secular Stagnation*, in *Foreign Affairs*, March/April 2016, pp. 2-9.

[39] C.M. Reinhart, K.S. Rogoff, *This Time Is Different. Eight Centuries of Financial Folly*, Princeton, 2009, p. XXXV.

Figure 23.1. US FIRE economy and manufacturing (added value per sector % of GDP, 1947-2009)

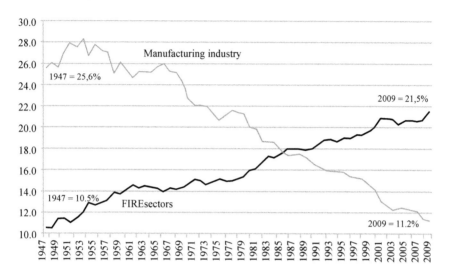

Note: FIRE economy (Finance, Insurance & Real Estate).

Source: US Bureau of Economic Analysis.

Figure 23.2. Global stock of debt and of principal financial products (1991-2010, in a sample of 79 countries)

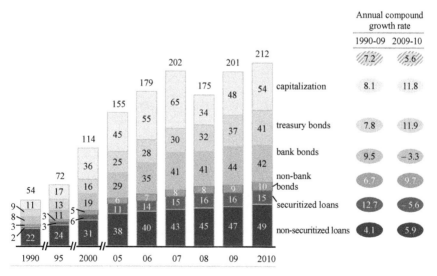

Source: Bank for International Settlements; Dealogic; SIFMA; Standard & Poor's; McKinsey Global Banking Pools; McKinsey Global Institute Analysis.

Figure 23.3. Total foreign investments (% of global GDP, in a sample of 79 countries, $trillion at constant 2010 exchange rates)

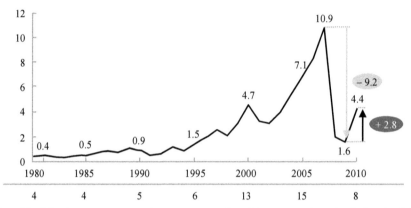

Note: Total foreign investments refer to assets purchased by non-residents (including banks) and include direct foreign investments, portfolio investments (shares and government bonds) and foreign loans.

Source: International Monetary Fund; Institute of International Finance; McKinsey Global Institute Analysis.

Bibliography

Rajan R.G., *Fault Lines. How Hidden Fractures Still Threaten the World Economy*, Princeton, 2010.

Reinhart C.M., Rogoff K.S., *This Time Is Different. Eight Centuries of Financial Folly*, Princeton, 2009.

Sorkin A.R., *Too Big to Fail. The Inside Story of How Wall Street and Washington Fought To Save the Financial System and Themselves*, London, 2009.

Stiglitz J.E., *Freefall. America, Free Markets, and the Sinking of the World Economy*, New York, 2010.

Strange S., *Mad Money*, Manchester, 1998.

Chapter 24
IN PRAISE OF HISTORY

The human race has certainly travelled a long way from the time when there were no cars or factories right down to the global society of the present day. Like all historians, we have had to choose which parts of the story to tell. This kind of choice is inevitable, but we need to be aware of what we are doing and to be honest about it with our readers.

Has our work been useful?

At times, when our students ask about the use of studying history, it is tempting to answer that it has none, because it certainly offers no new professional skills to anyone who wants to pursue a career in business or management, or to explore issues of theoretical or applied economics. Nevertheless, it can offer tools for understanding our position in the global world and our heritage in terms of culture and society, and help us to understand how these contribute to the ways we face the big and small problems we face every day.

In this case, it is clear that the affirmation "history has no use" is an affectation, a rhetorical way of pleasing the interlocutor. In this "shrinking" global world of continual contact and confrontation with others, historical analysis definitely has a purpose!

Is it possible to learn "lessons" from what history tells us? We tend not to view History as teaching us "lessons of life"; historical conditions are never repeated in quite the same way, and when conditions differ even slightly, individuals and groups may react quite differently from what was expected. All the same, we believe there are at least five recognizable "regular patterns":

1. Radical and unpredictable discontinuities can be seen. For example, the First World War drastically and pointlessly interrupts a phase of fertile development, the *belle époque* of the early 1900s.

2. Unpredictable before they happened, these discontinuities then reveal their dynamics after the event: "Nature does not make jumps" and "miracles" have no place in Economic History.

3. The great changes are never only a shift from one economic-technological paradigm to another that is more productive: the more general change in act also involves culture, the social order and institutions.

4. The famous maxim of Greek philosopher Heraclitus, *panta rhei* (eve-

rything flows) applies here; one type of economic behaviour may be positive, or very positive, in a certain period, but may be extremely damaging in a different period when conditions have changed. For example, while the hallmarks of Japan's "miraculous" success until 1990 were its conglomerates, the exchange of favours between government and strategic industries, jobs for life, and employees' loyalty to their company, in the following period these same features were actually difficult obstacles to overcome.

5. The struggle to achieve world economic supremacy is a zero-sum game, and there are always winners and losers. The 17th century was a period of decadence for Italy, but a golden age for the English, Dutch and French. While Europe and the USA have to contend with serious problems at present, China and India have become world economic leaders.

Finally, we started out with the "modest" aim of describing and explaining "how we became global" in just a few hundred pages. It is not for us to say whether we have succeeded, but we will be extremely satisfied if this book encourages you to do further reading in order to explore the problematic issues we have tackled here.

F.A.

AUTHORS

Franco Amatori is Professor of Economic History at Bocconi University, where he teaches History of Italian Business, Business History and Comparative Business History. He edited the volume; he is the author of chapters 6, 7, 24.

Andrea Colli is Professor of Economic History at Bocconi University, where he teaches Economic History, Business History and Global History. He edited the volume; he is the author of chapters 14, 15, 16, 17, 18.

Guido Alfani is Professor of Economic History at Bocconi University, where he teaches Globalization, Divergence and Inequality in Historical Perspective. He is the author of chapters 1, 2, 3.

Silvia A. Conca Messina is Assistant Professor in Economic History at the University of Milan, where she teaches Economic History and History of Economic Policy. She is the author of chapters 4, 5.

Gianluca Podestà is Professor of Economic History at the University of Parma, where he teaches Economic History and History of Financial Markets. He is the author of chapters 10, 11, 12, 13.

Marina Romani is Associate Professor of Economic History at the University of Genoa, where he teaches Economic History and History of Money and Financial Markets. She is the author of chapters 8, 9.

Luciano Segreto is Professor of Economic History at the University of Florence, where he teaches Economic History of Globalization, Business History in Global Economy and International Economic History. He is the author of chapters 19, 20, 21, 22, 23.

AUTHORS OF THEMATIC SECTIONS

Matteo Di Tullio (Bocconi University and University of Pavia): Demographic transition.

Roberto Giulianelli (Marche Polytechnic University): Mass Emigration from Europe.

Marina Nicoli (Bocconi University): Industrial Revolution.

Mario Perugini (Bocconi University): Workplace Organization and International monetary systems.

For Product Safety Concerns and Information please contact our EU
representative GPSR@taylorandfrancis.com
Taylor & Francis Verlag GmbH, Kaufingerstraße 24, 80331 München, Germany

www.ingramcontent.com/pod-product-compliance
Ingram Content Group UK Ltd.
Pitfield, Milton Keynes, MK11 3LW, UK
UKHW021019180425
457613UK00020B/993